*access to hi*

# The Crusades

## 1071–1204

MARY DICKEN AND NICHOLAS FELLOWS

The Publishers would like to thank the following for permission to reproduce copyright material.

**Photo credits: p14** Heritage Image Partnership Ltd/Alamy Stock Photo; **p34** Timewatch Images/Alamy Stock Photo; **p64** Granger Historical Picture Archive/Alamy Stock Photo; **p103** British Library Board. All Rights Reserved/Bridgeman Images.

**Acknowledgements:** *American Historical Review*, Vol. 55, 'The Problem of the Spurious Letter of Emperor Alexius to the Count of Flanders' translated by E. Joranson, 1950. Ashgate Publishing, *Robert the Monk's History of the First Crusade* by Carol Sweetenham, 2005. Bodley Head, *The Life and Legend of the Sultan Saladin* by Jonathan Phillips, 2019. Cambridge University Press, *The Crusades c.1071–c.1291* by Jean Richard, 1999. Charles Scribner's Sons, *A Sourcebook for Medieval History, Selected Documents Illustrating the History of Europe in the Middle Age* translated by O.J. Thatcher and E.H. McNeal, 1905. Continuum, *The First Crusade and the Idea of Crusading* by J. Riley-Smith, 2009. Folio Society, *Book of King Richard's Expedition to the Holy Land of Jerusalem*, 1958. Free Press, *The First Crusade* by T. Asbridge, 2005. Harvard University Press, *The First Crusade* by Peter Frankopan, 2012. Hodder Education, *The Crusades* by Jamie Byrom and Michael Riley, 2013. Jonathan Cape, *The Fourth Crusade* by Jonathan Phillips, 2004. Ktav Publishing, *The Jews and the Crusaders: The Hebrew Chronicles of the First and Second Crusades* edited and translated by Shlomo Eidelberg, 1996. Longman, *The Fourth Crusade* by Michael Angold, 2003. Oxford University Press, *The Oxford History of the Crusades* edited by Jonathan Riley-Smith, 1999; *The Crusades* by Hans Eberhard Meyer, 2009. Palgrave, *Defending the City of God* by Sharan Newman, 2014. Pearson Education, *The Crusades 1095–1197* by Jonathan Phillips, 2002. Penguin Books, *The Alexiad, Book III* edited by Peter Frankopan and translated by E.R.A. Sewter, 2009; *A History of the Crusades, Volumes II & III* by Steven Runciman, 2016; *God's War: A History of the Crusades* by Christopher Tyerman, 2007; *The Conquest of Constantinople* translated by Caroline Smith, 2008. Pimlico, *The Fourth Crusade and the Sack of Constantinople* by Jonathan Phillips, 2005. Routledge, *The Crusades and the Expansion of Catholic Christendom 1000–1714* by John France, 2005; *The Crusades 1095–1197* by Jonathan Phillips, 2014. Rowman & Littlefield, *The Concise History of the Crusades* by Thomas Madden, 1999. Simon & Schuster, *The First Crusade* by Thomas Asbridge, 2005; *The Crusades* by Thomas Asbridge, 2012. University of California Press, *Arab Historians of the Crusades* edited by Francesco Gabrieli and translated by E.J. Costello, 1969. University of Pennsylvania Press, *The First Crusade* edited by Edward Peters, 1971. University of Toronto Press, *The Crusades: A Reader* edited by S.J. Allen and Emilie Ant, 2010. Vintage Press, *Holy Warriors* by J. Phillips, 2009; *The First Crusade* by Peter Frankopan, 2013. W.W. Norton, *The Journey of Louis VII to the East*, edited and translated by Virginia Berry, 1948. Yale University Press, *The World of the Crusades*, by Christopher Tyerman, 2019.

Every effort has been made to trace all copyright holders, but if any have been inadvertently overlooked, the Publishers will be pleased to make the necessary arrangements at the first opportunity.

Although every effort has been made to ensure that website addresses are correct at time of going to press, Hodder Education cannot be held responsible for the content of any website mentioned in this book. It is sometimes possible to find a relocated web page by typing in the address of the home page for a website in the URL window of your browser.

Hachette UK's policy is to use papers that are natural, renewable and recyclable products and made from wood grown in well-managed forests and other controlled sources. The logging and manufacturing processes are expected to conform to the environmental regulations of the country of origin.

Orders: please contact Hachette UK Distribution, Hely Hutchinson Centre, Milton Road, Didcot, Oxfordshire, OX11 7HH. Telephone: +44 (0)1235 827827. Email education@hachette.co.uk Lines are open from 9 a.m. to 5 p.m., Monday to Friday. You can also order through our website: www.hoddereducation.co.uk

ISBN: 978 1 5104 6869 6



First published in 2020 by
Hodder Education,
An Hachette UK Company
Carmelite House
50 Victoria Embankment
London EC4Y 0DZ

www.hoddereducation.co.uk

Impression number 10 9 8 7 6 5 4 3 2
Year 2024 2023 2022 2021



Cover photo © Ivy Close Images/Alamy Stock Photo
Typeset by Gray Publishing
Printed in the UK by CPI Group Ltd

A catalogue record for this title is available from the British Library.

FSC www.fsc.org
MIX
Paper from responsible sources
FSC™ C104740

# Contents

## Dedication

**Keith Randell (1943–2002)**

The *Access to History* series was conceived and developed by Keith, who created a series to 'cater for students as they are, not as we might wish them to be'. He leaves a living legacy of a series that for over 20 years has provided a trusted, stimulating and well-loved accompaniment to post-16 study. Our aim with these new editions is to continue to offer students the best possible support for their studies.

# Introduction: about this book

This book has been written primarily to support the study of the following courses:

- AQA: 1A The Age of the Crusades c1071–1204
- OCR: Y203 and Y201 The Crusades and the Crusader States 1095–1192
- Pearson Edexcel: 1A The Crusades c1095–1204.

The specification grid on pages ix–x will help you understand how this book's content relates to the course that you are studying.

The writers hope that student readers will regard the book not simply as an aid to better exam results, but as a study which is enjoyable in itself as an analysis of a very important theme in history.

The following explains the different features of this book and how they will help your study of the course.

## Beginning of the book

### Context

Starting a new course can be daunting if you are not familiar with the period or topic. This section will give you an overview of the history and will set up some of the key themes. Reading this section will help you get up to speed on the content of the course.

## Throughout the book

### Key terms

You need to know these to gain an understanding of the period. The appropriate use of specific historical language in your essays will also help you improve the quality of your writing. Key terms are in boldface type the first time they appear in the book. They are defined in the margin and appear in the glossary.

### Profiles

Some chapters contain profiles of important individuals. These include a brief biography and information about the importance and impact of the individual. This information can be very useful in understanding certain events and providing supporting evidence to your arguments.

### Sources

Historical sources are important in understanding why specific decisions were taken or on what contemporary writers and politicians based their actions. The questions accompanying each source will help you to understand and analyse the source.

### Interpretations

These extracts from historians will help bring awareness of the debates and issues that surround this fascinating history topic.

### Chapter summaries

These written summaries are intended to help you revise and consolidate your knowledge and understanding of the content.

### Summary diagrams

These visual summaries at the end of each section are useful for revision.

### Refresher questions

The refresher questions are quick knowledge checks to make sure you have understood and remembered the material that is covered in the chapter.

### Question practice

There are opportunities at the end of each chapter to practise exam-style questions, arranged by exam board. The exam hint below each question will help you if you get stuck.

## End of the book

### Timeline

Understanding chronology (the order in which events took place) is an essential part of history. Knowing the order of events is one thing, but it is also important to know how events relate to each other. This timeline will help you put events into context and will be helpful for quick reference or as a revision tool.

### Exam focus

This section gives advice on how to answer questions in your exam, focusing on the different requirements of your exam paper. The guidance in this book has been based on detailed examiner reports since 2017. It models best practice in terms of answering exam questions and shows the most common pitfalls to help ensure you get the best grade possible.

### Glossary

All key terms in the book are defined in the glossary.

### Further reading

To achieve top marks in history, you will need to read beyond this textbook. This section contains a list of books and articles for you to explore. The list may also be helpful for an extended essay or piece of coursework.

# Online extras

This new edition is accompanied by online material to support you in your study. Throughout the book you will find the online extras icon to prompt you to make use of the relevant online resources for your course. By going to www.hoddereducation.co.uk/accesstohistory/extras you will find the following:

## Activity worksheets

These activities will help you develop the skills you need for the exam. The thinking that you do to complete the activities, and the notes you make from answering the questions, will prove valuable in your learning journey and helping you get the best grade possible. Your teacher may decide to print the entire series of worksheets to create an activity booklet to accompany the course. Alternatively they may be used as standalone activities for class work or homework. However, don't hesitate to go online and print off a worksheet yourself to get the most from this book.

## Who's who

A Level history covers a lot of key figures so it's perfectly understandable if you find yourself confused by all the different names. This document organises the individuals mentioned throughout the book by categories so you know your Saladin from your Nur ad-Din!

## Further research

While further reading of books and articles is helpful to achieve your best, there's a wealth of material online, including useful websites, digital archives, and documentaries on YouTube. This page lists resources that may help further your understanding of the topic. It may also prove a valuable reference for research if you decide to choose this period for the coursework element of your course.

# Specification grid

| Chapter | AQA | OCR | Pearson Edexcel |
|---|---|---|---|
| **Chapter 1 Context: The circumstances behind the Crusades** | | | |
| 1 The background to the Crusades | ✓ | ✓ | ✓ |
| 2 Western Europe in the eleventh century | ✓ | ✓ | ✓ |
| 3 The circumstances in the Palestinian lands before 1100 | ✓ | ✓ | ✓ |
| 4 The circumstances in the Byzantine Empire before 1100 | ✓ | ✓ | ✓ |
| **Chapter 2 The Council of Clermont and its impact** | | | |
| 1 The reasons behind Urban's appeal for a crusade to go to the east | ✓ | ✓ | ✓ |
| 2 Urban II's sermon at Clermont | ✓ | ✓ | ✓ |
| 3 The response to Urban II's sermon | ✓ | ✓ | ✓ |
| 4 The first crusaders and their motives | ✓ | ✓ | ✓ |
| 5 Key debate: What were the motives of those who went on the Crusade? | ✓ | ✓ | ✓ |
| **Chapter 3 The First Crusade (the People's Crusade)** | | | |
| 1 The failure of the first wave of the First Crusade | ✓ | ✓ | ✓ |
| 2 The second wave of the First Crusade led by the princes | ✓ | ✓ | ✓ |
| Key debate: Why was the First Crusade successful? | ✓ | ✓ | ✓ |
| **Chapter 4 The Crusader States of Outremer** | | | |
| 1 The establishment of the States | ✓ | ✓ | ✓ |
| 2 The problems facing the States | ✓ | ✓ | ✓ |
| 3 The survival of the Crusader States | ✓ | ✓ | ✓ |
| 4 Key debate: Why did the Crusader States survive? | ✓ | ✓ | ✓ |
| 5 The establishment of the Military Orders | ✓ | ✓ | ✓ |
| 6 Key debate: How important were the Military Orders in the survival of the Crusader States? | ✓ | ✓ | ✓ |
| **Chapter 5 The Second Crusade** | | | |
| 1 The fall of Edessa | ✓ | ✓ | ✓ |
| 2 The role of Bernard of Clairvaux in the Second Crusade | ✓ | ✓ | ✓ |
| 3 The roles of Louis VII and Conrad III in the Second Crusade | ✓ | ✓ | ✓ |
| 4 The events of the Second Crusade | ✓ | ✓ | ✓ |
| 5 The results of the Second Crusade | ✓ | ✓ | ✓ |
| 6 Key debate: Was the attack on Damascus a mistake? | ✓ | ✓ | ✓ |
| **Chapter 6 The Crusader States after the Second Crusade** | | | |
| 1 The rise of Nur ad-Din and developments in Islam | ✓ | ✓ | ✓ |
| 2 The Crusader States after the Second Crusade | ✓ | ✓ | ✓ |
| 3 The campaigns in Egypt | ✓ | ✓ | ✓ |
| 4 The rise of Saladin | ✓ | ✓ | ✓ |
| 5 The victory of Saladin at Hattin and his conquest of Jerusalem | ✓ | ✓ | ✓ |
| 6 Key debate: How should Saladin be viewed? | ✓ | ✓ | ✓ |

| Chapter | AQA | OCR | Pearson Edexcel |
|---|---|---|---|
| **Chapter 7 The Third Crusade** | | | |
| 1 The preaching of the Third Crusade | ✓ | ✓ | ✓ |
| 2 The roles of Frederick Barbarossa, Philip II and Richard I in the Third Crusade | ✓ | ✓ | ✓ |
| 3 The results of the Third Crusade | ✓ | ✓ | ✓ |
| 4 Key debate: What did the Third Crusade achieve? | ✓ | ✓ | ✓ |
| **Chapter 8 The Fourth Crusade** | | | |
| 1 The role of Pope Innocent III | ✓ | | ✓ |
| 2 The Treaty of Venice | ✓ | | ✓ |
| 3 The attacks on Constantinople | ✓ | | ✓ |
| 4 The results of the Fourth Crusade | ✓ | | ✓ |
| 5 Key debate: Why did the crusaders attack Constantinople? | ✓ | | ✓ |
| **Chapter 9 Conclusion (AQA): The Age of the Crusades, c1071–1204** | ✓ | | |
| **Chapter 10 Conclusion (OCR): The Crusades and the Crusader States 1095–1192** | | ✓ | |
| **Chapter 11 Conclusion (Pearson Edexcel): The Crusades c1095–1204** | | | ✓ |

CHAPTER 1

# Context: The circumstances behind the Crusades

The Crusades were a series of wars in which western Europeans attacked Muslims in the Middle East. This was because the Muslims controlled the holiest places associated with Christianity, such as Jerusalem. The wars lasted from the late eleventh century until the thirteenth century. They involved many Europeans, mostly men but some women, as well as people living in the territories of Byzantium and in the Middle East. This introductory chapter focuses on developments which resulted in the Crusades being launched through the following themes:

- The background to the Crusades
- Western Europe in the eleventh century
- The circumstances in the Palestinian lands before 1100
- The circumstances in the Byzantine Empire before 1100

**KEY DATES**

| | |
|---|---|
| **1054** | Schism between the eastern and western Churches |
| **1071** | Defeat of the Byzantines by the Turks at the Battle of Manzikert |
| **1073** | Gregory VII became pope |
| **1081** | Alexius II became the emperor of Byzantium |
| **1095–9** | First Crusade |
| **1147–9** | Second Crusade |
| **1189–92** | Third Crusade |
| **1202–4** | Fourth Crusade |

## 1 The background to the Crusades

■ *Where and when did the Crusades take place?*

Figure 1.1 (see page 2) shows the approximate geography of the countries in the eleventh century, when the Crusades began. The countries we know as Germany, France and Belgium did not exist. The Latin Christian kingdoms, or Latin West, are so-called because of the Catholic Church in Rome – the parts of the former Roman Empire where Latin, rather than Greek, had been spoken. The Latin West can also be used to describe the Catholic parts of medieval Europe. Rome had been the largest city in the world and the Roman Empire's influence was vast, including its official state religion, Christianity, which had been adopted by the ruler at the time, Constantine the Great, in 323. Around 395, the Roman Empire became permanently divided between east and west, with the eastern Roman Empire – called the Byzantine Empire – encompassing

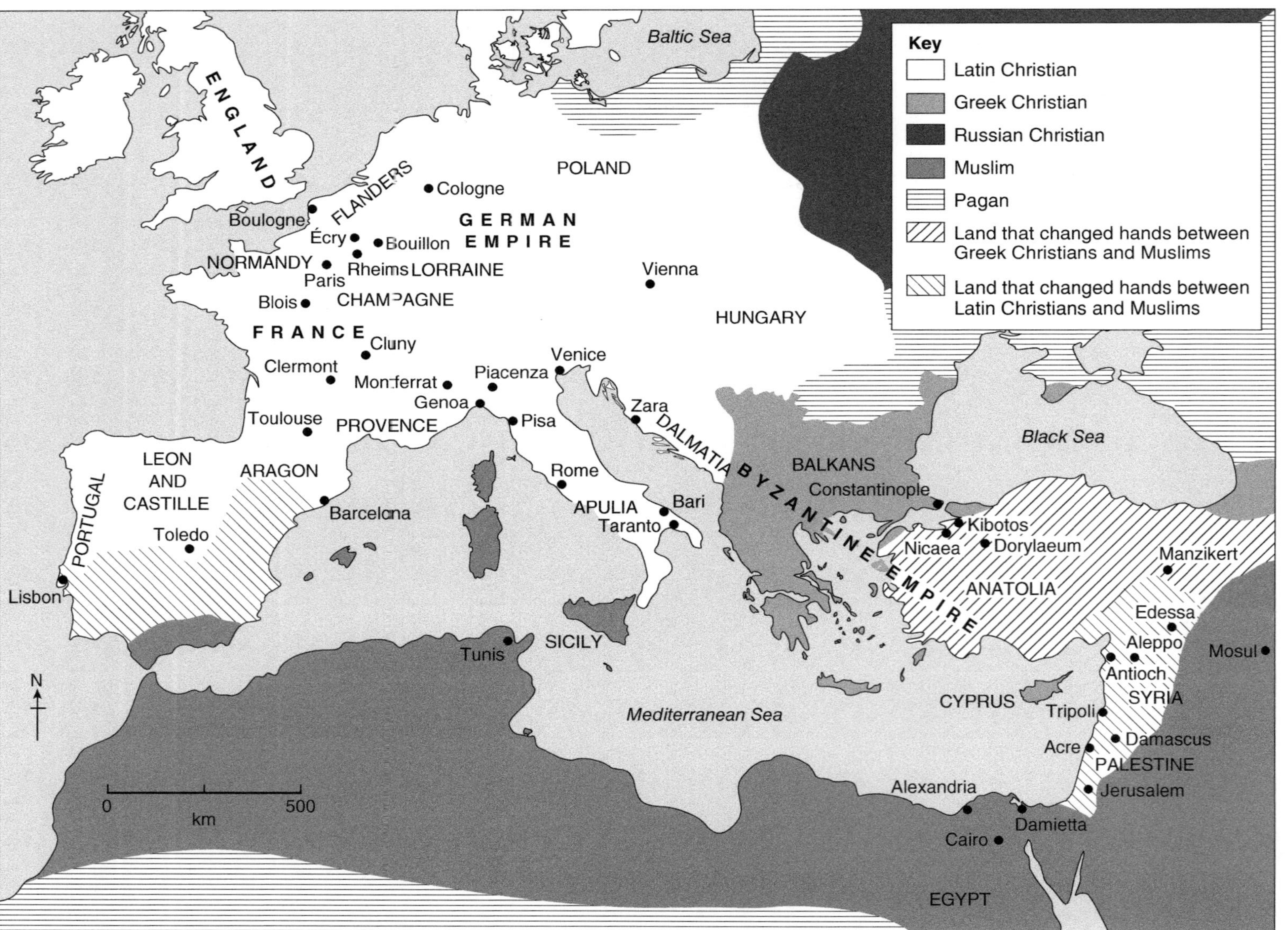


**Figure 1.1** Europe, Near East and north Africa at the time of the Crusades.

southern Italy, the Balkans, modern Turkey, Asia Minor and lands south of the Black Sea. Constantine now ruled from Byzantium (later, Constantinople), and the people of the Byzantine Empire could be called 'Greek Christian' as they were part of the Greek Orthodox Church. Constantinople became the centre of the Church instead of Rome. But, in 800, Pope Leo III (died 816) crowned **Charlemagne** as Holy Roman Emperor in Rome. This was seen as a challenge by the Byzantine emperors and relations became strained. The sack of Constantinople by a crusading force in 1204 weakened the Byzantine Empire, and its last years saw it as just one of several states in the eastern Mediterranean. Constantinople was finally taken by the Turks in 1453.

From 1095 onwards there were several crusades, or wars of the cross (although they were not called this at the time), taking place in the **Muslim Near East**. This book focuses on the first four wars:

- the First Crusade, 1095–9
- the Second Crusade, 1147–9
- the Third Crusade, 1189–92
- the Fourth Crusade, 1202–4.

The First Crusade arose from a combination of factors:

- In western Europe, the popes, in order to reassert their authority and unite **Christendom**, were eager to lead a crusading movement.
- The Byzantine Empire was on the verge of collapse in the 1090s, while many Christians living in the region felt under threat from Islamic forces.
- Stories circulating in western Europe about attacks on Christians in the Muslim Near East, and in Jerusalem in particular, where Christians had been allegedly persecuted and holy sites desecrated.
- The reform movement, led by the papacy, had intensified popular piety in the west, prompting Christians to share in a greater fascination with Jerusalem and the Holy Land.

History has tended, largely because of the writings of monks and clerics of the time, to focus on the central role of the pope in the crusading expeditions. This explanation was further reinforced by the creation of the Crusader States in the twelfth century. However, more recent work, particularly that of Peter Frankopan in his book *The First Crusade: The Call from the East* (published in 2012), has stressed the importance of developments within the Byzantine Empire and the role of its emperor, Alexius. Frankopan argues that Alexius' call for help in a last desperate bid to save the Byzantine Empire was the crucial factor in the development of the crusading movement. Frankopan further argues that the collapse of Byzantine administration in Anatolia, the capture of Ephesus and Nicaea, the military collapse of Byzantine forces, civil war and an attempted coup were at the centre of events and led Alexius to ask for help. Pope Urban II, as a result of a sudden change in his position, was able to seize the opportunity and use the appeal to try and reunite Christendom and secure his position.

### KEY FIGURE

**Charlemagne (c.742–814)**

Founder of the Carolingian Empire and ruled over what is now France, Germany and much of Italy and parts of eastern Europe. He was a fervent Christian, was crowned emperor by the pope and is seen as the first Holy Roman Emperor.

### KEY TERMS

**Muslim Near East**
The area near the eastern end of the Mediterranean Sea, approximately equivalent to what we know today as Greece, Turkey, Syria, Lebanon, Palestine, Israel and Egypt.

**Christendom**
The Christian parts of the world, largely in Europe at this time.

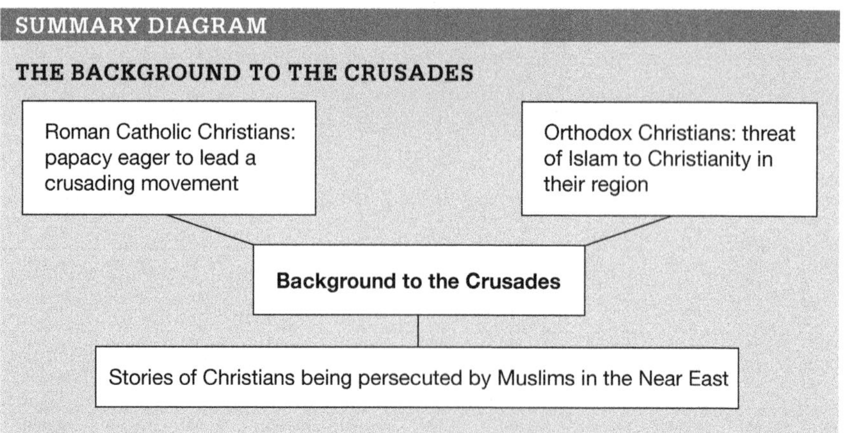


# 2 Western Europe in the eleventh century

■ *Why did the situation in western Europe encourage crusading?*

There are many explanations for why western Europeans took up the crusading movement. These include theoretical issues such as the idea of the Just War and the Peace and Truce of God movements. There are also practical motives, such as the desire of the popes to bolster their power, the wish to defeat the Muslims threatening Europe, and the need to preserve the position of the eastern Roman Empire. Finally, and most importantly, there was the issue of religion and the influence of the Church. Religion and the Church had a great hold over people's lives which, at the time, were often short and brutal. Hell was a very real fear and the offer from the Church to shorten your time there or avoid it altogether by undertaking pilgrimages or a crusade appealed to many. The issue of the right of pilgrimage to the holy places that the western Roman Empire wanted to maintain had become a major issue with the advance of the Turks into the region.

## The Just War

One of the reasons why crusading became an acceptable, and even desirable, duty for a Christian knight was that it was seen as morally justified. This belief in a Just War or holy war was derived from a number of sources, including the following:

- The Bible, especially the Old Testament, was full of examples of fighting heroes, such as Joshua, King David and Judas Maccabeus. The victories of the Israelites over their enemies were viewed as triumphs for God over heathen people.

- The Greek philosopher Aristotle (*c.*384–322BC) had used the phrase 'Just War' to describe war, which was, as he put it, 'for the sake of peace'.
- Roman writers, such as Titus Livius Patavinus, known as Livy (64 or 59BC to 12 or 17AD), added the idea of the *causa belli*, where war was justified if the enemy had broken an agreement. Marcus Tullius Cicero (106–43BC) believed that a Just War was one where lost goods could be recovered or where self-defence was involved.
- Early Christian writers reflected the changing situation once Christianity became the religion of the Roman Empire. They saw the protection of the lands which made up the empire as reasonable and a Just War, since the empire and the Church were so closely linked.
- Finally, Augustine of Hippo (AD354–430) defined the four essential characteristics of a Just War:
  - it must have a just cause
  - it must be for defence or to recover rightful possessions
  - it must be sanctioned by a legitimate authority
  - those who fight must have the right intentions.

When the Roman Empire in the west collapsed, it was more difficult for Christian warriors to continue to believe that God was on their side, since He had clearly not saved them from defeat. But the notion was so powerful that it was soon taken up by the heirs of the 'pagan barbaric tribes' who had overrun Europe. Men like the Emperor Charlemagne saw their wars of conquest as holy wars against pagan infidels and their victories as a sign of divine favour. The Church gave such warriors its blessing and successive popes were thankful for the support of Charlemagne, who was eventually crowned as Holy Roman Emperor in Rome in 800. The soldiers, in their turn, founded monasteries and gave lavish gifts to the Church, perhaps as a way of making up for the brutality of their way of life.

## The Peace and Truce of God movements

Along with the idea of a Just War, these movements contributed to the frame of mind which persuaded crusaders to embark on their journeys. They were instigated by the Catholic Church in the eleventh century with the hope of reducing the level of violence among nobles, who often took the law into their own hands and refused to recognise any central authority.

The *Pax et Treuga Dei* (the **Peace and Truce of God**) came about because Charlemagne's empire, known as the Carolingian Empire, had been divided among his heirs. This led to rivalry between them and their successors and caused much of what is now France to be poorly governed. The chaos led to the emergence of a feudal society, where local lords built castles and tried to preserve their positions themselves, since the king was too weak to keep order. Their anxieties were heightened by the approach of the millennium (the year 1000), popularly expected to be an apocalyptic event. The raids of

**KEY TERM**

**Peace and Truce of God** From about 1000, local nobles had begun to make agreements not to attack churches, unarmed persons and clergymen, and by 1040 this had developed so that fighting was forbidden on certain days of the week. 'Assemblies of peace' met to swear oaths to keep the peace, and 'leagues of peace' made up of clergy and nobles enforced this. The centre of this movement was the monastery of Cluny, where Urban had been a monk and was probably influenced by such developments.

the Vikings and their settlement in northern France were a further worrying factor. The *Pax Dei* was a peace proclaimed by local bishops who said that those who could not defend themselves (peasants, the clergy, and, later, women and children) were not to be attacked. The punishment for infringement was excommunication, but the penalty was removed if the offenders paid for what they had taken or provided some kind of reparation. The earliest peace councils were held in Aquitaine and Burgundy in the late tenth century. The *Pax Dei* was a permanent peace, but how far it was actually observed is questionable.

The Truce of God was initially a temporary ban on fighting and guaranteed the safety of all churches, monks, pilgrims and merchants. Eventually, it forbade hostilities during Advent, Lent and Rogationtide, and on Thursdays (the day of the Ascension of Christ), Fridays (the day of the Crucifixion) and Saturdays (the day of the Resurrection). Sundays and feast days had been observed as days of peace from an earlier period. A Church Council held at Arles (in Provence, France) in 1041 regularised these agreements, which left a mere 80 days available for fighting in each year. The whole aim was to limit the extent of conflict within France, and later Germany and Italy, but to make it acceptable if redirected to other regions, such as the Middle East.

Both the Just War and the Peace and Truce of God movements contributed to the reasons why Christians were persuaded to go on crusades.

## The idea of the pilgrimage

The destruction of much of Jerusalem in AD70 by the Romans meant that there were few remains of the city Christ had known. But, from the third century onwards, sites such as the cave at Bethlehem where he had been born, the Mount of Olives and the Garden of Gethsemane were visited by Christians for prayer and meditation. The conversion of Emperor Constantine to Christianity in 313, and the discovery of the **True Cross** by his mother, Helena (*c*.250–320), led him to build the Church of the Holy Sepulchre where Christ's body had been buried, which was thus the site of the Resurrection. This site attracted pilgrims immediately. Saint Jerome (*c*.374–420) lived in Bethlehem for a time and his disciples flocked there. There were fluctuations in the numbers of pilgrims according to how safe it was to travel in the Mediterranean, which was home to many groups of pirates.

**KEY TERMS**

**True Cross** Believed to be the cross on which Christ had been crucified. It had been found by Helena, the mother of Emperor Constantine, in about 327.

**Relic** A body part or a belonging from a holy person, kept as an object of reverence.

By the tenth century, the pirates were less troublesome and pilgrimages abounded from Italian ports to Palestine, often via Constantinople, where the vast Byzantine collection of **relics** could be viewed. The practice of pilgrimage was encouraged by the idea that visiting holy places possessed a spiritual virtue and could even lead to a pardon for sins being given by God. The prime destinations included Rome (Saints Peter and Paul) and Palestine (Jesus Christ). Pilgrimage was encouraged by the Abbey of Cluny, founded in 910, and numbers were recorded in their records.

From 1019, the Byzantine Empire controlled the Balkans and the overland pilgrimage route, which although longer than the sea crossing now became safer. Hostels were built for the pilgrims and, while great lords might travel with large **retinues**, protected by armed soldiers, it seems to have been perfectly possible for small groups to travel and arrive unscathed. Yet for this situation to continue, both the Byzantine and the Muslim worlds needed to be stable. All of these ideas and developments ensured that when Pope Urban II made his appeal at Clermont in November 1095 he was already preaching to a responsive audience.

## Europe in the late eleventh century

However, the situation in the Byzantine and Muslim world and western Europe in the eleventh century was far from stable. In western Europe, the century had seen Norman advances in both north-western Europe and Italy, in Spain Muslim forces were gradually being driven out, while in Germany there was unrest. The papacy was involved in a struggle with magnates throughout Europe, which often resulted in the pope excommunicating them. There was also division between the papacy and Byzantine Church (see pages 9–10). Finally, the position of the Church in the west was further weakened by the Investiture Contest (see page 9) and the installation of the **anti-pope**, Clement III, in 1084, which forced Gregory into exile.

## The role of the papacy

'Papacy' describes the realm and influence of the popes, the heads of the Roman Catholic Church, generally based in Rome. The pope in Rome ruled as the acknowledged heir of the apostle Saint Peter. His power was supported by the Donation of Constantine, a document which was supposedly a grant by Constantine to the popes of their supremacy over western Europe. (It was, in fact, an eighth-century forgery, issued to help boost papal supremacy.) Popes did not always find the rulers of Europe eager to recognise their superiority. Monarchs preferred the view that they held complete sovereignty over their realms. In certain circumstances they might appeal to the pope for support, as William of Normandy (*c*.1028–87) did in 1066 when he invaded England. Mostly, rulers such as Henry IV (1050–1106), the Holy Roman Emperor, defied the claims of the popes.

In the later eleventh century, popes were determined to enforce their control and to defend it by force if necessary. They raised armies, offering those who fought for them forgiveness of their sins, and categorised these wars as 'holy wars'.

### Gregory VII and the role of the papacy

In Pope Gregory VII's insistence on recognition of his rights in the Investiture Contest (see the box, page 9), he quarrelled in a major way with the emperor, Henry IV. This led to the unedifying spectacle of the pope excommunicating the emperor, and the emperor deposing the pope and establishing his own rival pope. This then meant the further involvement of the papacy in war: Gregory recruited soldiers from all over Europe to form the ***milites sancti Petri*** **(vassals of Saint Peter)**, offering them absolution of their sins and eternal salvation

**KEY TERMS**

**Retinues** Followers such as guards, soldiers and servants. The wealth and power of a lord were reflected in the size of his retinue.

**Anti-pope** A rival pope elected by opponents of a current pope. Each pope built up support where he could.

***Milies sancti Petri*** **(vassals of Saint Peter)** Knights throughout the Christian west who were bound by oath to offer armed service to the Church and to the pope as its head.

# Pope Gregory VII c.1025–85

Hildebrand, or Gregory VII, belonged to a reasonably prosperous family, possibly from Sovana in southern Tuscany. Gregory was educated in Rome and became a chaplain to Gregory VI. He went into exile with the pope and completed his education at Cologne. In 1058 he became archdeacon of the Roman Church. He supported the papal claim to sovereignty over the Church and over secular rulers. He favoured an alliance with the Normans in southern Italy and backed the invasion of England by William of Normandy. In 1073 he was elected pope and took the name Gregory VII.

He was determined to restore the supremacy of the papacy, to enforce **clerical celibacy** and root out **simony**. He held regular councils and wrote extensively to churchmen and rulers to enforce his views. However, his claims to overlordship were not recognised by William I of England or Philip I of France. Both kings had the backing of their bishops so there was little Pope Gregory VII could do. He excommunicated and **deposed** Henry IV in 1077, but this backfired. Henry reasserted his power, won the civil war in Germany and deposed the pope in 1080, marched on Rome and captured it in 1084. Gregory died in 1085, defeated and an exile, but his ideas about the papacy had a long-lasting impact in Europe.

### KEY TERMS

**Clerical celibacy** The belief that the clergy should not be married or have sexual relationships, so their focus was always on God.

**Simony** Paying to get an office or job in the Church.

**Depose** To remove a ruler or pope from their position.

for their souls. Such forces could be used by Gregory to discipline those who resisted his reforms and those who took up arms against him. He made it clear that his troops were fighting in the service of God. He even planned to lead an army to aid the Christians in the eastern Mediterranean. The terms in which he explained his aims, and the heavenly rewards that his soldiers would receive, were later echoed in the preaching of Pope Urban II (see pages 25–6). He also gave his blessing to Christian knights who fought in Spain against the Arab Muslims as the Arabs were not Christians, and promised them absolution for their sins, while maintaining that any lands they conquered were to be held from the pope as overlord. Gregory died in 1085 in exile from Rome, where his hostility to Henry IV had made him unpopular, with the anti-pope, Clement III, ruling in Rome. The emperor remained excommunicated and his subjects were not part of later crusading plans.

The cardinals loyal to Gregory elected the abbot of Monte Cassino as the new pope and he took the name Victor III, but he died in 1087 and it was not until early in 1088 that Pope Urban II was elected. However, his position was weak and he was rarely able to enter Rome.

Source A shows how Gregory VII asked for help against the Muslims.

### SOURCE QUESTION

In Source A, on what grounds is Gregory appealing for help?

### SOURCE A

**From a letter written by Pope Gregory VII in 1074 in response to appeals for help from Byzantium after the emperor had been defeated by the Turks at Manzikert in 1071, quoted in O.J. Thatcher and E.H. McNeal, translators, *A Sourcebook for Medieval History, Selected Documents Illustrating the History of Europe in the Middle Age*, Charles Scribner's Sons, 1905, p. 513.**

*We hereby inform you that the bearer of these letters on his recent return from across the sea [from Palestine] came to visit us. He repeated what we had heard from many others that a pagan race had overcome the Christians and, with horrible cruelty, had devastated everything, almost to the walls of Constantinople … and that they had slain many thousands of Christians … Therefore we beseech you by*

> *the faith in which you are united through Christ ... and by the authority of St. Peter, prince of the apostles, we admonish you that you be moved to proper compassion by the wounds and blood of your brethren and the danger of the aforesaid empire and that, for the sake of Christ, you undertake the difficult task of bearing aid to your brethren.*

### Investiture Contest

This was an issue between the pope and the emperor as both claimed supreme power. It began with the pope objecting to bishops being 'invested' with the symbols of their office by their lay lord to show their fealty. The pope thought their main loyalty was to him. He excommunicated Emperor Henry IV, who insisted on investing his bishops himself.

The quarrel between Gregory VII and Henry IV developed out of the Investiture Contest. Henry declared Gregory deposed in 1076. After Henry was excommunicated, his German subjects refused to obey him and he decided to beg Gregory's pardon, which was granted.

The anti-pope was Clement III, who was made pope by Henry IV as a rival to Gregory in 1080 and was consecrated in Rome in 1084. He crowned Henry IV as emperor and was the anti-pope to Pope Gregory VII and his successors, Victor III, Urban II and Paschal II. He died in 1100.

## Relations between Byzantium and Rome

In 1054 the Christian Church split. The division between the Latin and the Greek branches has never been healed.

The immediate cause of the schism between the Greek and Roman Churches in 1054 came from the Patriarch of Constantinople, Michael Cerularius (*c*.1000–59). He closed down Latin Churches and went on to deny the validity of the Roman Mass. The pope retaliated with the charge that Michael was the puppet of the Byzantine emperor. Papal representatives were sent to Constantinople to negotiate in 1054 but, while they were there, Pope Leo IX died. The relationship continued to deteriorate as the Byzantines made an alliance with the German enemies of the pope and the papacy made approaches to the Normans, the enemies of Byzantium. These complex relationships all added to the problems of the situation.

This situation formed part of the backdrop to the Crusades, although there were other causes of tension:

- *How much authority the pope had over the patriarchs.* The dominant figures in the Church at first were the Bishop of Rome (the pope), and the Bishops of Alexandria and Antioch, also known as patriarchs. Later, the Bishops of Jerusalem and Constantinople were also referred to as **patriarchs**.
- *Open rivalry between Rome and Constantinople.* This was due to the spread of Islam, leaving the patriarchs of Antioch, Alexandria and Jerusalem marginalised.

**KEY TERM**

**Patriarch** A bishop, in some eastern Churches.

- *Differences of language.* The western Church used Latin and the eastern Church used Greek. As time went on, fewer and fewer people understood both languages.
- *Territorial disputes.* These included disagreements about who had jurisdiction over parts of the Balkans, southern Italy and Sicily, where the inhabitants were mostly Greeks.
- *Different interpretations of the* **Trinity**. In the western doctrine, the Holy Spirit was referred to as 'proceeding' from the Father and the Son, while the eastern Church saw the Holy Spirit as proceeding only from God the Father.
- *Differences in perception.* The western Church was seen as more practical and logical while the eastern Church was more spiritual and mystical.
- *Clerical celibacy.* The western Church began to insist on this, while the eastern Church did not.

### KEY TERMS

**Trinity** The belief that God is one but has three persons: the Father, the Son and the Holy Spirit.

**Heresy** A belief that goes against the beliefs of the established Church.

However, under Pope Urban II relations improved. He was in such a weak position that he moved to conciliate Constantinople, sending a delegation in 1088. He saw that the best way to secure his own position was to become the unifier of the Church and restore relations with eastern Christians. He was fortunate that the Emperor Alexius viewed him as a better ally than the German-backed Clement. His position was further helped as many living in southern Italy had Greek links and wanted to see an improvement in relations with the emperor, which were given a boost in 1081 when Urban ended the excommunication of Alexius.

Urban's position was further helped when supporters of Henry IV, who had installed Clement III, began to defect, with his son Conrad and wife denouncing the emperor. This improvement in Urban's position was shown by his announcement that he would hold a council at Piacenza in March 1095. The venue was significant as it was territory which had previously been loyal to Henry and in the heart of Clement's original archbishopric of Ravenna. Although the meeting was designed to discuss ecclesiastical affairs, such as **heresy**, its impetus was changed when envoys arrived from Constantinople. They brought the news that the eastern empire was on the brink of collapse and needed help. Urban was quick to seize the initiative; he saw that he could use this to reunify the Church and announced that he would travel to Clermont. It was, therefore, the arrival of the envoys that led to Urban's call to arms, but it was the developments outlined earlier (see pages 4–6) that ensured that large numbers would respond to his call.

### SUMMARY DIAGRAM

#### WESTERN EUROPE IN THE ELEVENTH CENTURY

| Holy war: | | Reasons for a crusade: |
|---|---|---|
| • Just War<br>• Peace and Truce of God movement | **Western Europe in the eleventh century** | • Popes wanted to bolster their power<br>• Defeat the Muslims threatening Europe<br>• Preserve the position of the eastern Roman Empire<br>• Pilgrimage to holy places |

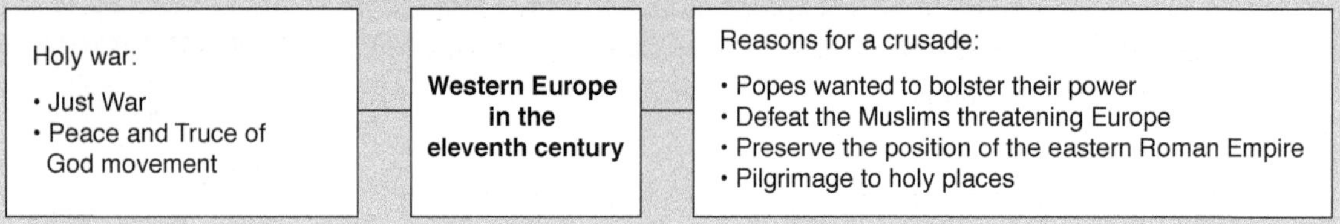

# 3 The circumstances in the Palestinian lands before 1100

■ *Why did circumstances in the Palestinian lands encourage crusading?*

The area of the Middle East (see Figure 1.1, page 2), including what is sometimes described as the Holy Land, had a difficult history. With a lack of natural frontiers and a key geographical position in the Mediterranean, it had been prey to successive conquerors. It was part of the Roman Empire but from the beginning there were tensions between the west and the east, which reached a climax with the conflict between Julius Caesar (100–44BC) and Marcus Antonius (83–30BC) and Cleopatra VII Philopator (69–30BC). The Roman provinces of Egypt and Syria were among the richest in the empire and thus very desirable.

## Byzantine rule

Most of the people living and trading in this area were Christians and they came to resent the authority of the Patriarch of Constantinople (see page 9), who was given precedence over Alexandria and Antioch. In addition, there was a strong Jewish presence in many of the larger cities, and the Jews were equally hostile to the Orthodox Christians. Descendants from all these groups were living in the area at the time of the Crusades and added to the instability there.

### Persian conquest: Persian defeat

King Chosroes II of Persia (590–628) was able to exploit the problems in the eastern Roman Empire and in the early seventh century captured most of Palestine. The True Cross was taken as loot back to Persia. In 630, after Chosroes had been murdered and the Persians defeated, the True Cross was restored to Jerusalem. Keeping control of Christian sites was to be a major focus of the Crusades.

## The rise of Islam

While the events outlined above help to explain why the Palestinian lands were so much in dispute, a major reason for the Crusades came from the emergence of the Prophet Muhammad and the establishment of Islam. Muhammad, born in the city of **Mecca** in what today is Saudi Arabia, in 570, had extraordinary qualities in both his religious message and his political grasp. In 622 he fled to Medina with a few friends. In 632 he died as the Lord of Arabia whose armies were advancing all across the area. In 638 the Arabs took Jerusalem. They moved on to Egypt and by the early eighth century held an empire which extended from Spain to central India.

These Arab conquests had the following effects:

- Christians were not persecuted for their faith, as they were a **People of the Book**; nor were their places of worship, in general, attacked.

**KEY TERMS**

**Mecca** The birthplace of Muhammad and the holiest city in Islam.

**People of the Book** An Islamic term referring to Jews, Christians and Sabians, or converts to Islam.

- Christians had to pay taxes to secure their safety; some converted to Islam.
- Nazareth, Bethlehem and Jerusalem continued to contain a significant number of Christians.
- Arabic became the language of administration and coinage bearing Arabic inscriptions took on standardised forms.
- An organised Islamic **polity** was created with a caliph at its head and governors appointed to oversee provinces.
- The Umayyad **caliphs** ruled from Damascus; the Umayyads, a leading Arab family, had taken control of Syria in 661.

**KEY TERMS**

**Polity** A form of civil government.

**Caliph** The head of an Islamic state, seen as a successor to Muhammad.

**Franks** Collective word for people who lived in France at the time.

**Holy Sepulchre** The burial place of Christ, and included a church built by Constantine, a sacred site.

***Jihad*** Meaning 'struggle' in Arabic; one of the duties of Muslims was to fight for the defence of their religion against non-Muslims or the infidel. The term was used to whip up enthusiasm for the war against the crusaders.

## Divisions in Islam

There were two main divisions in Islam: the Sunnis and the Shi'ites. The Sunnis acknowledged Abu Bakr, a close colleague of Muhammad, as his successor and as caliph. They believed that only they held fast to the correct Muslim tradition. The Shi'ites would only recognise Ali, Muhammad's cousin and son-in-law, as his heir. As Ali had several wives, the Shi'ites were divided as to which of his descendants would usher in the conversion of the whole world to Islam. Disunity among Muslims was to have a profound impact on the course of the Crusades.

## The Abbasid caliphate

In 750 the Shi'ite Abbasids established a caliphate at Baghdad and the Sunni Umayyads fled to Spain. The Abbasids were more fervent Muslims than the Umayyads but still employed many Christian administrators. They recognised that the Byzantine Empire might revive and threaten them, so they tried to build an alliance with Charlemagne. The caliph Harun-al-Rashid (763–809) allowed Charlemagne to found churches in Jerusalem. Charlemagne was also acknowledged as the protector of Christians in Palestine and built hostels for pilgrims to use. Later legends credited Charlemagne with making a pilgrimage himself. The **Franks** who went on crusade sometimes saw themselves as the heirs to Charlemagne.

## Byzantine revival

The improvement in the fortunes of Byzantium in the ninth century was partly due to the decline of the Abbasids, which led to civil war in their empire, and partly to the achievements of the Byzantine army. Successes included the reconquest of Syria, Antioch and Aleppo. The Byzantines saw these wars as being fought for the glory of Christendom, to free the **Holy Sepulchre** from the outrages of the Muslims and to destroy the power of Islam. Thus, they fought less to extend the empire and more to glorify God. The caliphs took up this theme themselves by proclaiming ***jihad***.

## The Fatimids

The Shi'ite Fatimids set up a caliphate in north Africa. They conquered Egypt in 969 and founded Cairo (Al Qahira) as their capital. They were initially a force for stability in the Middle East and on reasonably good terms with the Byzantines.

Fatimid rule in southern Syria and Palestine was no harder on Christians than the Abbasids had been. They agreed to let the Byzantine emperor carry out repairs to the Church of the Holy Sepulchre in 1027 and many Greeks came to the city to supervise the work.

By about 1050 the position in Jerusalem and Palestine seemed to be tranquil. The holy places were protected, trade was prosperous and pilgrimages could easily be made from Europe. However, the conquests of the Turks changed this situation.

### The Seljuk Turks

The **Seljuk Turks** were part of a large number of ethnic Turks from Central Asia who moved into the Muslim world from the late tenth century. Having adopted Sunni Islam, Seljuk-led armies seized control of large parts of the Middle East, creating a Turko-Persian Empire. In 1055, the Seljuks took control of Baghdad where a Seljuk sultan was installed as deputy to the Abbasid caliph.

From 1071, the Seljuks actively intervened in Syria. In 1078, a campaign of conquest was begun; by 1086, the Seljuks controlled a number of cities in Syria and Palestine, including Antioch, Aleppo and Jerusalem itself, which they had taken in the 1070s from the Fatimids.

The structure of the Seljuk Empire provides one of the reasons for its success: power was decentralised since the sultan would delegate control over territories to members of his family. These rulers were usually given the title of *malik*, literally meaning 'king', but often translated as 'prince'. Any of these 'princes' could in theory become sultan. However, the competition created by this structure would eventually work in the favour of the crusaders. On the death of Malik Shah in 1092, the cohesion of the empire was ruptured as the princes fought each other for the sultanate. Two years later, in 1094, this confusion would extend to the Fatimid caliphate in Cairo where a disputed succession occurred following the deaths of both the caliph and his deputy, the vizier.

From the 1070s, reports of a deteriorating situation for pilgrims to the Holy Land were being received in western Europe. A growing concern for Jerusalem emerged, anxiety that would be exploited by the Byzantine emperor, Alexius I Comnenus, and would contribute to the enthusiasm for a crusade to the east.

**KEY TERM**

**Seljuk Turks** A tribe from central Asia who moved west in the tenth century and converted to Sunni Islam. They captured Baghdad in 1055 and set up the Seljuk Empire. Under Alp Arslan and Malik Shah they extended their rule to include Iran, Mesopotamia, Syria, Palestine and the Sultanate of Rum. But they were later pushed back by the crusaders and attacked in the east by the Mongols.

## Cultural advancement of the east

In terms of science, learning and architecture, the Muslim world was more advanced than the Christian west at the end of the eleventh century. Islamic culture entered western Europe from the late eleventh and early twelfth centuries mainly through Sicily and Spain; but contact also developed after the establishment of the Crusader States. Muslim scholars had translated many ancient Greek texts at a time when these works were thought lost to the west. Aristotle's philosophical works, for example, survived in this way, and were rediscovered in western Europe particularly through Sicily and Spain in the twelfth century. By the early twelfth century, Islamic work on algebra and trigonometry were being translated for western European audiences, as were books on alchemy. Astronomical and mathematical works by great Muslim scholars like Muhammad al-Fazari were also introduced into the west in the twelfth century. Medical texts, such as Avicenna's (Ibn Sina) early eleventh-century encyclopaedia of medicine also grew in popularity. Islamic religious architecture, with its pointed arches, influenced the development of the Gothic style popular in the west from the early twelfth century. In short, by providing another means of cultural exchange between east and west, the crusades helped to open up the Christian west to the more advanced learning of the Muslim world.

## SUMMARY DIAGRAM

### THE CIRCUMSTANCES IN THE PALESTINIAN LANDS BEFORE 1100

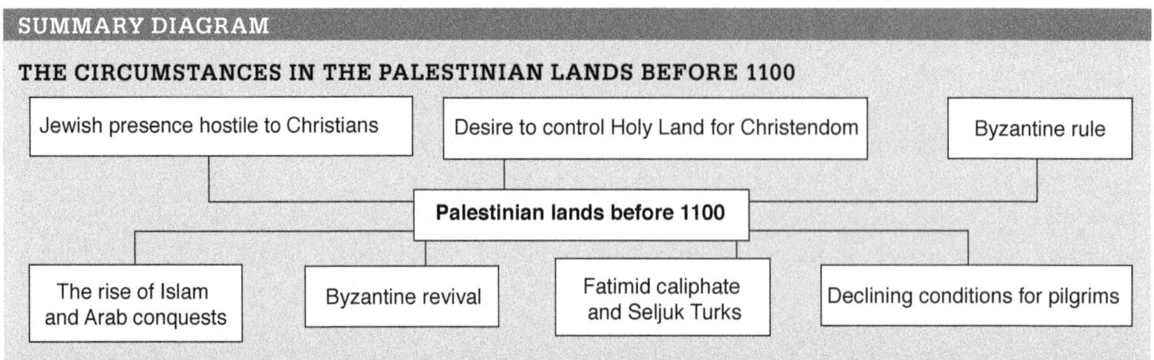


## SOURCE B

**SOURCE QUESTION**

How useful is Source B as evidence of the power and authority of Alexius?

The Byzantine Emperor Alexius I (left) being blessed by Christ (right), from a twelfth-century manuscript. Alexius, like Christ, is shown with a halo to suggest that he has been chosen and blessed by God.

# 4 The circumstances in the Byzantine Empire before 1100

- *Why did the circumstances in the Byzantine Empire encourage crusading?*

The Byzantine Empire had developed from the old eastern Roman empire, gradually becoming Greek in culture. It was the main barrier against the Islamic armies that were advancing from the east. However, by the start of the eleventh century it had become weak. The religion was Orthodox Christianity and the Church had grown apart from the Catholic Church in the west and in 1054 split completely with the Great Schism. There were attempts made to heal the division but they failed. A crusade would not only help to stop the Muslim advance, which the weakened empire could not do unaided, but might also lead to a restoration of religious unity between the eastern and western Churches.

Constantinople, the capital city of the Byzantine Empire, was one of the marvels of the early medieval world. It had huge fortifications, a series of stone walls up to twelve metres tall, and the population was far larger than that of the biggest cities in Europe. It attracted a vast range of merchants and fortune-seekers, and its inhabitants were more varied and cosmopolitan than in most cities. Its buildings were spectacular, with the vast dome of the Church of Hagia Sophia being one of the outstanding features. It was very attractive to crusading armies. The prosperity of the imperial family and friends of the emperor contrasted strongly with the poverty of the rest of the population, who were subjected to high taxes and a **debased coinage**.

## Threats to the Byzantine Empire

In the mid-eleventh century the empire came under threat from enemies on all sides:

- The Normans took over much of southern Italy.
- The aggressive tribe of the **Pechenegs**, based on the northern banks of the Danube, began to raid the Balkans.
- The Turks erupted on the eastern fringes of the empire and, in 1055, a tribal leader, Tughril Bey (990–1063), became the **sultan** in Baghdad.

There was little effective response from the rulers in Byzantium. In 1071 there was a disastrous defeat for the Greeks at the Battle of Manzikert near the eastern frontier. Romanos IV Diogenes (died 1072) was outmanoeuvred by the Turkish general, Alp Arslan (*c*.1030–72/3), and captured. Arslan released him and the generosity of the Turkish leader was much admired.

### KEY TERMS

**Debased coinage** Where the metal content of coins is less than their face value. The process leads to higher prices.

**Pechenegs** A Turkish tribe who had migrated from central Asia. They were much given to war with their neighbours but were finally defeated in 1091 by a combined force of their enemies.

**Sultan** A powerful ruler under the authority of the caliph.

The impact of the defeat on the Byzantines at Manzikert was considerable:

- Many Byzantines living in rural Asia Minor panicked and relocated to the safety of Constantinople.
- The movement of many people from the rural areas and the conscription of others into the army greatly reduced the numbers working on farms and therefore reduced food supplies.
- Byzantine commanders at Manzikert survived; losses in the battle were not significant enough to prevent future but costly campaigns against the Pechenegs.
- Taxes increased as a result of the growing financial crisis in the empire and widespread feelings of insecurity brought about by the defeat.
- Civil disorder followed in the late 1070s as leading aristocratic figures rebelled.
- Turks raided throughout Asia Minor, taking over much of Anatolia and even reaching the shores of the Bosphorus, restricting Byzantine power to an area around Constantinople.
- Robert Guiscard, the Norman leader in southern Italy, prepared to take advantage of the Byzantine defeat and the chaotic situation it created.

## Alexius I Comnenus

**SOURCE QUESTION**

According to Source C, what qualities did a Byzantine emperor need in order to be successful?

Alexius I had become emperor through a coup in 1081 and built up his power in several ways (see his profile, page 17). However, as a usurper, his rule lacked legitimacy and by the 1090s he was losing political authority. The life and achievements of Alexius I form the subject matter of *The Alexiad*, written by his daughter Anna Comnena, probably between 1143 and 1153. Source C shows how she admired her father.

**SOURCE C**

**From Anna Komnene (edited by Peter Frankopan and translated by E.R.A. Sewter), *The Alexiad*, Book III, Penguin revised edition, 2009, p. 85.**

*Alexius was not a very tall man, but broad-shouldered and yet well proportioned. When standing he did not seem particularly striking to onlookers, but when one saw the grim flash of his eyes as he sat on the imperial throne, he reminded one of a fiery whirlwind, so overwhelming was the radiance emanating from his countenance and from his very presence. His dark eyebrows were curved, and beneath them the gaze of his eyes was both terrible and kind … His broad shoulders, muscular arms and deep chest, all on a heroic scale, invariably commanded the wonder and delight of the people. The man's person indeed radiated beauty and grace and dignity and an unapproachable majesty. When he came into a gathering and began to speak, you were conscious from the moment he opened his mouth of the fiery eloquence of his tongue, for a torrent of argument won universal attention and captivated every heart.*

## Alexius I Comnenus (or Alexios I Komnenos) 1048–1118

Alexius was the nephew of Isaac I and had a military background. In 1081 he overthrew Emperor Nikiphorus, helped by the Doukas family, a rival to the Comnenus clan. He was able to do this as his wife, Irene, was a Doukas. He had both military ability and diplomatic skill and so was able to keep his many enemies at bay. He built up central authority in his empire, but his dependence on the feudal nobility, who had to be placated with gifts, weakened his revenue stream. Contemporaries saw him as the saviour of the empire, but a longer-term view would envisage him as more of a stopgap. He asked for help from the west against his enemies and the result was the First Crusade, which led to the loss of territories like Antioch. He did manage to maintain his control in parts of Anatolia but he could not exert much authority over the crusaders.

## Problems and solutions in Alexius I's early reign

Some of Alexius' problems spanned the entire period while others were solved by battle as they occurred (see Table 1.1).

**Table 1.1** Problems and solutions in Alexius I's early reign

| Problem | Solution |
|---|---|
| Alexius needed to build up support and ensure stability after a series of short reigns | Alexius gave appointments and positions to members of leading families to keep them loyal |
| Norman control of the Epirus, Macedonia and Thessaly | Alexius took personal command of the army and by 1084 had driven the Normans out |
| Pecheneg incursions in southern Thrace and threat to Constantinople | Alexius formed the largest army he could muster and defeated the Pechenegs totally in 1091 |
| Maintaining popularity | Alexius lived simply and his court was not extravagant |
| Religious divisions | Those deemed to be heretics were punished and senior clergy who favoured strictly orthodox views were appointed |

Alexius' first decade had been successful: he defeated the Norman and Pecheneg threats, minimised challenges to his position by effectively controlling the aristocracy, won over at this stage critics of his predecessors by adopting a modest lifestyle, and promoted the interests of the Orthodox Church. In addition, he went on to reform the coinage by replacing the debased currency, an initiative that would help to bring about financial recovery in the empire.

Yet his style of ruling and his preoccupation with military matters led to growing discontent within the empire. Furthermore, the problem Alexius could not solve alone was the issue of the Turks.

Initially, his relations with the Turks had been good and his position in Asia Minor in the 1080s appeared stable. After the defeat at Manzikert, Byzantine commanders had held out in many parts of Asia Minor. It was only in the 1090s when his position deteriorated, and he therefore sought help from the west. It is not easy to assess how severely he was threatened. *The Alexiad* tends to exaggerate the weakness of the situation in the empire on his accession, in order to magnify the extent of his achievements. In addition, Anna Comnena managed to gloss over some of the disasters which Alexius I suffered by implying that they had occurred before his reign began. Ambitious Byzantine families were another threat to Alexius I.

## Sulayman, ally of Alexius I

One of the Turkish chieftains in Asia Minor was Sulayman, who had fought under Alexius I as a mercenary and was now used by the emperor to keep control of much of Asia Minor under an agreement made in 1081. This left Alexius I free to deal with the Normans and the Pechenegs and meant he did not have to rely on possible rivals to police the region. But the power given to Sulayman led to resentment from other generals, and Sulayman was killed by rivals in 1085. Antioch, which he had recaptured, was lost again.

## Temporary recovery

Alexius I and the Sultan of Baghdad, Malik Shah (1053–92), the son of Alp Arslan (see page 16), formed an alliance. Malik Shah campaigned in person and retook Antioch. But he also ensured order in Asia Minor and did not intervene when some Turkish leaders were encouraged by lavish gifts from Alexius I to become Christians. However, the stability was not to last. While the empire seemed secure and safe by 1088, it became a very different story in the 1090s.

## Defeat and disaster

Alexius I was overcome by a combination of circumstances and misfortune:

- First of all, the Pechenegs turned out to be far from beaten, attacking and capturing Nikomedia, a town north of Nicaea and only about 80 kilometres from Constantinople.
- Another ambitious Turk, Chaka, set himself up in Smyrna. He developed a fleet and began to harry the coasts of Asia Minor. This disrupted food supplies and was very worrying to the people of Constantinople. The land defences of the city were impregnable, but the Byzantine capital was far more vulnerable to attack by sea. Hardships in the city led to complaints and hostile sermons from influential figures such as John the Oxite, the Patriarch of Antioch. He argued that God was punishing Alexius I for the emperor's seizure of the crown.
- In 1092 Malik Shah died, thus depriving Alexius I of his main ally against the hostile Turkish chieftains. There was no clear heir to the sultan and so the **warlords** were further emboldened. Alexius I tried to regain Nicaea by making an alliance with its ruler, Abu'l-Kasim (died 1092). But on returning to Nicaea, Abu'l-Kasim was murdered by Turks who opposed any alliance with Alexius I.

**KEY TERM**

**Warlords** Powerful nobles who recruited mercenary forces and controlled the land around their strongholds. They fought one another much of the time.

There were some successes, however. Nikomedia was retaken and, in 1091, the Pechenegs were utterly defeated and this time remained quiet. Some of them even joined Alexius' armies as mercenary soldiers.

It would be very difficult to argue against the view that Alexius' position was seriously threatened by 1094. His failure to defeat the Turks raised serious concerns among the Byzantines as to Alexius' suitability to rule. There had already been revolts in Crete and Cyprus in 1091 over heavy taxation, and trading privileges granted to Venice were seen as a threat to the position of local traders. His position was further weakened by nomad attacks in the Balkans and Serbian raids in the north-west of the empire. It was his decision to reinforce the strategically unimportant area of the north-west that seemed to confirm the need to replace him as emperor and a plot soon developed to replace him with Nikephoros Diogenes (c.1069–c.1094), the son of Romanos IV. When Alexius became suspicious he arrested Nikephoros and had him tortured until he confessed. The plot turned out to involve a large number of high-ranking figures at the Byzantine court, including family members, and Alexius proceeded to purge his government and began to rely more on foreigners and up-and-coming families from Thrace, rather than the traditional elite from Anatolia. But his hold on power remained precarious and he began to think that he needed a big success to win back the esteem of his people. Such a coup might be the recapture of Nicaea. But to do that he would need help.

## The letter to Robert of Flanders from Alexius

This letter was supposedly sent by Alexius in the early 1090s. There is some debate about whether it is genuine and many scholars have dismissed it as an implausible fabrication written in the twelfth century. It indicates that the empire had suffered heavy defeats at the hands of the Turks. There is also an argument that the lands had been lost to the Turks before 1081 and so the letter is based on a false premise. Moreover, it gives a list of the treasured relics of Constantinople, which could have encouraged attacks on the city, and so seems rather unlikely. The historian Peter Frankopan, writing in 2012, argues that it reflects the reality of the situation in the empire in this period, whether written by Alexius or not. Alexius had already received military support from Robert I of Flanders (*c.*1035–93) in the form of 500 knights to help in the defence of Byzantium and was hoping for more.

**SOURCE D**

**An extract from the letter to Robert of Flanders. From 'The Problem of the Spurious Letter of Emperor Alexius to the Count of Flanders', translated by E. Joranson, *American Historical Review*, Vol. 55, 1950, pp. 812–15.**

*O most illustrious count and especial comforter of the Christian faith! I wish to make known to you how the most sacred empire of the Greek Christians is being sorely distressed by the [Pechenegs] and the Turks, who daily ravage it and … seize its territory … There is widespread slaughter and indescribable killing … of the Christians … Accordingly, for love of God and out of sympathy for all Christian Greeks, we beg that you will lead hither to my aid and that of the Christian Greeks whatever faithful warriors of Christ you may be able to enlist … so that they may, for the salvation of their souls, endeavour to liberate the kingdom of the Greeks; since I, albeit that I am emperor, can find no remedy or suitable counsel, but am*

*[continued over the page]*

**SOURCE QUESTION**

What are the inducements that the writer holds out to those coming to aid him? From what you know of the reign of Alexius, how accurate is Source D as an account of his situation?

*always fleeing in the face of the Turks and the [Pechenegs] and I remain in a certain city only until I perceive that their arrival is imminent. And I think it better to be subject to your Latins than to the abomination of the pagans. Therefore, before Constantinople is captured by them, you most certainly ought to fight with all your strength so you may receive a glorious reward in heaven.*

As we have seen, such an appeal would receive a favourable hearing in the west. Given the number of knights who had already made the journey east and returned with stories of the horrific treatment of Christians at the hands of the Turks, Alexius had already been preparing the ground for an appeal with messages about the worsening situation in Jerusalem, which would strike a chord with many in the west. He was, therefore, able to exploit this concern for his own ends and link his problems to those of Jerusalem. Meanwhile, as we have seen on pages 7–10, political developments in the west provided Urban with an ideal opportunity and motive to respond.

## CHAPTER SUMMARY

The circumstances which led to the crusading movement arose from theories which suggested that a war against the Muslims was a Just War and from the ambitions of the papacy, which hoped to end the schism with Constantinople advantageously. The papacy had been weakened by the Investiture Contest and took this opportunity to raise its prestige. Further causes came from the expansion of Islam and the tensions within the Islamic world between various groups, which made pilgrimages to the holy places more perilous. The final cause lay within the Byzantine Empire, where Alexius I asked for help against the threat of the Seljuk Turks. Alexius I was a usurper and the Byzantine Empire was not easy to hold together. In view of the threat from the Turks, he felt he needed outside assistance.

## Refresher questions

Use these questions to remind yourself of the key issues in this chapter.

**1** What was the theory behind the idea of a Just War?
**2** What problems was the papacy facing?
**3** Why were pilgrimages popular?
**4** What was the connection of Muhammad with Jerusalem?
**5** Why was Constantinople so wealthy?
**6** What were the main problems facing Alexius I?
**7** What factors allowed Alexius I to overcome some of his problems?

CHAPTER 2

# The Council of Clermont and its impact

In 1095 Pope Urban II summoned a gathering of Christians to Clermont in France. Here, he appealed to those present to embark on a crusade to the east. His speech was met with an eager response and the result was that the first crusaders set out in 1096–7. This chapter focuses on Urban's sermon at Clermont through the following themes:

- The reasons behind Urban's appeal for a crusade to go to the east
- Urban II's sermon at Clermont
- The response to Urban II's sermon
- The first crusaders and their motives

The key debate on page 40 of this chapter asks the question: What were the motives of those who went on the Crusade?

### KEY DATES

| | | | |
|---|---|---|---|
| **1073** | Seljuk Turks captured Jerusalem | **1094** | Church Council at Piacenza |
| **1088** | Urban II became pope | **1095** | Church Council at Clermont |
| **1092** | Death of Sultan Malik Shah | | |

## 1 The reasons behind Urban's appeal for a crusade to go to the east

■ *Why did Urban II make his appeal for a crusade to go to the east?*

There were several reasons for Urban II's appeal. As mentioned earlier (see pages 7–10), the papacy had been through some difficult times, but with the changing political situation and Urban's experience he had the opportunity to revive the papacy.

### Urban II's involvement with the growing importance of the papacy

Urban II marked the papal revival by holding a Council at Piacenza in 1094, which was attended by both bishops and representatives of lay powers, and which exemplified the greater strength of his position (see page 10). The Council passed decrees against simony and **clerical marriage**, reflecting Urban II's commitment to the papal reform movement. It did not take immediate action against the French king Philip I and his adulterous relationship, showing

**KEY TERM**

**Clerical marriage**
Marriage for priests and bishops was (in theory) forbidden in the Roman Catholic Church, but not in the Greek Orthodox Church.

Urban II's diplomatic skills. The Council was also addressed by representatives of Alexius I, who asked for help in the form of mercenary soldiers to aid in the fight against the Turks (see page 10). They may have exaggerated the danger and perhaps stimulated the papal belief that only drastic actions could save Byzantium and the eastern Church.

Urban II wanted to build bridges with Byzantium and had lifted the excommunication of Alexius I in 1089. The Greek emperor had his own reasons for wanting to be on better terms with Rome, as his ambassadors had made clear. The differences between the Roman Catholic and Greek Orthodox Churches remained but were no longer seen as so important. The anti-pope, Clement III, lost his support among the Greeks by calling a council and condemning clerical marriage. Thus, the proclamation of the Crusade in Urban II's appeal could only set the seal on the increasing reputation of the papacy.

## Urban II and the Christians in the east

Urban II made the sufferings of Christians in the east a focus of his appeal. Historians have debated how far the Christians were suffering, but recent work by historians such as Frankopan has argued that Urban's speech did not exaggerate the situation and that his words would have been confirmed by stories from those who had returned from the east.

In many of the conquered areas, the Christians were a subject population who paid taxes but were free to worship to an extent. Sultan Malik Shah (see page 18) had restored order. There is no evidence of organised attacks on Christians and no appeals from them were sent to Constantinople or Rome. It is not even certain that Muslims were the majority population in Syria and Palestine in this period. But the death of Malik Shah certainly led to instability in the region. Civil war between his sons disrupted travel. In Syria there were disputes between rival warlords and Jerusalem was in the hands of yet another Turkish adventurer. The Fatimids seized the opportunity to reconquer southern Palestine, while another ambitious Turkish general, Kerbogha, formerly an Abbasid **atabeg**, began to attack the area around Aleppo.

Pilgrims were finding their journeys increasingly difficult. The rulers of many towns used the lack of central authority as an opportunity to levy tolls and taxes, and attacks from brigands and robbers were common.

**KEY TERMS**

**Atabeg** Hereditary Turkish noble title, given to the ruler of a province.

**Western Wall** Also called Kotel or the Al-Buraq Wall: the site where Muhammad tied his steed on his Night Journey to Jerusalem before ascending to paradise, and the holiest place where Jews are allowed to pray.

## Urban II's aim to capture Jerusalem

The city of Jerusalem had been captured by the Arab armies of Caliph Umar in 638, and remained in the hands of the caliphate for the next 400 years.

### The significance of Jerusalem

Jerusalem was a city sacred to Jews as the site of the Temple, until this was destroyed by the Romans in AD70. The **Western Wall** is one of the remnants of the Temple sanctified by pilgrimage and prayer.

## Pope Urban II c.1035–99

Pope Urban II's birth name was Odo. He came from a noble family in Champagne, was educated in France and then became an archdeacon in the diocese of Reims. He moved on to become a monk at Cluny and soon rose to be abbot. Hence, he was at the centre of the monastic reform movement. He was sent to Rome in 1084 and made a cardinal by Pope Gregory VII. He then went to Germany as papal legate, but remained loyal to Gregory in the papal struggle with Henry IV. Gregory was succeeded by Victor III who died in 1087, so Urban was elected pope in 1088. His approach was more moderate than that of Gregory and he focused on reform more than the investiture issue (see page 9). He called the Council of Clermont and preached the First Crusade in 1095. In his fifties, he was young enough to hope to be able to reform the papacy. At first his position was weak and insecure. Emperor Henry IV (1050–1106) had been crowned by the rival pope and was triumphant in Germany and northern Italy. It was not until 1093 that Urban could spend Christmas in Rome. Henry IV had been weakened by the revolt of his son, Conrad, which the pope had quietly encouraged, and France and Spain recognised Urban II once it became clear that he would not insist on the extravagant claims which Gregory VII had made. The Normans in southern Italy and Sicily also backed him. He hoped to reunite the Greek and Roman Churches but hostility in Byzantium defeated him. He launched the First Crusade in 1095 but died before learning of the capture of Jerusalem in July 1099.

## Kerbogha

Kerbogha was the atabeg of Mosul and faced the crusaders in the siege of Antioch in 1098. He paused on his way to relieve the siege to attack Edessa and so arrived too late to save Antioch, although he then besieged the crusaders who had taken the city. One version of this story says he had 75,000 men in his army, but that they came from different areas, owing allegiance to different emirs, and he found it hard to keep them united. His mother, aged about 70, travelled from Aleppo to urge him not to attack the crusaders as their God was so powerful, He would defend them. This story may be a later insertion to boost the reputation of Christianity. In the end, his troops deserted and he returned to Mosul in some disgrace.

For Christians, Jerusalem was equally a holy city as the place where Jesus had been crucified and risen again. The Church of the Holy Sepulchre was believed to have been built on the site of the tomb where Christ's body had rested.

For Muslims, Jerusalem was significant as the place to which Muhammad had made his Night Journey, when he was taken miraculously by the angel Gabriel to pray at Jerusalem, nearly 1250 kilometres away, and returned to Mecca in a single night. It was also the place from where he had ascended into heaven. The Shrine of the Dome of the Rock marked the holiest spot.

Under Muslim rule, Jews and Christians were seen as deserving of toleration, although the superiority of Islamic teachings was made clear. Thus, Christian visits to Jerusalem were allowed and, in the eleventh century, pilgrimages had become very common. Travelling to Jerusalem was difficult, costly and wearisome, as much of the journey would have to be on foot, and as a result won the pilgrim great spiritual rewards.

The capture of Jerusalem by the Seljuk Turks in 1073 and then by the Fatimids in 1098 made little difference to the treatment of pilgrims. The powerful attraction of Jerusalem as a destination for crusaders was because of its central role in

Christian beliefs. The city was widely believed to be the place from which the Last Judgement would be brought about by God: after the Holy Roman Emperor had surrendered his earthly power, the heavenly power would take over.

Both Gregory VII and Alexius I had mentioned the liberation of Jerusalem as a possible aim for a crusading or mercenary army, and Urban II took up this idea. As a reformer he dreamed of restoring the Church to the purity of its earthly days under the apostles in Jerusalem. 'Freeing' the city was an essential first step towards this goal. It was, therefore, hardly surprising that his emphasis was more on freeing Jerusalem than in providing the Emperor Alexius with aid. Source A (below) shows how he felt.

## Urban II's aim to instigate penitential warfare

The idea of fighting for the remission of one's sins (see the box, page 25) had begun with Gregory VII, and the Crusades as collective acts of penance were distinct from other holy wars. The crusader was fighting not only for the Church and the future of Christianity, but also to save his own soul from the torments of hell. The religious developments and movements outlined in Chapter 1 meant that the pope was able to draw on the religious passion and fervour of the time, as well as the desire for adventure. Urban II took up this belief and his message that he wanted a war of liberation where the crusaders would fight as an act of penance resonated well in France. The central power of the state in France was very limited and the result was an anarchic situation where personal safety was far from being guaranteed. The Peace and Truce of God movement (see page 5) had partly been a response to this situation. The Church was trying to channel all this aggression in society into more worthy aims. Urban II, whose family was part of the knightly class, was a keen exponent of this view and his ideas had been much influenced by his time at Cluny, one of the powerhouses of the reform movement. But what he was doing was to put the act of warfare in the same class as other meritorious acts such as prayer and fasting, which was a different way of looking at warfare.

**ONLINE EXTRAS** OCR **WWW**

Learn how to plan an effective essay by completing Worksheet 1 at **www.hoddereducation.co.uk/accesstohistory/extras**

**ONLINE EXTRAS** Pearson Edexcel **WWW**

Learn how to write effective opening sentences by completing Worksheet 1 at **www.hoddereducation.co.uk/accesstohistory/extras**

**SOURCE A**

**Bernold of Constance gives an account of the Council at Piacenza, quoted in Peter Frankopan, *The First Crusade*, Vintage Press, 2013, p. vii.**

*An embassy of the emperor of Constantinople came to the synod and implored his lordship the Pope and all the faithful of Christ to bring assistance against the heathen for the defence of this holy church, which had now been nearly annihilated in that region by the infidels who had conquered her as far as the walls of Constantinople. Our Lord Pope called upon many to perform this service, to promise by oaths to journey there by God's will and to bring the emperor the most faithful assistance against the heathen as very best as they were able.*

**SOURCE QUESTION**

What does Source A suggest about the relationship between the pope and the emperor? How accurate is this view from your own knowledge?

## Penance

Remission of sins was an essential part of Roman Catholic doctrine. Catholics believed that their sins must be fully forgiven in order for them to reach heaven and that they were weighed down by the burden of sinfulness. Going to confession and performing acts of penitence helped them to gain absolution, but visiting shrines, going to holy places where relics of saints were displayed and going on a pilgrimage were ways of gaining extra forgiveness.

The pope could also grant plenary indulgences, that is, to remove all temporal punishment from sinners because all their sins would be forgiven. The conditions under which the indulgence was granted were laid down by the pope.

SUMMARY DIAGRAM

**THE REASONS BEHIND URBAN'S APPEAL FOR A CRUSADE TO GO TO THE EAST**

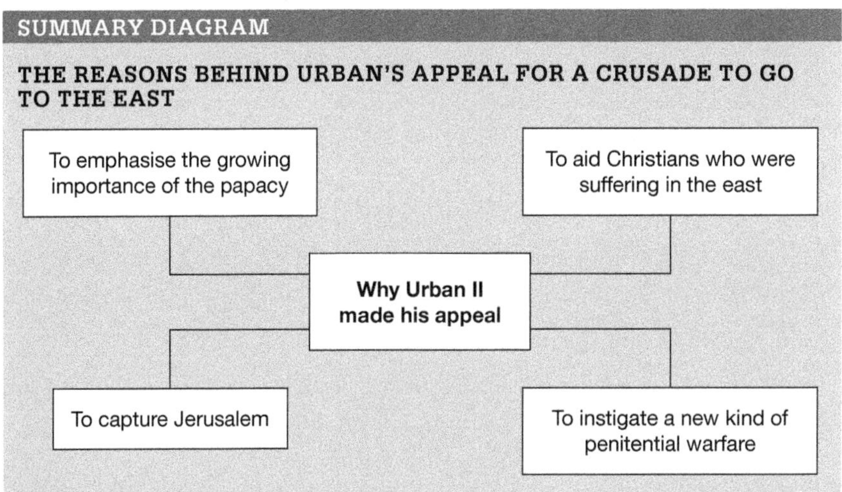


# 2 Urban II's sermon at Clermont

- *What happened at Clermont?*

Building on his success at the Council of Piacenza, Urban II decided on a tour of France to underline his control of the Church. The key moment was to be the Council at Clermont.

## The route to Clermont

Urban II arrived in Provence in July 1095 and finally left France in September 1096 after a journey which covered about 3000 kilometres. He was accompanied by many other clerics, often high-ranking bishops, archbishops and cardinals. He wore his tiara and the procession in which he rode was probably the most magnificent ever seen by those who witnessed it. His route was a strategic one. He took in Le Puy, whose Bishop Adhémar of Monteil was to be a leader in the

Crusade. It was from here, possibly after conferring with Adhémar, that he sent out the summons to Clermont. He celebrated the feast of the Assumption at this major Marian shrine and then moved on to Saint-Gilles, part of the lands of Raymond of Saint-Gilles, the Count of Toulouse. As Raymond had fought the Muslims in Spain, the pope hoped he would join the new crusade. In October, Urban returned to Cluny to dedicate the high altar of the new church being built there. The monks at Cluny were told stories by those who stayed in their hostels of the problems faced by pilgrims. It is clearly evident that Urban used the time from his arrival in France until the Council at Clermont to prepare and win support for his crusade, reflected in the immediate response to his message from Adhémar and Raymond of Toulouse, which would ensure that recruitment got off to a good start. However, he avoided the territory of the Capetian French king, Philip I (1052–1108), who was no friend to Urban, and also the northern parts of France where William II 'Rufus' (c.1056–1100) was in dispute with his brother, Robert of Normandy (c.1051–1134).

## The Council at Clermont

The Council opened on 18 November 1095 and sat for ten days. About 300 churchmen were present. The initial discussions were along familiar lines:

- Decrees were passed against simony, lay investiture and clerical marriage (see pages 8, 9 and 21).
- Philip I of France was excommunicated for his adulterous marriage to Bertrade of Montfort.
- The Truce of God (see pages 5–6) was to be universally recognised.

On 27 November, Urban II held a public session of the Council. Great crowds assembled so the meeting was held out of doors rather than in the cathedral as

## Raymond of Toulouse 1041/2–1105

Raymond IV of Saint-Gilles succeeded his brother, William IV, as Count of Toulouse in 1088. He was a much-respected man with genuine religious feeling and supported the papal reform programme. His instant response to the call for the First Crusade was probably agreed with Urban II before the sermon at Clermont. He was the oldest and the richest of the leaders of the First Crusade and was accompanied by his wife and son, as well as Bishop Adhémar. He refused to swear fealty to Alexius but did take an oath of friendship. He was a man of his word and tried to persuade Bohemund to return Antioch to the emperor after the crusaders captured it. But he was also ambitious for himself and diverted to attack Tripoli on the march to Jerusalem. He returned eventually to join in the attack and capture of Jerusalem, taking the Tower of David and then refusing to give it up to Godfrey of Bouillon. But he rejected the throne of Jerusalem which was offered to him, saying he could not rule in a city where his saviour had suffered. He took part in the defeat of the Fatimid attack at the Battle of Ascalon in 1099, but then formed an alliance with Alexius II. His forces blocked the advance of Bohemund from the territory of Antioch. He built a castle, Mons Peregrinus, outside Tripoli as a base from which to continue his attack. He died there in 1105 and Tripoli fell to his troops soon afterwards. One of his clerks, Raymond of Aguilers, accompanied him and wrote an account of the Crusade.

had happened before, and it was here that Urban II delivered his sermon calling for the Crusade.

## Urban's appeal

There is no one reliable account of what Urban said. Versions from five chroniclers are given in Table 2.1 (see below and page 28). These were all written after the outcome of the First Crusade was known and depend to an extent on the information available to the different chroniclers at the time.

**Table 2.1** Summaries of Urban's appeal at Clermont

| Chronicle | Date | Written by | Details of the account |
|---|---|---|---|
| *Gesta Francorum* (*Deeds of the Franks*) | For the Crusade itself the author made notes and then wrote his account a few years later in 1104–5 | A knight who went on the Crusade. His account is valuable as most other versions were by churchmen, but he was probably not present at Clermont and was therefore writing from what he had been told | The author stressed the need for the crusader to save his soul and to suffer in the name of Christ to gain a heavenly reward |
| *A History of the Expedition to Jerusalem* | Written between 1101 and 1128 | Fulcher of Chartres, a priest. Fulcher was at Clermont and went on the Crusade with Stephen of Blois | • Reference to the acceptance of the Truce of God<br>• Other ways in which the Christian knight can serve God<br>• The conquests of the Turks and Arabs in the east<br>• Ill-treatment of Christians<br>• The granting of remission of sins for all who die on the Crusade<br>• An eloquent appeal to all who can fight in the cause |
| *Historia Hierosolymitana* (*History of Jerusalem*) | After 1106 | Robert the Monk of Reims. There is little information about Robert. He claims to have been at Clermont but was not a crusader. He used the *Gesta Francorum* as his basic text but added to its theological content | • Reference to the special regard the people of France have for the Church<br>• Sad news from Jerusalem and Constantinople about the invasions by the people of Persia<br>• Descriptions of how Christians had been ill-treated and enslaved, with much gory detail<br>• Descriptions of how much land had been conquered from the Greeks<br>• Appeal to remember Charlemagne and his son Louis, who destroyed Turkish kingdoms and established Christianity<br>• Holy places being treated with dishonour by an 'unclean' people<br>• Descriptions of how men are so poor and short of food they are fighting one another, but the victors can rule over a land flowing with milk and honey |

*[continued overleaf]*

| Chronicle | Date | Written by | Details of the account |
|---|---|---|---|
| *Historiae Hierosolymitanae Libri IV (History of Jerusalem, Book IV)* | Written between 1107 and 1111 | Written by Baldric of Dol, who was Archbishop of Dol in Brittany. He was not at Clermont and did not go on the Crusade, but he knew people who did. He, too, used the *Gesta Francorum* as a basic source but improved the language and the theology | • Vivid references to the sufferings of the Church under the Turks, with sacred sites being profaned and Christians tortured or killed<br>• Descriptions of how disgraceful it is that Jerusalem, the city in which Christ suffered, should be in pagan hands<br>• How equally disgraceful it is that Christian knights fight each other<br>• An appeal to the knights to fight instead for Christ in defence of the eastern Church and drive out the Turks in righteous warfare<br>• Noting that the possessions of the enemy will be bestowed on the victorious knights<br>• An appeal to the other bishops and clergy present to preach the same in their churches |
| *God's Deeds Through the Franks* | Written between 1106 and 1109 | Guibert of Nogent, who was abbot of the Benedictine Monastery at Nogent. He, too, used the *Gesta Francorum* and elaborated on its rather basic content | • The need to cleanse the polluted and sacred shrines in Jerusalem, the holiest place on earth<br>• How men had fought unjust wars eagerly enough so should now fight a Just War with a glorious reward<br>• How, if neither the words of scripture nor the papal appeal stir men to fight, then the sufferings of the Christians should do so<br>• Pilgrims are being ill-treated and forced to pay excessive taxes to travel to Jerusalem and tortured if they refuse, with plenty of detail about the tortures<br>• The need to fight in the name of Christ |

The summaries in Table 2.1 show that capturing Jerusalem was the goal of the Crusade, although it is not included in the work of Fulcher of Chartres, whose report is the one closest to the actual event. Historian Hans Eberhard Meyer, writing in 1965, argues that the letters which Urban II wrote after Clermont to urge others to join the Crusade initially referred to the need to save the eastern Churches as the main aim. By 1086, however, he was writing about the 'march to Jerusalem to free the Church of God'. Meyer suggests that there was a lack of overall planning and that it was during 1086 that public opinion led Urban to revise his thinking.

**ONLINE EXTRAS OCR** WWW

Develop your understanding of Urban's motives for the Crusade by completing Worksheet 2 at **www.hoddereducation.co.uk/accesstohistory/extras**

Historian H.E.J. Cowdrey, writing in 1970, suggests that there is evidence that refers to the march to Jerusalem as the focus of the Crusade, since it was the heart of the eastern Church. However, Meyer argues that this was unlikely as Urban II would have no wish to promote a new rival to Rome, although Meyer does concede that Cowdrey's evidence has some merit.

Historian Peter Frankopan, writing in 2013, takes the view that Urban II's main emphasis initially was on the spiritual benefits to be obtained, the relief from having to perform penance for all sins committed, forgiveness of specific sins and a share in the sufferings of Christ. He also suggests that these prospects had less power in enticing men to join the Crusade than the attraction of liberating Jerusalem. It is also likely that details of the expedition would be vague, as the pope saw Alexius as in charge of the army and that it would be up to him to organise the details once the force had arrived. Source B gives one version of part of Urban II's sermon.

**ONLINE EXTRAS** WWW
OCR

Learn how to write an argument rather than an assertion by completing Worksheet 3 at **www.hoddereducation.co.uk/accesstohistory/extras**

## SOURCE B

**Robert the Monk's account of the closing words of Urban's sermon, quoted in Carol Sweetenham, *Robert the Monk's History of the First Crusade*, Ashgate Publishing, 2005, p. 81.**

*Jerusalem is the navel of the earth. It is a land more fruitful than any other, almost another earthly paradise. Our Redeemer [Jesus] dignified it with his arrival, adorned it with his words, consecrated it through his Passion, redeemed it by his death and glorified it with his burial. Yet this royal city at the centre of the world is now held captive by her enemies and enslaved by those who know nothing of the ways of the people of God. So she begs and craves to be free and prays endlessly for you to come to her aid. Indeed it is your help she particularly seeks because God has granted you outstanding glory in war above all other nations. So seize on this road to obtain the remission of your sins, sure in the indestructible glory of the Heavenly Kingdom.*

**SOURCE QUESTION**

Identify all the ways in Source B that the pope uses to try to encourage men to join the Crusade.

## SUMMARY DIAGRAM

**URBAN II'S SERMON AT CLERMONT**

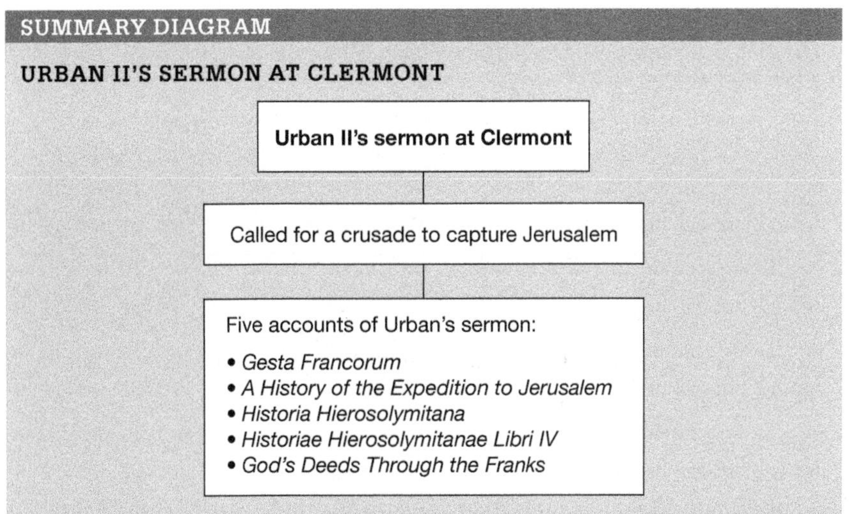

Urban II's sermon at Clermont
Called for a crusade to capture Jerusalem
Five accounts of Urban's sermon:
• *Gesta Francorum*
• *A History of the Expedition to Jerusalem*
• *Historia Hierosolymitana*
• *Historiae Hierosolymitanae Libri IV*
• *God's Deeds Through the Franks*

# 3 The response to Urban II's sermon

- *What was the response to Urban II's sermon?*

**KEY TERMS**

**Confession** The prayer in which worshippers asked for forgiveness for the sins they had committed.

**Absolution** The act of forgiveness, which only a priest could undertake.

**Surcoat** A garment worn over medieval armour, often embroidered with heraldic arms.

**Plenary indulgence** Absolved someone from all punishments incurred by their sins.

Urban II had not even finished his sermon before some of the crowd began to shout *'Deus le volt'* ('God wills it'), further evidence that call for the Crusade was carefully staged to ensure that there was large-scale support. As soon as the pope stopped speaking, the Bishop of Le Puy knelt before him and begged for permission to join the Crusade, again suggesting that this had all been carefully organised during Urban's time in Provence. The support of a renowned bishop would help to ensure that other high-profile Christians would join the call. Even at the actual site of the sermon, hundreds of those assembled followed suit. They were led to repeat the words of the **confession** and the pope gave them **absolution** and sent them home.

Although it might be argued that this was perhaps a rather more enthusiastic response than Urban had dared to hope for, it is more likely a clear sign that the preparations he had made since his arrival in Provence had been a success. However, those present at Clermont were not the most influential or powerful lords, but that was rectified the next day when envoys from Raymond of Toulouse arrived and pledged his backing for the Crusade and his support provided the major figure for it to be effective. In the meantime, the pope consulted with his bishops and issued further instructions about the mechanics of the Crusade:

- All who took part and who had confessed their sins would receive full remission of penance or a **plenary indulgence**.
- The worldly belongings of those on crusade would be protected by their bishops while they were away.

All crusaders should wear the sign of the cross with a red cross sewn on the shoulder of their **surcoat**.

- The old and infirm should not go.
- Monks needed permission to join.
- The Crusade was not solely a war of conquest and the Greek Christians should have their possessions restored to them.
- Those taking part should be ready to leave by the Feast of the Assumption (15 August) 1096 and assemble in Constantinople.

The view that much of the response was orchestrated is supported by some historians, such as Christopher Tyerman (2006), who suggests that Urban was clear from the start about what he hoped to achieve. Urban carried with him relics of the True Cross, possibly provided by Alexius, and the symbolism of 'taking the Cross' was linked to the association with Jerusalem as the place of crucifixion. His sermon outlined his new concept of holy war to liberate the eastern Christians as an act of penitential piety and with the benefit of full remission of sins. Source C (see below) illustrates this point.

The unfamiliar message needed a prearranged response, which was the role of the Bishop of Le Puy. The sewing of crosses on the tunics of the crusaders was a physical response to the sermon, which underlined its impact, but again their availability suggests that it was planned. In some later meetings where the Crusade was preached, Tyerman references the placing of those already converted at the front of the audience, so they could come forward first and then others would follow.

Urban then went on to complete a preaching tour to gather more volunteers and he urged all his bishops to preach the crusade in their dioceses. Clergy went to the Loire, Normandy, Limousin and England to raise support. The target was the aristocracy; men who were used to fighting and who would welcome a legitimate enemy against whom they could show their skills. He tried to discourage some of those who responded so eagerly to his call, as there was no role for non-combatants, so the infirm and women and children were recommended to stay at home. Clerics and monks needed permission from their bishop or abbot to go crusading, and newly married young men were expected to get the blessing of their wives before joining the Crusade. Urban also told the knights of northern Spain that they would be more profitably employed in continuing the fight there against the Muslims, rather than joining in the march to the east.

### SOURCE C

**Guibert of Nogent (*c*.1055–1124) explains how the cross became the symbol for the crusaders, quoted in Edward Peters, editor, *The First Crusade*, University of Pennsylvania Press, 1971, p. 37.**

*The most excellent man concluded his oration and by the power of the blessed Peter absolved all who vowed to go and confirmed those acts with apostolic blessing. He instituted a sign well suited to so honorable a profession by making the figure of the cross, the sign of the Lord's Passion, the emblem of the soldiery, or rather of what was to be the soldiery of God. This, made of any kind of cloth, he ordered to be sewed upon the shirts and cloaks of those about to go. He commanded that if anyone, after receiving this emblem or after openly taking this vow, should shrink from his good intent through base change of heart, or affection for his parents, he should be regarded as an outlaw forever, unless he repented and again undertook his pledge.*

**SOURCE QUESTION**

What light does Source C throw on what was in the pope's mind at this point?

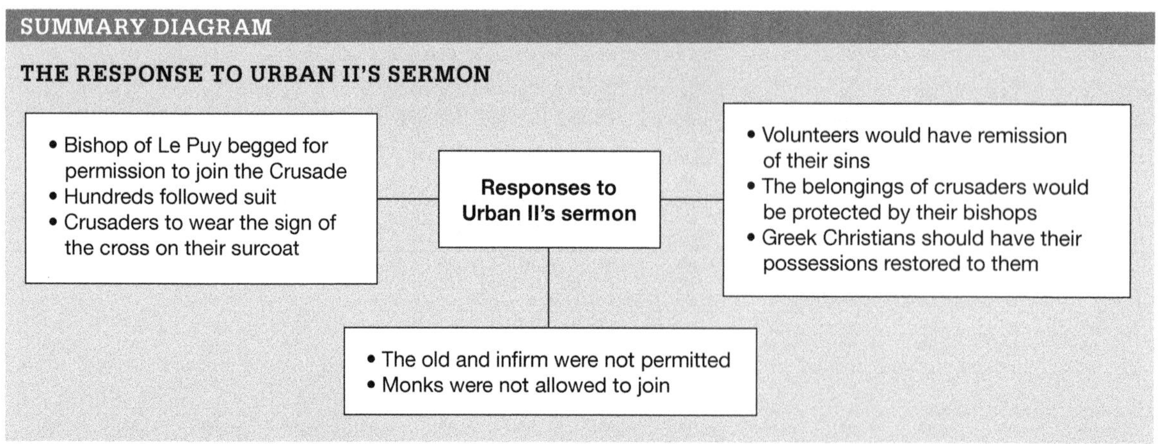

SUMMARY DIAGRAM
THE RESPONSE TO URBAN II'S SERMON
Responses to Urban II's sermon
• Bishop of Le Puy begged for permission to join the Crusade
• Hundreds followed suit
• Crusaders to wear the sign of the cross on their surcoat
• Volunteers would have remission of their sins
• The belongings of crusaders would be protected by their bishops
• Greek Christians should have their possessions restored to them
• The old and infirm were not permitted
• Monks were not allowed to join


# 4 The first crusaders and their motives

■ *Who were the first crusaders and why did they go on crusade?*

The reasons for people leaving their homes varied, with probably as many different motives as people who went on the Crusade. Urban's appeal at Clermont and use of highly emotive language certainly resulted in a massive wave of recruits for a holy war, producing a mass movement that would not be repeated. It led to an army of peasants, women and children, as well as knights, and was certainly more than either he envisaged or Alexius wanted.

Urban certainly had his own motives for his sermon. Although some of the chroniclers and early historians of the Crusades made the sermon at Clermont seem a spontaneous reaction by Urban II to the appeals from the east, recent research has shown that much careful thought had gone into Urban II's decision to preach the sermon.

Urban II had a number of issues to bear in mind:

- The Investiture Contest had weakened the papacy in that there was a rival pope and it was not always safe for popes to live in Rome. Urban II needed to show he had overcome this.
- Reform movements in the Church were strengthening.
- The situation in the Holy Lands was thought to be deteriorating.
- Alexius I was under pressure in Byzantium.

The pope was faced with a situation in which he could show his leadership, express his reforming credentials and give assistance to the Greek Church, and so smooth over the schism and win back for the Christians the sacred spaces which were so important to them.

Urban was also concerned to put a stop to the violence of the warring kingdoms in Europe and his message at Clermont specifically targeted the nobility of northern France and northern Europe. The pope, and many in the Church, believed that society was breaking down in western Europe. Local bishops had already attempted to bring about peace in what was called the Peace and Truce of God movement (see page 5), and this concern is reflected in Urban's sermon when he mentioned the violence of Christian against Christian. Rather than knights fighting each other he wanted them to help their Christian brothers, put an end to civil war in their own countries and go to the Holy Land.

## Why did people go on the Crusade?

One of the main debates about the Crusades concerns the reasons why people joined to travel vast distances and often to suffer tremendous hardship, with the chance of never returning. Although the reasons for people undertaking such a vast and dangerous enterprise varied considerably, it is helpful to group them in three possible reasons:

- Religious reasons. Historians working in a more secular age can underestimate the strong beliefs and the genuine faith of many crusaders, but the current consensus among historians is that reverence for the holy places and the promise of remission of sins were sufficient for most (see page 25).
- Political reasons. This probably applied most to the pope and his representatives. The pope wanted to increase his political power (see page 22) and some would see the benefit of being his ally.
- Territorial reasons. Some knights and princes had no land and saw the opportunity to establish their own power and kingdom. However, for ordinary crusaders it may have been the chance to acquire loot and plunder.

### Poverty

In some cases, it is difficult to find evidence for the motivations of those who joined the Crusades. The poor did not keep crusading diaries and probably were illiterate. They may have been influenced by the growing population, which affected inheritances. In cultures where the land was divided equally among the heirs, as more children in the family survived, the size of the land which passed to each heir shrank and eventually became insufficient to maintain the peasant and his family. In addition, prior to 1096, there had been several years of poor harvests in France as a result of droughts, which led to famine. One of the outcomes was an epidemic of **ergotism**. As symptoms included mania and seizures, the superstitious often believed that those affected were victims of witchcraft. This added to rural tensions. Thus, there were good reasons for the poor to leave their villages, and the propaganda stressed the prospects of a new life in a new land. However, as stated earlier, it is not possible to know for certain why they went.

**KEY TERM**

**Ergotism** A disease prevalent in areas where rye bread was eaten. It was caused by eating rye that was affected by a fungus. Symptoms included convulsions, hallucinations and gangrene. Sufferers often died.

**SOURCE QUESTION**

What impression does Source D intend to create about the crusaders?

**SOURCE D**

A crusader knight from a thirteenth-century psalter.

## Hope of gaining territory

Some say the knightly class were men of violence and saw the Crusade as a splendid opportunity. The tenacious way in which men such as Bohemund of Taranto and Baldwin of Boulogne fastened on to the territories they conquered supports this view. However, even if Bohemund went with conquest in mind (and the fears of Alexius I suggest that his contemporaries thought that was his aim), it is difficult to find other examples. Moreover, some knightly families built up a tradition of crusading and several family members went, such as the Montlhéry, whose descendants included Baldwin II (died 1131), Joscelin I of Edessa (died 1131) and Hugh I of Jaffa (died 1112/16). In any case, initially, the Crusade was viewed as helping a Greek enterprise under the emperor and it was expected that Alexius I would take over lands conquered, which had once been part of his empire. It was the refusal of Alexius I to go far from Constantinople which led to the Crusades becoming independent ventures.

## Plunder

Some of those who joined the Crusades might have done so for motives of plunder. The Crusades in Spain had certainly made some participants rich and the Council at Clermont was worried that 'money' might be a motive. Attacks on Jewish people in the first wave of the Crusade included extortion and looting, and this continued in the march to Antioch. Yet, a certain amount of foraging was inevitable, and there was a thin line between legitimate transactions and pillage. Certainly, few returned from the Crusades with bags of gold. The problems of transporting bulky objects defeated most who acquired them. Those who left Jerusalem in 1099 loaded with treasure were usually poor again by the time they reached northern Syria.

## Primogeniture and younger sons

A popular explanation for men going on crusade is that they were younger sons of landed families, for whom there was no future at home. As **primogeniture** became the norm, excess heirs were a burden on the estate and needed an outlet. But the evidence does not support this view. Going on a crusade was a costly business. A knight needed a horse, servants and animals to carry his baggage. Moreover, knights knew from the accounts of pilgrims that it was a long way to Jerusalem and a difficult journey. Charters in monasteries and cathedrals show knights selling their land or possessions to finance their travel.

## Family settlements

Families often took joint decisions about financing a crusading member. One trend noted is that they made good use of the opportunity to settle outstanding disputes, so that the crusader could depart with a clear conscience. If family land was at stake, other family members might buy it, or a religious institution might advance money with the land as security. When it came to having to dispose of land, families chose to sell land where titles were in dispute or where the land was already mortgaged.

Thus, travelling 3000 kilometres on a crusade was expensive, and to do so on the off-chance of gaining land when one got there, or of returning with enhanced status, would have been foolhardy. The most reasonable explanation is that the knights mentioned in this section were motivated by genuine religious devotion. In addition, the numbers going on crusade were only a proportion of the knightly class. In the French-speaking parts of Europe there were probably 50,000 knights, while on the First Crusade the total number of knights was about 10,000. The majority of knights stayed at home and, perhaps, endowed a monastery or enriched their local church, instead.

# The main crusaders and their motives

Urban's appeal at Clermont was to the nobility of western Europe, particularly of France and Flanders. He did not ask a king to lead the Crusade because this was a papal expedition. The political leaders of Europe were also divided, the

**ONLINE EXTRAS** AQA WWW

Learn to identify a range of factors by completing Worksheet 1 at **www.hoddereducation.co.uk/accesstohistory/extras**

**ONLINE EXTRAS** OCR WWW

Develop your analysis of factors by completing Worksheet 4 at **www.hoddereducation.co.uk/accesstohistory/extras**

**ONLINE EXTRAS** OCR WWW

Develop your understanding of economic motives for the Crusades by completing Worksheet 5 at **www.hoddereducation.co.uk/accesstohistory/extras**

**KEY TERM**

**Primogeniture** The right of succession belonging to the firstborn son. This was common in western Europe, where the eldest son inherited all the lands of his parents.

**ONLINE EXTRAS** Pearson Edexcel WWW

Learn how to write a balanced argument by completing Worksheet 2 at **www.hoddereducation.co.uk/accesstohistory/extras**

**ONLINE EXTRAS** Pearson Edexcel WWW

Develop your analysis of causation by completing Worksheet 3 at **www.hoddereducation.co.uk/accesstohistory/extras**

**ONLINE EXTRAS** Pearson Edexcel WWW

Get to grips with planning an essay by completing Worksheet 4 at **www.hoddereducation.co.uk/accesstohistory/extras**

**KEY TERM**

**Frankish knights** Men from the landowning classes and influenced by the code of chivalry and the legends of the past. Chivalry in this sense was the honourable conduct expected from a knight, such as courtesy to ladies and undertaking of worthy tasks. (It was more notable for the theory than for the observance.) The Frankish knights fought on horseback, and their equipment and entourage were expensive to maintain.

Holy Roman Emperor Henry IV was still excommunicated, as was Philip I of France, while William II of England had little interest in the Church. As a result, those who were invited to join the Crusade were some of the greatest nobles of Europe, including **Frankish knights**. Some were princes, which has led to some calling this Crusade 'the Princes' Crusade'.

## Adhémar, Bishop of Le Puy

Adhémar (died 1098) had already been on a pilgrimage to Jerusalem and had probably discussed the possibility of a crusade with the pope. Hence, he was able to be the first to volunteer, which gave him some kind of precedence, and he was appointed as the official papal representative. He was a skilled negotiator and needed all of his diplomacy as the Crusade proceeded. Adhémar was not an experienced knight and the Crusade needed military leadership.

## Count Raymond of Toulouse

Raymond (1041/2–1105) sent messengers to Urban while the pope was still at Clermont, saying that he and many of his nobility were ready to join the crusade. His message came too soon for him to have heard about the Crusade, so he had presumably been informed by Urban earlier as to his intentions. As the first nobleman to join, he expected to be acknowledged as the leader, and he was one of the oldest of the crusaders. He showed the seriousness of his commitment by handing over many of his possessions to the monastery of Saint-Gilles. Later accounts suggested that he had fought against the Muslims in Spain and lost an eye, or even that he had been on a pilgrimage to Jerusalem and refused to pay the heavy taxes demanded of pilgrims. Thereupon the Muslims had torn out his eye as a punishment and he carried the eyeball around with him as evidence for what he had suffered. Both of these stories were made up to account for Raymond's loss of an eye. They illustrate how crusaders were represented as epic heroes in the chronicles.

Raymond was a friend of Adhémar and was hoping to be named as the commander of the Crusade. Urban II did not oblige him, possibly because it was expected that Alexius I would be the ultimate leader, since the first aim of the Crusade was to bring help to Byzantium.

## Bohemund of Taranto

Bohemund (*c*.1054–1111) was the son of Robert Guiscard, the Norman conqueror of southern Italy, and was a very experienced soldier. He had fought to establish Norman power in the Balkans at the expense of the Byzantine Empire. In 1082 he had been present when his father ended a long and difficult siege of the Greek city of Durazzo, by taking it through betrayal from within. Bohemund duly took note. He had personal knowledge of the Muslim mercenaries employed in the Byzantine army. The death of his father in 1085 had limited his prospects, as his brother Roger inherited the Italian lands, and his uncle, also

Roger, ruled Sicily. Left almost landless, he managed to conquer territory around Taranto and Bari. Hence, he had all the military expertise the pope could ask for, although he was viewed with some suspicion by Alexius I. His motives in taking the cross were suspected by some as being more for ambition than religion. He had generally given his support to the reformed papacy and may have been present at Piacenza.

## Tancred

Tancred (1075–1112) was Bohemund's nephew and he was one of many Norman knights who followed Bohemund in joining the Crusade. He was only about twenty years of age but was a powerful and energetic fighter.

## Godfrey of Bouillon

Godfrey (*c.*1060–1100) was an unlikely recruit as he came from Lotharingia, an area which was hostile to the reforming papacy and which Urban had not visited on his preaching tour. Godfrey had been an ally of Henry IV and even joined in besieging Rome, but, nevertheless he took the cross (took the oath to join the Crusade). His father was the Count of Boulogne. His brother had succeeded to the title so he had his own way to make. But he had been lucky in inheriting lands from a childless uncle. He had no great experience of war and seems to have joined the Crusade largely because everyone else was doing so. But he was to prove a worthy crusader and wholly committed to the pilgrimage to the Holy Land.

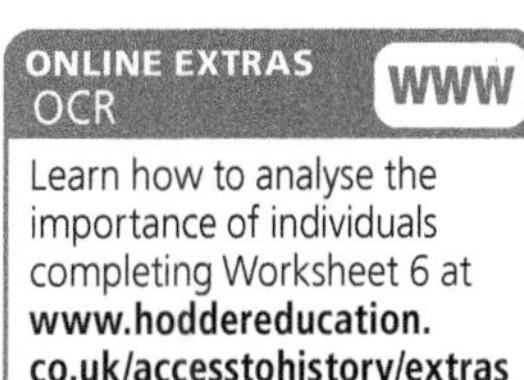


## Baldwin of Boulogne

Baldwin (*c.*1058–1118) was Godfrey's brother and joined very much at the last minute. Like Tancred he was to boost his reputation by his deeds on the Crusade.

## Godfrey of Bouillon c.1060–1100

Godfrey was the son of Eustace of Boulogne and descended from Charlemagne. He inherited Bouillon from his mother and went on to fight for Henry IV in the emperor's wars against Saxony. He joined the First Crusade with his brothers Eustace and Baldwin, the only major German prince to do so, although he was French-speaking. His motives are not clear as he had shown no special devotion to the Church. Legal documents he drew up before leaving show that he intended to return home and not to settle in the east. His army was the first to leave for the Holy Land. On the march to Antioch he took the territory of Tilbesar, which was a prosperous area and helped him with supplies. It had been under Byzantine rule originally, but he refused to return it to Alexius. He felt he had only taken an oath to the emperor under duress. Following the capture of Jerusalem, he accepted the crown of Jerusalem after Raymond of Toulouse declined, but would not take the title of king, becoming instead Defender of the Holy Sepulchre. He defeated an attack from Egypt soon afterwards, but was unwise in becoming a vassal of the Patriarch Daimbert as this led to later problems over the role of Church and State. He died in 1100 and was succeeded by his brother, Baldwin. He was later idolised as an ideal Christian knight. His tallness, fair hair and good looks may have contributed to this view of him.

## Baldwin of Boulogne c.1058–1118

Baldwin was the younger brother of Godfrey of Bouillon and joined him on the First Crusade. On the march across Anatolia, he campaigned against the Seljuk Turks with Toros, the Christian prince of Edessa. Toros agreed to recognise Baldwin as his heir in return for his aid, whereupon Baldwin overthrew him and took control of Edessa in 1098. He married the daughter of a local Armenian noble family to cement his power base. After Godfrey died in 1100, Baldwin was invited to become Defender of the Holy Sepulchre. He led a successful campaign against the Fatimids and was then crowned as King of Jerusalem. He was opposed by Daimbert, the Patriarch of Jerusalem, and eventually Baldwin deposed Daimbert and appointed the next patriarch himself. He took all the coastal cities apart from Tyre and Ascalon and built castles to protect his southern borders. He forced his wife to become a nun so he could marry another woman, but he died on a raiding expedition in 1118, childless. His achievement was impressive as he held his kingdom for eighteen years against the enmity of Egypt and Syria, depending heavily on the loyalty of his vassals at Tiberias, Haifa and Caesarea.

## Bohemund (or Bohemond) c.1050s–1109

Bohemund was the son of Robert Guiscard, the Norman adventurer who dominated southern Italy from the late 1050s, eventually as duke of Apulia and Calabria. He was named after a legendary giant and grew up to be a tall, strong knight, with a big reputation. Little is known of his childhood and his date of birth cannot be pinned down. His mother died when he was young and his father chose to make the son of his second wife his heir, so Bohemund was landless and hence eager to embark on the First Crusade. He played a leading role at Nicaea and Dorylaeum and even more so at Antioch, where his guile and negotiation with a traitor allowed the crusaders to capture the city. He remained there and held Antioch in defiance of Alexius, to whom he had sworn an oath of allegiance. But while defending Antioch he was captured and imprisoned by the Turks. On his release, he went to Rome and France, where he married the daughter of Philip I, hoping to get more supporters. But his campaigns against the Byzantines failed and eventually he accepted Alexius' terms, becoming his vassal in return for Antioch. His reputation was thus much diminished. One of his sons succeeded him as Count of Antioch.

### Hugh of Vermandois

Hugh (1057–1101) was the brother of the French king Philip I, but his lands were not extensive and he came with a small force. The king stayed behind. He was still excommunicated for his bigamous marriage and refused to give up the lovely Bertrade.

**ONLINE EXTRAS** AQA 

Learn how to analyse a range of factors by completing Worksheet 2 at **www.hoddereducation.co.uk/accesstohistory/extras**

### Robert of Normandy

Robert (*c.*1051–1134) was the eldest son of William of Normandy. He found Normandy difficult to govern and was under pressure from his younger brother, William Rufus, the English king. A later tradition even suggested that he joined the Crusade to get away from his problems. He brought with him Stephen of Blois (*c.*1045–1102), a wealthy French lord who was married to Robert's sister, Adela (*c.*1067–1137). He also brought Robert II of Flanders (*c.*1065–1111), the son of Robert I (*c.*1035–93) who had met Alexius I and sent 500 knights to help in the defence of Byzantium (see pages 19–20).

**ONLINE EXTRAS** AQA 

Practise reaching a judgement by completing Worksheet 3 at **www.hoddereducation.co.uk/accesstohistory/extras**

## Baldwin II, died 1131

Baldwin came from Bourcq in the Ardennes area of France and was cousin to Godfrey and Baldwin I. When Baldwin I became King of Jerusalem in 1100, he was named as ruler of Edessa. He was captured in 1104 by the Seljuk Turks and ransomed in 1108. He then had to fight to win back Edessa from the regent, Tancred. In 1118 he was crowned as King of Jerusalem, leaving Jocelyn of Courtenay to rule Edessa. He was instrumental in the founding of the Templars (see pages 88–90) and gave them the supposed site of the Temple of Solomon as their base. He helped to maintain the other crusader territories, as governor of Antioch after Roger was killed at the Field of Blood, until Bohemund II came of age. Similarly, he went to keep order in Edessa in 1123 when Jocelyn was captured, only to fall into the hands of the Turks himself. He had to pay a large ransom and leave his daughter, Yveta, as a hostage. He married an Armenian, Morfia, and they had four daughters. Alice married Bohemund II and Hodierna married the Count of Tripoli, so Baldwin was well placed to keep an eye on all the crusader kingdoms. He began the building of the new Church of the Holy Sepulchre. He was described as a very tall man with a blond beard reaching to his waist. He was also very pious and his knees were calloused from the amount of time he spent in prayer.

## The experience of the crusaders

Generally, crusaders did not have experience of fighting abroad, and loyalties tended to be to the leader of each contingent rather than to the whole. There was some tension, too, between those from northern France and southern France. No monarchs took part in the First Crusade. Philip I of France was, as we have seen, excommunicated. Henry IV, the emperor, was an enemy of the papacy and William II of England was equally hostile to Urban. In any case, Urban II wanted the Crusade to be very much his own initiative.

It is very hard to give a precise figure for how many went on the First Crusade. Thomas Asbridge, writing in 2004, suggests that there were 7000 knights and 35,000 infantry with an accompanying band of between 20,000 and 60,000 others. The departure of a crusader could be a very emotional moment, as Source E illustrates.

### SOURCE E

**Fulcher of Chartres describes what he envisaged as the leave-taking of a crusader, quoted in Edward Peters, editor, *The First Crusade*, University of Pennsylvania Press, 1971, p. 57.**

*However many tears were shed by those remaining for those going, they were not swayed by such tears from leaving all that they possessed; without doubt believing they would receive an hundredfold what the Lord promised to those loving him. Then the wife reckoned the time of her husband's return, because, if God permitted him to live, he would come home to her. He commended her to the Lord, kissed her and promised as she wept that he would return. She fearing that she would never see him again, not able to hold up, fell senseless to the ground; mourning her beloved as though he were dead. He, having compassion, it seems, neither for the weeping of his wife, nor feeling pain for the grieving of any friends, and yet having it, for he secretly suffered severely, went away with a determined mind.*

**SOURCE QUESTION**

Explain the emotions described in Source E which Fulcher thought a departing crusader and his wife might feel.

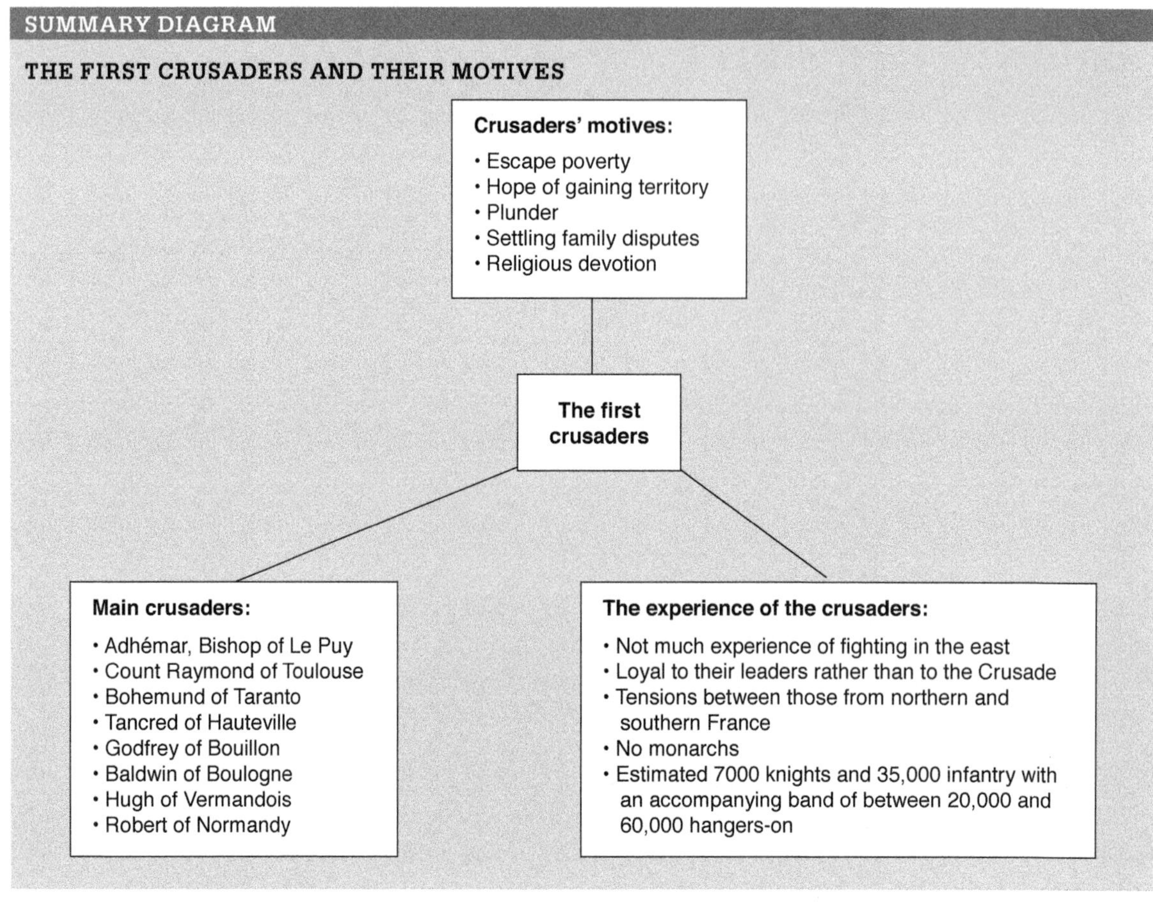

SUMMARY DIAGRAM
THE FIRST CRUSADERS AND THEIR MOTIVES
Crusaders' motives:
• Escape poverty
• Hope of gaining territory
• Plunder
• Settling family disputes
• Religious devotion
The first crusaders
Main crusaders:
• Adhémar, Bishop of Le Puy
• Count Raymond of Toulouse
• Bohemund of Taranto
• Tancred of Hauteville
• Godfrey of Bouillon
• Baldwin of Boulogne
• Hugh of Vermandois
• Robert of Normandy
The experience of the crusaders:
• Not much experience of fighting in the east
• Loyal to their leaders rather than to the Crusade
• Tensions between those from northern and southern France
• No monarchs
• Estimated 7000 knights and 35,000 infantry with an accompanying band of between 20,000 and 60,000 hangers-on


# 5 Key debate

■ *What were the motives of those who went on the Crusade?*

Historians have long debated the motives of those who went on the Crusade, with the most common divide between those who have argued that it was for adventure and plunder, and others who have suggested that it was the promise of spiritual reward. However, even though two clear schools of thought have emerged, it is also worth remembering that different social classes probably had different motives.

Most of the peasant-pilgrims were driven by the desire to reach Jerusalem; even if they were diverted to attack Jewish people in Europe, the Crusade was a clear expression of the strength of lay piety. The use of **charter evidence** by historians such as Jonathan Riley Smith (1997) has revealed the importance of connections between the local nobility and ecclesiastical institutions and has clearly

**KEY TERM**

**Charter evidence** Evidence from charters, which are medieval records of, for example, grants, sales or exchanges of land or rights, an agreement between two parties, or even a list of possessions.

demonstrated that there was a strong religious drive even among the secular knights of the west. This view has been further supported by Jonathan Phillips in *The Crusades* (2002) and by Marcus Bull in his work *Knightly Piety and the Lay Response to the First Crusade* (1993). Bull argues that the pre-existing religious values of knights had to be considered for a full understanding of their response to a crusade. Bull points out that these lords were well aware of their sinfulness, but they also respected the consequences of their sins and had long sought the remission of their sins through pilgrimage and acts of public benediction. Thus, when Pope Urban II preached the First Crusade as an armed pilgrimage, it provided knights with an opportunity to continue in their pilgrimage tradition while performing an act of self-sacrifice to please God.

Bull's work supports the view of Smith and challenges that of Carl Erdmann (1977) and Hans Eberhard Mayer (1988). Erdmann argues that the real reason for the Crusade was to answer the request for help sent by the Byzantine emperor, but this view has been successfully challenged as the Turkish threat was receding by 1095 and Urban himself did not mention supporting the Greeks in the account of any of his speeches at Clermont. Mayer argues that material gain was the main concern of the crusaders. His work focuses on the economic pressures resulting from societal changes of the time, such as inheritance practices, as being the driving motive. Although it is undoubtedly true that many of the knights hoped to gain land and riches, in a similar way to the Norman conquests of England and southern Italy, in the name of God, most recent work has stressed the spiritual element and the desire to liberate fellow Christians.

### EXTRACT 1

From Jonathan Phillips, *The Crusades 1095–1197*, Pearson Education, 2002, pp. 14 and 17.

*The holy city was such a potent image that the pope could not have used it as a decoy solely to help the Greeks and to facilitate a union with the Orthodox Church. It was the ideas of liberating the Christians of the Levant [the Middle East] and the city of Jerusalem that stirred the hearts and minds of those who planned the expedition and those who took the cross. Furthermore, by intending to recapture Christ's patrimony the crusade had a just cause, which was a prerequisite for the justification of Christian violence.*

*Spiritual issues were a prominent factor governing people's lives at the time of the First Crusade. It was an intensely religious age: the number of saints' cults was increasing, along with interest in relics and the observation of feast days. Pilgrimage and monastic life flourished. Sin was ubiquitous in everyday life, particularly in the violent society of the late eleventh century and the need for all people – whether rich or poor – to atone for their actions is vital in explaining the level of enthusiasm for the First Crusade.*

**INTERPRETATION QUESTION**

Which of the two interpretations, Extract 1 or Extract 2, do you find more convincing as an explanation for the motives of those who went on the First Crusade?

**ONLINE EXTRAS** AQA **WWW**

Practise your interpretation analysis skills by completing Worksheet 4 at **www.hoddereducation.co.uk/accesstohistory/extras**

**ONLINE EXTRAS**
**AQA** WWW

Practise your interpretation analysis skills by completing Worksheet 5 at **www.hoddereducation.co.uk/accesstohistory/extras**

**ONLINE EXTRAS**
**Pearson Edexcel** WWW

Practise your interpretation analysis skills by completing Worksheets 5 and 6 at **www.hoddereducation.co.uk/accesstohistory/extras**

**EXTRACT 2**

From Hans Eberhard Mayer, *The Crusades*, Oxford University Press, 1988, pp. 36–7.

*Naturally not all crusaders were moved by piety. In the Middle Ages too there were sceptics and the motives for going on crusade were many, various and tangled, often social and economic in character. But the offer of indulgence must have had an irresistible attraction for those who did not doubt the Church's teaching, who believed in the reality of the penalties due to sin. Such believers must have made up a great part of those who went on the First Crusade.*

# CHAPTER SUMMARY

Pope Urban II wanted to emphasise papal power, but was also concerned about conditions for pilgrims. He used the appeal for aid from Alexius I as an opportunity to preach the Crusade at Clermont when he held a Council. This was a key moment in the development of the crusading movement. The response was very favourable and many knights took the cross. Their reasons for doing so are much debated, but the general view is that few went hoping for material gain and most were focused on religious factors.

## Refresher questions

Use these questions to remind yourself of the key issues in this chapter.

**1** What problems did Urban II face when he became pope?
**2** Why had travelling as a pilgrim to Jerusalem become more challenging?
**3** What is penitential warfare?
**4** Why did Urban II call the Council of Clermont?
**5** Why is it difficult to be certain what Urban said at Clermont?
**6** Who responded positively to Urban II's call?
**7** What motives have been suggested for men joining the Crusade?
**8** What was the aim of the Crusade?

## Question practice: AQA

### Essay questions

**1** 'The outcome of the Battle of Manzikert in 1071 was the most important reason for the calling of the First Crusade in 1095.' Explain why you agree or disagree with this view. [AS level]

**EXAM HINT** You will need to explain the importance of the outcome of the battle in relation to other reasons for calling the First Crusade. Reach a detailed conclusion which explains your argument.

**2** To what extent was there more continuity than change in the relationship between the West and Byzantium in the years 1071–99? [A level]

**EXAM HINT** Your answer must avoid a narrative descriptive approach. Think in terms of themes across the period of years. Ideally, outline your argument in the introduction so that your arguments flow from this.

**3** 'Material gain was the most significant motive for people joining the First Crusade.' Assess the validity of this view with reference to the years 1071–99. [A level]

**EXAM HINT** You will need to analyse the various motives, one being material gain. Try to outline your overall argument in the introduction and then base your arguments throughout the essay on this opening.

## Question practice: OCR

### Essay questions

**1** Which of the following was of greater importance in the appeal for the First Crusade? i) The desire to increase papal power. ii) The Battle of Manzikert. Explain your answer with reference to both i) and ii). [A level]

**EXAM HINT** The importance of the two factors in the appeal for the First Crusade's success should be explained and a supported judgement reached as to which was the most important.

**2** Assess the reasons for the success of Urban's appeal for a crusade. [A level]

**EXAM HINT** Responses should consider a range of reasons for the success of Urban's appeal and their importance should be explained. A judgement should be reached as to their relative importance in the success of his appeal.

## Question practice: Pearson Edexcel

### Essay questions

**1** Was the guarantee of a plenary indulgence the main reason why men went on the Crusades? [AS level]

**EXAM HINT** Explain the importance of the indulgence for medieval Christians. Other relevant factors might include the Church reform movement, Seljuk conquests and the aim to free Jerusalem from Muslim rule.

**2** To what extent was Urban II's appeal at Clermont the main reason for the First Crusade? [A level]

**EXAM HINT** Consider the impact of the sermon at Clermont. Link this with other factors, such as the plenary indulgence, and the support given by leading European princes.

# CHAPTER 3

# The First Crusade (the People's Crusade)

The First Crusade began with a disorderly rabble marauding their way across Europe and ended with the capture of Jerusalem. This chapter explores why the early failures did not lead to total disaster through the following themes:

- The failure of the first wave of the First Crusade
- The second wave of the First Crusade led by the princes

The key debate on page 66 of this chapter asks the question: Why was the First Crusade successful?

**KEY DATES**

| | |
|---|---|
| **1095** | The first wave (People's Crusade) of the First Crusade set off for the Holy Land |
| **1096** | The second wave of the First Crusade set off for the Holy Land |
| | Area around Nicaea attacked |
| | Massacre of Jews in several areas of Germany |
| **1097** | Nicaea capitulated |
| **1098** | Capture of Edessa |
| | Siege of Antioch |
| | Kerbogha defeated by the crusaders |
| **1099** | Raymond of Toulouse left for Jerusalem |
| | Pope Urban II died and was succeeded by Paschal II |
| | Jerusalem captured by the crusaders |

## 1 The failure of the first wave of the First Crusade

*Why did the first wave of the First Crusade fail?*

The response to the preaching of Urban II was so strong that it was impossible to control the message. As a result, crusaders set off in different groups and at different times:

- The so-called first wave, usually known as the People's Crusade, consisted of those who were eager to fight but were often inexperienced. These included women and children and people from less well-off groups, so they could leave promptly as they had few affairs to settle. However, more recent work has also shown that the group did include some knights and members of the lesser aristocracy.
- The second wave consisted of the trained knights, who were the people Urban II really wanted on the Crusade.

**Key figures of the First Crusade**

Pope Urban II
Adhémar, Bishop of Le Puy
Alexius I
Baldwin of Boulogne
Bohemund of Taranto
Count Raymond of Toulouse
Godfrey of Bouillon
Hugh of Vermandois
Robert of Normandy
Stephen of Blois
Tancred of Hauteville
Walter Sansavoir

## The first wave

This first wave is often referred to as the People's Crusade, which would imply that it was largely made up of peasants, but the leaders were from the knightly classes. This group was the result of the appeal of the preacher Peter the Hermit (c.1050–1115) who proclaimed the Crusade in what is now the Rhineland and other areas of Germany. As the area was ruled over by Henry IV, Urban II did not visit the region. The lawlessness of those who were part of this wave cannot be put down to their being ill-disciplined men from the lower orders. But the lack of discipline in the crusading forces was certainly a factor. As their leader, Peter the Hermit has been blamed for the failure, being depicted as a sincere but naïve preacher who was overtaken by events which he could not control.

### Who was Peter the Hermit?

What we know of Peter the Hermit comes from the chroniclers, who were all churchmen and were writing not that long after the events. They were often eyewitnesses or had accounts from eyewitnesses. For the chronicler Robert the Monk, Peter was a 'famous hermit, who was held in great esteem'. **William of Tyre** (*c.*1130–85) added that he came from Amiens and was a hermit 'both in deed and nature', who was known for his fervency. According to William and the chronicler Albert of Aachen, who wrote between 1125 and 1150, Peter had been on a pilgrimage to Jerusalem already and had been horrified by the high taxes levied on pilgrims. It was even claimed that he had met the pope. Anna Comnena (see page 16) added that Peter had suffered much ill-treatment at the hands of the Turks. He lived an **ascetic life** and abstained from bread and meat, although Robert the Monk adds a caustic comment that 'this did not stop him enjoying wine and all other kinds of foods whilst seeking a reputation for abstinence'. Guibert of Nogent was more admiring, saying 'he wore a wool shirt and over it a mantle reaching to his ankles; his feet and arms were bare. He lived on wine and fish; he hardly ever ate bread'.

**KEY FIGURE**

**William of Tyre c.1130–85**

Born in Palestine and studied at both Paris and Bologna. He returned to the Kingdom of Jerusalem in 1164 and was tutor to the future Baldwin IV. He became chancellor of the kingdom and Archbishop of Tyre in 1175. His *Historia rerum in partibus tranmarinis gestsarum*, completed in 1184, was the first history of Jerusalem. Various dates have been suggested for his death, from 1184 to 1186.

**KEY TERM**

**Ascetic life** A simple life characterised by denial of the pleasures of the secular world.

Peter was an enthusiastic preacher and may have been spreading the word about the situation in the Holy Land even before Urban II began to preach. Some contemporaries claimed that it was Peter who had the idea of the Crusade in the first place. Where Urban II carried parts of the True Cross (see page 6) with him, Peter claimed a direct message from heaven. In some versions this took the form of a precious letter. His sermons stressed the urgency of the situation and the need to set out at once. Anna Comnena added that a divine voice had inspired him to proclaim that all should set out from their homes to worship at the Holy Sepulchre. He also concentrated on an area which Urban II had not visited, what we now know as the Rhineland. He was astoundingly successful in the number of followers he attracted and herein lay one of the basic reasons for his eventual failure. Guibert said he had never seen anyone else receive such support, and Albert of Aachen asserted that he was joined by churchmen, noble laymen and the common people, both the chaste and the sinful. If this was true, welding such a disparate force together would be a challenge for an experienced leader, let alone Peter, who was 'small in stature and his external appearance contemptible', according to William of Tyre.

Peter faced several problems:

- He had no plan. There was no set date for the Crusade to depart and anyone who wanted to go could join in.
- He did not have the approval of the Church.
- His followers were worked up by his message and saw anyone who opposed them as part of the enemy.
- There was a strong element of anti-Semitism or hostility towards Jewish people among the followers and this would have a considerable influence on early events.
- Peter had no real control over those who went.
- The proportion of non-combatants was probably higher than was desirable.

Some historians have argued that Peter did inspire some members of the knightly class. One of these was Walter Sansavoir (died 1096), also known as the 'Penniless'. Walter had eight knights under him and they moved in advance of those with Peter, reaching Hungary in May 1096 (see page 50). Historian Christopher Tyerman, writing in 2004, suggests that this shows Peter had some organisational ability. Peter was probably also instrumental in the recruitment of armies in both southern and northern Germany, where he was joined by Count Emich of Flonheim (an area of present-day Germany).

**ONLINE EXTRAS**
OCR

Learn how to support an argument with evidence by completing Worksheet 7 at **www.hoddereducation.co.uk/accesstohistory/extras**

## The attacks on Jewish people

The first wave of the crusaders was also notable for its attacks on the Jews before they even left Germany. These took place in a number of cities where there were large Jewish communities:

- In May 1096 Count Emich's forces attacked Jews in Speyer, killing some who refused to be baptised as Christians, but the local bishop intervened to protect them.
- Later in May, Emich moved on to Worms, where local peasants joined in enthusiastically to kill hundreds of Jews.
- Further slaughter occurred in Mainz, even though Jews offered the archbishop money to protect them and also tried to buy off Emich. The slaughter and destruction lasted two days. The synagogue was burned down and many Jewish people killed themselves rather than be killed by the Christians or forced to convert, as happened in Worms, Mainz and Prague. Possibly as many as 1000 Jews died and unknown amounts of loot fell into Christian hands.
- By the end of May, Emich reached Cologne. The Jews here had fled to the countryside, but the synagogue was destroyed and they were hunted down in the countryside. Again, there was much looting.
- Other groups attacked Jews in the area of Trier and Metz in June.

- In July the Cologne region was targeted again, as well as the area north around Xanten.

Source A describes a typical attitude towards Jewish people.

**SOURCE QUESTION**

What does Source A show about the relationship between Jews and Christians?

**SOURCE A**

**An account of what happened in Mainz, from the chronicle attributed to Solomon bar Samson, a Jewish writer, written in the 1140s, quoted by Shlomo Eidelberg, editor and translator, *The Jews and the Crusaders: The Hebrew Chronicles of the First and Second Crusades*, Ktav Publishing, 1996, p. 24.**

*The leaders of the Jews gathered together and discussed various ways of saving themselves. They said: 'Let us elect elders so that we may know how to act, for we are consumed by this great evil.' The elders decided to ransom the community by generously giving of their money and bribing the various princes and deputies and bishops and governors. Then, the community leaders who were respected by the local bishop, approached him … and … asked: 'What shall we do about the news that we have received regarding the slaughter of our brethren in Speyer and Worms?' [He] replied: '… Bring all your money into our treasury. You, your wives and your children, and all your belongings shall come into the courtyard of the bishop until the hordes have passed by. Thus you will be saved from the errant ones.' Actually, [he] gave this advice so as to herd us together and hold us like fish that are caught in an evil net, and then to turn us over to the enemy, while taking our money. This is what actually happened in the end, and 'the outcome is proof of the intentions'. … All the bribes and entreaties were of no avail to protect us on the day of wrath and misfortune.*

**KEY TERM**

**Pogrom** The deliberate persecution of an ethnic or religious group.

## Why were Jews attacked?

The reasons for the **pogroms** against Jewish people were not just related to greed and envy, although these deadly sins were undoubtedly partly to blame. The role of some Jews as moneylenders has been seen as a reason for them being the targets of violence, but evidence from the Rhineland suggests that the interest rates they charged were around eight per cent, which was not excessive for the period. It is possible that some crusaders, who had sold up their possessions to equip themselves for their journey, saw Jews as easy pickings and a chance to recoup losses.

Jews were also seen as the people responsible for the crucifixion of Christ. As a result, there may have been an element of vengeance in these attacks. The use of the cross as an important symbol in the crusading movement could have influenced the thinking of some of the attackers.

It is also likely that because Jews were not Christians, they were seen as infidels or non-believers and were therefore on a par with the Muslims. There is certainly evidence from the attacks on the Jews of Speyer, Mainz, Trier and Cologne that the crusaders twisted the pope's call to 'kill the infidel' to include Jews and take their wealth.

**ONLINE EXTRAS** OCR WWW

Get to grips with analysing the importance of factors by completing Worksheet 8 at **www.hoddereducation.co.uk/accesstohistory/extras**

The attacks on Jews were symptomatic of the diverse aims and lack of unity of the first wave of the Crusade. Killing Jews was largely condemned by the Christian writers. The chronicler Albert of Aachen said, 'by some error of mind they rose in a spirit of cruelty'. He believed that the wiping out of Emich's force in Hungary was a just punishment for their sins in slaughtering Jews, even though 'the Jews were opposed to Christ'. Ekkehard of Aura, a German monk writing between 1098 and 1115, commented that men were 'scandalised and concluded that the whole expedition was vain and foolish'.

## The march to Constantinople

Those historians who see Peter as a leader of some ability emphasise his establishment of a regular military command and his advance to Cologne, a convenient mustering point, in April 1096. His force was effective and well funded and, according to Albert of Aachen, numbered 15,000 with as many knights as infantry. There may have been up to 20,000, since the line of the pilgrims stretched out over a mile. Emich of Flonheim followed behind Peter. The sheer number of crusaders who responded to Peter's message was a clear indication of not only the success of his appeal but also the religious fervour that gripped Europe at the time. Some have argued that they were poorly provisioned and that this was made worse by setting off earlier than the official departure date of August 1096. It may have been this that led to the pillaging and attacks on Jewish communities, even though Jews were supposed to be under the protection of the Church.

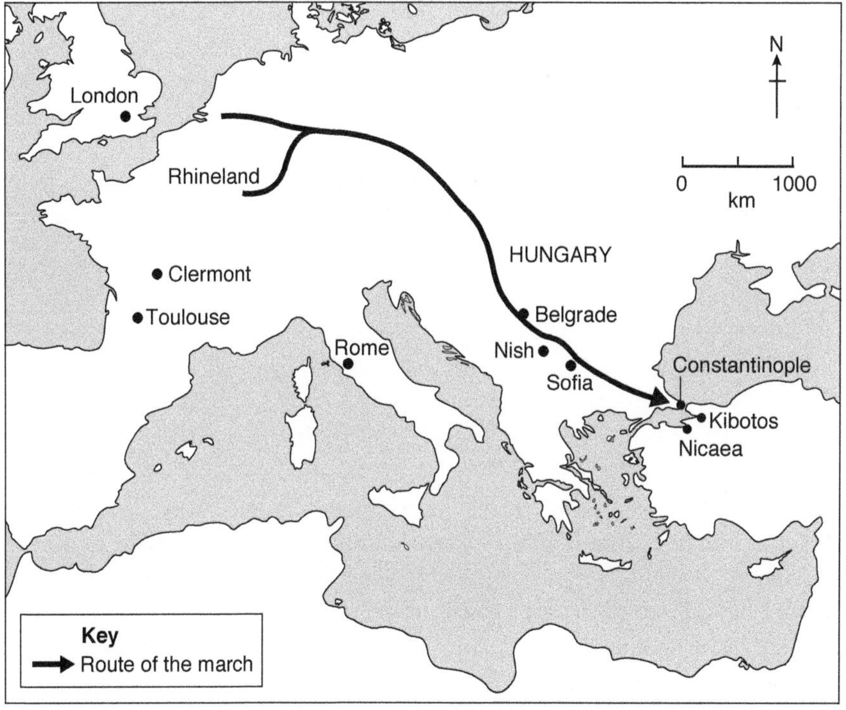


**Figure 3.1** The route of the 1095–6 march to Constantinople.

Whatever the merits of Peter as a leader, it cannot be denied that the march to Constantinople was marked by problems and some serious defects:

- Walter Sansavoir found getting supplies through difficult.
- Once he had crossed into the Byzantine Empire, there were further problems over food. He was travelling at the time of the year when supplies were low.
- Some of Walter's troops were killed in a row over food.
- Alexius I was alarmed at the sight of the crusaders, who were not the experienced fighters he had hoped for.
- By May, Peter's followers forced Jews in the area they had reached to be baptised.
- Disputes over supplies and rumours about the way Walter's army had been treated by the Byzantines led to the sacking of a town in June.
- In July there was a battle at Nish, and Peter may have lost up to a third of his men. Alexius I intervened and sent escorts to bring the remnants to Constantinople by the beginning of August.

Although Peter could be commended for reaching Constantinople in so short a time, the exhausting marches, covering about 30 kilometres a day, the uncertainty of food supplies and the problems in maintaining communications over a long, drawn-out journey had taken their toll.

As for the armies following Peter, they were all wiped out in what we now know as Hungary, where the king had no desire to see the problems caused by Walter and Peter's men multiplied. A force of Saxons and Bohemians led by Folkmar, a priest, was destroyed. Another priest, Gottschalk, leading a band from the Rhineland, was forced to surrender, while Emich of Flonheim gave up on the Hungarian frontier by July 1096. These disasters meant that Peter and Walter had fewer soldiers at their disposal than they had expected.

## The final failure of the first wave

Alexius I not only did not want an undisciplined army at large in Constantinople, but was not pleased by the arrival of a force that lacked fighting experience. As a result, he arranged for them to be transported across the Bosphorus in August 1096 to a base out of harm's way. Peter's role was reduced to one of diplomacy and he was often in Constantinople negotiating about supplies. As a result, the leadership fell into the hands of some of his captains who wanted a more active role. This led to several ill-advised attacks on the Turks, often fuelled by rivalries between the different national groups among the crusaders. In one of these, an Italian faction, attempting to outdo the French by capturing a castle near Nicaea, was taken and the leader saved his life only by converting to Islam. This kind of event was hardly likely to go unnoticed and led to demands for vengeance from the rank and file. Walter and the other knights resisted but were talked down.

**ONLINE EXTRAS**
Pearson Edexcel WWW

Learn how to write effective opening sentences by completing Worksheet 7 at **www.hoddereducation.co.uk/accesstohistory/extras**

An attack on Nicaea followed from 1096 to 1097. The Sultan of Rum, Kilij Arslan I (1079–1107), took command of the Turkish troops in person and on 21 October completely defeated the Christians. Walter was killed in 1096. Much of the army was massacred and saved only from complete annihilation by the arrival of a Byzantine relief force. Peter survived and he returned to Constantinople to await the arrival of the main army. However, the behaviour of the first wave of crusaders had raised doubts about the value of asking for help and would also play a significant role in the reaction of Alexius to the arrival of the main wave of crusaders, particularly as one of his enemies, Bohemund of Taranto, was one of its leaders.

**SOURCE B**

**Anna Comnena describes the massacre of the People's Crusade at Nicaea. Anna Komnene, *The Alexiad*, Book X.**

*When the mention of plunder and riches was heard, they straightway set out in tumult on the road which leads to Nicaea, forgetful of their military training and of observing discipline in going out to battle. For the Latins are not only most fond of riches, as we said above, but when they give themselves to raiding any region for plunder, are also no longer obedient to reason, or any other check. Accordingly, since they were neither keeping order nor forming into lines, they fell into the ambush of the Turks around Draco and were wretchedly cut to pieces. Indeed, so great a multitude of French and Normans were cut down by the Ishmaelite sword that when the dead bodies of the killed, which were all lying about in the place, were brought together, they made a very great mound, or hill, or lookout place, lofty as a mountain.*

**SOURCE QUESTION**

What can we learn from Source B about those who took part in the People's Crusade?

## Kilij Arslan I 1079–1107

Kilij was the ruler of the sultanate of Rum. In his youth he had been a hostage for his father's good behaviour at the court of Sultan Malik Shah. He was released in 1092 and established himself at Nicaea, removing Ghazni, the governor appointed by the sultan. He married the daughter of the Emir of Chaka to build up a wider alliance, but his father-in-law betrayed him. Kilij had his revenge by inviting his wife's father to a banquet and murdering him while he was in a drunken stupor. He defeated the armies of the People's Crusade in 1098 and may have killed as many as 30,000 of them. He did not expect the main crusade to be much of a threat, but lost Nicaea and his family was captured and sent to Constantinople. However, Alexius returned them and did not exact a ransom as he wished to keep on good terms with Kilij. Kilij was defeated again at Dorylaeum, but harassed the crusaders as they advanced and in 1101 he inflicted defeats on crusading armies, showing that they were not invincible.

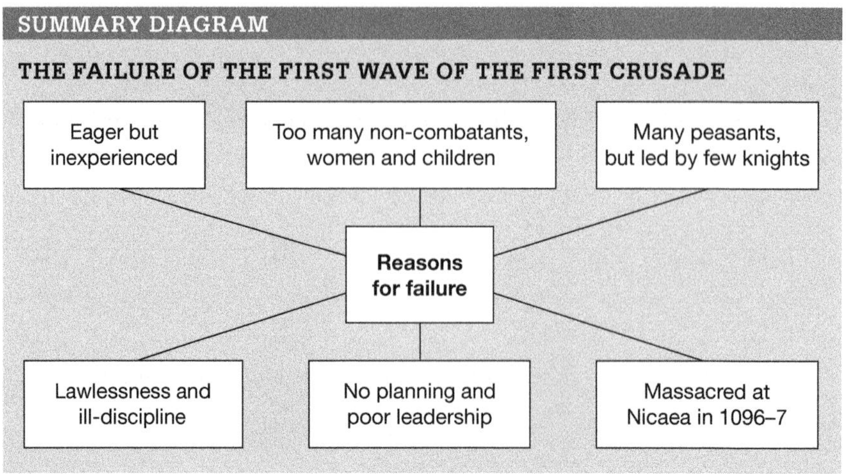


# 2 The second wave of the First Crusade led by the princes

■ *What was the result of the second wave of the First Crusade?*

## The journey to Constantinople

Like the first wave, the second wave travelled in several groups *en route* to Constantinople, although they were more disciplined. Godfrey of Bouillon and his brother Baldwin (see pages 37 and 38) set off first and went through southern Germany to the border with Hungary. Here they came to terms with the king, who had already wiped out a large part of the People's Crusade. Baldwin had to allow himself to be a hostage for the good behaviour of the army and Godfrey issued strict orders against **pillaging**. Their route was overland. Raymond of Toulouse also avoided a sea voyage, but his route was through northern Italy and thence to the Balkans, part of the Byzantine Empire. The northern French journeyed across France and Italy, to the Norman territories in Italy where they had friends. Robert of Normandy and Stephen of Blois spent the winter of 1096–7 there and then sailed across the Adriatic from Bari. Hence, they had a shorter distance to travel on the last stage to Constantinople. Bohemund had the shortest journey, crossing from Brindisi.

**KEY TERM**

**Pillaging** During war, stealing or robbing a place or something.

There were a few mishaps on the way but nothing like the problems which the first wave had experienced. The Bishop of Le Puy was ambushed by bandits and only escaped with his life when some of his fellow crusaders rescued him. Hugh of Vermandois was shipwrecked and lost all his possessions. However, most crusaders reached Constantinople safely. This was largely the result of careful planning by Alexius I. After the fiasco of the expedition of Peter the Hermit (see pages 46–51), he was much better prepared for the more serious crusade.

There were no problems over supplies, as the emperor's officials made sure that the towns near the crusader routes had food ready for them and controlled its arrival. Bodyguards were sent out to accompany the crusaders and keep them to the roads which would bring them to the capital quickly. The only leader who seems to have been ready to forage on his own was Bohemund, but even he became cooperative when promised food and treasure in abundance.

## The aims of Alexius I

Alexius I was careful to ensure the different groups had minimal contact with each other, as he did not want to find a large and possibly hostile army approaching his capital. He had already experienced problems when Godfrey of Bouillon arrived and refused at first to go to the holding camp. There were skirmishes between Godfrey and Byzantine soldiers and the outskirts of Constantinople were pillaged. In the end, Alexius I cut off supplies to Godfrey and so forced him to go to the camp. To keep the crusaders out of trouble they were not allowed into the city except in small groups and at particular times. Another of Alexius I's tactics was to detach the leaders from their troops as they got closer and invite them to come on ahead to Constantinople, where they were lavishly entertained. He wanted to get them to agree that all the lands they conquered which had once been part of his empire should be returned to him. He also hoped he might persuade the individual leaders to swear fealty to him personally and so gain more control over them.

**ONLINE EXTRAS** WWW
OCR

Get to grips with analysing effectiveness by completing Worksheet 9 at **www.hoddereducation.co.uk/accesstohistory/extras**

### How Alexius I achieved his aims

Hugh of Vermandois, Robert of Flanders, Robert of Normandy, Stephen of Blois and eventually Godfrey of Bouillon all swore an oath of allegiance to Alexius I. Bohemund, possibly encouraged by Tancred, held out for better terms. Alexius I agreed that Bohemund could keep lands he might conquer around Antioch, as these were well away from Byzantine frontiers and would provide a buffer between the empire and the Turks. Bohemund was so pleased with this prospect that he put pressure on Raymond of Toulouse, who was adamant that he would not swear fealty. Eventually, Raymond agreed to promise that he would not act against Alexius I. This was really what Alexius I wanted, as his main fear was that the crusading army might turn against him. In appealing to Pope Urban II (see pages 19–20) he had hoped for some mercenaries (soldiers) to help him against his enemies, both internal and external: he had no intention of falling victim to those who were meant to be his salvation.

## The journey from Constantinople to Antioch

There may have been an expectation that Alexius I would take command and march with the crusaders. He did certainly consider doing so as a way of keeping a close eye on their activities, but he decided that the danger that he might be overthrown while he was away was too great for him to risk it. Alexius I's priority was to regain lands lost by Byzantium. This was not what the crusaders had come to do, but it was why Alexius I had asked for help in the first place.

## Nicaea

However, Alexius I accompanied the crusaders on the first leg of their journey as Nicaea was one of his prime targets. The city was strongly defended and the Turks had known that the crusaders were gathering, and so had laid in plenty of supplies. But the Turks may not have expected to face such a strong force, given how easily they had overcome the first wave of crusaders. In the end, a combination of the skills learned by the Normans in siege warfare in Italy and some tactical decisions by Alexius I led to the fall of Nicaea in June 1097. Alexius I prevented the defenders from bringing in supplies by calling on ships from his navy to stop relief arriving across the Ascanian Lake. His archers also played a vital role in the final assault, and he began negotiations for the surrender of the city, offering good terms to the defenders.

The crusaders were much encouraged by this victory and saw it as a clear sign of divine approval. Alexius I now decided to return to Constantinople, but he insisted that those, like Tancred, who had not taken an oath to him now did so. Nicaea was duly handed over to him in accordance with all the agreements made as the Crusade set out. Alexius I left Tatikios, one of his experienced generals, to lead the way for the crusader armies. Tatikios' local knowledge was another factor in the success of the march. The crusaders were also encouraged as some towns now deserted Kilij Arslan I and returned to the overlordship of Byzantium. Alexius I was able to come to terms with Kilij Arslan I and a truce was agreed.

## Dorylaeum

The army split into two sections on leaving Nicaea. One section, commanded by Bohemund, was ambushed by the Turks under Kilij Arslan I close to the ruined city of Dorylaeum. A fierce battle followed and was won only by the determination of Bohemund, who rallied his troops, led from the front and deployed his men tactically. Detachments from the other part of the army came to his aid and the troops from Provence in France, possibly led by the Bishop of Le Puy, attacked the Turkish rear and so they were defeated. The crusaders rejoiced again in the favour God had shown them, while their commanders reflected on the fighting spirit of the Turks, their very competent bowmen and their impressive horsemanship.

# The march to Antioch across Anatolia

This was one of the most demanding parts of the journey:

- The rate of advance was very slow, ten to twenty kilometres a day.
- Many horses had died and so some knights had to walk.
- It was hot by day and very cold at night.
- Much of the terrain was mountainous and inhospitable.
- A lack of food and a greater lack of water debilitated the armies.
- The non-combatants suffered severely.

After the march was completed, probably about half of those who originally set out had perished. However, those who survived did so because:

- Tatikios chose a route which, although far from direct, allowed for supplies to be maintained and for strategic towns to be captured to safeguard the rear of the crusaders.
- The Turks were on the defensive. Much of the area was Christian rather than Muslim and so their control was harder to maintain.

## The Capture of Edessa 1098

Baldwin of Bolougne and Tancred both led splinter groups which captured towns such as Edessa, although the two leaders fell out over the spoils. This meant that large areas were cleared of hostile forces and so supplies could be maintained. It also paved the way for the main crusader army as it approached Antioch.

Baldwin, indeed, was invited to become the ruler of Edessa and he took over with enthusiasm: adopting Byzantine dress, growing his beard in Arab fashion and marrying a local princess as his wife had died. It could be argued that, as a younger son, he had got what he came for and wanted to go no further, but the possession of Edessa was important strategically (see Figure 4.1, page 73) and the region was fertile and prosperous, allowing it to supply food and other resources for the Crusader States that were established further south in less fertile areas.

## The siege of Antioch

The siege of Antioch was the crucial turning point for the Crusade. There had been victories on the march, but if the aim of capturing Jerusalem was to be fulfilled, Antioch needed to be taken first. Antioch was important to the Christians as the place where Saint Peter had established his first church. It had, in its time, been variously ruled by the Greeks, Romans, Byzantines, Persians and Arabs, and had changed hands frequently. In 1085 it had fallen to the Turks, but Alexius I hoped he could recover the city. It commanded northern Syria and to move on past it would have left the crusader rear dangerously exposed to Turkish attacks. However, it was very well defended by mountains and the River Orontes and surrounded by massive walls, which the crusader army was unable to surround. An imposing citadel (fortress) near the summit of one of the mountains completed the defences. Once the crusaders saw it, they knew that an all-out assault would be pointless.

There were other factors which made Antioch a difficult prospect:

- The Turkish garrison of about 5000 men was well supplied.
- The Turkish commander, Yaghi Siyan, was experienced and resourceful.
- Food supplies for the crusaders, abundant at first, soon became scarce.
- Winter rain and snow sapped the strength of the army.
- The crusaders could not stop supplies going in to Antioch.

- The commander could maintain communications with other Arab leaders.
- By early 1098 morale was low among the besiegers. Peter the Hermit tried to desert but was brought back.
- Tatikios left the camp and returned to Alexius I, although he claimed to be going for reinforcements.
- By early 1098 the crusaders were probably down to 30,000 men.

But the crusaders also had some advantages:

- The Turkish state was unstable and control of Antioch was disputed between two nephews of the Shah, **Ridwan of Aleppo** (died 1113) and **Duquq of Damascus** (died 1104).
- There was no immediate source of reinforcements for the commander of Antioch.
- They were able to keep open communication with several ports and so some supplies came in that way.
- Bohemund led at least two attacks on Muslims in the surrounding area.
- Bohemund defeated an army coming from Damascus.
- In February, Bohemund with a strong cavalry charge defeated the forces of Ridwan of Damascus and was recognised as the sole leader in the field of battle.
- The Turks did not unite against the crusaders and the Fatimids of Egypt held aloof, being Shi'ite Muslims.

The siege lasted for seven and a half months and was a huge challenge to the crusaders. The cost of food supplies was a major problem and the less wealthy leaders suffered the most. Bohemund was worn down by the sight of so many of his men and horses starving that he threatened to leave, and both Godfrey of Bouillon and Robert of Flanders ran short of funds. In March 1098 fresh supplies arrived by sea, with craftsmen and material for building a siege tower to help in taking Antioch. This fleet came from an English garrison and, historian Peter Frankopan argues, writing in 2012, that it was sent by Tatikios, who had thus fulfilled his promises when he returned to Constantinople. As the **supply train** moved slowly from the coast to Antioch, protected by Bohemund and Raymond, it was attacked by Yaghi Siyan and fierce fighting ensued. The victory of the crusaders was a real boost for their confidence. They had also destroyed some of the best troops of the defenders.

With the coming of summer in 1098, morale improved further as their grip on the city tightened, helped by the new tower. The Muslims in Antioch became more subdued with fewer provocative demonstrations, while Christians in the city began to show their support for the crusaders. The minds of the besiegers were powerfully affected by the news that a relieving army was approaching, led by Kerbogha (see page 57).

### KEY FIGURES

**Ridwan of Aleppo (d. 1113)**

The son of Tutush, grandson of the Seljuk Sultan Alp Arslan, and the nephew of the Sultan Malik Shah. On Tutush's death in 1095, Ridwan, aged thirteen, succeeded to his father's Syrian lands. On the arrival of the crusaders, Ridwan was attempting to put down a revolt led by his younger brother Duqaq.

**Duqaq of Damascus (d. 1104)**

Younger brother of Ridwan of Aleppo, he led a revolt against Ridwan. The appearance of the westerners was enough to put an end to Duqaq's revolt, but he did not work with his brother Ridwan in defeating the newcomers.

### KEY TERM

**Supply train** Horses carrying supplies to help the crusaders.

## The capture of Antioch 1098

Bohemund had now hatched a plan to take Antioch, spurred on by an agreement among the leaders that he could keep the city if his troops were the first to enter it. However, it would eventually have to be handed over to the emperor to whom they had all sworn oaths. Raymond of Toulouse stood out against this suggestion but the other leaders all agreed. They were then told by Bohemund that he was in touch with Firouz, one of the captains of the garrison, who had agreed to help in the capture of Antioch by the crusaders.

The plan was relatively simple. Under cover of a diversionary attack on one part of the walls, Firouz would admit a small detachment of Bohemund's men and they would overpower the immediate defenders and then join up with the other crusaders to overrun the city. But not everyone was convinced it would work and Stephen of Blois withdrew on 2 June, claiming he was ill. However, over 2–3 June the agreed strategy worked surprisingly well. It depended on co-ordinating the two attacks, a silent approach and climbing of the ladder let down by Firouz. This then led to the rapid defeat of the troops within Antioch. Yaghi Siyan fled and was killed outside the walls. The only failure was that the citadel was not captured. The crusaders then embarked on a dreadful slaughter of the Muslims in Antioch. On 4 June the army led by Kerbogha arrived, and the besiegers now became the besieged.

Kerbogha was a bruising general and he had the advantage of larger of numbers and fresh horses. He kept up his attacks on Antioch so the crusaders had little rest. He captured some of the forts around its walls and his grip tightened to prevent supplies coming in. Furthermore, his allies still held out in the citadel, leaving the crusaders caught between two sets of enemies.

**ONLINE EXTRAS** OCR **WWW**

Learn how to assess the impact of events by completing Worksheet 10 at **www.hoddereducation.co.uk/accesstohistory/extras**

**ONLINE EXTRAS** OCR **WWW**

Learn how to write an argument rather than an assertion by completing Worksheet 11 at **www.hoddereducation.co.uk/accesstohistory/extras**

### The Holy Lance

According to all the chronicles, the crusaders seemed stuck – but it was the miraculous discovery of the Holy Lance, the spear that had pierced the side of Christ on the cross, that put new heart into the crusaders. Peter Bartholomew (died 1099), a peasant from Provence, told Raymond of Toulouse and the Bishop of Le Puy (see page 36) that it had been revealed to him in a vision that the Holy Lance would be found buried in the Church of Saint Peter in Antioch. On 14 June, part of it was recovered after digging in the church. It may have been just a small fragment of metal but it had a mighty impact. A relic linked to the sufferings of Christ resonated especially with the crusaders. They now resolved to bring Kerbogha to battle.

However, historian Thomas Asbridge, writing in 2004, argues that the influence of the Holy Lance may have been overstated as it was not until 28 June that the crusaders actually attacked Kerbogha. He suggests that two factors were decisive in leading to the crusader attack:

- *The possibility of reinforcements had vanished.* Alexius had been active in south-west Asia Minor in expelling the Turks and was ready to march to Antioch, when he was warned by the retreating Stephen of Blois that the crusaders were on the verge of total defeat. Alexius, therefore, decided to concentrate on upholding his control of Anatolia. Whether the crusaders knew of his decision before 28 June is not certain, but they had probably abandoned any hope of getting any more fighting men.

- *Victory or death – no surrender.* On about 24 June a deputation was sent to Kerbogha, led by Peter the Hermit (see page 46). Whatever its aim, it failed as Kerbogha had no intention of giving up his advantageous position. A range of sources offer different reasons for the sending of the deputation:
  - that it was to show defiance and bravery on the part of the beleaguered crusaders
  - it was a simple spying mission
  - it was to propose a trial by battle with the best men on each side fighting it out.

The chroniclers describe the sending of Peter to Kerbogha as an exploration of what would happen if the crusaders offered to surrender. They wanted Kerbogha to promise to let them leave Antioch in his hands and to go on with their journey. When Kerbogha rejected this, the crusaders knew it was victory or death, and so chose to bring Kerbogha to battle before their situation got any worse.

**Table 3.1** Why the crusaders won

| The historical explanation | The explanation from the chronicles |
|---|---|
| • They took Kerbogha by surprise – he was playing chess in his tent and did not believe the crusaders would be so foolhardy as to risk a set battle<br>• The crusaders were so short of horses that they fought largely on foot and Bohemund as commander proved able to marshal and rally his forces effectively<br>• Bohemund had a clear plan of action with the troops in four divisions<br>• Kerbogha hesitated about how to react when he was first attacked. He could not decide whether to reply at once as the crusaders marched out of Antioch or to wait and fight on ground of his choosing. As a result he missed attacking the crusaders when they were most vulnerable, crossing the River Orontes<br>• In the end, Kerbogha made a late attack on the crusader advance, but the crusaders held firm, thanks to Bohemund's control<br>• The failure of the Arabs to break the crusader line led to panic and desertion<br>• Kerbogha's army came from different parts of northern Syria and so was not welded together and broke up under the strain<br>• Kerbogha was a harsh and unpopular general and some of his troops were mutinous anyway<br>• Only 200 knights under Raymond of Toulouse were left in Antioch and the troops in the citadel could have easily defeated them and captured the city, but Kerbogha did not realise this in time | • The battle was preceded by solemn fasting and prayer<br>• Priests lined the walls reciting blessings as the crusaders marched out<br>• Raymond of Toulouse carried the relic of the Holy Lance and Kerbogha was paralysed by seeing it<br>• Many supernatural knights (believed to be Greek warrior saints) joined in the fighting<br>• God sent a divine shower which filled the crusaders with the will to fight |

## The battle, 28 June 1098

The crusaders were short of food and needed a quick victory. They offered prayers and fasted, while giving full rations to their horses so the animals would be in top condition.

The battle between the crusaders and Kerbogha was a significant episode in the Crusade. It was another instance where failure could well have meant the end of the whole enterprise.

Whatever the cause, the victory was climactic and celebrated by the crusaders.

**SOURCE C**

**An account of the battle by Fulcher of Chartres, quoted in Edward Peters, editor, *The First Crusade*, University of Pennsylvania Press, 1971, pp. 82–3.**

*On the eve of the feast day of Apostles Peter and Paul, trusting in God and confessing our sins, we went out of the gates of the city with all our war equipment. We were so few that they were sure that we were not fighting against them, but fleeing. All our men having been prepared, and certain ranks both of foot-soldiers and knights being arranged in order for battle, with the Lord's Lance we boldly sought where their greater courage and strength lay, and forced them to flee from their most advanced positions. As was their custom, they began to scatter on all sides, occupying hills and paths and trying to surround us. For they thought they could kill all of us in this manner. But our men, having been trained in many battles against their trickery and cleverness, God's mercy so came to our aid that we, who were very few in comparison with them, drove them all close together. Then with God's right hand fighting with us, we forced them to flee and to leave their camps with everything in them. Having totally conquered them, having put them to flight and having killed many thousands of their soldiers, we returned to the city, glad and cheerful.*

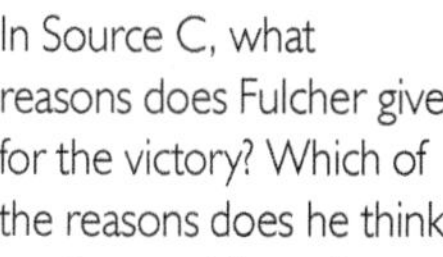

**SOURCE QUESTION**

In Source C, what reasons does Fulcher give for the victory? Which of the reasons does he think are the crucial ones?

## The journey to Jerusalem

The crusaders now prepared to march to their final destination. However, it was not possible for them simply to collect their forces together and take the road south. They needed to secure Antioch. Herein lay a problem.

Bohemund had been promised the city by his fellow crusaders and had satisfied the conditions of the promise, but Raymond of Toulouse stood by the vow he had taken, albeit reluctantly, to Alexius I, and urged that the city should be restored to Byzantium. Historians have been generally critical of Bohemund and depict him as solely out for his own ends, but Raymond was equally ambitious. He was using the supposed superiority of his oath to Alexius I as a weapon against Bohemund. Raymond had no real intention of giving Alexius I Antioch, but he did mean to stop Bohemund from having the city.

Yet Bohemund was in possession of the citadel, which had fallen to the crusaders in the aftermath of the battle. Here, too, Raymond challenged Bohemund when his troops took control of the areas outside Antioch which controlled the supply routes. Raymond also used his connection with the Holy Lance (when he carried it; see page 57) so that he looked like the natural leader. The council of princes which had overseen the Crusade so far now decided to send a deputation to the emperor to see whether he intended to come to take control of Antioch, but this led to more delay as a rapid response could not be expected. Hugh of Vermandois and Baldwin of Hainault were put in charge of the mission.

The capture of Antioch had other results:

- The churches were restored and the Greek Patriarch, John the Oxite, was confirmed in his position on the insistence of the Bishop of Le Puy.
- Supplies were still a problem. Now that Antioch was taken, the surrounding area could not be treated as enemy territory and plundered, so the different groups of crusaders were assigned different areas.
- Some crusaders sought employment with Baldwin of Boulogne in Edessa.
- Groups of knights began to fight the Turks for their own benefit, but some were defeated and killed.
- The weakened troops fell prey to illness and many, including Adhémar of Le Puy, died in August 1098.

News came that Baldwin of Hainault had been killed by the Turks, and Hugh delayed his journey to Constantinople. The crusaders now sent an appeal to Urban II to come to Antioch and take on the leadership of the Crusade. But Urban was not to be tempted and the crusaders remained leaderless, with Raymond and Bohemund locked in competition. Their rivalry was worsened when Raymond instigated the siege of the city of Marrat an-Numan, only to be joined in the attack by Bohemund. The capture of the city in December led to widespread murder and looting and did not ease the ill-feeling between the crusader factions. Raymond even tried to win over the other leaders with hefty bribes. Worse still, he failed to maintain supply lines to Marrat, with the result that the men holding the town were cut off and starving, so much so that they were reduced to cannibalism.

Raymond now made a decisive move. In January 1099 he announced that he would set out for Jerusalem. He was joined by Robert of Normandy and by Tancred, who was breaking away from his uncle, Bohemund. But Godfrey of Bouillon and Robert of Flanders refused to join Raymond, while Bohemund simply took advantage of his departure to secure Antioch more thoroughly. Eventually, Raymond made the foolish decision to besiege the town of Arqa. He could not proceed further with his depleted army so he needed to keep it occupied while he awaited reinforcements. But the siege did not go well and he feared a Turkish attack. He sent desperate messages to Robert of Flanders and Godfrey of Bouillon and they rushed to his aid, although some suspected that it was merely a ruse on Raymond's part to get the crusaders all gathered in one place.

Raymond tried to raise morale by using the prophetic talents of Peter Bartholomew (see page 57), who reported fresh visions and God's call for the evil to repent. However, Peter had lost some of his appeal. He was challenged and agreed to undergo trial by fire to prove he was a genuine prophet. Unfortunately, he was badly burned and died soon afterwards. Raymond's prestige was damaged and support for the siege of Arqa fell away. Messages were then received from Alexius I ordering the crusaders to await his coming before attacking Jerusalem. This was enough to spur them on to try to take the city on their own. They set off in May 1099.

This part of the Crusade was far from being a great success, but the crusaders did finally move off to march on Jerusalem. One helpful factor was their brutality in both obtaining supplies and capturing hostile bases. This encouraged local rulers to come to terms and avoid such consequences. This also put plenty of wealth in the pockets of the crusaders and eased supply problems considerably.

**ONLINE EXTRAS** WWW
AQA

Develop your analytical skills by completing Worksheet 6 at **www.hoddereducation.co.uk/accesstohistory/extras**

## The capture of Jerusalem 1099

As the crusaders approached and besieged Jerusalem, they faced the following obstacles:

- The speed of their final advance had taken the Fatimids by surprise, but by leaving cities like Acre (see Figure 4.1, page 73) unconquered the crusaders were dangerously exposed.
- They had a small but very experienced army of about 12,300 men, but they were divided, with Godfrey, Robert and Tancred besieging one section and Raymond and the southern French attacking another.
- They recognised the need to construct siege engines, but supplies of wood locally were sparse.
- Food was plentiful in the summer, but the weather was hot and thirst was a problem, especially as the Fatimids (see page 13) had poisoned the wells outside the city.
- A fleet arrived from Genoa with wood and craftsmen, but links to the ports were cut off.
- As the siege engines were being built, arguments about who would rule Jerusalem once it was captured continued.

Despite all their problems, the crusaders were inspired and determined and their frontal assault on 14–15 July succeeded. The chroniclers described the tactics and the success with great satisfaction. The key factors lay in the construction of two fearsome siege towers, which meant the Fatimids had to split their forces to defend two parts of the walls. Overnight on 13–14 July, the crusaders moved one of the siege towers, which meant partly dismantling and rebuilding it, to a position which was less well defended by the Fatimids. The crusaders had also built a vast battering ram, many catapults, scaling ladders and screens made from **wattle** which protected the attackers. But their activities were in full view of the besieged, who made their own preparations.

**KEY TERM**

**Wattle** Woven strips of wood forming panels used for fencing or for walling.

On 14 July the battering ram made a breach in the walls, but the Fatimids resisted fiercely. The next day Godfrey of Bouillon led the assault from the top of one of the siege towers. The tower was wheeled very slowly up to the walls, and was so well protected that all the various missiles hurled by the defenders did not damage it. It also had the advantage of being taller than the walls so the men at the top could rain down arrows on the Fatimids. Godfrey was able to take advantage of a fire in one of the other turrets to get on to the walls. Once the Franks were in the city, resistance crumbled. The Fatimid governor of Jerusalem, Iftikhar ad-Daulah, surrendered to Raymond and was one of the few defenders to survive. The slaughter and pillage were immense. Up to 70,000 Muslims were killed in the bloodbath. Yet the crusaders rejoiced in coming to the Church of the Holy Sepulchre and gave thanks to God. Killing, sacking and worshipping all went hand in hand. Source D illustrates this point.

**ONLINE EXTRAS**
Pearson Edexcel **WWW**

Learn how to address the concept of significance by completing Worksheet 8 at **www.hoddereducation.co.uk/accesstohistory/extras**

**SOURCE QUESTION**

How would you explain the contradictions apparent in Source D between the different actions of the crusaders?

**SOURCE D**

**Robert the Monk describes the scenes in the Temple of Solomon, quoted in Carol Sweetenham, *Robert the Monk's History of the First Crusade*, 2005, Ashgate Publishing, pp. 200–1.**

*When day seemed to be drawing to a close our men, worried that the sun would set, found a new rush of courage, broke into the temple and put its occupants to a wretched death. So much human blood was spilt there that the bodies of the slain were revolving on the floor on a current of blood. Arms and hands that had been cut off floated on the blood and found their way to other bodies, so nobody could work out which body the arm had come from, which was attached to another headless body. Even the soldiers who were carrying out the massacre could hardly bear the vapours rising from the warm blood … Then they ran through the streets and squares, plundering whatever they found. Jerusalem was full of good things and nobody lacked any delight. Made thus immensely rich, they made their way joyfully to the Lord's Holy Sepulchre. They thanked Him who was buried there and laid down their mortal sins … Once they had completed this act of solemn devotion, they returned to the houses which the Lord had destined for them, surrendering to the needs of nature, they gave their exhausted bodies food and rest in sleep.*

## Why was the First Crusade a success?

There can be little doubt that the capture of Jerusalem was a remarkable success, but why had a force which had walked thousands of miles and was depleted by disease and deaths been able to capture Jerusalem? There were a number of reasons for this:

- The Arabs were not prepared for the attack. They had easily won at Manzikert in 1071, captured Antioch in 1084 and had easily defeated the People's Crusade, and believed that the crusader force would be just as straightforward to defeat.

- The Muslims were divided between Sunnis and Shi'ites. These groups hated each other more than they hated the crusaders and were willing to form alliances with the crusaders to defeat their Muslim enemies.
- There was rivalry between Turkish emirs, or chieftains, and Seljuk atabegs, the Fatimids' hold on Palestine was weak, while the Abbasid caliph in Baghdad ruled under the supervision of the Turkish sultan. The crusader army never faced a united opposition. There was a power vacuum in Anatolia as a number of rulers were fighting for leadership in the region.
- The Muslim weaknesses encouraged the crusaders to believe they could recapture lands. The march on Jerusalem was helped as the local Arab communities were divided and acted virtually independently. The Fatimids in Egypt did not come to help, and the emirs of Shaizar, Homs and Tripoli gave money and gifts to the crusaders to keep away, while Beirut, Sidon, Tyre and Caesearea paid ransoms to avoid being taken and provided the crusaders with supplies.
- The support of Byzantium in the early stages.
- The crusaders' military tactics. They were quick to learn. At the Battle of Dorylaeum they became accustomed to the lightly armed mounted Turkish archers. Victory against them gave them confidence.
- The crusaders used the heavy cavalry charge, which the Turks were not accustomed to facing.
- The capture of towns and cities on the way meant that they could not be attacked in the rear. The capture of places such as Edessa, which was a prosperous and fertile area, meant that food supplies were available.
- The use of siege towers, both at Antioch and at Jerusalem. Ladders were used effectively to get men into both cities.
- Religious zeal helped the crusader army, particularly when times were very difficult during the siege of Antioch during the winter months. Their religious zeal may have encouraged the belief in the Holy Lance and in the breakout from Antioch that they were accompanied by 'supernatural' knights, which appeared to add to the size of their force. It was religious zeal after the capture of Edessa and Antioch that drove the force after the death of Adhémar and learning that the emperor would be joining them.
- Supplies from the west. The Genoese navy brought timber for the building of the siege machines and catapults that were used to capture Jerusalem.
- The leadership and fighting skills of men such as Bohemund.
- The Turks also faced difficulties in Persia and this meant that their forces were divided.

After a long and fraught journey, the second wave of the First Crusade had ended in victory for the crusaders and the successful capture of Jerusalem.

**ONLINE EXTRAS** AQA WWW

Get to grips with analysing the importance of factors by completing Worksheet 7 at **www.hoddereducation.co.uk/accesstohistory/extras**

**ONLINE EXTRAS** AQA WWW

Learn how to write an effective introduction by completing Worksheet 8 at **www.hoddereducation.co.uk/accesstohistory/extras**

**ONLINE EXTRAS** OCR WWW

Learn how to plan an effective essay by completing Worksheet 12 at **www.hoddereducation.co.uk/accesstohistory/extras**

**ONLINE EXTRAS** Pearson Edexcel WWW

Learn how to address the concept of significance by completing Worksheet 9 at **www.hoddereducation.co.uk/accesstohistory/extras**

**ONLINE EXTRAS** Pearson Edexcel WWW

Learn how to use specific examples by completing Worksheet 10 at **www.hoddereducation.co.uk/accesstohistory/extras**

**SOURCE E**

The capture of Jerusalem in 1099, from a fourteenth-century French biography of Godfrey of Bouillon. Godfrey is shown wearing a crown. The image includes a mysterious knight who appeared on the Mount of Olives to direct the attack by waving his shield.

**SOURCE QUESTION**

How useful is Source E as evidence for the capture of Jerusalem by the crusaders?

# The impact of the capture of Jerusalem

## Impact on Jerusalem

- On 17 July order was restored, the streets were cleared, for fear the rotting bodies would cause disease to spread, and the corpses were burned.
- Godfrey was appointed as Advocate of the Holy Sepulchre on 22 July, ruler of the city in fact, but not given the title of king in order to placate Raymond.
- The rivalry between Raymond of Toulouse and Godfrey of Bouillon continued as Raymond at first refused to hand over the defences of Jerusalem

which he had captured, and, when he did so, he retired to a camp outside the city.

- A Frenchman, Arnulf, was chosen as the new Patriarch of Jerusalem, making it part of the Catholic Church, rather than the Greek Church.
- A Fatimid army coming to the aid of Jerusalem was defeated in a battle near Ascalon, taken by surprise in a night attack.

## Impact on the Latin West

- In September most of the crusaders left to return home, including Robert of Flanders, Robert of Normandy and Peter the Hermit, which suggests that their motives had been religious rather than the gaining of land and wealth. About 300 knights stayed to support Godfrey in Jerusalem.
- Enthused by the success of the Crusade, Pope Paschal II, who had replaced Urban II, who died in 1099, encouraged a 'third wave' led by Raymond of Toulouse, Stephen of Blois and Hugh of Vermandois, all possibly trying to retrieve their reputations. It was wiped out by the Turks in Asia Minor in 1101. Hugh and Stephen were killed. Raymond just survived, but apparently lost the Holy Lance in the process.
- The crusader leaders began to create kingdoms for themselves (see pages 71–6), suggesting a decline in the influence of the papacy.

## Impact on the Byzantine Empire

- The success of the crusading armies gave Alexius the opportunity to regain his former possessions.
- Alexius was on his way to aid the crusader army when Stephen of Blois told him the crusaders had been defeated at Antioch.
- Alexius was later sent a message by the crusaders inviting him to take possession of Antioch, evidence that the crusaders still considered that their oath to Alexius was binding.
- Alexius declined the offer to join in the march on Jerusalem as he was not interested in the city and was negotiating with the Egyptians.

## Impact on the Muslim Near East

- The threat from Persia prevented the Turks from bringing an army to confront the crusaders.
- The success of the Crusade was a psychological shock to the Turks, particularly after the failure of the People's Crusade.
- More land and territory was lost in the period 1100–30 (see page 77).
- Divisions continued in the Muslim world which allowed the Crusader States to become established.

**ONLINE EXTRAS** WWW
AQA

Learn how to plan an effective essay by completing Worksheet 9 at **www.hoddereducation.co.uk/accesstohistory/extras**

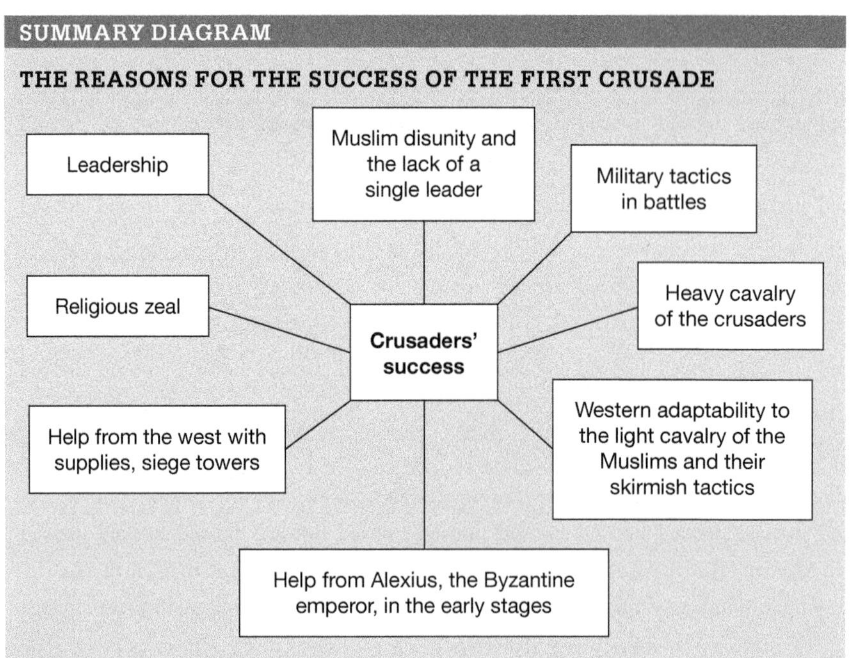


## 3 Key debate

■ *Why was the First Crusade successful?*

Historians have put forward a number of reasons for the success of the First Crusade. These have included religious fervour, which was a culmination of the reform movement, and had been seen clearly with the inspiration that the crusaders had gained from the discovery of the Holy Lance. This religious fervour would also play a key role in the crusaders' ultimate success before the walls of Jerusalem. Religious motives were also stressed by Thomas Madden (1999), who highlighted the genuine concern and motivation of the crusaders to liberate the oppressed Christians in the east, building on the work of Jonathan Riley Smith (see the key debate in Chapter 2, page 40). However, others, such as John France (2005), have argued that it was the military capabilities of the crusaders that led to their triumphs. He has suggested that the crusading army became more effective as the campaign proceeded. There is certainly some truth in the military skill of the crusaders, as was also seen at Jerusalem with their building of the siege towers.

In contrast, the work of Moshe Gil has emphasised the divisions within the Muslim world as playing a key factor in the triumph of the crusader armies. This factor has also been explored by Thomas Asbridge (2005), who commented that 'this argument should not be ignored as once the Muslims were united under Jihad they proved a much more formidable force and the Crusaders were not able to retake Jerusalem during the Third Crusade'. Others, such as Peter Frankopan (2012), have argued that the aid the crusaders received from Byzantium was crucial and, as with Muslim disunity, this issue should not be dismissed as subsequent crusades lacked such aid and failed to achieve their goal.

### EXTRACT 1

From Thomas Asbridge, *The First Crusade*, Simon & Schuster, 2005, p. 307.

*Two overriding emotions empowered their efforts – desperation and devotion. Having endured such an immense struggle simply to reach Jerusalem, and now facing the palpable threat of Fatimid counterattack, most Crusaders were driven by an unshakable determination to conquer the Holy City and complete their pilgrimage to the Holy Sepulchre. Without such an inspirational goal, or such impending danger, the expedition might well have been ripped apart by division. As it was, the crusaders' spiritual fervour and survival instinct coalesced, providing just enough impetus to hold the few remaining threads of Frankish unity in place.*

### EXTRACT 2

From John France, *The Crusades and the Expansion of Catholic Christendom 1000–1714*, Routledge, 2005, p. 81.

*But the crusader victory was the more remarkable because it was won by an almost entirely infantry army. We have very good reason to believe that … the crusader army had only about 200 horses left because a substantial number of our sources report the fact. … It was the suddenness of the crusader strike and the speed and vigour with which the crusaders flung themselves into the battle which enabled them to defeat the enemy in detail before his [Kerbogah's] massive forces could be gathered and brought to bear. This aggressiveness was the hallmark of Bohemond, and it was he who gained enormous prestige from the victory.*

### EXTRACT 3

From Thomas Asbridge, *The First Crusade*, Simon & Schuster, 2005, p. 334.

*Had the Muslims of the Near East united in the face of the First Crusade it could not possibly have prevailed. The combined forces of Damascus, Aleppo and Mosul would surely have crushed the Franks outside the walls of Antioch; facing the collective might of the Abbasid and Fatimid caliphates, the Latins could never have mounted the sacred walls of Jerusalem. In the years to come, hundreds of thousands of Franks sought to equal the achievements of these First Crusaders, but in the face of burgeoning Islamic solidarity, none prospered.*

**INTERPRETATION QUESTION**

Which of the interpretations in Extracts 1–4 for the success of the First Crusade do you find most convincing? Explain your answer using your own knowledge.

**ONLINE EXTRAS** WWW
AQA

Learn how to develop your interpretation analysis by completing Worksheet 10 at **www.hoddereducation.co.uk/accesstohistory/extras**

**ONLINE EXTRAS** WWW
Pearson Edexcel

Learn how to develop your interpretation analysis by completing Worksheet 11 at **www.hoddereducation.co.uk/accesstohistory/extras**

**ONLINE EXTRAS** WWW
AQA

Get to grips with extract analysis by completing Worksheet 11 at **www.hoddereducation.co.uk/accesstohistory/extras**

**ONLINE EXTRAS** WWW
Pearson Edexcel

Learn how to develop your interpretation analysis by completing Worksheet 12 at **www.hoddereducation.co.uk/accesstohistory/extras**

**EXTRACT 4**

**From Peter Frankopan, *The First Crusade*, Harvard University Press, 2012, p. 206.**

*But it is one man, above all others, who stands out. Alexios I Komnenos put in motion the chain of events that introduced the Crusades to the world. The call from the east was to reshape the medieval world, massively expanding the geographic, economic, social, political and cultural horizons of Europe. After more than 900 years in the gloom, Alexios should once again take centre stage in the history of the First Crusade.*

# CHAPTER SUMMARY

The First Crusade began with a force led by Peter the Hermit. This went through Germany, where massacres of Jewish populations took place. Once in Asia Minor, the inexperienced crusaders were wiped out by the Turks, although Peter survived. The Princes' Crusade left from France and Germany and came together at Constantinople. Emperor Alexius wanted such a large army moved on rapidly. The crusaders moved on through Asia Minor to Antioch with some heavy losses. The capture of Antioch was helped by the scheming of Bohemund and the finding of the Holy Lance. The journey to Jerusalem was difficult. The siege of Jerusalem succeeded but was followed by a massacre of the defenders.

## Refresher questions

Use these questions to remind yourself of the key issues in this chapter.

**1** Why did people join Peter the Hermit?
**2** Why was Peter the Hermit's Crusade a failure?
**3** Why was Alexius I afraid of the crusader armies?
**4** Why did the crusaders win the battle at Dorylaeum?
**5** How did the crusaders overcome the difficulties of fighting and marching in unfriendly terrain?
**6** What was the importance of Bohemund?
**7** How did the crusaders take Antioch?
**8** Why was the siege of Jerusalem successful?

## Question practice: AQA

### Essay questions

**1** 'By 1099 the Byzantine Empire had recovered from its weaknesses.' Explain why you agree or disagree with this view of the years 1071 to 1099. [AS level]

**EXAM HINT** Argue for and against the proposition and then reach a detailed conclusion that is clearly argued.

**2** To what extent did the papacy successfully expand its authority in the years 1071–99? [A level]

**EXAM HINT** Make sure that you avoid a narrative approach. Examine aspects that agree with the proposition and aspects which do not, and then reach a clearly argued conclusion.

**3** 'By 1099 the First Crusade had achieved its objectives.' Assess the validity of this view of the years 1071 to 1099. [A level]

**EXAM HINT** Consider the full date range to this question in breadth. While it is tempting to simply consider events from the Council of Clermont onwards there should be a clear attempt to define the longer-term aims. What, for example, were the consequences of the Battle of Manzikert, or of the Great Schism, or of the attempts by a politically resurgent papacy to establish control over the Church in the east?

### Interpretation question

**1** Using your understanding of the historical context, assess how convincing the arguments in Extracts 1, 2 and 3 (page 67) are in relation to the reasons for the success of the Franks during the First Crusade. [A level]

**EXAM HINT** Identify the main thrust or the main point being made in each extract. Then, suggest if it is convincing or not with evidence from contextual knowledge in support of your view. Identify a secondary argument if you can and again establish if it is convincing or not. Aim to give a balanced view. Hence, the main thrust of Extract 1 is that religious factors motivated the crusaders. A second element is that desperation borne out of a simple instinct for survival kept the crusaders focused on success. You should use your contextual knowledge to assess these views.

## Question practice: OCR

### Essay questions

**1** Which of the following was more important in causing the failure of the People's Crusade? i) Peter the Hermit's leadership. ii) The actions of Alexius I. Explain your answer with reference to both i) and ii). [A level]

**EXAM HINT** The importance of the two factors in causing the failure of the People's Crusade should be explained and a supported judgement reached as to which was more important.

**2** 'Muslim disunity was the most important reason for the success of the First Crusade.' How far do you agree? [A level]

**EXAM HINT** As the named factor, responses should explain the importance of Muslim disunity in the success before analysing other factors that were responsible for the success of the Crusade. A judgement as to the relative importance of factors should be reached.

## Question practice: Pearson Edexcel

### Essay questions

**1** How far do you agree that the weakness of Muslim forces was the main reason for the success of the First Crusade? [AS level]

**EXAM HINT** Compare the numerical strength, and the qualities of leadership displayed by both Christian and Muslim forces, and the different factors which motivated both sides.

**2** How significant was the capture of Antioch in explaining the success of the First Crusade? [A level]

**EXAM HINT** Examine the reasons for the Christian victory at Antioch, including the Holy Lance. Link this point to the Christians' subsequent success in capturing Jerusalem.

CHAPTER 4

# The Crusader States of Outremer

The victories of the First Crusade led to the establishment of four Crusader States under the rule of European princes. This chapter examines the founding of the States and their later history by focusing on the following themes:

- The establishment of the States
- The problems facing the States
- The survival of the Crusader States
- The establishment of the Military Orders

The key debate on page 86 asks the question: Why did the Crusader States survive? And the key debate on page 91 asks the question: How important were the Military Orders in the survival of the Crusader States?

**KEY DATES**

| | |
|---|---|
| **1098** | Edessa established by Baldwin of Boulogne |
| | Antioch established by Bohemund |
| **1099** | Capture of Jerusalem – Godfrey of Bouillon became king |
| **1100** | Baldwin I became King of Jerusalem |
| **1101** | Capture of the port of Caesarea |
| **1104** | Capture of the port of Acre |
| **1109** | Capture of Tripoli |
| **1110** | Capture of Beirut and Sidon |
| **1113** | Hospitaller Order became independent |
| **1119** | Battle of the Field of Blood |
| | Templar Order founded |
| **1124** | Capture of the port of Tyre |
| **1129** | Templar Order given official Church support |

## 1 The establishment of the States

*Why and how were the States established?*

The four Crusader States all resulted from the successes of the First Crusade, with their establishment starting even before the capture of Jerusalem. They were ruled by noble knights from western Europe. The kingdoms developed in the following ways:

- A king was chosen to rule the kingdom.
- Further land and territory was captured in the period 1100–30.
- The outlying territories were formed into three provinces: County of Antioch, County of Edessa and County of Tripoli.

- They were organised in the same way as European feudal states, with land being allocated to lesser barons who gave the rulers armed support when it was needed.
- The legal and political structures of the kingdoms were similar to those in western Europe, with the king as a feudal overlord.

**KEY TERM**

**Outremer** French for overseas. The term came into use after the First Crusade and described the County of Edessa, the Principality of Antioch, the County of Tripoli and the Kingdom of Jerusalem. It was later used more broadly to cover the Levant or the Holy Land.

They were collectively known as **Outremer** and sometimes referred to as the Latin East. However, as most of the crusaders returned home, it left only a few thousand to establish and hold the States and therefore their survival was not certain and would depend on a number of factors, including:

- the lack of unity in the Muslim world
- alliances formed with Muslim tribes and leaders
- aid from the west
- the establishment of the Military Orders
- the building of castles.

But despite these developments, the States did face a number of challenges as the period progressed. Aid from the west declined, relations with the emperor in Byzantium deteriorated such that he was actively seeking Muslim aid against the crusaders, the development of *jihad* provided a rallying point for the Muslim world and there was growing internal instability, particularly over succession issues in some of the States.

## County of Edessa

Edessa was the first State to be founded. It was ruled by Baldwin I (of Boulogne), who had captured it in 1098 from its Byzantine ruler, and who became Count of Edessa. It was strategically placed in Armenia and possession of Edessa was helpful in keeping Antioch secure. The State was also fertile in comparison to the regions to the south and was therefore a crucial source of food. Within a short period of time, Baldwin was able to acquire a great deal of treasure, married a local princess and adopted many Arab habits. He was ready to include the local inhabitants in his government, but control was maintained by the Franks and his hope was that the new State would see a fusion of its different groups to make a stable settlement. Muslims were granted religious toleration, but, after experiencing their unreliability as allies, Baldwin was reluctant to trust them with much power. His achievements were not admired much by dedicated crusaders, who did not feel that Muslims should be given freedom of worship and felt Baldwin had rather sold out on the aims of the Crusade.

In theory, Edessa should have been returned to the emperor in accordance with the oath Baldwin had sworn, but, as the man in possession, Baldwin was in control. When Baldwin became King of Jerusalem (see page 76), his cousin, Baldwin Le Bourcq, became the Count of Edessa and in 1118 became King of Jerusalem as Baldwin II. Baldwin II was later joined by another cousin, Joscelin I of Courtenay (died 1181), who managed to extend his rule in the direction of

Aleppo. Edessa suffered extensively from Muslim raids and crusader rivalries and was no longer the rich city it had been when first taken by the crusaders. A powerful earthquake in 1114 made the situation worse.

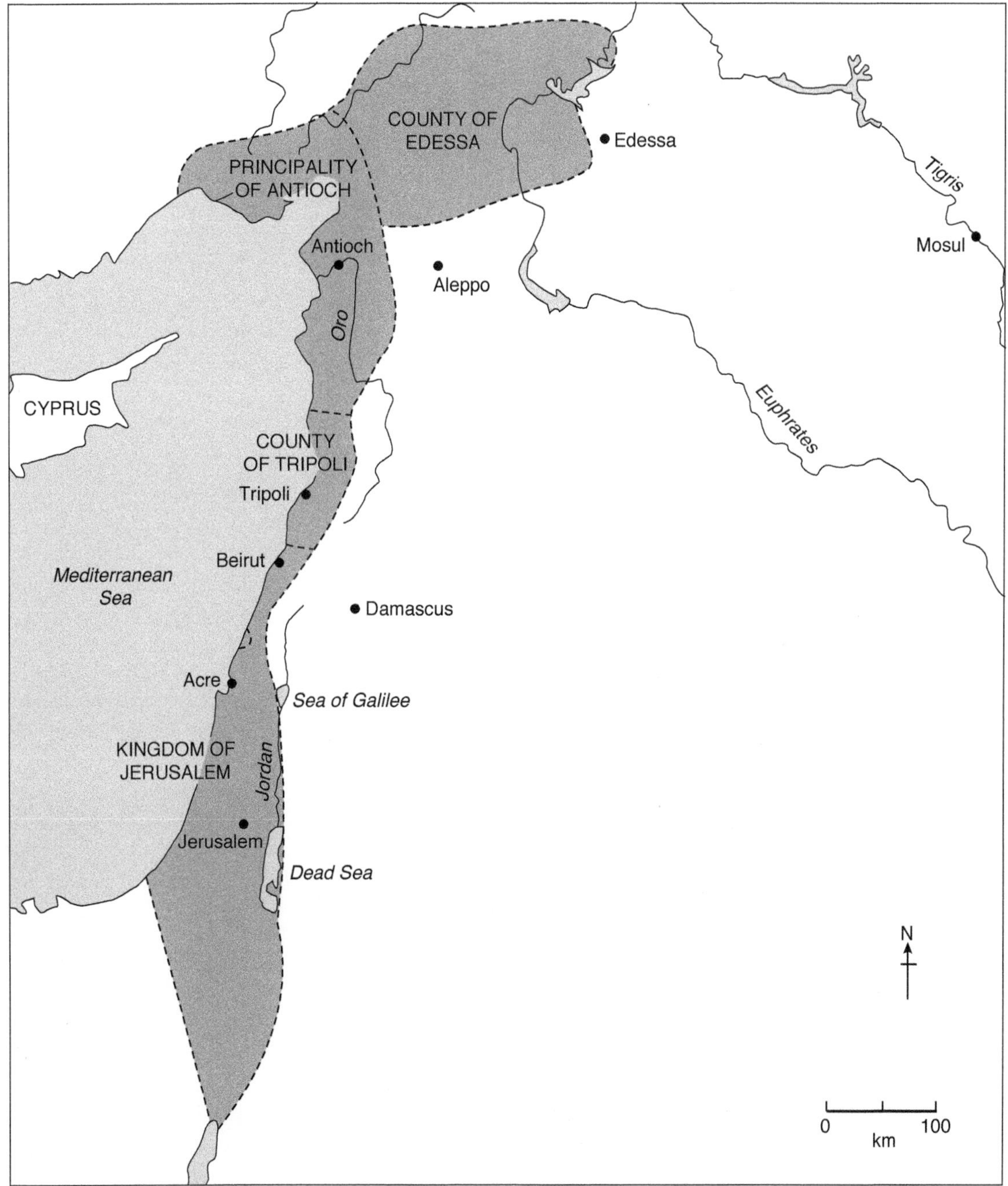


**Figure 4.1** The Crusader States in the early twelfth century.

## Timeline of rulers of Edessa

| | |
|---|---|
| 1098–1100 | Baldwin of Boulogne the first Count of Edessa |
| 1100–18 | Baldwin of Le Bourcq |
| 1104–5 | Tancred while Baldwin was in captivity |
| 1105–8 | Richard of Salerno |
| 1119–31 | Joscelin I of Courtenay when Baldwin I became King of Jerusalem. Joscelin I was captured in an ambush in 1122 and freed the next year |
| 1131–59 | Joscelin II – he was captured by the troops of Nur ad-Din in 1150 (see page 121) and his final years were spent as a captive |

**KEY TERM**

**Danishmends** A Turkish tribe ruling in Anatolia.

**KEY FIGURE**

**Ilghazi**

Muslim ruler of Mardin from 1108 or 1109 until 1122, achieved the first major Muslim victory against the Franks when he defeated and killed Roger of Salerno, regent of Antioch, at the Battle of Balat. The battle itself marked an important moment in the growth of the idea of *jihad*, with a renowned religious scholar preaching to Ilghazi's army prior to the fighting.

# Principality of Antioch

This was under Bohemund, but he struggled to maintain his position against local Armenian and Byzantine warlords who had their own ambitions, and he was then captured by the **Danishmends** when trying to take the city of Melitene. He was imprisoned between 1100 and 1103 and then totally defeated at Harran in 1104. He eventually left the east in 1105. His nephew, Tancred, ruled, first as regent (1101–3) and then as prince (1105–12). He was able to expand the territory of Antioch, helped by another Norman, Roger of Salerno (died 1119) who was killed at the Battle of Balat by **Ilghazi** of Mardin. Tancred's administration was similar to that of the former Byzantine rulers but he relied on Norman officials, whom he could trust. When attacked by local Muslim rulers, he avoided pitched battles, therefore preserving his limited manpower, and constructed a network of alliances built up on his borders to frustrate their intentions, allowing the State to survive.

## Timeline of rulers of Antioch

| | |
|---|---|
| 1098–1105 | Bohemund I of Taranto |
| 1101 | Tancred as Regent and from 1108 prince |
| 1113–19 | Roger of Salerno |
| 1119–26 | Baldwin II as regent |
| 1126–30 | Bohemund II, who married Alice, daughter of Baldwin II |
| 1130–6 | Fulk of Anjou (see page 80) as regent chose Raymond of Poitiers to marry Constance, the heiress of Antioch, in 1136 |
| 1136–49 | Raymond of Poitiers |
| 1149–53 | Constance |
| 1153–61 | Reynald of Châtillon, second husband of Constance, imprisoned by Nur ad-Din (see page 124) in 1161 |
| 1161–3 | Constance |
| 1163–1201 | Bohemund III |
| 1201–16 | Bohemund IV |

Of these, Tancred died young, Roger, Bohemund II and Raymond were killed in battles they had initiated, and Reynald spent sixteen years in prison in Aleppo.

## County of Tripoli

Raymond of Toulouse was the founder of this State. Despite being one of the first to sign up for the Crusade, he had been constantly elbowed out by his rivals and so made no gains in either Antioch or Jerusalem. As a result, he decided to look elsewhere for his opportunity to set up a State and had the support of other crusaders whose gains had, thus far, been minimal. He captured Tortosa in 1102 and then advanced on Tripoli, the main port for Damascus and so a useful strategic gain. He built a castle on a mound known as Mount Pilgrim, but he died in 1105, before Tripoli had been captured, and left a disputed succession behind him. Tripoli was ultimately taken in 1109 despite a late attempt to relieve the siege by the Muslim military leader **Toghtekin**.

**KEY FIGURE**

**Toghtekin**

Atabeg of Damascus from 1105 to 1128. Shortly before the fall of Tripoli, he attempted to relieve the siege but was ultimately unsuccessful. He pursued his own political ambitions, even taking control of Busra al-Sham in 1106 from his own rivals.

### Timeline of rulers of Tripoli

| | |
|---|---|
| 1103–5 | Raymond IV of Toulouse and I of Tripoli |
| 1105–9 | William-Jordan, cousin of Raymond |
| 1109–12 | Bertrand, illegitimate son of Raymond |
| 1112–37 | Count Pons, son of Bertrand |
| 1137–52 | Raymond II |
| 1152–87 | Raymond III after a regency by his mother Hodierna, a daughter of Baldwin II. He was in captivity 1164–74 |
| 1187–1233 | Bohemund IV of Antioch |

## Raymond III of Tripoli c.1140–87

Raymond succeeded his father as Count of Tripoli when Raymond II was assassinated in 1152. The county had been created by Raymond of Toulouse, but it lacked resources for its defence and depended on support from Jerusalem and Antioch. As a result, the counts brought their troops to the feudal muster of the kings of Jerusalem and the King of Jerusalem was regent for Raymond until he was of age. He was taken captive by Nur ad-Din (see page 83) in 1164 and held for eight years, during which period he became fluent in Arabic. He was ransomed largely by funds from the Knights of St John, to whom he granted land on which they built castles, including Krak des Chevaliers. In 1174 he acted as regent in Jerusalem for his cousin, Baldwin IV, and remained active in affairs there after Baldwin was of age. But one faction in Jerusalem resented his role and he was sent home in 1180. However, the growing threat from Saladin made him a useful ally and he was recalled in 1184 as regent for Baldwin, chosen by the High Court of nobles. It was agreed that if Baldwin's heir died before reaching his majority then the succession would be decided by the pope, the emperor, and the kings of France and England. Baldwin IV died in 1185 and Raymond tried to buy some time by a four-year truce with Saladin. Baldwin V died in 1186, but the agreement was ignored by Baldwin's mother, Sibylla, and her husband, Guy de Lusignan. Raymond withdrew in disgust to Tiberias, a stronghold belonging to his second wife, Eschiva of Bures (his first marriage to Hodierna, sister of Sibylla, had been turbulent and led to a separation). Raymond kept up the truce even when Jerusalem was at war again with Saladin, but was then horrified when some Muslims, to whom he had granted a safe conduct, attacked and killed some of Guy's supporters. Those who died were mostly Templars (see page 88) and Raymond saw their severed heads displayed on Muslim lances and so was reconciled with Guy and joined in the war. He fought at Hattin (see pages 138 and 139), where he was wounded and he died soon after. The character Tiberias in the 2005 Ridley Scott film, *Kingdom of Heaven*, is said to be modelled on Raymond. He was a controversial figure. The Templars believed he was conspiring with Saladin, which was why the crusaders were defeated at Hattin, whereas his defenders point to the charge he led at the battle which failed only because he lacked sufficient troops.

## Kingdom of Jerusalem

This came under the rule of Godfrey of Bouillon after its capture, but he died in 1100. He had previously agreed to hold the city from Daimbert of Pisa (died 1105), who was the new Patriarch of Jerusalem and who had put forward the claim of the Church to the Holy City. Godfrey needed military support and a fleet from Pisa was at hand to enforce Daimbert's views. Hence, Godfrey had reluctantly agreed. But, when Godfrey died, it was by no means clear who his heir was. Daimbert was not in Jerusalem at the critical moment and so Godfrey's supporters sent an urgent message to Baldwin of Edessa, Godfrey's brother, to come to take over. The possibility of a civil war loomed but the most likely backers of Daimbert, Bohemund and Tancred, were otherwise occupied. By Christmas 1100 Baldwin was crowned by Daimbert as 'King of the Latins in Jerusalem'.

### Timeline of rulers of Jerusalem

| | |
|---|---|
| 1099–1100 | Godfrey of Bouillon |
| 1100–18 | Baldwin I of Boulogne |
| 1118–31 | Baldwin II, cousin to Baldwin I |
| 1131–43 | Fulk of Anjou associated with his wife, Melisende (see page 80), daughter of Baldwin II |
| 1143–63 | Baldwin III, son of Baldwin II, although Melisende continued to stress her rights until 1152. He had no children |
| 1163–74 | Amalric I, brother of Baldwin III |
| 1174–85 | Baldwin IV, who was a leper (see page 134) |
| 1185–6 | Baldwin V (see page 138) |
| 1186–92 | Guy de Lusignan with his wife, Sibylla, daughter of Amalric I |
| 1192–1205 | Isabella with Conrad I 1192, Henry 1192–7 and Aimery 1197–1205 |

**ONLINE EXTRAS** OCR **WWW**

Learn how to write a balanced essay by completing Worksheet 13 at **www.hoddereducation.co.uk/accesstohistory/extras**

**ONLINE EXTRAS** Pearson Edexcel **WWW**

Get to grips with note taking by completing Worksheet 13 at **www.hoddereducation.co.uk/accesstohistory/extras**

## Baldwin III 1129–63

Baldwin was the son of Fulk and Melisende (see page 80). He had early experience in warfare, leading armies from the age of fourteen. He became joint ruler of Jerusalem with his mother in 1143 at a time when the failure of the Second Crusade had weakened the Latin kingdoms. In 1152 he became sole ruler but had to deal with his mother's supporters who opposed his rule, sending Manasses into exile. He faced numerous problems, from the instability in Antioch and Tripoli, where he had to intervene, to financial difficulties, along with the constant warfare against Nur ad-Din (see page 83). He managed to capture Ascalon and fortify Gaza, but could not prevent the loss of Damascus. His struggle with Nur ad-Din was constant between 1155 and 1158 and had mixed success. He was a respected ruler and noted, according to William of Tyre, for his sociability as he never refused a request for an audience. He married Theodora Comnenus, the niece of Manuel I (see page 121) in 1158, and her dowry reduced his worries about money. He was able to maintain the loyalty of his vassals by keeping taxation low and giving them lands generously. His early death was seen as a potential disaster. He left no children, so his brother, Amalric, the holder of the County of Ascalon, succeeded him.

## Expansion and consolidation of territory after the First Crusade 1100–24

The Christian hold on lands after the First Crusade was tenuous, but in the period to 1124 there were a number of notable acquisitions, as well as a significant defeat at the Battle of the Field of Blood in 1119. The King of Jerusalem, Baldwin I, held just Jerusalem, Bethlehem and the port of Jaffa. In 1101 the port of Caesarea was taken, but still the kingdom was isolated, with Antioch, the crusaders' other main base, over 480 kilometres away. As a result, many of those who had deserted the First Crusade were called back and they helped to secure the kingdom.

Baldwin I's reign saw considerable expansion, with Acre taken in 1104, and Beirut and Sidon in 1110, and in 1115 a castle was built at Montreal in Transjordan, which controlled the trade routes from Damascus to Egypt and helped to secure crusader control.

In 1108, following Bohemund's return to Europe, a new 'crusade' was launched and although this attacked part of the Byzantine Empire, some crusaders did then go on to Jerusalem and help to consolidate the area.

However, in 1119 Baldwin II's position as the new King of Jerusalem was threatened by a Muslim attack. Roger of Antioch's army was defeated near Aleppo and 700 knights and 3000 foot soldiers were killed. This forced Baldwin to move north to Antioch and restore order, but the defeat had seriously depleted the fighting strength of the crusaders. As a result of the attack, relations between Christians and Muslims became more difficult. At the Council of Nablus in 1120 it was decided that sexual relations between the Christians and Muslims should be forbidden. The Council also recognised the weak position of the States and this resulted in the founding of the Templars and the call for another 'crusade'. The result was significant as, although only Venice responded to the call, it led to the capture of the port of Tyre in 1124, with the result that the Muslims' only port was Ascalon, making it much harder for them to bring in supplies.

The States of Outremer were largely established by crusading leaders. They had been able to carve out principalities for themselves, taking advantage of the disunity among the many and varied Muslim states. Holding on to what they had won with relative ease would prove far more difficult.

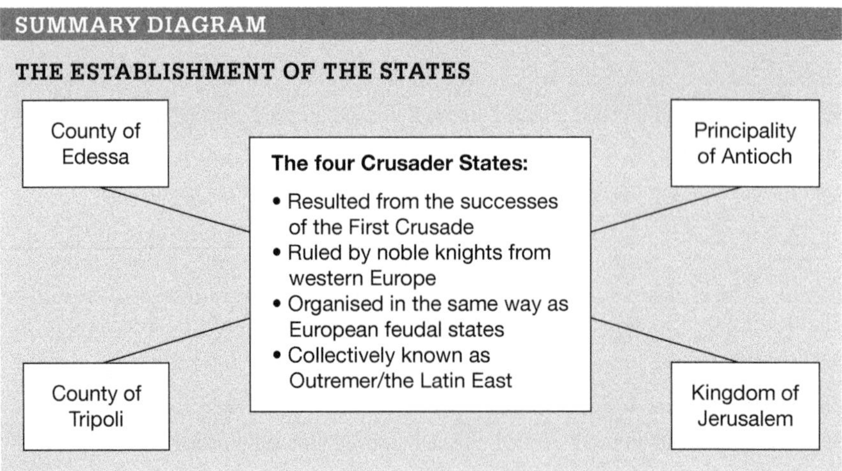

SUMMARY DIAGRAM
THE ESTABLISHMENT OF THE STATES
County of Edessa
Principality of Antioch
The four Crusader States:
• Resulted from the successes of the First Crusade
• Ruled by noble knights from western Europe
• Organised in the same way as European feudal states
• Collectively known as Outremer/the Latin East
County of Tripoli
Kingdom of Jerusalem


# 2 The problems facing the States

*What problems did the Crusader States face?*

The geographical position of the States was a major problem from the outset. The Mediterranean Sea provided them with a clearly defined boundary to the west, but there were no natural or defensible borders to the east: flat desert land stretched from the States towards Aleppo in the north and Damascus in the south. Medieval European states rarely had clearly defined political boundaries, and the Crusader States never established the divisions between States with any certainty.

The problems which the States encountered also came from both without and within. Muslim hostility varied in intensity, but always had to be reckoned with, and reinforcements from the west were not large. The Crusader States were always short of men and without the disunity of the Muslim forces it is unlikely that the States would have survived in these early years. The lack of manpower also meant that the States had to attempt to establish peaceful relations with the Muslims, who not only were their neighbours but made up part of the population. Alliances were made with Muslims, sometimes against fellow Christians, even if they did not last long. Settlers often married local women, which helped to reinforce unity, while merchants and labourers were encouraged to carry on trading and farming.

Internal divisions, often about the succession to the rule of the States, and rivalry between the crusader lords themselves were further factors. The Crusader States would always be vulnerable, as they were newly established lordships in an understandably unfriendly environment. Nevertheless, the persistent struggles within the Muslim world between Mosul, Damascus and Aleppo often worked in favour of the Christians.

## External problems faced by the Crusader States

The following shows the external problems the new states faced from existing Muslim rulers:

- 1104: the Muslim rulers of Mosul and Mardin, who had been fighting each other, joined together to defeat the crusaders who were trying to take Harran, south-east of Edessa. Both Baldwin I and Joscelin I were captured and, while they were unavailable, Tancred acted as regent until 1105, when Richard of Salerno (died 1119) took over. Tancred's clear hopes of taking Edessa for himself did not endear him to Baldwin, and relations after Baldwin was released were frosty. Both men tried to gain allies among the Muslim warlords, which made the situation of Edessa even more perilous. Tancred died in 1112 and relations improved.
- 1119: the ruler of Mardin defeated the forces of Antioch under Roger of Salerno at the Field of Blood, partly because Roger engaged in battle rather rashly, forgetting the principle that battles against the Muslims were best avoided. Roger was killed.
- 1128: the new ruler, or atabeg, of Mosul, Imad ad-Din Zengi (*c.*1085–1146), occupied Aleppo, thus cutting off an area of possible expansion for the Latins and allowing him to threaten Damascus. Combined forces from Antioch, Edessa and the Byzantines could not dislodge him. His conquests included Baalbek, which he put under the control of Naim ad-Din Ayyub (died 1173), the father of Al-Malik al-Nasir Salah ad-Din Yusuf, better known in the west as Saladin (1137–93) (see page 133).
- 1144: while Joscelin II of Edessa was campaigning in the area of Aleppo, the city of Edessa fell to Zengi after just four weeks and the eastern part of the county was lost for ever. Zengi claimed that Joscelin had been helping Zengi's Muslim enemies and so the attack was justified.

### Zengi (or Zangi or Zingi) c.1085–1146

Zengi was the atabeg, or local chieftain, who ruled Mosul, Aleppo and Edessa. His father had governed Aleppo under Malik Shah but was executed for treason, and Zengi was brought up by Kerbogha in Mosul. He was made atabeg of Mosul and then Aleppo by Sultan Mahmud II whom he had aided against a rival. Zengi is one of the twelfth-century counter-crusaders associated with the Muslim religious revival and call for *jihad* that would eventually lead to the unification of Syria, Egypt and Palestine. While he is celebrated as the first great proponent of *jihad*, his commitment to the idea has been doubted, with many historians arguing that he exploited the religious revival to fulfil his own political ambitions. For example, in 1130, when he proclaimed a *jihad* against the Franks, his attention was focused on Muslim-held Hama and Damascus. During his career, Zengi often fought other Muslims, including five Seljuk sultans and three Abbasid caliphs. He captured Edessa in 1144 (see page 97), thus inflicting the first real setback on the crusaders. He returned to Iraq to suppress a rising and was killed by a servant with a grudge. Nur ad-Din was his son.

## Queen Melisende 1105–61

Melisende was the daughter of Baldwin II and Morfia of Melitene. She was brought up in Edessa, but in 1118 her father was elected King of Jerusalem, partly on the advice of Joscelin I, his former rival in Edessa, who was now ruler of Galilee. She was raised as his heir, since he had no sons. Melisende then moved to Jerusalem with her three younger sisters. Her father was captured by Muslims and imprisoned in 1123–4, and only released when his youngest daughter was given up as a hostage to ensure that Baldwin paid the vast ransom demanded. This tactic worked as he raided far and wide to raise the necessary sum and free his daughter.

In 1126 Baldwin arranged for his second daughter to marry Bohemund II, which suggests that he intended Melisende to be his heir. This was reinforced when, shortly afterwards, the next daughter, Hodierna, was betrothed to the heir of Raymond I of Tripoli.

Eventually, Baldwin II decided to seek a husband for his eldest daughter. He asked Louis VI, King of France, for advice about a husband for Melisende and Louis suggested Fulk of Anjou (1092–1143), father of Geoffrey and some 23 years older than Melisende. Fulk was one of the most brutal and godless men of his day, although even he travelled three times to Jerusalem to obtain forgiveness for his many sins, which included burning his first wife at the stake as a punishment for her adultery. The marriage in 1129 was not all that happy but two sons were born, the elder being another Baldwin, born in 1130. Fulk had insisted that he should be the undoubted King of Jerusalem and that the pope should confirm Baldwin's title. He and Melisende were to govern Acre and Tyre until Baldwin died in 1131. Melisende and Fulk then became joint rulers in Jerusalem. Their relationship became fraught with tension as he insisted on ruling alone and attempted to promote his Angevin favourites, which was resisted by Melisende. In 1134 Count Hugh of Jaffa led a rebellion, a clear indication that relations between the crusader nobles and the outsider Fulk were not harmonious. There were also rumours that Hugh had become too friendly with Melisende, which led to further unrest as he made a deal with the Muslims in Ascalon and forced Fulk to march south and besiege Jaffa. Hugh was killed while waiting to leave the Holy Land, winning him much sympathy and forcing Fulk to consult more closely with his wife and the crusading nobles. As a result of his wife's power and the influence of the native crusaders he had attempted to bring in his own supporters from France, but this had caused resentment and was the ultimate cause of unrest and rebellion. Fulk died in a hunting accident in 1143. Baldwin III was just thirteen so he was crowned as king with his mother as queen. For the first time in Jerusalem, a ruler had come to the throne by inheritance as opposed to election. She was reluctant to give her son Baldwin much power and as he grew older this led to a civil war. Melisende retired to Nablus, where she died in 1161. She was a controversial figure and her tenacious hold on power was not always popular.

In the longer term the greatest threat to the States came from the re-emergence of *jihad,* literally 'struggle' or holy war (see page 97). As well as this, if the new States were to survive, aid from the west would be important, particularly as many crusaders, having fulfilled their vows of reaching Jerusalem, had returned home. Manpower would be a continual problem, with only a few thousand of the crusader army remaining behind. Some noble families did send their sons to the States to maintain the supply of nobles, seeing the kingdom as a sort of province of feudal Europe. However, after the euphoria of the success of the First Crusade, numbers going to the States did decline and there needed to be regular appeals for further support and aid.

### Problems of succession

The following shows the internal problems the new states faced from the crusaders themselves:

- 1104: while Count Baldwin II was in captivity, Tancred tried to claim he had the right to have Edessa and called on Muslim allies for help.
- 1109: Bertrand, the illegitimate son of Raymond of Toulouse, claimed Tripoli with the help of Baldwin I of Jerusalem against William-Jordan (died 1109), Raymond's cousin, who had the backing of Tancred.
- 1116: Baldwin I of Jerusalem died childless despite two marriages, and factions at court backed different candidates to succeed him. Baldwin II of Le Bourcq became king but when he was later captured, questions were asked about whether he should be replaced.
- 1126: Baldwin II of Jerusalem became concerned that his cousin Joscelin might take over Antioch and rule it alongside Edessa. Hence, he made contact with Bohemund II, who was in Italy and now in his late teens. Bohemund II was glad to come to Antioch and succeed to his father's lands, and he married Baldwin's second daughter, Alice.
- 1130: on his death, Bohemund II left an infant daughter, Constance (1128–63), but his nearest male heir was Roger II of Sicily (1095–1154). Roger II was not seen as a desirable ruler as it was feared that Antioch would become just an outpost of Sicily, so Fulk of Anjou (1092–1143), the King of Jerusalem, chose Raymond of Poitiers (*c.*1115–49), who married Constance. But there was a brief period when Alice (*c.*1110–after 1136), Baldwin's daughter and Bohemund's widow, tried to take over in Antioch herself.
- 1131: the death of Baldwin II led to further problems over the succession in Jerusalem as his daughter, Melisende (1105–61), was associated by him with her husband Fulk of Anjou and different court factions favoured Melisende and Fulk.
- 1133–4: Hugh, Count of Jaffa, plotted against King Fulk of Jerusalem. He was accused of treason by one of Fulk's supporters and offered to be tried by combat. But he did not arrive on the appointed day and was condemned in his absence and exiled for three years. While waiting to leave, Hugh was assassinated. There were even suggestions that his relationship with Queen Melisende was too friendly. This illustrates the tension in Jerusalem, where Fulk was unpopular and Hugh was supported by much of the native crusader nobility.

Source A describes the situation in Jerusalem.

**SOURCE A**

**From William of Tyre, *A History of Deeds Done Beyond the Sea* (written between 1170 and 1184), quoted in Jonathan Phillips, *The Crusades 1095–1197*, Routledge, 2014, p. 228.**

*But one sentiment hung on the lips of all, that this crime [the murder of Hugh] could not have been committed without the knowledge of the king. Through the crowd ran the cry that the count [Hugh] had been suffering unjustly from a charge of which he*

*[continued over the page]*

**SOURCE QUESTION**

What does Source A suggest about the relative power of Fulk and Melisende? How does Source A indicate that Fulk was not popular?

> ONLINE EXTRAS OCR WWW
>
> Practise supporting ideas with evidence by completing Worksheet 14 at **www.hoddereducation.co.uk/accesstohistory/extras**

> ONLINE EXTRAS OCR WWW
>
> Practise making judgements about issues by completing Worksheet 15 at **www.hoddereducation.co.uk/accesstohistory/extras**

*was innocent ... Accordingly the count grew in universal favour and good will and it was felt that the accusations against him, of whatever nature, proceeded entirely from malice ... From that time all who had informed against the count and thereby encouraged the king fell under the displeasure of queen Melisende and were forced to take diligent measures for their own safety ... It was not safe for these informers to come into her presence ... Even the king found no place was entirely safe among the kindred and partisans of the queen. At length, through the mediation of certain intimate friends her wrath was appeased and the king, after persistent efforts finally succeeded in gaining a pardon for the other objects of her wrath.*

In addition, there were the following problems:

- Joscelin II of Edessa (died 1159) was not a strong leader and lacked the resources to build the castles which other rulers were constructing (see pages 84–5), which weakened Edessa.
- Most of the States went through periods when their rulers were taken prisoner by the Muslims.
- The influence of Byzantium was a cause of dispute, since the emperor claimed control of Antioch and both Prince Raymond II of Tripoli (1116–52) and Prince Reynald (*c*.1125–87) had to accept the emperor as their overlord with their lands under his lordship and perform homage (swear obedience).
- There were conflicts between Church and State in Antioch, with quarrels between Reynald and the Patriarch Aimery (died *c*.1196) over who had the ultimate power.
- The independence of Antioch depended very much on support from Jerusalem, either against the Muslims or to settle disputes about the succession.
- Tripoli remained a loose association of lordships with little distinctive culture, depending very much for defence on castles such as Krak des Chevaliers.

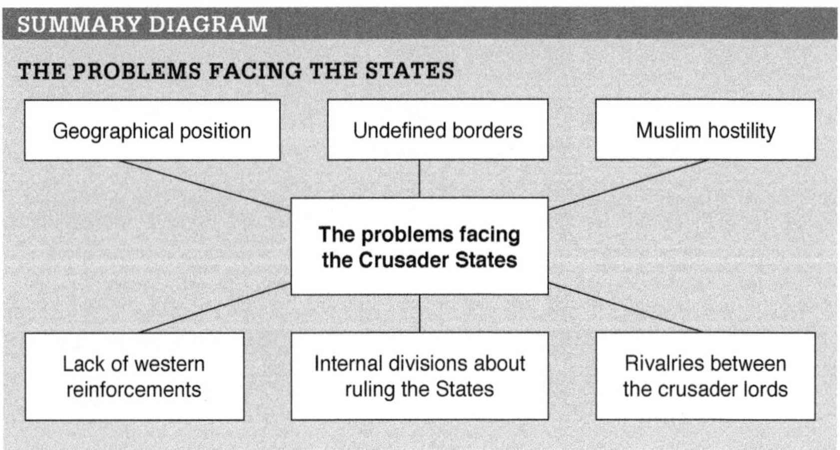

# 3 The survival of the Crusader States

*How successful were the Crusader States?*

The number of problems the States faced could suggest that they enjoyed little success. However, by 1130 the States were established. Conquests in the period 1100–18 had helped to secure the coastline and the provinces of Tripoli, Antioch and Edessa. Admittedly, Edessa was a short-lived Crusader State and by 1150 was in the hands of Nur ad-Din (see Chapter 5). But Antioch survived, largely thanks to the determination of rulers such as Tancred and Roger. Their administration built on both Byzantine and Norman models and their barons remained loyal in order to maintain the independence of the principality. They were pragmatic rulers who recognised the need to be on good terms with at least some of their Muslim neighbours and who avoided the fierce anti-Muslim rhetoric of some of their fellows.

## Jerusalem

Another success story was in the kingdom of Jerusalem, where Melisende was generous to Christian institutions of all kinds, Latin, Syrian and Armenian. She particularly wanted to set up a convent at Bethany, so that her youngest sister could be abbess there eventually, as Melisende felt it was not fitting for a king's daughter to be subject to the authority of a lower-born abbess. The convent of St Lazarus was later built and generously endowed by Melisende. Another monastery, also dedicated to St Lazarus, was set up outside Jerusalem for the care of lepers. Under the patronage of Melisende and Fulk, the scriptorium of

### Nur ad-Din (or Nureddin) 1117–74

The new ruler, or atabeg, of Mosul, Imad ad-Din Zengi (*c.*1085–1146), occupied Aleppo. Zengi continued his attempts to take Damascus in 1145, but he was assassinated by a Frankish slave named Yarankash in 1146. Zengi was the founder of the eponymous Zengid dynasty. In Mosul he was succeeded by his eldest son Saif ad-Din Ghazi I, and in Aleppo he was succeeded by his second son Nur ad-Din, born in 1117.

Nur ad-Din became the atabeg based in Aleppo in 1146, under the Abbasid caliphate of Baghdad. His elder brother took the lands further east, based around Mosul, and so Nur ad-Din could concentrate on Syria and Egypt. He was determined to reverse the Muslim defeats which he saw as caused by disunity. He defeated a crusader attempt to retake Edessa after its fall in 1144 and captured Antakiya in 1149 and the vital city of Damascus in 1154, by collaborating with the military governor of the region. In 1149 he defeated and killed Raymond of Antioch and sent the prince's severed head as a trophy to the caliph in Baghdad. He built up a loyal following by making land grants hereditary. He was a very capable general and noted for his piety and temperance. He used the loot he took to build mosques, schools and hospitals, as well as the House of Justice in Damascus where officials attended regularly to hear cases. In 1169–71 he conquered Egypt, so that he now ruled Syria and parts of Asia Minor and Egypt. His reign saw *jihad* become established as a vital factor in the Muslim advance and he founded many madrasas, or religious schools, where *jihad* was taught.

the Church of the Holy Sepulchre flourished and one of its products was the beautifully decorated Melisende Psalter, which was a fusion of eastern and western styles. The Church of Notre Dame de Josaphat was another given presents by Melisende. This was reputed to be the site of the tomb of the Virgin Mary and Melisende chose to be buried there. Her patronage also enabled craftsmen such as goldsmiths to flourish, and housing and selling to visiting pilgrims was another stimulus to trade and commerce. Hence Jerusalem prospered.

## Rulers

The most successful rulers were in Jerusalem. Here Baldwin I established himself by capturing some coastal ports and repelling Fatimid attacks from Egypt. He was an ambitious younger son with his fortune to make. He married three times for worldly advancement, although he was probably homosexual. One of his lovers was a converted Muslim. Baldwin's chaplain, Fulcher of Chartres, wrote a vivid account of his doings, never claiming that he was noted for his piety. Baldwin attracted settlers to his kingdom and built up a web of dependency, binding men to him by granting them revenue from the land rather than the land itself, which he kept in his own hands. Baldwin II continued many of these practices. In 1124, with help from the Venetians, his troops captured Tyre, a useful seaport.

Much, therefore, depended on the abilities of the rulers and on a smooth succession, which made the States similar to those developing in Europe and also reflected the common practice in the Middle East, where small militias could seize control of a few towns and villages and establish a relatively independent territory.

## Castles

One of the keys to holding on to power in the States was the construction of castles. The crusaders had learned from their own experience on the First Crusade how difficult it was to capture fortresses like Antioch and Jerusalem. As a result, they proceeded to build their own. These castles, as in the west, served many purposes, both defensive and administrative. They were certainly important in ensuring the survival of the States through their military function, controlling passes and valleys as well as dominating areas. The first castles tended to be based on existing sites, using Arab or Byzantine fortifications, often in major cities. But in time, castles were constructed in more rural settings, probably for administrative purposes. Others in the south were more offensive in nature, with the building of Chastel Hernault, Ibelin, Blanchegarde and Bethgibelin putting pressure on Ascalon and the fertile fields which surrounded the city. Montreal was built to control the area around the Dead Sea and Aqaba, while the greatest of the crusader castles, Krak des Chevaliers, dominated the Homs Valley.

The crusaders built a series of castles which defended the valleys and coastal plains, but the lack of men meant that they could be deployed only in defending the castles or on the battlefield. In trying to capture castles, the Muslims relied on frontal assault or mining as their mastery of siege engines was less effective than that of the Christians. But Nur ad-Din made much more use of heavy engines and this led to new castles being built which were far stronger, but also very expensive to construct. These were often handed over by the crusaders to the Military Orders to maintain. Despite some of the difficulties associated with castle construction and their manning, they did play a crucial role in consolidating the crusaders' hold over the States.

## Trade

A key feature of the States was the establishing of successful trade routes, to and through the States. The Muslim lands to the east included the great trading cities of Aleppo and Damascus. Trade routes from Syria had been long established, and continued throughout the twelfth century. The crusader ports on the Mediterranean Sea, notably Acre, Beirut, Tripoli and Tyre, provided links not only to the Muslim lands to the east but established important trading connections with Europe and Byzantium. These were established through the Italian city states, many of which had representatives in Constantinople. Byzantine silk, for example, was sought after not only in Europe but also in the Crusader States.

## Relations between Crusader States and indigenous peoples

Despite obvious barriers of religion, language and culture, the Crusader States survived for generations. Frankish communities lived side by side with indigenous groups, with relations between the incomers and the local population shaped by economic factors, notably the need for tax. Each community – whether Christian, Muslim or Jewish – governed itself, but it was the Franks who ruled, largely through the creation of lordships. Some cooperation between different faiths did exist: the hospital in Jerusalem, for example, run by the Hospitallers, was open to all, regardless of religion, and the Templars in the holy city accommodated Muslim guests wishing to pray to Mecca. However, Christians who were not from the west and Muslims were technically excluded from Frankish citizenship and were therefore prevented from joining the ruling elite. Conversion, however, to western (or Latin) Christianity, for both Muslims and local Christians, could provide a route to citizenship. In Frankish eyes, Muslims were an economic resource, useful as labourers or taxpayers. Jewish people, too, tended to be seen in a similar light. Nor were relations with Orthodox Christians and older groups associated with early Christianity, such as Armenian Christians, any smoother. Society in the Crusader States was certainly diverse, as the evidence of architecture and artistic patronage suggests. But while concessions were made to other faiths and relations between different communities were often shaped by pragmatism rather than antagonism, each community remained distinct.

**ONLINE EXTRAS** OCR **WWW**

Learn how to analyse the importance of issues by completing Worksheet 16 at **www.hoddereducation.co.uk/accesstohistory/extras**

**ONLINE EXTRAS** AQA **WWW**

Get to grips with writing a balanced essay by completing Worksheet 12 at **www.hoddereducation.co.uk/accesstohistory/extras**

**ONLINE EXTRAS** OCR **WWW**

Learn how to plan an effective essay by completing Worksheet 17 at **www.hoddereducation.co.uk/accesstohistory/extras**

**ONLINE EXTRAS** Pearson Edexcel **WWW**

Develop your understanding of causation by completing Worksheet 14 at **www.hoddereducation.co.uk/accesstohistory/extras**

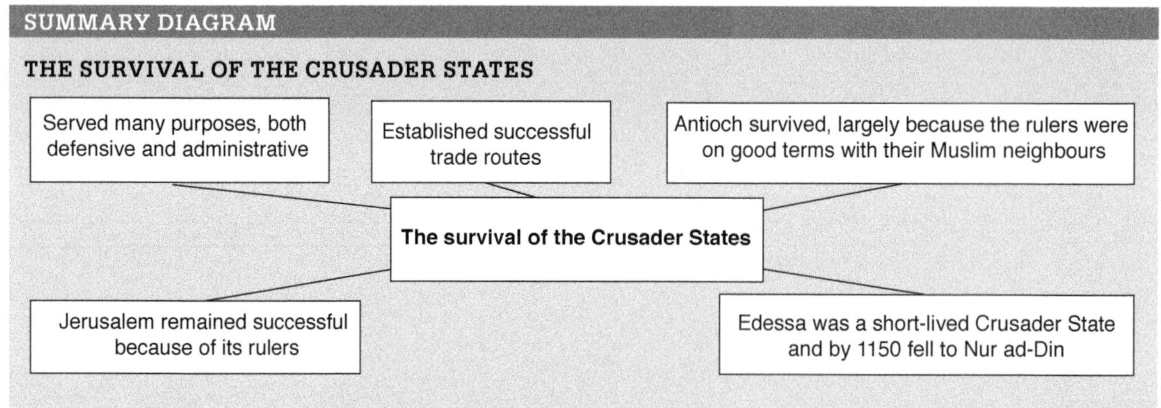

SUMMARY DIAGRAM
THE SURVIVAL OF THE CRUSADER STATES
Served many purposes, both defensive and administrative
Established successful trade routes
Antioch survived, largely because the rulers were on good terms with their Muslim neighbours
The survival of the Crusader States
Jerusalem remained successful because of its rulers
Edessa was a short-lived Crusader State and by 1150 fell to Nur ad-Din


# 4 Key debate

*Why did the Crusader States survive?*

Following the capture of Jerusalem and the success of the First Crusade, most of the crusaders returned to Europe. This meant that those who remained not only faced the prospect of trying to establish new crusader kingdoms but were heavily outnumbered by Muslim forces. The survival of these kingdoms was, in the early years, precarious and historians have suggested a number of reasons for their survival, many of which are similar to the reasons given for the success of the First Crusade. One reason, in particular, was the disunity within the Muslim world, as seen in the writing of historian Thomas Asbridge in Chapter 3.

However, it has also been suggested that the structures established by the crusaders played a crucial role in this survival. There has been some argument that the decision to elect kings and import the feudal structure from the west helped to strengthen the newly established kingdoms, while others, such as Jonathan Phillips (2002), have suggested that it was fortifications, such as castles, that were crucial in these formative years (see Extract 1).

**INTERPRETATION QUESTION**

Why did the Crusader States survive? Explain your answer with reference to the different interpretations in Extracts 1 and 2.

**EXTRACT 1**

Jonathan Phillips, *The Crusades 1095–1197*, Routledge, 2014, pp. 81–2.

*While battles could exert a decisive influence on Frankish power, the key to holding on to territory was the control of castles and fortified sites, which included towns and rural manor houses. … The knowledge gained in the course of the [first] crusade proved invaluable in taking other castles and fortifications of the Levant, as the Franks established their rule. It was then the settlers who had to refortify, develop and construct their own defences in order to preserve their hold on the Holy Land and to provide centres of authority.*

Not only does Phillips stress the role of castles, but he also suggests that success on the battlefield played a crucial role, as early conquests further helped to strengthen the crusader kingdoms and gave the impression of their invincibility. Such an interpretation has been suggested by French historian Jean Richard, writing in 1999, as we can see in Extract 2.

**ONLINE EXTRAS** **AQA** **WWW**

Get to grips with extract analysis by completing Worksheet 13 at **www.hoddereducation.co.uk/accesstohistory/extras**

**ONLINE EXTRAS** **Pearson Edexcel** **WWW**

Develop your interpretation skills by completing Worksheets 15 and 16 at **www.hoddereducation.co.uk/accesstohistory/extras**

**EXTRACT 2**

Jean Richard, *The Crusades c.1071–c.1291*, Cambridge University Press, 1999, pp. 104 and 105.

*In case of the Muslims we need to distinguish between the time of conquest and their later situation within the Frankish states. During the conquest, they [the Muslims] suffered badly. The capture of fortified towns entailed violence and massacres, some of which have been described in lavish detail, for Jerusalem, Ma'arrat, Caiphas or Beirut among others. When a town was stormed, such excesses were sadly only too common. … Of the women captured in Caesarea, conquered in 1104, the historian tells us that 'beautiful or ugly, they had to turn the grindstone of the mills', that is, they became domestic slaves.*

But it was not just fear among the Muslims that led to the survival of the States. A coexistence between Muslims and Christians also developed, particularly while the Muslims were divided, as many saw it as the best way to ensure their own survival and the opportunity to make money through trade with the new settlers. However, the new States also received help from the west through the ports that they had captured. In particular, according to Malcolm Barber (2012), it was the arrival of these supplies through the ports, usually from Italian city-states, that allowed the kingdoms to flourish.

## 5 The establishment of the Military Orders

- *What were the Military Orders and why were they established?*

The defence of the Crusader States was a challenge which the crusaders found difficult to meet. Most crusaders did not stay indefinitely in the Holy Land. They had families and estates to which they needed to return. Despite appeals for settlers to come to Palestine, few arrived as time progressed. This was a major problem as men were needed to garrison the castles and guard the trade and pilgrim routes. The formation of the Military Orders in the period 1100–30 – religious orders of soldier-monks, who took vows to defend the Holy Land, but also to live as monks – was a solution to this problem.

The concept of a soldier-monk was new. These men were members of religious orders who had taken vows of chastity, poverty and obedience but spent their time garrisoning castles and attacking Muslim land.

## The Order of the Hospitallers

**KEY TERM**

**Papal bull** Public decree issued by a pope.

The Order of the Hospitallers emerged soon after the First Crusade, building on the institution established in Jerusalem (in the early 1080s) in the grounds of the monastery of St John the Baptist. The monastic order was set up by Gerard Thom, soon after 1099. In 1113 Pope Paschal II in a **papal bull** recognised the Order of the Hospital of St John as an independent order. Daughter hospices were also established in parts of Europe and they sent funds to the east to support the hospices there. The scale of endowments, donations and manpower grew rapidly and this provided a vital supply line for the monks and hospitals in the east.

The aim of the order was to channel the zeal of those who believed that the Church needed to minister to the poor and sick, as if ministering to Christ himself, and to ensure that those who died received a fitting burial. This was nothing new, but the Hospitallers described themselves as the 'slaves' and 'serfs' of those they served, showing the extent of their dedication.

### Treatment of the sick

The Hospitallers were soon endowed with gifts from Baldwin II and others throughout the Latin West and they needed these generous grants to fulfil their aspiration. People were admitted, whatever their illnesses, apart from lepers. The patients included Muslims and Jews and there were careful arrangements to respect the dietary needs of all, with a separate kitchen to prepare chicken for those who declined to eat pork.

The standard of care was very high, with separate wards for women with female attendants. One was for obstetrics, with little cots for the babies so they did not have to share the maternal bed. Indeed, all patients had their own beds, something almost unknown at the time. They were given white loaves, meat three times a week and large amounts of vegetables and fruit. Bedding was changed regularly, and cloaks and sandals were supplied for visits to the latrines.

There could be up to 1000 patients being treated at any time in the main hospital in Jerusalem, and, in emergencies, 2000 could be taken in. They were cared for by a staff of the brothers and sisters of the order, trained physicians and surgeons, and male and female servants who did most of the nursing. Some devout souls from Europe travelled to Jerusalem to work in the main hospital. All in all, there were probably about 600 staff involved. In addition to the hospital, the order ran an orphanage for abandoned children, a rudimentary ambulance service and a mobile unit to accompany armies, all of which cost a great deal to run and depended on the large endowments and donations.

### Military role

Only later did the Hospitallers take on a military role, perhaps inspired by the Templars. They served in armies and, by 1136, were being entrusted with the garrisoning of castles on the borders of the Crusader States, with Fulk granting them the castle of Bethgibelin. By 1144 they controlled the fortress at Krak des Chevaliers and this military role continued to increase into the 1160s. However, numerically, they were never a large group. About 300 brothers and sisters were stationed in the Middle East at any one time.

## The Knights Templar

The Knights Templar were established to provide protection for pilgrims on the road from the coast to Jerusalem and then on to Jericho. Two French knights, Hugh de Payns (*c.*1070–1136) and Godfrey of St Omer, set up a group in 1119, and were licensed by the Patriarch of Jerusalem to follow monastic vows. In 1120 the Council of Nablus gave them official backing. Their base, given to them by Baldwin II, was in the area of Jerusalem where the Temple of Solomon was believed to have stood and they took their name from this. They attracted influential figures such as Fulk of Anjou, later to be king in Jerusalem, who stayed with them for a year. It was said that at first they were so poor that they had to share a horse, which gave rise to the seal of the Templars, showing two men on a horse.

From 1127 to 1129 Hugh de Payns travelled all through western Europe with the dual aim of attracting gifts for the order and recruits for the coming attack on Damascus. He was enormously successful as extensive grants of land and money filled the coffers. He was welcomed all over France, in Flanders, England and Scotland. By the time he reached Troyes in 1129, where a Church Council was being held, presided over by a papal legate and attended by Bernard of Clairvaux (see pages 98–100), his reputation was so high that the Council agreed to confirm the foundation and draw up a rule for it to follow. This reflected the religious revival trend in Europe in the twelfth century, where monastic orders were established and organised so that they could become international in their scope.

### How the Templars ruled

The rule of the Templars included vows of chastity, obedience and poverty, as with other orders, but also included useful guidance on the care of weapons and discipline in battle. Templars were allowed to have their own priests and so were in total control of their affairs. The granting of pardons to those who gave them donations encouraged generosity, while some laymen joined at the end of their lives to benefit from burial in their cemeteries for the good of their souls. By 1150 the Templars were a very wealthy organisation and the temples they built in London and Paris attested to their power and influence. They enjoyed full remission of their sins and wore the red cross on their white robes like other crusaders. Their presence was a real boon for the crusaders as there was a perpetual shortage of soldiers. Life expectancy in Outremer was not high, especially for men. Crusaders often came from the west, fought for a couple of years and then returned home. The Templars were a permanent presence who cost nothing and could afford to build and maintain castles.

### Justification for Military Orders

There was some contemporary feeling that the demands of monastic life were incompatible with those of the military life and unease was expressed about the apparent contradictions. These doubts were answered by vigorous propaganda, especially from Bernard, but were never entirely stilled. Bernard argued that the Templars were a new kind of knight, motivated by right intentions, calling them the 'soldiers of Christ', in contrast with the more traditional knights who fought only for material gain. Their faith and trust in God gave the Templars the edge in battle, Bernard asserted. The idea of Military Orders was taken up in many parts of Europe.

## The achievements of the Templars

Like the Hospitallers, the number of Templars in the Middle East was small: about 500 at any given time. One of their main roles was as custodians of castles, but they were also given large tracts of land, so much so that by 1187 they were the chief landowners in Outremer. Some local churchmen resented their coming but could do little since the pope supported them and many Palestinian nobles joined their ranks. Amalric I of Jerusalem was furious when they attacked some Muslim envoys with whom he had been negotiating. He imprisoned their leaders and might have challenged their independence had he lived. William of Tyre was a critic and referred to the time at the siege of Ascalon in 1152, when a group of Templars breached the walls and refused to let anyone else in as they wanted all the loot for themselves. As a result, they became trapped and were all killed, which seemed a just result to the chronicler. They also suffered very heavy casualties in some engagements. The maintenance of their fortifications (the defences of a city or town, which could include walls and turrets, and the building of castles as military bases) was a great expense as they had to pay mercenaries to oversee the walls. This meant that their great resources, when fully utilised, could become overstretched.

**ONLINE EXTRAS** AQA **WWW**

Learn how to make judgements about factors by completing Worksheet 14 at **www.hoddereducation.co.uk/accesstohistory/extras**

**ONLINE EXTRAS** AQA **WWW**

Get to grips with exam-style questions by completing Worksheet 15 at **www.hoddereducation.co.uk/accesstohistory/extras**

**ONLINE EXTRAS** OCR **WWW**

Learn how to make supported judgements by completing Worksheet 18 at **www.hoddereducation.co.uk/accesstohistory/extras**

**ONLINE EXTRAS** OCR **WWW**

Learn how to plan a balanced essay by completing Worksheet 19 at **www.hoddereducation.co.uk/accesstohistory/extras**

**ONLINE EXTRAS** Pearson Edexcel **WWW**

Test your understanding of the strengths and weaknesses of the Crusader States by completing Worksheet 17 at **www.hoddereducation.co.uk/accesstohistory/extras**

Templar independence was also a problem as kings had no control over them, since their allegiance was to the pope. The lands they held did not entail any feudal dues and their tenants paid no taxes to the Church. They had representatives in the High Courts of Jerusalem, Antioch and Tripoli, but tended to give advice based on solely military requirements. When they disliked a proposal, they would not agree. They also were great rivals with the Hospitallers and would rarely fight alongside them. They also felt free to negotiate with Muslims on their own authority and thus undermine royal authority.

The Military Orders were feared by the Muslims. As a result, they would execute any of their members if they captured them, rather than imprisoning or ransoming them. To some extent, the Military Orders did help to solve the manpower problem, but the survival of the States in these early years also owed much to the efforts of men such as Baldwin, Bohemund, Tancred and Roger of Antioch. However, the Battle of the Field of Blood was a clear indication of the vulnerability of the States, which the Military Orders and castles could only do so much to combat. Once they faced a united Muslim challenge from Nur-ad-Din and Saladin, their weaknesses would become even more evident.

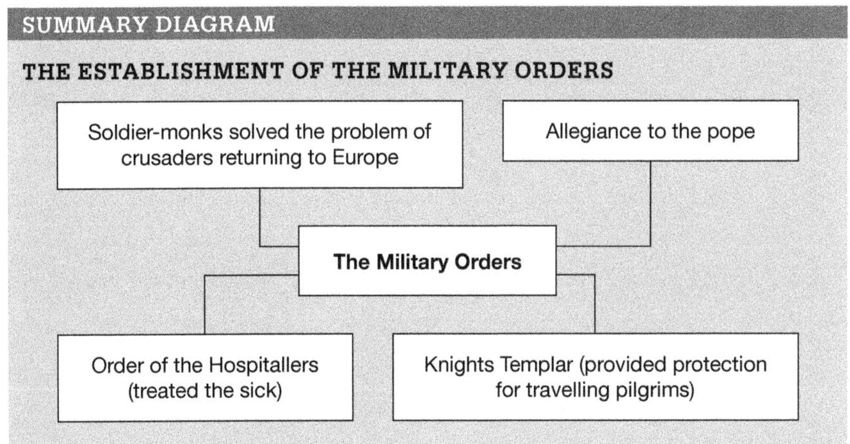


# 6 Key debate

*How important were the Military Orders in the survival of the Crusader States?*

The debate about the Military Orders and the importance and nature of their role has been affected by popular perceptions. As the later suppression and persecution of the Templars is well known, there is a tendency to look back and find in their earliest history the flaws for which they were later condemned. There is also an issue in that there is a view that the orders were hypocritical as they fought and killed and yet claimed to be inspired by Christian principles. Some of this latter critique has been reduced as more recent interpretations of the Crusades have emphasised the importance of spirituality in the thinking of the time and its impact on the elites who often formed the membership of the orders. Another factor affecting the way the orders are evaluated lies in the lack of source material relating to their early days. William of Tyre who is generally seen as the most reliable of the writers began his History in 1175. He was hostile, especially to the Templars, and he claimed that they were a poor and simple group of men, numbering only nine in 1129. Their seal showed two knights on a single horse to demonstrate their poverty. But William used these details to make a contrast with the great wealth which the orders later held and to show how far they had diverted from their original circumstances. An alternative version, supported by Helen Nicholson (2001), suggests that they stressed their earlier poverty as a reminder that they needed to maintain their riches in order to fulfil the purposes for which they had been founded.

Malcolm Barber (1994), a specialist on the orders, suggests that they would never have developed into military organisations or as defenders of the Church against infidels, had it not been for the need to protect pilgrims. He also argues that their development was much aided by St Bernard, who wrote *In Praise of the New Knighthood* (c.1136) to support them. Barber sees this as crucial because it led to generous donations which gave them independence. It was also the lack of manpower in the kingdoms which made the role of the orders necessary to compensate for their military weakness. In another view, Helen Nicholson (2001) argues that the orders were not always a benefit as their rashness led to the failure to take Ascalon in 1153 and she cites further examples in fighting against Saladin, in which two successive Masters of the Temple were killed, leading to the interpretation that their military achievements were not especially outstanding.

Extract 3 outlines how the orders contributed to the crusading movement.

**INTERPRETATION QUESTION**

Which of the two interpretations, Extracts 3 and 4, do you find the more convincing as an explanation of the contribution of the Military Orders to the crusading movement?

**EXTRACT 3**

**From Alan Forey, 'The Military Orders 1120–1312' in Jonathan Riley-Smith, editor, *The Oxford History of the Crusades*, Oxford University Press, 1999, pp. 188–9.**

*Despite their limited numbers, at least in the East the brethren's bravery and determination were held in high regard by their opponents: the chronicler Ibn al-Athir, for example, described a Hospitaller castellan [the castle's governor] of Crak des Chevaliers as 'a bone in the gullet of the Muslims'. The brethren also provided a more disciplined force than many secular contingents. The Templar Customs include strict regulations about conduct in camp and on the march, and the brethren of all orders were, of course, bound by a vow of obedience, which was reinforced by the threat of severe penalties for disobeying orders in the field. In all leading orders the punishment for desertion in battle was expulsion, while Templars who launched an attack without permission lost their habits for a period. The threat of censure could not eliminate all acts of disobedience in the field, but several crusade theorists agreed with the view of the Templar master, James of Molay, that, because of their vow of obedience, brethren were superior to other troops. Some theorists also saw the military orders in Syria as having the advantage of experience. Certainly leading officials in the orders had usually given long service, although in the Temple the rank-and-file knightly brethren were normally fairly recent recruits, who served in the Holy Land for only a limited period, while they were still young.*

Extract 4 suggests that the orders contributed in other ways.

**EXTRACT 4**

**From Christopher Tyerman, *The World of the Crusades*, Yale University Press, 2019, p. 156.**

*The two Military Orders became leading political players in Outremer. Although frequently at odds with each other, the Orders featured prominently in deciding military strategy. Jurisdictionally independent of all except the distant papacy, they could act as supposedly neutral arbiters in politics and financial management. As the costs of defence rose, decreasingly matched by the resources of the crown and local secular nobility, the Orders' power and influence increased as they controlled more castles and former military sites. By the 1180s, the combined Templar and Hospitaller contribution of around 700 knights to the full muster of the kingdom of Jerusalem was roughly equal to that from all other sources. The orders grew into large international corporations, their fighting knights an elite minority.*

**ONLINE EXTRAS** AQA **WWW**

Develop your extract analysis skills by completing Worksheet 16 at **www.hoddereducation.co.uk/accesstohistory/extras**

# CHAPTER SUMMARY

Four Crusader States emerged from the First Crusade. From the first they faced problems regarding the succession of rulers and continued attacks from their enemies. But they had some successes, notably the rule of Fulk and Melisende in Jerusalem. They built a network of castles for their protection. The setting up of the Military Orders was a further security measure.

## Refresher questions

Use these questions to remind yourself of the key issues in this chapter.

1. How were the Crusader States established?
2. What were the strengths and weaknesses of the kingdom of Jerusalem?
3. Why were castles built?
4. What was the contribution of the Hospitallers?
5. What was the contribution of the Templars?
6. What criticisms were made of Melisende of Jerusalem?

## Question practice: AQA

### Essay questions

**1** 'The Military Orders were the most significant factor in the consolidation of the Crusader States in the years 1119–49.' Explain why you agree or disagree with this view. [AS level]

**EXAM HINT** The question is really asking you to assess the reasons for the consolidation of the Crusader States. Ensure that you have a clear opinion expressed in your introduction. There are probably four different factors that you will wish to consider, but avoid simply describing these. Instead, prioritise these factors and justify your choice.

**2** To what extent does personal rivalry among the Christians explain the weaknesses of the Crusader States in the years 1119–49? [A level]

**EXAM HINT** Clearly identify the weaknesses of the States – the answer might lose cohesion if this is not done. The weaknesses are a given factor so you should not really challenge the premise of the question. Try to avoid having bland definitions as part of the introduction but integrate them into your judgement that drives the entire answer.

**3** 'Muslim disunity accounts for the establishment and expansion of the Crusader States.' Assess the validity of this view with reference to the years 1099–1130. [A level]

**EXAM HINT** Consider the importance of Muslim disunity. Do not write a narrative response. Try to consider what specific examples there are of disunity and argue the link if there is one to the establishment and expansion of the Crusader States. Identify three other factors that might be responsible for the success of the States and argue if they were more or less significant than Muslim disunity.

## Interpretations question

**1** With reference to Extracts A and B below, and your understanding of the historical context, which of these two extracts provides the more convincing interpretation of the role of Melisende in Outremer in the years 1131–52? [AS level]

**EXAM HINT** Consider areas in which there are similarities and differences in the two extracts. You may find that there is a similar interpretation about the role of Melisende, but that the evidence varies between the extracts making one more convincing than the other. Remember balance, and that you should find in each extract reasons to agree and to disagree but do not lose your overall judgement about which is the more convincing. You may find that one extract blames Baldwin, suggesting that Melisende was forced into her actions by the inadequacies of Baldwin as an individual and as a ruler.

### EXTRACT A

From Sharan Newman, *Defending the City of God*, Palgrave, 2014, pp. 216–17.

*Historians have seen Melisende's actions through a lens of centuries of primogeniture. If she had been male, then Baldwin would have been seen as an upstart and a traitor. As it was, it is clear that there were many who were satisfied with her governance and not comfortable with allowing Baldwin complete control. None of the chroniclers living at that time in the Near East have said she was power hungry. In a time and place where nearly every ruler spent most of his time trying to expand his territory, she was fairly consistent. If her son's forays into enemy territory had been successful she might have decided on graceful retirement. Or she might have arranged that he handle military matters and she run the home front.*

*But one thing makes me wonder: why wasn't Baldwin married as a teenager? Even if he had been homosexual, he could have done his duty and produced heirs as other homosexual kings had done. I haven't found any reference to ambassadors making the rounds looking for acceptable brides. Was Melisende so determined to hold on to her son that she didn't want to compete with a wife? I doubt it. Baldwin didn't marry until 1158, long after Melisende had lost control over his actions.*

### EXTRACT B

From Hans Eberhard Meyer, *The Crusades*, Oxford University Press, 2009, pp. 108–9.

*The king [Baldwin III] was now [1149] nineteen and disliked sharing the government with his mother, Melisende. When he came of age at fifteen, she had given no sign that she would terminate the regency, because the institution of joint rule gave her a share of her own in the kingdom. The majority of the barons disliked the arrangement just as much as the king ... Melisende was by no means without allies. Above all she could rely on the support of the Church. She had pushed loyal men into great crown offices, notably into the most important office of constable ... Only very gradually was Baldwin III able to match this strength by building up a power base of his own in the crown estates in the north between Tyre and Acre. From 1149 onwards the relationship between mother and son was more than chilly ... She built up her own household with her own officials separate from the royal household proper. These actions violated the principles of joint rule as established by Baldwin II ... and came close to dividing the kingdom ... In 1150 those vassals who acknowledged allegiance only to the queen mother, took the unprecedented step of openly ignoring the king's summons to follow him up north.*

## Question practice: OCR

### Essay questions

**1** Which of the following was of greater importance in the survival of the Crusader States? i) Castles. ii) Military Orders. Explain your answer with reference to both i) and ii). [A level]

**EXAM HINT** The importance of the two factors in the survival of the Crusader States should be explained and a supported judgement reached as to which was more important.

**2** 'Muslim weaknesses were the most important reason for the survival of the Crusader States in this period.' How far do you agree? [A level]

**EXAM HINT** As the named factor, responses should explain the importance of Muslim weakness in the survival of the states before analysing other factors that aided their survival. A judgement as to the relative importance of factors should be reached.

## Question practice: Pearson Edexcel

### Essay questions

**1** How far do you agree that the Military Orders of Templars and Hospitallers were the most important reason for the survival of the Crusader States in the years 1100–92? [AS level]

**EXAM HINT** Note the vast wealth accumulated by the religious orders, enabling them to protect the Crusader States, and to establish a network of castles. Other relevant points may include establishing trade routes with Europe and changing relations with the local Muslim population.

**2** How accurate is it to say that growing divisions within the ruling elite were the most important problem facing the Crusader States in the years 1100–92? [A level]

**EXAM HINT** Examine growing divisions within the elite, especially under Baldwin III and Baldwin IV. Also consider the growth of Muslim power under Nur ad-Din and Saladin, and the failure of European states to provide assistance for the Crusader States.

CHAPTER 5

# The Second Crusade

The capture of Edessa by Imad ad-Din Zengi in December 1144 was greeted with horror in Europe, but not by much enthusiasm for a military response. The real impetus for the Second Crusade came from the preaching of Bernard of Clairvaux. This chapter examines the Second Crusade by focusing on the following themes:

- The fall of Edessa
- The role of Bernard of Clairvaux in the Second Crusade
- The roles of Louis VII and Conrad III in the Second Crusade
- The events of the Second Crusade
- The results of the Second Crusade

The key debate on page 116 of this chapter asks the question: Was the attack on Damascus a mistake?

**KEY DATES**

| | |
|---|---|
| **1144** | Fall of Edessa to Zengi |
| **1145** | Eugenius III issued the papal bull *Quantum praedecessores* |
| **1146** | Preaching tour of Bernard of Clairvaux |
| **1147** | German Crusade against the Wends<br>Departure of Conrad III and Louis VII |
| **1148** | Failure to capture Damascus and return of Conrad III to Germany |
| **1149** | Return of Louis VII to France |

## 1 The fall of Edessa

■ *Why did Edessa fall?*

Zengi, the Muslim ruler of Aleppo and Mosul, captured the Crusader State of Edessa on 22 December 1144. The state had suffered from internal divisions over the succession (see Chapter 4) and had also been threatened from the Byzantine Empire over the control of Antioch. It was the fall of Edessa that prompted letters to be sent to the west asking for help and these appeals led to the Second Crusade under the command of Louis VII of France and Conrad, the German emperor. The pope, Eugenius III, saw it as an opportunity for the papacy to regain control of the crusading movement, which had been lost at the end of the First Crusade.

## What was the importance of the idea of *jihad* in the capture of Edessa?

*Jihad*, meaning struggle, was not a new idea. The notion of holy war was found in the **Qur'an** and in the sayings of Muhammad, where the rewards of *jihad* were emphasised. The greater *jihad* was seen as a personal struggle against sin, while lesser *jihad* was the obligation to defend Islam from unbelievers through armed struggle. The zeal of the crusaders was perceived as a kind of *jihad* and Muslim preachers at the time, including as-Sulami in Damascus, urged Muslims to show similar zeal in defence of their beliefs. Source A (see below) illustrates the importance of *jihad*.

**KEY TERM**

**Qur'an** The central text of Islam, believed to have been directly revealed to Prophet Muhammad by God in Arabic over a period of 23 years (609–32).

*Jihad* was used by Zengi to give authority to his political ambitions and his supporters were able to use it to rally fellow Muslims against the crusaders, with the result that Zengi became the focus for holy war ideology and recruitment. He was able to use *jihad* as a means to construct alliances and to defeat his Muslim enemies. During the 1130s and 1140s he had developed his power so that he dominated the region, launching raids into both Christian and Muslim lands. By December 1144 he was able to lay siege to Edessa, which was defended only by Archbishop Hugh, who lacked resources. Zengi acted quickly, building wooden towers, digging tunnels under the walls and bombarding them until they collapsed. His quick action prevented other crusaders from coming to the aid of the city. Its fall led to the deaths of some 15,000 people, including Hugh, while churches and monasteries were also destroyed.

Edessa was difficult to defend because of its remoteness, but the speed of Zengi's actions and the lack of help from other crusaders and the Byzantine Empire further weakened the city's position.

**SOURCE A**

**Ibn al-Qalanisi (c.1071–1160) describes the capture of Banyas in 1157, quoted in Francesco Gabrieli, editor, and E.J. Costello, translator, *Arab Historians of the Crusades*, University of California Press, 1969, pp. 67–8.**

*In less time than it takes to tell the enemy was completely overwhelmed and the fighting was over. Almighty and all-conquering God had sent his supporters victory and condemned the infidel rebels to hell … The Muslim army lost only two men … Both died as martyrs for the Faith, deserving a heavenly reward. May God have mercy on them … This was a great victory and a glorious triumph sent by Almighty God the bringer of victory to honour Islam and its believers … A huge crowd of citizens came out to see the glorious victory granted by God to all Muslims, and they praised and blessed Him for permitting His friends to triumph and enabling them to defeat the adversary. They praised the just king Nur ad-Din sincerely and unceasingly for being their defender and champion … .*

**SOURCE QUESTION**

What light does the passage in Source A throw on the use made by Nur ad-Din of the idea of *jihad*?

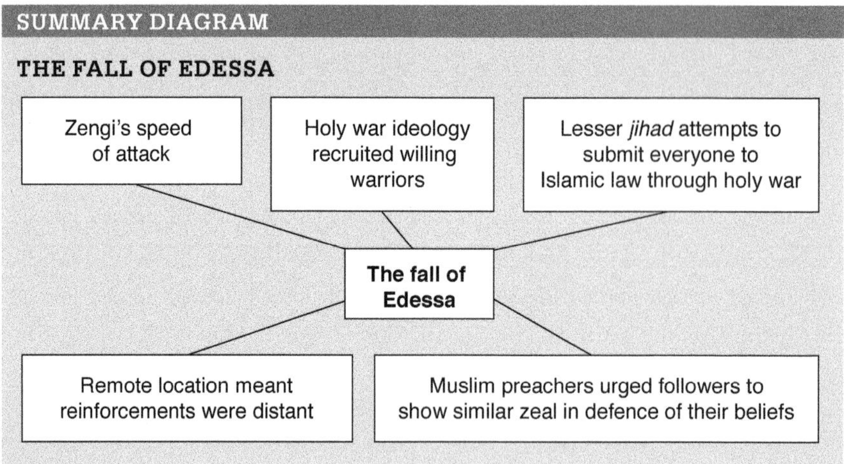
SUMMARY DIAGRAM
THE FALL OF EDESSA
Zengi's speed of attack
Holy war ideology recruited willing warriors
Lesser *jihad* attempts to submit everyone to Islamic law through holy war
The fall of Edessa
Remote location meant reinforcements were distant
Muslim preachers urged followers to show similar zeal in defence of their beliefs

# 2 The role of Bernard of Clairvaux in the Second Crusade

- *How important was St Bernard in the calling of the Crusade?*

The bishops of the east lost no time after the fall of Edessa in sending a delegation to Rome to ask for aid. The pope, Eugenius III (*c*.1080–1153), had only just been elected and he saw an opportunity to illustrate his authority in the Church. He thus issued a general letter, *Quantum praedecessores* (*How much our predecessors*) calling for crusaders to retake the city of Edessa, promising them remission of sins, even for those who might die on the journey, and decreeing that their property should be protected and no interest be due on their debts while they were away. He was careful to stress the links between the appeal he was making and that of Pope Urban II – to note the part played by those who had been defending the places gained since 1099 and to argue that the fall of Edessa was a clear threat to the survival of the Church, even if there was no danger to Jerusalem or the other States. His main hope was for a quick response in France, as experienced by Urban II over the First Crusade, but the French knights had initially held back. To some extent this was welcome, as the pope did not want a repeat of the events of the First Crusade when the passionate preaching of men such as Peter the Hermit had led to the massacre of large numbers of Jews. This time, the pope entrusted the preaching to Bernard of Clairvaux and his mandate was designed to ensure that other 'official preachers' gave the same message. Only he, and other official preachers, would recruit for the Crusade. Bernard toured the Rhineland and the Low Countries for seven months offering eternal salvation and the chance to partake in a holy

**ONLINE EXTRAS** OCR WWW

Learn how to analyse the importance of factors by completing Worksheet 20 at **www.hoddereducation.co.uk/accesstohistory/extras**

war. However, despite the much tighter control over the preaching it did not prevent an unauthorised preacher, Rudolph, from stirring up attacks on Jews in Germany.

**SOURCE B**

**From Pope Eugenius III's papal bull *Quantum praedecessores*, 1 March 1146, quoted in Jonathan Phillips, *The Crusades 1095–1197*, Routledge, 2014, pp. 180–1.**

*We recognise how great the danger is that threatens the Church of God and all Christianity because of this [the fall of Edessa] and we do not believe that it is hidden from your understanding. It will be seen as a great token of nobility and uprightness if those things acquired by the efforts of your fathers are vigorously defended by you, their good sons. But if, God forbid, it comes to pass differently, then the bravery of the fathers will have proved to be diminished in the sons. … We, providing with a father's concern for your peace of mind and the abandonment of the eastern Church, by the authority given us by God concede and confirm to those who, inspired by devotion, decide to take up and complete so holy and very necessary a work and labour that remission of sins which our aforesaid predecessor Pope Urban instituted.*

**SOURCE QUESTION**

In Source B, why does the pope refer to 'the efforts of your fathers'?

In March 1146 Bernard began his tour in a field at Vézelay where, with the King of France, Louis VII, at his side, he read out the *Quantum praedecessores* letter and added his own sermon. The response was so great that he ran out of cloth for crosses and had to use pieces torn from his own habit, possibly a deliberately orchestrated procedure. He followed this up with letters and other sermons. His appeal was directly to the knightly class and he had no interest in encouraging those who were not qualified to fight to go. By November he had reached Frankfurt, and at the Christmas Mass held during the assembly at Speyer impressed on Emperor Conrad III (see page 105) that the **Day of Judgement** would be disastrous for him, if he had not heeded the call to crusade.

The appeal of Bernard was a brilliant piece of rhetoric, as the surviving letters he wrote prove. He also, along with Pope Eugenius III, was moving on from the theology of Pope Urban II. The crusaders were assured that just going on a crusade was so unpleasant that it was enough of a penance to win them remission. Bernard encouraged them to believe that it was God's mercy, transmitted through the papal **Power of the Keys**, which would ensure that their sins were forgiven.

Bernard urged, 'Take the sign of the Cross and you will obtain in equal measure remission of all the sins which you have confessed with a contrite heart. If the cloth itself is sold, it does not fetch much; if it is worn on a faithful shoulder it is certain to be worth the kingdom of God.' The taking of the cross was less to imitate the sacrifice of Christ than to show that the crusader had submitted himself to the mercy of God. There was also the point that the gains of the First Crusade and the courage shown by the crusaders then should not all be thrown away.

## Key figures of the Second Crusade

Pope Eugenius III

Bernard of Clairvaux

Conrad III of Germany

Louis VII of France

Byzantine Emperor Manuel I

Roger II of Sicily

**KEY TERMS**

**Day of Judgement** The day when Christ would return to earth and everyone would be judged and be sent to either heaven or hell.

**Power of the Keys** The power given to St Peter in the Gospels to forgive sins, which was passed on to all the popes as heirs of St Peter.

## Bernard of Clairvaux 1090–1153

Bernard's parents came from the Burgundian nobility. He was the third of seven children, of whom six were sons. His mother died when he was nineteen and this may have been what propelled him to become a monk. In 1112 he joined the abbey at Cîteaux, near Dijon. This house was a recent foundation, established by Robert of Molesme (1028–1111) in 1098 as a reformed abbey, returning to the original discipline of the Benedictine rule. Such was his personal impact that 30 of his friends and relations joined with him.

In 1115, after just three years as a monk, he was sent to Clairvaux in the diocese of Langres with twelve others to establish a new Cistercian house (the Cistercian order emphasised a simple life of manual labour and self-sufficiency). Here he led such an austere life that he was often ill, but he attracted over 130 new monks including his father and all his brothers. In 1119 the first General Chapter or assembly of the order was held and the pope confirmed its rules. In 1120 Bernard published the first of his many writings, the *Apologia*, defending his order against attacks from the Benedictines of the great abbey at Cluny.

Bernard played a large role at the Church Council of 1128 at Troyes and in 1130 was chosen to judge which of two rivals was the true pope. He picked Innocent II and travelled extensively to persuade European rulers to recognise Innocent. Among those he visited were William X of Aquitaine (1099–1137) and Roger II of Sicily (1095–1154). He was also involved in a dispute with Peter Abelard (1079–1142), a teacher at the University of Paris, whose views were judged to be heretical. The Council of Sens in 1141 found that Bernard was in the right. His sermons were described as 'sweet as honey' and so he became known as the Doctor Mellifluous.

Thus, Bernard had the highest possible reputation when he began to preach the Second Crusade in 1144, and its poor outcome saddened his last years. In his final book, *The Considerations*, he tried to defend himself by suggesting that the sins of the crusaders were to blame for their failure. He died in 1153.

The result was that the Second Crusade was much larger than the first in terms of numbers. Many of those who joined came from families where other members had been on crusade and reflected the prominence that crusading was beginning to have in the thinking of knightly circles. By 1144 accounts of the First Crusade were available for the literate to read, such as the anonymous *Gesta Francorum*, and personal stories were no doubt also circulating. For the less literate, popular songs extolling heroic deeds were being commonly performed, so the First Crusade was far from being forgotten.

Bernard was also determined that the events which had stained the reputation of the First Crusade should not be repeated. When he heard that Rudolf, another Cistercian monk, was preaching the Crusade in Germany and stirring up feeling against Jews there, Bernard went to Mainz and disciplined the monk, who was preaching illegally as he had no permission from the local bishop. Rudolf had succeeded in developing anti-Semitism among the lower classes but the lords and knights extended protection to Jewish people this time and casualties were far lower than in the First Crusade. It was the activities of Rudolf which largely led to the preaching of the Crusade being extended to Germany. Pope Eugenius III had probably originally intended that it should be a largely French affair.

**ONLINE EXTRAS** WWW
OCR

Learn how to write argument rather than assertion by completing Worksheet 21 at **www.hoddereducation.co.uk/accesstohistory/extras**

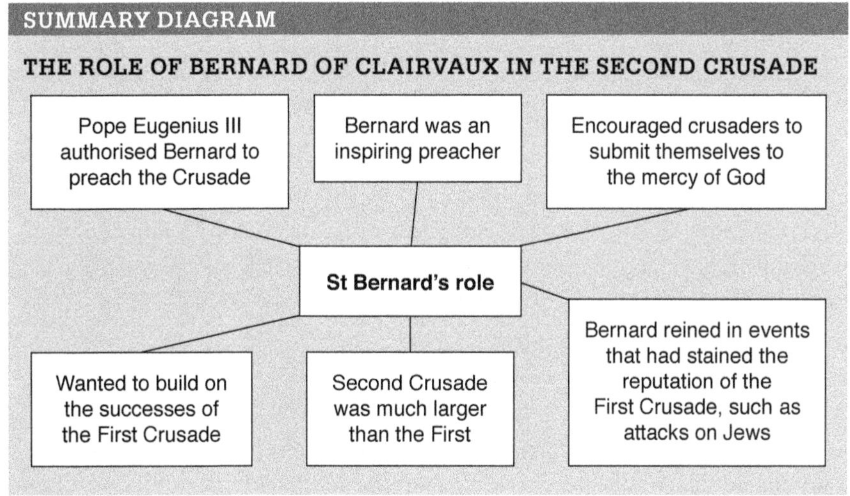
SUMMARY DIAGRAM
THE ROLE OF BERNARD OF CLAIRVAUX IN THE SECOND CRUSADE
Pope Eugenius III authorised Bernard to preach the Crusade
Bernard was an inspiring preacher
Encouraged crusaders to submit themselves to the mercy of God
St Bernard's role
Bernard reined in events that had stained the reputation of the First Crusade, such as attacks on Jews
Wanted to build on the successes of the First Crusade
Second Crusade was much larger than the First

# 3 The roles of Louis VII and Conrad III in the Second Crusade

- *Why did Louis VII and Conrad III join the Second Crusade?*

Unlike the First Crusade, the leaders of the Second Crusade were kings, Louis VII of France and Conrad III of Germany. It was a new departure for monarchs to lead a crusade, as the First Crusade had been led by princes, and it would lead to tension and rivalries between the two men over who should have predominance. Each man had his own particular reasons for responding to the call, as can be seen below.

## Why did Louis VII join the Second Crusade?

Louis VII of France (1120–80) was 25. He had become King of France unexpectedly in 1137 after his elder brother, Philip (1116–31), was killed in a freak accident in the streets of Paris, involving a runaway pig and a frightened horse. Louis VII had originally been intended for the Church and his mindset was serious and spiritual. Louis VII's uncle, Hugh of Vermandois, had been on the First Crusade (see page 38). Louis VII was married to Eleanor of Aquitaine (1122–1204), whose father, William X of Aquitaine, had been a crusader. These were all reasons why Louis decided to go on crusade himself. However, he had an additional reason for wanting to crusade. In 1143 he had besieged the town of Vitry-sur-Marne, 200 kilometres east of Paris, in the course of a war against the Count of Champagne. The inhabitants had taken refuge in the church, but the building caught fire from the burning arrows being used against the castle and most of those sheltering in the church had died. Their screams are said to have haunted Louis VII. He felt the need for forgiveness and thought going on crusade would achieve this.

Eleanor was also eager to participate. It was not unknown for women to go on crusade, but she was one of the highest ranked to do so. Her marriage to Louis VII had produced only one daughter, Marie (1145–98), and she hoped the blessings from the Crusade might lead to the birth of a male heir. Eleanor was no favourite of Bernard, who disapproved of her frivolous lifestyle, while she consistently ignored his advice and resented his influence on her husband.

Louis VII held a council and appointed regents to rule while he was away. The most important of these was Suger, Abbot of St Denis (*c.*1081–1151), one of Louis VII's most influential advisers. Louis VII's departure from France was marked by a ceremony at **Saint Denis**, presided over by Pope Eugenius III himself.

**KEY TERM**

**Saint Denis** The burial place of Denis, the first Bishop of Paris, martyred in about 250 on the hill of Montmartre. An abbey was established there and most French kings were buried there, so it was a very sacred site.

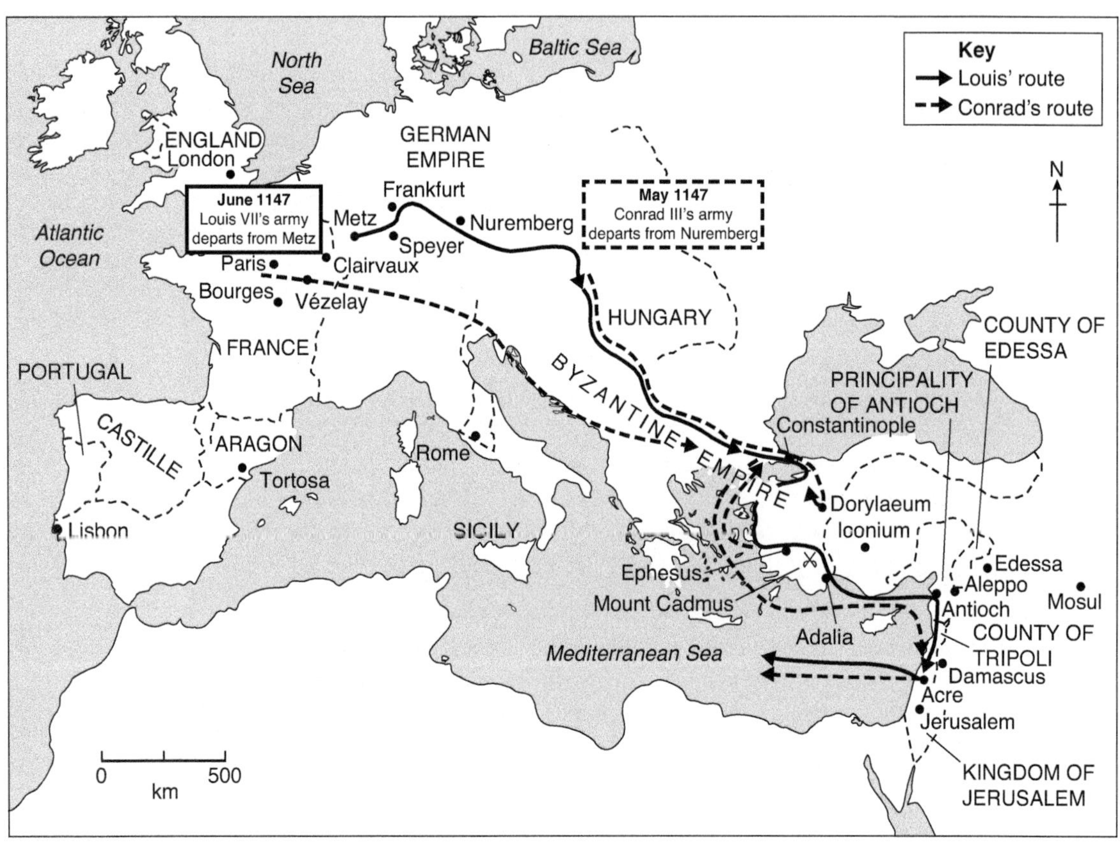


**Figure 5.1** The journeys of Louis VII and Conrad III on the Second Crusade.

## Louis VII c.1120–80

Louis succeeded his father, Louis VI (1081–1137), as King of France in 1137. He married Eleanor, daughter of William X, Duke of Aquitaine and so extended his lands to the Pyrenees. He continued the efforts of the Capetians to build up the prestige of the French monarchy and to improve the administration. He was asked by Pope Eugenius III to organise a crusade and persuaded Bernard of Clairvaux to preach it. Conrad III of Germany joined him in a rare example of Franco-German cooperation. But the Crusade failed at Damascus in 1148. He was also on good terms with Pope Alexander III and supported him against Frederick Barbarossa (see pages 150–2). Alexander spent some of his exile from Rome in France. Another exile welcomed by Louis was Archbishop of Canterbury Thomas Becket, fleeing from the wrath of England's Henry II. Louis' main enemies were the **Angevins**, Geoffrey of Anjou and his son Henry (who became Henry II). When Louis divorced Eleanor for misconduct in 1152, she married Henry almost at once. Louis' second wife died but his third finally gave him a son, Philip, known as Dieudonné as his birth seemed like a gift from God. Louis was no real match for Henry II but was helped by the quarrels Henry pursued with his family and with Becket, which weakened him. Suger, the Abbot of Saint-Denis and one of his chief advisers, wrote the chronicle of Louis' reign. He managed to live long enough for his son to be old enough to succeed without needing a regent which may have damaged the monarchy.

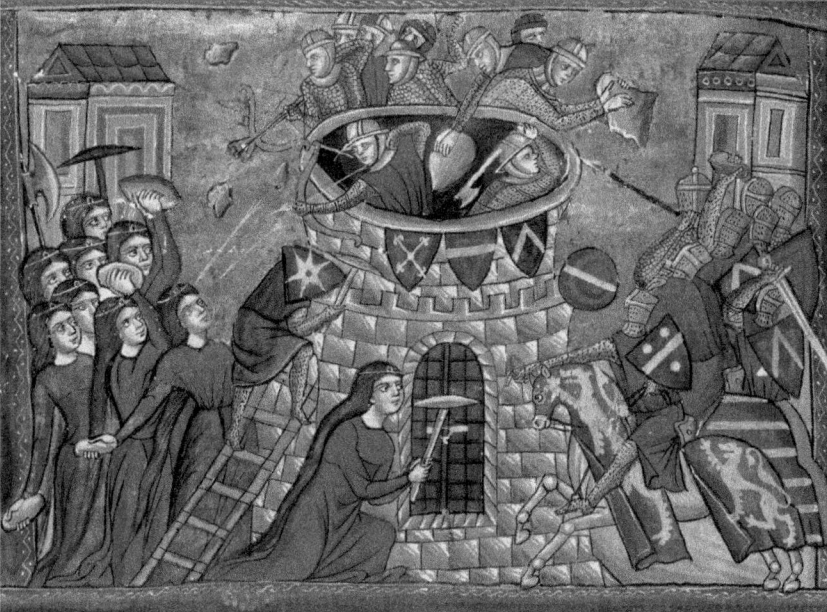

**SOURCE C**

**A thirteenth-century illustration showing women besieging a tower. Although women were discouraged from going on crusade, some still chose to do so.**

### KEY TERM

**Angevin** The Angevins were a royal house that ruled England and much of France in the twelfth and early thirteenth centuries; its monarchs were Henry II, Richard I and John.

**SOURCE QUESTION**

Why did the artist of Source C depict women on a crusade, despite them being discouraged from participating?

## Why did Conrad III join the Second Crusade?

Conrad III was the first German king of the house of Hohenstaufen and had been elected in 1137. He then faced a civil war from rival claimants, but by 1142 he had beaten his enemies. Aged 54 in 1147, he was much older than Louis, and was concerned that he might not return alive. Thus, he persuaded the German nobles to elect and crown his heir, Henry (1136/7–50), as king.

Conrad had been to the Holy Land before, in 1124, after vowing to fight for Christ in Jerusalem, possibly after some kind of conversion experience. He was the only European ruler to campaign there twice.

Bernard helped to make it easier for Conrad III to crusade by working endlessly to bring some degree of peace to an unstable Germany and so allow Conrad III to leave the country without too much worry about being overthrown in his absence. His chief rival in Germany, Welf VI (1115–91), who had been in rebellion against Conrad, was persuaded to take the cross as well. Similarly, Henry of Bavaria, Welf VI's main enemy, was also persuaded to join the Crusade. The absence of these removed the most serious potential for conflict in Germany during Conrad's absence. Conrad's nephew, Frederick III of Swabia (1122–90), another possible source of trouble at home, also joined the Crusade.

**ONLINE EXTRAS** WWW
OCR

Learn how to write an argument rather than an assertion by completing Worksheet 22 at **www.hoddereducation.co.uk/accesstohistory/extras**

## The plan for the Second Crusade

The fact that, unlike the First Crusade, the Second was led by two kings should have ensured that it was a great success, but instead it was a disaster. Not only was the original aim of retaking Edessa not achieved, but the crusaders were defeated outside the walls of Damascus.

Such a major undertaking required forward planning. Louis VII had to decide how to travel: the land route via the Danube and the Balkans, or the sea route from southern Italy. The preparations took him the best part of a year. He was in touch with rulers whose realms would be affected, and was given permission by the Hungarian king to use the land route and by Roger II of Sicily for the sea route. Although he was later criticised for taking the land route, it had considerable advantages:

- The land route was the cheapest for most of the French travelling from Flanders and northern France as supplies were available in France and they could forage in Germany. Given the monetary cost of crusading, this was a real benefit.
- Transport of horses by sea was problematic.
- Many French knights lived far inland and fitting up a fleet was outside their experience.
- An offer of help with sea transport came from Roger II of Sicily, an enemy of both Conrad III and the Emperor Manuel I (see page 108) because of Roger II's ambitions in Italy and the eastern Mediterranean, and so best avoided.
- Once the Germans had decided to join the Crusade, it was a sound idea to follow the same route as they did.

**ONLINE EXTRAS** WWW
AQA

Learn how to write an effective introduction by completing Worksheet 17 at **www.hoddereducation.co.uk/accesstohistory/extras**

## Conrad III 1093–1152

Conrad's father was Frederick I, Duke of Swabia, and his uncle was Henry V of Germany. When Henry died in 1125, the electors ignored the claims of Conrad and chose Lothar, Duke of Saxony and Bavaria. This led to civil disorder and the situation was reversed in 1137 when Lothar died and Conrad was elected. This annoyed Lothar's son, Henry the Lion, and further fighting broke out, with Henry being deprived of Saxony. These events laid the foundation for the long-running Guelf–Ghibelline rivalry in Germany. Conrad was generally an ineffective ruler, apart from a successful expedition to Bohemia. He joined the Second Crusade, having his son Henry crowned as king before he left to secure the succession. He spent time in Constantinople recovering from illness and made an alliance with Manuel I (see page 108), who married Conrad's sister-in-law. On his return home in 1148, he faced further problems from unruly vassals. He never went to Rome so was never crowned as emperor. His son Henry died and so his heir was Frederick of Swabia, known as Barbarossa.

## Roger II of Sicily 1095–1154

Roger II became one of the most powerful rulers in Europe. Descended from the Normans who had conquered Sicily, he was just a child when he inherited Sicily. His mother acted as regent for him and later married Baldwin I of Jerusalem. Her marriage was declared invalid by the Church and this may explain Roger's refusal to go crusading.

Roger inherited Apulia in southern Italy but had to fight the pope and local nobles to be recognised as its ruler. He backed the rival pope, Anacletus (died 1138), and was rewarded with the crown of Sicily in 1130. He had to fight a long civil war to hold on to his lands but was eventually the winner.

Roger established an absolutist but well-administered government. Sicily was noted for its wealth and trade, the tolerance of Roger II and the splendour of his court. His navy, under George of Antioch (died 1151/2), controlled the eastern Mediterranean Sea. He took advantage of the Second Crusade to attack Manuel I (see page 108).

Some French soldiers and the English contingent who sailed from Dartford did go by sea, stopping off at Lisbon *en route* (see pages 106–7). Conrad III used the land route reaching the Danube via Nuremberg and Regensburg. His troops helped the French by building new bridges over some of the rivers. The aim was that the two forces would meet in Constantinople.

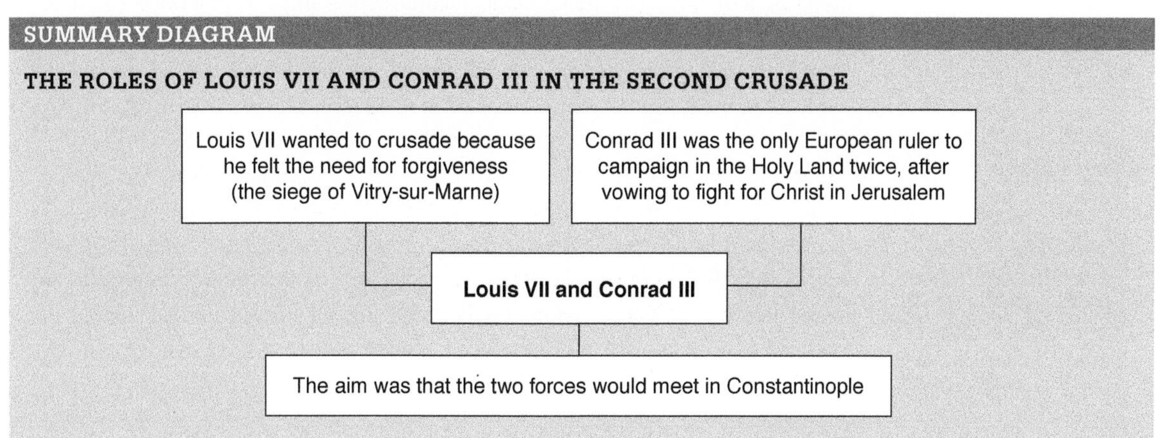

SUMMARY DIAGRAM
THE ROLES OF LOUIS VII AND CONRAD III IN THE SECOND CRUSADE
Louis VII wanted to crusade because he felt the need for forgiveness (the siege of Vitry-sur-Marne)
Conrad III was the only European ruler to campaign in the Holy Land twice, after vowing to fight for Christ in Jerusalem
Louis VII and Conrad III
The aim was that the two forces would meet in Constantinople

# 4 The events of the Second Crusade

■ *What happened during the Second Crusade?*

The Second Crusade began with wars in areas that were not the Holy Land, and with people who were not Muslims.

## The conversion of the Wends to Christianity

The Wends were a pagan Slav race who lived beyond the north-east border of Germany. In 1147 the Saxon princes who had signed up to the Crusade made it clear that they would prefer to fight against the Wends, somewhat nearer to home than Edessa. Bernard of Clairvaux was especially eager for this to happen and proposed that the Wends should be given the choice of death or conversion. Pope Eugenius III, however, only mentioned conversion. The crusaders, who were largely Danes and Saxons, were to receive the same spiritual benefits as those journeying much further. The Wendish prince did not wait to be attacked and moved against the forces of Henry the Lion, Duke of Saxony (1129/31–95), and the other German leaders. There was no clear victor. The Wends agreed to be baptised, and the Christians claimed success. The whole episode deprived the Crusade of troops who could have been useful in the Holy Land and set a precedent that crusading could take place outside it, so long as the enemy was non-Christian. However, it ensured that potentially troublesome elements of the German nobility were kept occupied while Conrad was away, and as most taking part in the Crusade were Danes and Saxons, the impact on the numbers who went to the Holy Land was quite limited.

## The siege of Lisbon

In May 1147 a fleet of up to 200 ships with about 10,000 men on board left Dartmouth, on the southern coast of England, with the intention of sailing to Jerusalem to help in the Crusade. It consisted of ships from what we now know as England, Scotland, Belgium, the Netherlands, Luxembourg and the Rhineland. The fleet had no acknowledged leader and most of those involved were from the ranks of traders and merchants, rather than the knightly classes. When these men reached Lisbon in June, they were persuaded by Alfonso Henriques (1106/11–85), who was trying to set up an independent Portuguese state, to join him in attacking the **Moors** in Lisbon. Not all of the crusaders wanted to do this, but Alfonso argued that the pope had authorised other battles against the Moors, and that this was simply a brief digression; Jerusalem remained the chief goal. Alfonso sealed the bargain with a promise that the crusaders could keep all the loot once Lisbon was taken. The siege lasted until October, but Lisbon was captured and returned to Christianity. Some of the crusaders chose to stay there as Alfonso needed settlers to replace those killed in

**KEY TERM**

**Moors** Used by medieval and early modern Europeans to variously describe Arabs, north African Berbers and Muslim Europeans.

the sacking of the city. Others carried on after the winter to the Mediterranean. Here they became involved in the siege of Tortosa (see Figure 5.1, page 102), on the Catalan border, which the Genoese and Catalans were undertaking. Once Tortosa was captured, again, some crusaders settled there, so that those who finally reached the Holy Land were a very small proportion of those who had set out. However, the composition of those involved in this event again suggests that its impact on the main crusader army would have been limited as most were merchants and traders rather than knights.

## The crusaders depart

As mentioned, Louis VII, the King of France, and Conrad III, the King of Germany, played key parts in the Second Crusade. Conrad III and the Germans left Regensburg in May 1147, while Louis VII set out from Metz a few weeks later. The German army made good progress, but there were tensions within its ranks between the Germans and the Slavs, while the French-speaking troops were disliked by all. Conrad III was not the man to weld the disparate groups into a single fighting force. Further problems arose when the army reached the Byzantine Empire. There were quarrels over the food supply, attacks on the local population and severe losses in a flash flood. Manuel I (see page 108) sent troops to keep order but the Germans then attacked these soldiers too. When the army reached Constantinople in September, Manuel I was so frustrated that he refused to meet Conrad III.

The French army was slightly smaller than the German, but better disciplined, and reached the border of the empire in August. The Byzantines tried to hurry them along and some even caught up with the Germans in front. But the Germans were distinctly unfriendly and the troops from Lorraine decided to throw in their lot with the French army where they were better understood. These tensions did not bode well for the future.

## The situation in the Byzantine Empire

Manuel I was no more secure than Alexius I, his grandfather, had been when the First Crusade arrived. The Turks were still raiding his borders and his efforts to build a line of defensive forts to deter them had not been wholly successful, although divisions among Muslims worked to his advantage. He had also been able to make alliances with some Turkish leaders against other Turks. In 1147 he had agreed to a truce with the Turks, as he feared the threat of Roger II of Sicily (see page 105) and was concerned about the exact aims of the Crusade. Unlike the First Crusade, the Byzantine emperor had not asked for help, and on this occasion was more concerned as to whether the crusading forces might actually attack Constantinople. His intention, therefore, was to move the crusaders out of Constantinople as soon as he could. His fears were somewhat justified, as there were some within the French army who favoured attacking Constantinople in alliance with Roger II of Sicily and this may have encouraged him to strengthen the walls of his capital. Manuel I even tried to obtain a guarantee of the crusaders' good behaviour from the pope, such were his concerns.

However, Louis VII refused to agree to any attack on Constantinople and argued that the pope had not sanctioned it. Despite this apparent reassurance, once Manuel I had put a safe distance between the capital and the crusader armies, he was less helpful. He was also concerned that if the crusaders retook Edessa it would encroach on Byzantine territory and this gave him even less reason to support them.

## Advance into Asia

Problems now began to pile up to challenge the crusaders:

- Conrad III ignored advice from Manuel I to stay in Byzantine territory and to send non-combatants home. He eventually split his forces into two, but still decided to follow the route of the First Crusade, overestimating the distance his army could travel in such harsh terrain day by day.
- Thus, Conrad III failed to ensure adequate water supplies for his men, and they were ambushed near Dorylaeum and most of them killed. Conrad III's camp was looted, he lost everything and fell seriously ill.
- The French lingered in Constantinople until Manuel I spread rumours that the Germans had won a victory, so they hurried off to share in the spoils.
- Manuel I made Louis VII swear an oath that he would give back any possession of Byzantium that he might recover, in return for supplies.
- Louis VII caught up with Conrad III and was dismayed to find the Germans in such disarray as he had thought they were winning.

## Manuel I Comnenus 1118–80

Manuel was the son of John II and Irene, a princess from Hungary, and succeeded his father in 1143 as Byzantine emperor. One of his great interests was the courtly culture of the west and he introduced jousting tournaments to Byzantium. He was more concerned with events in western Europe than with the threat from the Turks at the start of his reign, seeing Roger II of Sicily as his main enemy. Manuel had married Conrad III's sister-in-law as a way to gain an alliance.

Manuel was defeated in Sicily and his influence there was ended. He then turned to face the Turkish Sultan of Iconium in the 1140s, but with little lasting success. He managed to force the rulers of Antioch and Jerusalem to recognise him as their overlord, while his interventions in Croatia, Bosnia and Hungary increased his lands and influence in the Balkans.

Manuel married Maria of Antioch as his second wife. He was responsible for repairing the two main Christian churches, the Holy Sepulchre in Jerusalem and the Church of the Nativity in Bethlehem, although they were staffed by Latin Christians. One of his contributions to the Church of the Nativity was a frieze showing the early councils of the Church, which had mostly taken place in Byzantine territory, and thus illustrated his claims. But his preoccupation with trying to revive the Roman Empire in Europe meant that he did not devote enough time to the affairs of the east, and his defeat at Myriocephalum weakened his position considerably.

In 1169 and in 1177, Manuel provided naval support for the invasion of Egypt. In 1171 he accepted the homage of King Amalric I. His death in 1180 was a major blow to the crusaders. His hopes of reviving the Roman Empire and ending the schism in the Church were never even close to being realised.

- Conrad III returned to Constantinople to convalesce.
- The French continued their march, taking the route close to the sea, which was safer, but which meant Edessa was further away than ever.

Despite all these difficulties, Louis VII did defeat a Turkish force in December 1147 at the Battle of Ephesus. This proved that the crusaders were not destined to lose every battle, and did the job of heartening the army, as Source D shows.

**SOURCE D**

**From Odo of Deuil, *The Journey of Louis VII to the East*, edited and translated by Virginia Berry, W.W. Norton, 1948, p. 135.**

*From the Greeks then, the Turks learned that our knights had no horses and, taking advantage of this security prepared to attack the army in full force. This was made known to the king, and, for a move against the Turks he concealed with him the Templars and the wealthy knights who still kept their chargers even though they were starving. Appearing suddenly before the advancing Turks, he killed some, thus forcing the rest to re-cross the river without using a bridge and to believe from that time that the army had plenty of horses. Meanwhile the Greeks furnished ships at an outrageous price as was true of their other wares. A few poor vessels were presented to the king as if they were a free gift from the commander and were divided among the barons and bishops [for the voyage to Antioch]. Although the king wanted ships he resented the high price, but he buried his complaints in silence and sought the vessels promised for the rest of the army. The Greeks delayed for a long time and, by such villainy robbed both the poor and the wealthy of their possessions.*

**SOURCE QUESTION** 

What does Source D indicate about the leadership qualities of Louis VII? Consider why the Greeks were so unhelpful to the crusaders.

## Antioch 1148

Louis VII and his army reached Antioch in March 1148 (see Figure 5.1, page 102). The latter stages of their journey had been challenging. While crossing mountains the troops had become dangerously strung out. These were circumstances made for the Turkish archers on horseback, who could swoop in and out of a confused crusader line. There were severe losses of horses and men and the morale of the crusaders slumped again. To prevent such a disaster recurring, the Templars took over marshalling the forces. The men were put together in smaller groups, all the members of which swore an oath of loyalty to their comrades. When they were close, Louis VII and his immediate retinue sailed to Antioch, leaving the rest of the army to follow the difficult land route, under the command of one of the Templars (see page 110).

If the Crusade was to move on Edessa (see Figure 5.1, page 102), then Louis VII would need to march north. Raymond of Antioch (*c*.1115–49), who was uncle to Eleanor, Louis VII's wife, was eager to join with Louis VII in fighting in northern Syria, while Conrad III, still in Constantinople, had claimed to be simply waiting for reinforcements to arrive before embarking on the march to Edessa. But this is not what happened.

Why did the crusaders abandon the plan to recapture Edessa? There were several reasons for a change of plan:

- Raymond of Antioch had little interest in recovering Edessa and was on bad terms with Joscelin II of Edessa (died 1159). Raymond argued that Aleppo would be a better target as Nur ad-Din (see page 83) was now established there and its capture would make the Outremer far more secure.
- Raymond may have even hoped to regain lands which his father had lost, and may have been aiming to take Edessa for himself.
- Louis VII recognised that Edessa was a lost cause since much of the city had been destroyed in the second attack on it in 1146.
- Louis' army had been severely weakened by the Turks in January 1148 in a battle in the Cadmus mountains, French morale was so low that Templars took command and led the army to Antioch.
- Louis VII saw no point in fighting for the benefit of Antioch, especially since Raymond was officially the vassal of Manuel I and so any gains would merely benefit the Byzantine emperor.
- Louis VII was increasingly hostile to Raymond, since Eleanor was perceived as being rather too close to her uncle.
- Louis VII saw his pledge to go on pilgrimage to Jerusalem as of the greatest importance.

Hence, the crusaders moved on to Jerusalem, where Louis VII and an extremely reluctant Eleanor (it was said that Louis VII had to use force to make her accompany him) arrived in the spring of 1148.

## Were the rumours about Eleanor and Raymond justified?

It was rumoured that Raymond was having an affair with his niece, Eleanor. This caused considerable scandal. Arguments that the rumours were justified come from William of Tyre, who was writing 30 years after the event, but who says specifically that 'contrary to her royal dignity, she disregarded her marriage vows and was unfaithful to her husband'. Thierry Galeran, the king's secretary, is also said to have advised Louis to remove Eleanor from Antioch as soon as he could, although Galeran was a eunuch who was detested by Eleanor and was the butt of her mockery. The manner of her removal was taken to add force to the argument, not to mention the fact that Eleanor asked Louis VII for a divorce in March 1148 and wanted to stay in Antioch with Raymond.

But the arguments against the accusation being true seem more convincing. Eleanor was Raymond's niece, since he was her father's youngest brother. Hence, a sexual relationship would have been considered incestuous and even Eleanor, with her frequent disregard for convention, is unlikely to have seen this as acceptable. Also, she was only in Antioch for ten days. In addition, Raymond's wife, Constance, was present in the city. She had been the heiress to Antioch and so Raymond's title as prince came through Constance. Raymond was not a man likely to humiliate his wife and jeopardise his position. The hostility of the chroniclers to Eleanor led to exaggeration. In one version by the anonymous minstrel of Reims, Eleanor was depicted as trying to elope with Saladin, who in 1147 was actually a child of about ten (see page 133).

## The Council at Acre

Louis and his companions arrived at Jerusalem in May 1148. They were welcomed by Queen Melisende, her son, Baldwin III (1130–63), and Conrad III, who having recovered from his illness had made his way to Jerusalem. Reinforcements were expected to arrive by sea, so the crusaders moved to the port of Acre to greet them and here they held a council to decide what to do next. Among the new arrivals were the remnants of those who had set out from England and had then been diverted to Lisbon, other members of the families of those who were already in the Holy Land, and a contingent from Italy.

There should have been troops from Provence, but an unfortunate event had prevented their arrival. Their leader was Alphonse-Jordan (1103–48), the son of Raymond I of Tripoli (*c*.1041–1105). He had been born in the east and baptised in the River Jordan, hence his name. Raymond II of Tripoli (*c*.1115–52) feared that Alphonse-Jordan might lay claim to his lands, as Raymond II's claim to Tripoli was by being an illegitimate son of Raymond I. In the event, Alphonse-Jordan died almost as soon as he arrived, which gave rise to ugly rumours that he had been poisoned. His troops returned to Provence and took no part in the rest of the Crusade. Raymond II of Tripoli decided to stay at home and did not venture to Acre. As a result, those present at the Council were largely the rulers and nobles of Jerusalem, their bishops, and the leaders of the Hospitallers and Templars. The meeting considered the crusaders' next move.

There was little value in attacking Edessa as a second assault on it had destroyed much of the city and, although the Franks still held some land in the region, it was probably not worth trying to reconquer. Moreover, the lack of cooperation from Raymond meant that military activity in the north was unlikely.

This meant that their choice of targets lay between Ascalon, the only port on the Levantine coast which was still held by the Muslims and a Shi'ite city, and Damascus, held by Sunnis. The abandonment of the original aim of the Crusade and the lack of a clear alternative may have further weakened the morale of crusader forces who had already suffered considerable losses in battle.

Damascus was the major Muslim power nearest to Jerusalem. It was a very rich prize, noted for its fruit orchards and grain fields, watered by the River Amana. It was also famed for the skill of its weavers, who produced the damask named after the city, and for its metalworkers. Swords of Damascene steel were much valued by crusaders who were lucky enough to possess one. As a result, the crusaders chose to attack Damascus. This decision has been much criticised.

**ONLINE EXTRAS** WWW
OCR

Get to grips with assessing the impact of events by completing Worksheet 23 at **www.hoddereducation.co.uk/accesstohistory/extras**

However, it seemed likely that Nur ad-Din (see page 83), who had just married the daughter of the governor of Damascus, would soon capture the city. Thus, the more united the Muslims became, the greater threat they would pose and so the decision to attack before this could happen could be justified. There had been a truce with the governor of Damascus since 1139 but the recent alliance between the governor and the Turkish leader was seen as a breach of the agreement.

## The siege of Damascus

Both sides were sure they had divine support. The Christians carried a piece of the True Cross, kept in the Church of the Holy Sepulchre, while the Muslims had a copy of the Qur'an, which had belonged to the first caliph, Uthman (579–656), and was stained with his blood. The inhabitants of Damascus feared the worst and begged for help from Nur ad-Din, sending him messages by carrier pigeon. The crusaders took up an advantageous position on 24 July amid the orchards and gardens on the north-western outskirts of Damascus. Then, fearing that reinforcements would soon come to the rescue of the besieged, they moved their camp to the eastern side, where they thought the walls were

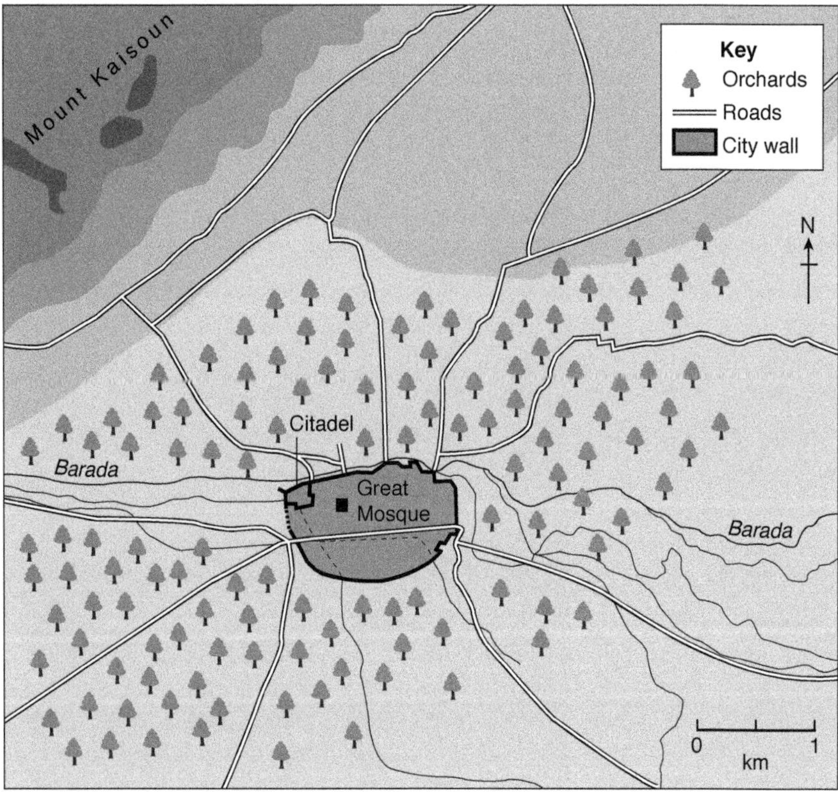


**Figure 5.2** The siege of Damascus, July 1148.

weaker. They hoped to capture the city without delay. This move proved to be an error as the eastern sector was poorly supplied with water and the walls were not as weak as had been expected. The Muslims had quickly occupied the position vacated by the crusaders, leaving the latter little choice but to withdraw, which they did on 28 July. The siege had lasted just four days.

## Why did the Second Crusade fail?

There had been great hopes for the Crusade, particularly as it was led by powerful monarchs. Its failure caused a great deal of resentment in both the Crusader States and Europe and raised questions as to why it had failed. A number of reasons were put forward and included:

- The lack of a clear aim once the retaking of Edessa was abandoned.
- Divisions between Conrad and Louis, which resulted in a lack of cooperation.
- Conrad III was sure that the settlers in Jerusalem had been bribed by the men of Damascus to give up the siege. He had been repelled by the degree of sympathy and cooperation he had witnessed between Christians and Muslims in Jerusalem and elsewhere.
- Prince Raymond of Antioch also attracted much ill-feeling, although exact details about what he had done to influence events in Damascus were sparse.
- Odo of Deuil (1110–62), a chronicler who was on the Crusade, was of the opinion that the treachery of the Greeks had damaged the Crusade in its early stages and the presence of non-combatants had slowed it down.
- Arab writers had another explanation. Ibn al-Qalanisi (died 1160), who was in Damascus at the time, referred to the religious fervour of the defenders. They prayed daily in the **Great Mosque** built by the Umayyads (see page 12) and they revered Damascus as the burial place of many holy men of Islam. He also stressed that reinforcements were beginning to arrive. Nur ad-Din had reached Homs, only 150 kilometres away, and had been joined there by troops from Mosul.
- The old rivalry between the chief Muslim rulers had been overcome in the face of the threat from the crusaders.
- There was also a suspicion that the governor of Damascus had handed over money to the nobles of Jerusalem to encourage them to retreat, just as Conrad III had suspected. Ibn al-Athir (1160–1231), writing in Mosul in the thirteenth century, certainly was of this opinion.

**KEY TERM**

**Great Mosque** A centre of religious life for the Muslims which dated back to 634.

**ONLINE EXTRAS** OCR **WWW**

Get to grips with analysing the importance of factors by completing Worksheet 24 at **www.hoddereducation.co.uk/accesstohistory/extras**

**ONLINE EXTRAS** Pearson Edexcel **WWW**

Learn how to back up your statements with evidence by completing Worksheet 18 at **www.hoddereducation.co.uk/accesstohistory/extras**

**ONLINE EXTRAS** Pearson Edexcel **WWW**

Learn how to use diagrams to organise your information by completing Worksheet 19 at **www.hoddereducation.co.uk/accesstohistory/extras**

**SUMMARY DIAGRAM**

**THE EVENTS OF THE SECOND CRUSADE**

**The Second Crusade**

**In Europe:**

- Wars in areas that were not the Holy Land and with people who were not necessarily Muslims (Wends near Germany; Moors in Lisbon)

**The Council at Acre:**

- Louis and his companions arrived at Jerusalem in May 1148
- Welcomed by Queen Melisende, her son, Baldwin III, and Conrad III

**Advance into Asia:**

- Conrad III failed to ensure adequate water supplies
- Ambushed near Dorylaeum and many troops killed
- Camp was looted and Conrad lost everything
- Louis VII caught up with Conrad III and was shocked at what he found
- In return for supplies, Manuel I made Louis VII swear he would give back any of Byzantium that he might recover
- Conrad III returned to Constantinople to convalesce
- The French continued, taking the route close to the sea

**The siege of Damascus:**

- The Christians carried a piece of the True Cross, kept in the Church of the Holy Sepulchre
- The Muslims had a copy of a Qur'an that had belonged to the first caliph, Uthman
- Damascus feared the worst and begged for help from Nur ad-Din
- The crusaders were defeated
- The siege had lasted just four days

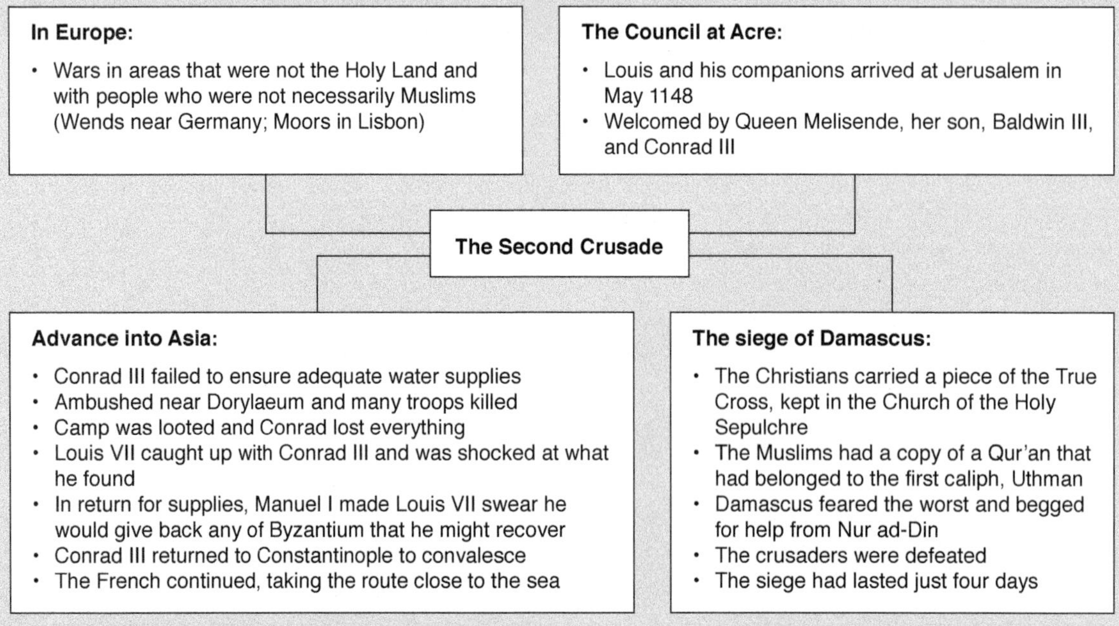

# 5 The results of the Second Crusade

*What was the impact of the Second Crusade?*

## The impact on the west

Whatever the cause, the Crusade could not be seen as anything other than a disaster for the crusaders. It saw a series of reverses which undermined the advances that the crusaders had made previously. Edessa was not regained and they failed to take Damascus. It was the first time that kings had gone on a crusade and so reflected badly on them. Bernard of Clairvaux (see page 100), who had been certain of victory, had to be particularly agile intellectually to defend himself. He took the view that the hearts of the crusaders had not been pure enough for them to succeed and other commentators noted that humbler forces had captured Lisbon, while the proud and mighty had failed at Damascus, and shown far less determination. The failure was, therefore, a serious blow to the pride of the west and particularly to the prestige of the papacy. It also turned many in the west against the idea of crusading and may have ensured that in future crusades were just military expeditions with limited aims. Finally, it also destroyed the belief in the military invincibility of the west that had been built up as a result of the success of the First Crusade and advances made in the period 1100–18 (see page 77).

On 9 September Conrad III left for home. On his way, he made a treaty with Manuel I against Roger II of Sicily, showing how the peace in Europe negotiated by Bernard had fallen apart. In the end, Conrad III's plans came to nothing, however. Roger II forestalled him and fomented a rebellion by the rival Welf family in Germany which kept Conrad III busy at home and with no time to fight Roger II.

Louis VII lingered on. He was, perhaps, unwilling to face up to the facts of his failure. Eventually, he and Eleanor sailed from Acre in April 1149, on different ships, such was the hostility between them. They suffered from stormy weather during which their ships became separated. They were eventually reunited at the court of King Roger II. It was here that Eleanor learned that Raymond of Antioch had foolishly taken on Nur ad-Din, with only a few hundred knights and about 1000 foot soldiers. His army was soon surrounded and he was killed. His head and right arm were sent in a silver box to the Caliph of Baghdad. Eleanor blamed Louis VII even more for not helping her uncle, but they decided to visit Pope Eugenius III on their way home to try to put their respective cases before the pontiff. While in Rome, Pope Eugenius III prepared a special bed for the estranged couple, with the result that a second daughter, Alice, was born nine months later. This was not enough to save the marriage, however.

While at Roger II's court, Louis VII had agreed to renew the alliance with the Sicilian king and talk of another crusade was being fostered by Bernard, However, the pope refused to join an alliance with Roger II, and Louis VII feared that Roger II might ask too much in return. The French knights had no appetite for another crusade, so peace was restored. However, public trust in the crusading movement had been severely damaged and it would not be easy to bring such a large force together again.

## The impact on relations between the west, Byzantium and the Crusader States

If relations between the west and Byzantium were not strained before the Crusade, they were now. In the west the behaviour of the Byzantines was seen as treacherous and trust between the two broke down even more.

Similarly, rulers and princes in the west and the settlers in the Crusader States also lost trust in and respect for each other, which may explain why the numbers going east and aid from the west reduced.

## The impact of the Crusade on the Muslim world

The success of Zengi, after the defeats of the First Crusade, was psychologically important. It showed not just the Muslim world, but also the west, that Zengi's troops were a military force able to inflict defeats. They had been able to capture

**ONLINE EXTRAS** AQA **WWW**

Get to grips with continuity and change by completing Worksheet 18 at **www.hoddereducation.co.uk/accesstohistory/extras**

**ONLINE EXTRAS** AQA **WWW**

Learn how to identify a range of causes by completing Worksheet 19 at **www.hoddereducation.co.uk/accesstohistory/extras**

**ONLINE EXTRAS** AQA **WWW**

Learn how to consider consequences by completing Worksheet 20 at **www.hoddereducation.co.uk/accesstohistory/extras**

**ONLINE EXTRAS** OCR **WWW**

Practise analysing the importance of factors by completing Worksheet 25 at **www.hoddereducation.co.uk/accesstohistory/extras**

**ONLINE EXTRAS** Pearson Edexcel WWW

Learn how to use criteria to support your argument by completing Worksheet 20 at **www.hoddereducation.co.uk/accesstohistory/extras**

**ONLINE EXTRAS** Pearson Edexcel WWW

Develop your analysis of events by completing Worksheet 21 at **www.hoddereducation.co.uk/accesstohistory/extras**

and hold Christian territory. This helped to bring the Muslim states closer together and unite for further attacks against the Crusader States, encouraging *jihad* and the assault on Jerusalem in 1187.

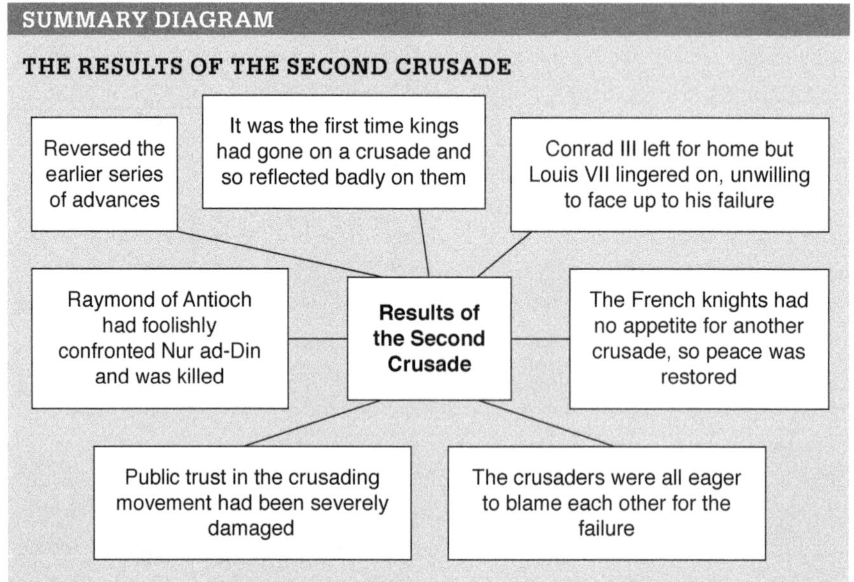

SUMMARY DIAGRAM
THE RESULTS OF THE SECOND CRUSADE
Reversed the earlier series of advances
It was the first time kings had gone on a crusade and so reflected badly on them
Conrad III left for home but Louis VII lingered on, unwilling to face up to his failure
Raymond of Antioch had foolishly confronted Nur ad-Din and was killed
Results of the Second Crusade
The French knights had no appetite for another crusade, so peace was restored
Public trust in the crusading movement had been severely damaged
The crusaders were all eager to blame each other for the failure


# 6 Key debate

*Was the attack on Damascus a mistake?*

The nature of the Second Crusade has given rise to debates among historians. Giles Constable (1953) argues that the papacy saw the whole enterprise, including all the expeditions and not just that to the Holy Land, as part of a concerted campaign against the infidels. This view is reflected in the title of Jonathan Phillips' account of the Crusade, published in 2008, which was subtitled *Extending the Frontier of Christendom*. This so-called pluralist view of the Crusades led to some definition of what constitutes a crusade being sought. The conclusion of Jonathan Riley-Smith was that papal authority was the key feature and Phillips agrees that Eugenius was in control of the crusading movement in its various forms. S.J. Edgington illustrates this view by arguing that some of those who joined the expedition, which took Lisbon, were inspired by the preaching of Bernard of Clairvaux. Phillips used methodology pioneered by Riley-Smith to identify individual crusaders and assess their roles. His book is the first detailed account of the Crusade since the nineteenth century and analyses the historiography in detail.

Some critics, such as Alan Forey (1984), suggest that the pluralist view exaggerates what the papacy could achieve and point out that Eugenius III and St Bernard could only inspire and not command. They certainly could not force Louis VII and Conrad III to work together. In addition, the pluralist view may be seen as not entirely in accordance with contemporary ideas about crusading, where local interests often predominated. It has also been suggested that historian Richard Fletcher was too dependent on the work of Helmold of Bosnau, writing shortly after the Crusade, who argued that the expeditions to the east, to Spain and to the Baltic were all part of the one movement.

The attack on Damascus is another key debate for the Crusade. Phillips maintains that up to this point Edessa was still seen as the goal for the Crusade and it was only at the Council at Acre that it was agreed this was impractical. At the time the diversion to Damascus had been condemned as a betrayal. One of the problems with interpreting this decision is that the sources are few and lack essential detail and the failure of the siege led some chroniclers to assert that it never had any chance of success, making good use of their knowledge of the outcome. Steven Runciman (1954) argues this case with some vigour. Phillips and Forey, however, maintain that the decision had sound rationale behind it, as Damascus was a key city both strategically and because of its strong biblical connections and that the siege could well have been successful had the crusaders not moved their camp.

Extract 1 suggests that the decision to attack Damascus had some merit.

**EXTRACT 1**

From Thomas Madden, *The Concise History of the Crusades*, Rowman & Littlefield, 1999, p. 58.

*On 24 June 1148 the two kings [Conrad III and Louis VII] convened an assembly at Acre of all the barons and leading clergy of the kingdom of Jerusalem. Together they commanded a powerful force. The question was what to do with it. Many options were debated, although the original purpose of the crusade, the recapture of Edessa was not among them. Aleppo was the obvious target, but it received minor consideration. At last they settled on an attack on Damascus. Jerusalem and Damascus were allies of course, but that was easily dispensed with. It had not escaped the notice of Baldwin III, who had just reached the age of majority and the other Palestinian lords, that Nur ad-Din had recently married the daughter of the atabeg of Damascus. Many Christians felt that it was only a matter of time before Nur ad-Din captured the city, putting Jerusalem in grave danger. Still, it was a risk. In an attempt to shore up a defensive line against Nur ad-Din, the knights of Palestine would have to chance creating a new and nearby enemy. For the recently arrived crusaders there were no such qualms. They did not understand how a treaty with infidels could have been made in the first place and they saw no reason to honour it now.*

**INTERPRETATION QUESTION**

Using your own knowledge, what are the strengths and weaknesses of the two interpretations in Extracts 1 and 2 about the Second Crusade?

**ONLINE EXTRAS** AQA **WWW**

Practise your extract analysis by completing Worksheet 21 at **www.hoddereducation.co.uk/accesstohistory/extras**

**ONLINE EXTRAS** AQA WWW

Develop your analysis of interpretations by completing Worksheet 22 at **www.hoddereducation.co.uk/accesstohistory/extras**

**ONLINE EXTRAS** AQA WWW

Learn how to assess the arguments of historians by completing Worksheet 23 at **www.hoddereducation.co.uk/accesstohistory/extras**

**ONLINE EXTRAS** Pearson Edexcel WWW

Practise your interpretation analysis by completing Worksheet 22 at **www.hoddereducation.co.uk/accesstohistory/extras**

Extract 2 argues that the decision to attack Damascus was deeply flawed.

**EXTRACT 2**

**From Steven Runciman, *A History of the Crusades, Volume II*, Penguin Books, 2016, first published 1954, pp. 228–9.**

*We do not know what was the course of the debate [at Acre], nor who made the final proposal. After some opposition the assembly decided to concentrate all its strength on an attack against Damascus. It was a decision of utter folly. Damascus would indeed be a rich prize and its possession by the Franks would entirely cut off the Muslims of Egypt and Africa from their co-religionists in northern Syria and the East. But, of all the Muslim states, the Kingdom of Damascus alone was eager to remain in friendship with the Franks for, like the farther-sighted Franks, it recognised its chief foe to be Nur ad-Din. Frankish interests lay in retaining Damascene friendship until Nur ad-Din should be crushed, and to keep open the breach between Damascus and Aleppo. To attack the former was the surest way to throw its rulers into Nur ad-Din's hands. But the barons of Jerusalem coveted the fertile lands that owed their allegiance to Damascus. To the visiting crusaders Aleppo meant nothing, but Damascus was a city hallowed in Holy Writ, whose rescue from the infidel would resound to the glory of God. It is idle to try to apportion blame for the decision, but the greater responsibility must lie with the local barons, who knew the situation, rather than with the newcomers to whom all Muslims were the same.*

# CHAPTER SUMMARY

The Second Crusade was set in motion by the pope, Eugenius III, and much assisted by the preaching of St Bernard, with the intention of recapturing Edessa. Their aim was that French knights should be the main participants. Louis VII took the cross and was accompanied by his wife, Eleanor of Aquitaine. Conrad III of Germany also joined. There was a large following, including non-combatants. Other crusaders fought against the Wends on the north-eastern borders of Germany and against the Muslims around Lisbon. The Crusade failed to take any Muslim-held territory. Conrad III's troops were defeated early on. The crusaders did not even go to Edessa but decided to besiege Damascus. This was a total failure. The result was to discredit the idea of a crusade and to show the Muslims that the crusaders could be defeated.

The side-tracking of the Second Crusade into other arenas has been blamed for its eventual failure, and Bernard and Eugenius III can be seen as too keen to diversify. However, it is only speculation to suggest that the Crusade would have been more successful if all the participants had fought together for Edessa.

## Refresher questions

Use these questions to remind yourself of the key material covered in this chapter.

1. Why did Pope Eugenius III want another crusade?
2. What was the importance of the preaching of Bernard of Clairvaux?
3. Why did Louis VII join the Crusade?
4. Why did Conrad III join the Crusade?
5. What problems did the crusaders face on the journey to Constantinople?
6. What problems did the crusaders face on their journey to Antioch?
7. Why did Louis VII refuse to help Raymond of Antioch?
8. Why did the crusaders decide to besiege Damascus?
9. Why was the siege of Damascus a failure?
10. What were the main results of the Crusade?

## Question practice: AQA

### Essay questions

**1** How far was the lack of support from the west the reason for the continued difficulties facing Outremer in the years 1119–47? [A level]

**EXAM HINT** It is easy to allow your response to become a description of the difficulties faced. However, this is not the route to a successful essay. Neither is the task to describe and detail the lack of support from the west. The best approach is to determine which factors clearly led to specific difficulties, such as the lack of manpower. It can be difficult to argue how the absence of a factor led to something else, so avoid becoming caught up here in counter-factuals or accounts of what might have happened if there had been support. Instead, identify where there was little support and detail how this had an effect.

**2** 'The fall of Edessa in 1144 was the main reason for the calling of the Second Crusade.' Assess the validity of this view with reference to the years 1119–47. [A level]

**EXAM HINT** You need to analyse the various reasons for the calling of the Second Crusade in relation to the whole period. Ideally, you will be able to outline your overall argument in the introduction and then let the essay flow from this.

## Question practice: OCR

### Essay questions

**1** Which of the following was more important in bringing about the failure of the Second Crusade? i) Louis VII. ii) Conrad III. Explain your answer with reference to both i) and ii). [A level]

**EXAM HINT** The importance of the two rulers in bringing about the failure of the Second Crusade should be explained and a supported judgement reached as to which was more important.

**2** 'Lack of clear aims was the most important reason for the failure of the Second Crusade.' How far do you agree? [A level]

**EXAM HINT** Responses should analyse a range of factors responsible for the failure of the Crusade. It might be helpful to start with the named factor, lack of clear aims, and assess the role it played in the failure before going on to other issues. A judgement as to the relative importance of the factors should be reached.

## Question practice: Pearson Edexcel

### Essay question

**1** To what extent was the growth of Muslim military power the main reason for the failure of the Second Crusade? [A level]

**EXAM HINT** Assess the relative significance of a number of factors, perhaps including the leadership of Zengi and Nur ad-Din, the lack of clear aims for the crusade, and the divisions between Conrad III and Louis VII.

# CHAPTER 6

# The Crusader States after the Second Crusade

The Crusader States felt much less secure after the failure of the Second Crusade, and with good reason. This chapter examines the pressures on the States from 1149 to 1187 by focusing on the following themes:

- The rise of Nur ad-Din and developments in Islam
- The Crusader States after the Second Crusade
- The campaigns in Egypt
- The rise of Saladin
- The victory of Saladin at Hattin and his conquest of Jerusalem

The key debate on page 143 of this chapter asks the question: How should Saladin be viewed?

**KEY DATES**

| | | | |
|---|---|---|---|
| **1153** | Capture of Ascalon by the crusaders | **1179** | Capture of Jacob's Ford by Saladin |
| **1163** | Start of King Amalric's attacks on Egypt | **1187** | Battle of Hattin |
| **1174** | Saladin in control of Damascus | | Fall of Jerusalem to Saladin |
| **1176** | Defeat of Manuel I at Myriocephalum | | |

## 1 The rise of Nur ad-Din and developments in Islam

*What was the significance of the rise of Nur ad-Din?*

Nur ad-Din was one of the key figures of the Crusades (see page 83). The damage Nur had inflicted on Edessa (see pages 96–8) meant that the crusaders saw no point in trying to recover it. In 1147 and 1148 he had taken some of the most fertile territory of Antioch. But he made no further move during the Second Crusade, apart from coming to relieve Damascus in 1148.

However, in 1149 he attacked Inab, a fortress belonging to Antioch, and defeated Raymond and the small band of knights who went to its relief (see page 115). The death of Raymond made Nur a famous warrior for Islam and played a key role in his consolidation of power. Nur followed up this victory with an attack on Antioch itself and raided the surrounding countryside, even reaching the coast, where the Muslims had not previously penetrated. He went so far as to bathe in the Mediterranean Sea to show off his achievements to his troops. Once he had shown the people of Antioch the strength of his power, he retreated. He also had a stroke of luck in that Joscelin II of Edessa was captured in 1150 by a local lord while out hunting near his remaining stronghold of Tel Bashir. The lord knew that Nur ad-Din would pay a good price for the prisoner. Joscelin II was handed over and would later die in prison in Aleppo.

Nur ad-Din was also able to take control of Damascus in 1154. Damascus had once been an ally of the Franks, but relations had cooled even before the unsuccessful attempt at taking the city in July 1148 during the Second Crusade. Nur al-Din's commitment to *jihad* allowed him to win over many Damascenes and take over the city. This meant that the two key cities of Damascus and Aleppo were governed by the same man and shows how the disunity of the Muslims, which had been so helpful to the early crusaders, was coming to an end. Nur ad-Din married the daughter of the previous ruler of Damascus to bolster his control there.

## *Jihad* in practice

Nur ad-Din saw himself as a warrior for Islam. After recovering from a serious illness, he made the pilgrimage to Mecca, the holy city of Islam, in 1157–8, and in 1163 he suffered a rare defeat at the hands of the Franks in the Battle of al-Buqaia. These two experiences led him to a more austere way of life. He became more closely linked to men of religion and pursued the higher form of *jihad*, namely the purification of the soul, as well as the more worldly demand for the renewal of holy war.

For Nur ad-Din, politics and religion were closely entwined, as, indeed, was the case in much of Christendom. As a result, he was focused not only on the Franks as enemies, but equally on the Shi'ite Muslims, to whom he was also hostile. He set up mosques and schools to promote Sunni beliefs and used poets and writers to press the message home. He was famed as a lawgiver and held weekly courts where he dispensed justice. He also provided bathhouses, hospitals and orphanages for his people. Above all, he stressed the importance of Jerusalem as a place of pilgrimage and the need to bring the sacred city back to the rule of the faithful followers of the prophet. Source A gives one view of him.

**ONLINE EXTRAS** OCR WWW

Get to grips with assessing the importance of factors by completing Worksheet 26 at **www.hoddereducation.co.uk/accesstohistory/extras**

**SOURCE QUESTION**

How similar were the characteristics admired by Muslims and Christians as described in Source A?

**SOURCE A**

**A description of Nur ad-Din written by Ibn al-Athir, quoted in Francesco Gabrieli, editor, and E.J. Costello, translator, *Arab Historians of the Crusades*, University of California Press, 1969, pp. 70–1.**

*Nur ad-Din was a tall, swarthy man with a beard but no moustache, a fine forehead and a pleasant appearance enhanced by beautiful melting eyes. His kingdom stretched far and wide and was even acknowledged in Medina and Mecca … Among his virtues were austerity, piety and a knowledge of theology. His food and clothing and all his personal expenditure came out of income from properties bought with his legal share of booty … He had a good knowledge of Muslim law, but he was not a fanatic … He would not permit the imposition of any illegal tax anywhere in his domains, but abolished them all … On the battlefield he had no equal … Among his public works he built walls for all the cities and fortresses of Syria. He built the Great Mosque of Nur ad-Din at Mosul … He honoured scholars and men of religion and had the deepest respect for them. He would rise to his feet in their presence and invite them to sit next to him. He was always courteous to them and never contested what they said ... His expression was grave and melancholy because of his great humility. Many were his virtues, innumerable his merits; this book is not large enough to encompass them all.*

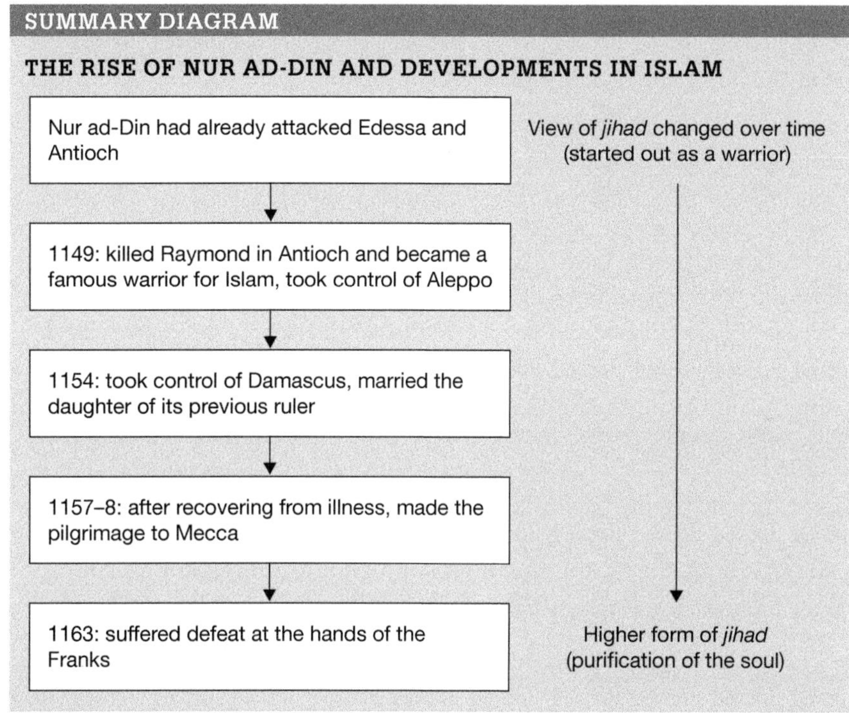

SUMMARY DIAGRAM
THE RISE OF NUR AD-DIN AND DEVELOPMENTS IN ISLAM
Nur ad-Din had already attacked Edessa and Antioch
1149: killed Raymond in Antioch and became a famous warrior for Islam, took control of Aleppo
1154: took control of Damascus, married the daughter of its previous ruler
1157–8: after recovering from illness, made the pilgrimage to Mecca
1163: suffered defeat at the hands of the Franks
View of *jihad* changed over time (started out as a warrior)
Higher form of *jihad* (purification of the soul)


# 2 The Crusader States after the Second Crusade

■ *How strong were the Crusader States politically and militarily?*

The problems which have already been noted with regard to the Crusader States remained difficult to solve after the Second Crusade.

## Edessa

Edessa was no longer a viable state; the city had been largely destroyed and was under Muslim control. The capture of Joscelin II left his wife struggling to carry on and defend Tel Bashir. In the end it proved too much of a challenge and she was forced to sell her estates to the Byzantine emperor, Manuel I, in return for an income for herself and her children.

## Antioch

The kings of Jerusalem held a traditional protectorate over the principalities in Syria, so, on the death of Raymond in 1149, Baldwin III travelled north to rule these areas and, perhaps, to escape from the control that his mother, Melisende, still exerted over him. The situation in Antioch was further complicated by the overlordship claimed by Manuel I and even more so by the problem of the succession.

### The problem of the succession

Constance (1128–63), Raymond's widow, had inherited Antioch from her father Bohemund II (1107/8–30). She had four young children, Maria (1145–82), Philippa (1148–78), Bohemund (1148–1201) and Baldwin (died 1176), but the Franks felt she needed the guidance of another husband. Constance begged to differ. She claimed that none of those offered to her as possible mates was worthy of her status, although William of Tyre maintained that it was her desire to live a free and independent life which motivated her. Under the laws drawn up later, but based on earlier practice, an heiress was to be given a choice of three men as possible husbands and, if none of them was suitable, three more, and if she refused them all, she could choose her own husband. Constance then asked Manuel I for his advice as her overlord. Manuel I was pleased with this opportunity to increase his influence in Antioch but he blundered. He sent his brother-in-law John Roger (died after 1166) to woo her. John Roger was middle aged and far less handsome than Raymond had been. Constance was not impressed and remained unwed.

### Council at Tripoli

In 1150 Baldwin III called a council to discuss what to do about the obstinate Constance. It was attended by Baldwin III and by Melisende, although by then they were on very bad terms. Also at the council was Hodierna (*c.*1110–*c.*1164), Melisende's sister, who was married to Raymond of Tripoli, but unhappy in the relationship. The aunts tried to persuade Constance to do as she was told but failed. They may not have tried all that hard, since neither had found marriage especially rewarding. It could also be the case that no candidate had the backing of both Baldwin III and Melisende, so Constance did not want to risk offending one of them and so reducing the amount of support she could expect from Jerusalem. Constance had some support from Aimery (died *c.*1196), the Patriarch of Antioch. He probably felt that his own power would be diminished by the arrival of a new lord in Antioch.

### Constance's choice

In 1153 Constance made her own choice. This was Reynald of Châtillon (*c.*1125–87), a dashing adventurer with no money and no following. Baldwin III gave his approval but Reynald proved to have little political ability. Aimery's fears turned out to be justified. The patriarch and Reynald fell out and Reynald had Aimery arrested. He was tied up in the sun for an entire day with his face smeared with honey, thus providing a feast for a hive of bees which were released nearby. Although Baldwin III insisted that Aimery be restored to his position, the patriarch decided he would prefer to live in Jerusalem, where he felt he would be safer. However, such struggles further undermined the unity of the State.

## Tripoli

The marital affairs of Raymond of Tripoli reached a crisis in 1152 when Hodierna refused to stay with her husband. Melisende tried to mediate and suggested that Hodierna come to Jerusalem for a time. The two women were on their way when they got the news that Raymond was dead. He had been murdered by the Assassins.

The Assassins were based in the mountains near Tortosa and saw murder as an acceptable political weapon. They were strict Shi'ites so their victims tended to be Sunni Muslims and their reasons for choosing Raymond are unknown. They owed their allegiance to Sheikh Rashid ad-Din Sinan (1132/5–93), known as the 'Old Man of the Mountains'. Their chosen weapon was the dagger and their courage was enhanced by the use of hashish, which gave them their name. The result was the need for a regency in Tripoli and a murderous assault by the Franks on the native population, both of which further weakened the State.

Hodierna returned to Tripoli with her children, Raymond (1140–87) and Melisende, and assumed the regency. Baldwin III was thus the titular regent for underage heirs in both Antioch and Tripoli. Moreover, both States in the meantime had female rulers. While these circumstances could not be helped, they did not make it any easier to defend the States from Muslim attacks as it was expected that rulers would lead their armies into battle, something that at the time was considered unheard of for women.

## Jerusalem

The tension between Melisende and her son, Baldwin III, increased. Melisende had been building up her power. In 1151 she made her younger son, Amalric (1136–74), the Count of Jaffa, which gave her control of the central section of the coast and helped her plan to isolate Baldwin in Acre. But she made an error in allowing her chief adviser to marry the wealthy widow of one of the barons. The baron had three sons who saw their inheritance melting away and so transferred their allegiance to Baldwin III. This increased support emboldened the young prince and in 1152 he requested that the patriarch crown him a second time as sole ruler of Jerusalem. When the patriarch refused, Baldwin III appeared alone in public wearing the crown, thus asserting his right to be sole ruler. A brief civil war ensued, further evidence of the divisions and weakness within the State. Melisende was forcibly removed from Jerusalem and died in 1161. Her only return to Jerusalem was in 1153 to act as regent when Baldwin III was absent.

## How powerful were the kings of Jerusalem?

Historians have argued both that the kings were and were not powerful. The study of charters has revealed that the monarchy tried its best to dominate the nobles. In the early years of the kingdom, the Crown made substantial grants of land to the nobles, but, as time went on, much of this land reverted to the king. Many nobles died, others were bankrupted by the heavy defence costs. The king could thus reward his own supporters with the land that came into his hands. The two largest holdings were Galilee and Jaffa, and the revolt of Hugh of Jaffa in 1134 showed the danger of letting a noble control so much land. The kings therefore tried a variety of ways to maintain their power:

- Large holdings could have smaller parcels of land hived off and given to other lords. Galilee became an example of this.
- Important holdings, such as Jaffa, were retained by the king.
- Land holdings could be widely dispersed so that no large single unit was built up by the lord.
- Royal castles could remain in the king's hands in the midst of a granted area.
- Ownership of land by the Church or the Military Orders was encouraged.
- The under-vassals of great lords paid homage directly to the king and so were prevented from joining their lords in revolt.
- The coinage emphasised the role of the king as protector of the holy places and helped to give the impression of his power.

# Other events: the capture of Ascalon

Baldwin III's absence in 1153 (see page 125) was due to his attack on Ascalon. This was the only port still in Muslim hands on the central part of the coast. Baldwin III had made long-term plans for the capture of Ascalon by continuing the policy of encircling the city which had been begun by his father, Fulk. He had built a castle on the site of the ancient city of Gaza, which blocked the route connecting Ascalon to the land ruled by the Fatimids in Egypt. In January 1153 he began the siege of Ascalon. The city resisted strongly but Baldwin persisted and it surrendered in August. The garrison were given three days in which they could leave. The plunder from Ascalon was immense and Baldwin was able to reward his men lavishly. His brother, Amalric, was made Lord of Jaffa and Ascalon, which marked an improvement in relations between the brothers as Amalric had been loyal to Melisende in the civil war. The mosque in Ascalon became the Cathedral of St Paul and a bishop was elected. But this drew protests from the Bishop of Bethlehem, who insisted that Ascalon came within his diocese, thus illustrating the tensions which arose so easily in the Crusader States.

## The consequences of the capture of Ascalon

The capture of Ascalon was an undoubted triumph for Baldwin III, but could also be seen as a mixed blessing with some unintended consequences. The port had presented no real threat to Jerusalem, but its capture drew the eyes of the king south and away from the north where the Muslims were more menacing. The realm of the Fatimids was rich and minimally fortified, a temptation to which Baldwin III succumbed. In time this was to prove disastrous as the threat to Egypt brought Nur ad-Din and later Saladin southwards (see page 133), and ended with the encirclement and fall of Jerusalem, albeit some 30 or more years later. Another result was that Baldwin III had run up large debts in mounting his attacks and this meant he was unable to send aid to the north when Nur ad-Din struck.

However, in the short term, the security of Jerusalem was improved as the Egyptians no longer had a port on the eastern Mediterranean coast. This limited the range of their naval activities as ships needed supplies of fresh water close at hand. Thus, Frankish ports were safer, and trading vessels and pilgrims could travel more securely, bringing useful income with them.

## Military stalemate in the north

Despite the success of Nur ad-Din in taking over Damascus, the crusaders continued to fight back, but with variable results. They suffered a serious defeat at Jacob's Ford in 1157 (see map on page 135) and a severe earthquake inflicted further damage. They were heartened, however, by the arrival of Count Thierry of Flanders (1099–1168), an experienced crusader who had fought in the east in 1139 and on the Second Crusade. He was related to Baldwin III as his wife was Baldwin's half-sister and he came from a wealthy noble family. As he was a pious man, devoted to the defence of the Holy Land, he was an ideal addition to the Frankish forces. He assisted Baldwin in the siege of Shaizar, a strategic crossing point on the River Orontes, taking advantage of Nur ad-Din's illness, which limited the resistance of the Muslims.

Two of the factors which often affected developments in the Crusader States then became apparent; namely the rivalry between Antioch and Jerusalem and attitudes to those seen as newcomers. Baldwin was proposing to give Shaizar to Thierry as a fief, but Reynald of Antioch objected, claiming it was his to give. Thierry refused to perform homage to Reynald, claiming he swore only homage to kings and not to mere princes. Reynald went away in disgust and the siege collapsed. This seemed to be a petty quarrel, but Reynald may have thought Baldwin's actions were a threat to Antioch's control of northern Syria. Reynald, as an outsider, was not wholly popular in Antioch. In any case, Nur ad-Din recovered from his illness, and the opportunity for further crusader gains was lost.

## Relationships with Byzantium

At this point, Manuel I was the overlord of Antioch and Raymond had travelled in 1145 to pay homage to him. Reynald took the relationship much less seriously at first and even went so far in 1156 as to raid Cyprus, part of the Byzantine Empire. The governor was killed and troops from Antioch marauded around the island. This action shocked Baldwin III of Jerusalem, who was hoping to build better links with Constantinople against their common enemies, particularly after the deterioration in relations after the Second Crusade. The restoration of a good relationship was important given the lack of military resources and supplies available to the Crusader States, particularly as aid from the west had also declined. Moreover, Baldwin III had recently become betrothed to Manuel's niece. Manuel I was infuriated and embarked on a punitive expedition to northern Syria. When Manuel reached Antioch, the unfortunate Reynald had to beg pardon and was humiliated by having to prostrate himself in the dust at Manuel's feet. Baldwin III arrived later and undertook his usual mediating role. The emperor relented and agreed to marry one of Reynald's step-daughters. The emperor and Baldwin III seem to have become genuine friends. When Baldwin III broke his arm, Manuel I acted as surgeon and set the injured bones.

There was a serious side to this tripartite alliance. In 1159 the three rulers advanced on Aleppo. Nur ad-Din did not want to risk an all-out battle and so came to terms, agreeing to release many prisoners whom he held, some since the Second Crusade. From Manuel I's point of view this was a successful undertaking. The conquest of Aleppo could have made Antioch strong enough to seek to become more independent from Byzantium. As it was, Nur ad-Din's ambitions were checked and Manuel was able to insist that an Orthodox patriarch be appointed in Antioch, one of his long-term aims.

**SUMMARY DIAGRAM**

**THE CRUSADER STATES AFTER THE SECOND CRUSADE**

**The Crusader States after the Second Crusade**

**Edessa:**

- No longer viable
- Capture of Joscelin II forced his wife to sell up

**Tripoli:**

- Raymond of Tripoli murdered by the Assassins
- Hodierna assumed the regency

**Antioch:**

- On Raymond's death in 1149, Baldwin III travelled north to fulfil this role and escape his mother, Melisende
- Further complicated by the overlordship claimed by Manuel I
- Even more complicated by the problem of the succession
- Melisende still in charge

**Jerusalem:**

- Baldwin III appeared in 1152 wearing a crown, asserting his right to be sole ruler
- Civil war
- Melisende forcibly removed from Jerusalem and died in 1161

# 3 The campaigns in Egypt

- *Why did Egypt become a target for the crusaders and with what results?*

Baldwin III died suddenly in 1163. He was only 33 and had proved an able ruler once free of his mother's control. He was childless and was succeeded by his younger brother, Amalric I. The succession did not go entirely smoothly and there was dispute among the nobility about who should rule, only settled by the prevailing power of the patriarch. The patriarch insisted that Amalric I give up his wife, Agnes, the daughter of Joscelin II of Edessa, to whom he was related. Amalric I agreed, once the legitimacy of his children was guaranteed. It may have been that there were fears among the nobles that Agnes would insist on provision for her brother, now landless, and his followers being made out of the lands of Jerusalem. The focus of the new king, aged 27, was to be Egypt. Egypt was attractive for a number of reasons:

- The Fatimid dynasty was in decline. It had lost Jerusalem in 1099 and Ascalon in 1153.
- Egypt was very wealthy and these riches would pay for troops.
- The land was fertile and therefore would provide supplies.
- The port of Alexandria on the north coast was the main port in the eastern Mediterranean.

## Egypt at the time of the Crusades

Egypt was ruled by the Shi'ite Fatimids and the dynasty was in decline. The rulers had degenerated and real power lay with the **viziers**, who were often engaged in vicious power struggles among themselves. The bureaucracy, in the hands of the Copts (Christians), was very advanced and efficient. The kings of Jerusalem had regularly targeted Egypt. Baldwin I died on his way back from an expedition there and Baldwin II had attacked in 1125. The capture of Ascalon, the frontier castle (see pages 126–7), was partly aimed at enabling crusader expansion into Egypt. In the 1160s Baldwin III was strong enough to demand tribute and he had tried to weaken the commerce of Egypt by banning the import of shipbuilding materials, an action made possible by his taking of Ascalon. The problem with the weakness of Egypt was that if the crusaders did not take it, then Nur ad-Din, a devoted Sunni, would step in and then the Crusader States would be threatened on the east and from the south by the same enemy.

**KEY TERM**

**Viziers** Chief ministers of a Muslim ruler.

## Amalric I's campaigns in Egypt

Amalric I attacked Egypt throughout the 1160s. He had much need of the wealth which a conquest might bring him, from the agriculture of the Nile valley to the alum mines (alum was an essential in the dyeing of cloth). The trade in Sudanese slaves and the exchange of goods with India on one side and Byzantium and the west on the other added to the attractions of the country. The rivalry between two aspiring viziers, Dirgham and Shawar (died 1169), led each of them to look for allies.

Nur ad-Din was much alarmed by the prospect of Christian control of Egypt and he retaliated with attacks on northern Syria, where he took the city of Harim, and then in 1164 captured Banyas in the kingdom of Jerusalem. The Muslims followed this up with a victory at Artah, in which both Bohemund III of Antioch and Raymond of Tripoli were captured. Raymond remained in prison for ten years although Bohemund was ransomed. By now the whole of the principality of Antioch east of the Orontes had been taken by the Muslims and would never be recovered by the crusaders. Another extensive earthquake in 1164 led to a temporary truce.

ONLINE EXTRAS
OCR
WWW

Learn how to write an argument rather than an assertion by completing Worksheet 27 at **www.hoddereducation.co.uk/accesstohistory/extras**

## Amalric I's efforts to gain assistance

The king needed men and money and tried a number of ways to obtain both:

- He appealed to the pope, and **Alexander III** (*c*.1100/05–81) issued papal bulls calling for a new crusade. Some French nobles responded, such as William IV of Nevers (died 1168), but he died in Acre from illness.
- He raised money in Jerusalem with a ten per cent tax on movable property.
- He even made an alliance with Shawar, the ruler of Egypt who was threatened by Nur ad-Din's general, Shirkuh (died 1169). The sultan was to pay the Christians to stay in Egypt until Shirkuh was defeated.
- In 1167 he married a niece of Manuel I at Tyre and hoped for Byzantine aid in his conquests.

**KEY FIGURE**

**Alexander III (c.1100–81)**

He was pope from 1159 to his death in 1181. He had been born in Siena and probably studied at Bologna. In 1153 he became papal chancellor and led the cardinals opposed to the German emperor, Frederick Barbarossa I. His election as pope was disputed, but over time he gained support from monarchs such as Henry II, but was still forced to spend most of his time as pope outside Rome. Disputes continued with the anti-popes until the death of Frederick Barbarossa in 1176, but even after this he faced challenges.

Amalric had some temporary success. He even briefly held Alexandria before he withdrew in 1167. But he had problems. He was very dependent on the support of the Hospitallers and his capture of the city of Bilbais was to further their aims of advancing into Egypt. Shawar, who had emerged the victor in the struggles in Egypt, was a double-crosser who made alliances both with the Franks and with Shirkuh. In 1168 the Franks were too weak to continue their campaigns but by the end of 1169 Shawar had been assassinated and Shirkuh was dead. However, the new general was Shirkuh's nephew, Saladin (1137/8–93), and a greater challenge to the crusaders.

## Conflicts at home

In Jerusalem, Amalric I faced more challenges. He was never personally popular, having a dour personality, and was regularly booed by his subjects as he went about his affairs in Jerusalem. His readiness to let his friend, Miles of Plancy (died 1174), who was the head of the administration, exert real power added to noble resentment. Amalric I eventually married Maria Comnena (*c*.1154–1208/17), the great-niece of Manuel. They had a daughter, Isabella. This increased tensions at court with the rival claims of the children of each of his marriages, each of whom had a following among the powerful and ambitious men in Jerusalem. Agnes, the discarded wife, was a further disruptive factor as she married Hugh of Ibelin (1130/3–69/71), Lord of Ramlah, in 1163. Then, after Hugh died on a pilgrimage to Compostela in 1170, she married Reynald Grenier (1130s–1202), Lord of Sidon. Thus, she had links with leading noble families and remained the mother of the likely heir to Amalric I. These complications over the succession were a continuing problem in the kingdom of Jerusalem and further weakened the State.

As Reynald of Châtillon of Antioch was in the hands of the Muslims from 1161, and Joscelin II of Edessa and Raymond III of Tripoli were captured in 1164, Amalric I was the sole free ruler of the Crusader States for much of the 1160s. Thus, he had few powerful allies on whom he could call for help.

## Appeal of Frederick, Bishop of Tyre

As the situation in the east worsened, the crusaders sent envoys of increasingly higher status to the west to beg for help, a clear indication of the weakness and concerns of the States. Frederick, Bishop of Tyre (died 1174), stressed the threat to pilgrims, to the holy places and the sufferings of the Christians in the east. Alexander III issued a new papal bull and urged people to respond with service rather than money, but neither of the main targets, Louis VII of France or Henry II of England (1133–89), reacted favourably. The main reason was the tension between them. Henry II ruled much of France and Louis hoped to remedy this situation and to benefit from crises in the Angevin lands. Henry was also embroiled in a quarrel with his Archbishop of Canterbury, Thomas Becket (*c.*1119/20–70). Bishop Frederick saw that reconciling the two parties might advance the Crusade and so tried to mediate between them. But his efforts were made fruitless by the murder of Becket in December 1170.

**ONLINE EXTRAS** OCR **WWW**

Get to grips with the strengths and weaknesses of the Crusader States by completing Worksheet 28 at **www.hoddereducation.co.uk/accesstohistory/extras**

## Appeal of Amalric I to Constantinople

In 1170 the High Court met in Jerusalem and Amalric I made clear his desire to go in person to Constantinople to ask Manuel I directly for assistance. His chronicler, William of Tyre, who wrote at the request of Amalric I, described his reception in detail, but had less to say about what was agreed. This was almost certainly because Amalric I was forced to acknowledge the suzerainty of Manuel I in some way.

**ONLINE EXTRAS** OCR **WWW**

Get to grips with assessing factors by completing Worksheet 29 at **www.hoddereducation.co.uk/accesstohistory/extras**

## Appeal of Amalric I to the Assassins

This was one of the most surprising appeals since the Assassins were Muslims, albeit Shi'ites and so persecuted by Nur ad-Din, and it shows how desperate Amalric I was.

**ONLINE EXTRAS** OCR **WWW**

Learn how to support a judgement by completing Worksheet 30 at **www.hoddereducation.co.uk/accesstohistory/extras**

## Appeal to Henry II

After the murder of Becket, Henry II had to promise to send knights to the east to serve with the Templars and to go on the Crusade himself within three years before he could be absolved. But Henry was prevented from travelling by a serious rebellion on the part of his heir, the young Henry (1155–83), and could not possibly leave his realms.

In 1174 both Nur ad-Din and Amalric I died, the latter from a sudden attack of dysentery, aged only 38.

**ONLINE EXTRAS** WWW
Pearson Edexcel

Get to grips with the concept of turning points by completing Worksheet 23 at **www.hoddereducation.co.uk/accesstohistory/extras**

## Henry II 1133–89

Henry was the son of Geoffrey of Anjou and Empress Matilda. He inherited Anjou, Maine and Normandy from his father and his claim to England from his mother. His marriage to Eleanor of Aquitaine brought him that duchy and Poitou. He ruled more of France than the French king, Louis VII, Eleanor's first husband. He became King of England in 1154 on the death of Stephen and restored law and order there ruthlessly, despite his youth. He was notorious for his red hair, his bad temper and his womanising, but he was a skilful warrior and an excellent administrator. His quarrel with Thomas Becket, Archbishop of Canterbury, and Becket's exile, return and murder, scandalised and divided Europe. Henry was forced to perform penance at Canterbury and to promise to join a crusade. His infidelity antagonised Eleanor and she joined with their sons against him. But Henry defeated the rebellion and imprisoned his wife. His plans for the division of his lands among his sons incensed his son Richard, and Philip II encouraged the rift, which was to his advantage. Henry was defeated and had to give in to all Richard's demands. He died almost alone at his castle at Chinon.

### SUMMARY DIAGRAM

**THE CAMPAIGNS IN EGYPT**

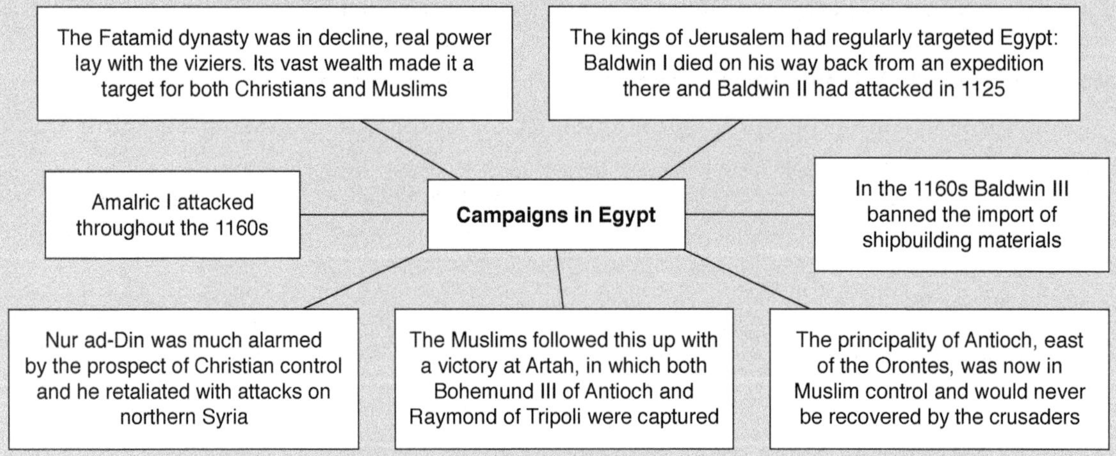

**Campaigns in Egypt**

- The Fatamid dynasty was in decline, real power lay with the viziers. Its vast wealth made it a target for both Christians and Muslims
- The kings of Jerusalem had regularly targeted Egypt: Baldwin I died on his way back from an expedition there and Baldwin II had attacked in 1125
- Amalric I attacked throughout the 1160s
- In the 1160s Baldwin III banned the import of shipbuilding materials
- Nur ad-Din was much alarmed by the prospect of Christian control and he retaliated with attacks on northern Syria
- The Muslims followed this up with a victory at Artah, in which both Bohemund III of Antioch and Raymond of Tripoli were captured
- The principality of Antioch, east of the Orontes, was now in Muslim control and would never be recovered by the crusaders

# 4 The rise of Saladin

■ *Why was Saladin able to challenge the crusaders?*

It is easy to depict the rise of Saladin as inevitable, given the problems which faced the crusader kingdoms in the late twelfth century, although it did take him thirteen years to establish his control over the Muslim lands.

## Who was Saladin?

Saladin rose to power through his family's relationships with Zengi and Nur al-Din. His father, Shirkuh, had taken control of Egypt in the years 1169–74 and in 1174 had also taken Damascus. In 1175, the caliph of Baghdad invested Saladin with the government of Egypt, Yemen and Syria. As the son of a mercenary, and as a member of a Kurdish family, Saladin was seen as an upstart by the Turkish nobility; he was therefore quick to take steps to secure greater legitimacy, marrying, for example, Nur al-Din's widow in 1176, which also helped secure his position as Nur al-Din's successor. Saladin remained keen to establish his links to Nur al-Din, installing the latter's *minbar* (pulpit), for example, in the Aqsa Mosque after his conquest of Jerusalem in 1187. He also shared Nur al-Din's concern to promote an image of piety. Saladin's commitment to the culture of *jihad* was key in this context, since it helped to legitimise his position by highlighting his spiritual merits and aligning his rule with Qur'anic models of leadership. His belief in *jihad* might have been sincere; religion mixed with politics for Saladin, Zengi and Nur al-Din. But it is striking that he established far fewer religious schools than Nur al-Din. Saladin's aim was to unify the different elements of the Muslim world to eject the Franks from the Holy Land. His particular skill lay not so much in military tactics but in the recognition that diplomacy and negotiation could be as effective as force. However, as a Sunni, he faced enemies within Islam, some of whom were motivated by concern over

### Saladin 1137/8–93

Saladin was born into a Kurdish family. His father moved to Aleppo to serve the Turkish leader, Zengi (or Zangi or Zingi), who was the governor of Syria. He went, with his uncle, Shirkuh, to fight in Egypt as part of the army of Nur ad-Din, Zengi's son. Here Shirkuh died and the vizier Shawar was assassinated, so Saladin emerged as sultan. His family connections coupled with his own abilities account for his rapid rise to power. In 1171 he ended the Fatimid caliphate and returned Egypt to Sunni rule, When Nur ad-Din died, Saladin acted as regent for his young son and gradually brought Syria and Palestine under his control. He was inspired by the concept of *jihad*, but was also a firm disciplinarian as a commander. One of his greatest victories was at Hattin in 1187 (see pages 137–41), which enabled him to overrun the kingdom of Jerusalem and take the city. He seemed totally triumphant, but he could not take Tyre and the extent of his victories led to the Third Crusade and much bitter warfare. His troops were raised by feudal levies and so could be reluctant to fight at times. Moreover, Richard I was a worthy opponent. Eventually, the crusaders retired, still in possession of a foothold on the coast, and Saladin retreated to Damascus, where he died. His family continued to rule Egypt until the Mamluks took it in 1250.

his expansion from Egypt into Syria. Others believed that he might have been exploiting *jihad* to further his own ambitions. It was believed that he made treaties with the crusaders to enable him to deal with co-religionist rivalries.

## Saladin's challenges to the crusaders

Saladin had to deal with resistance from Aleppo, where Nur ad-Din's family dominated, and from Shi'ites like the Assassins. His position had been strengthened by being recognised by the Sunni caliph of Baghdad as the ruler of Egypt, Yemen and Syria. He also dealt firmly with the Assassins, who tried twice to kill him, by destroying their fortifications and ravaging their lands. He then took control of Damascus in 1174.

As with the divisions among Muslims, so there were divisions among Christians. To understand these divisions, some background to Baldwin IV is needed.

### Baldwin IV

Baldwin IV (see below) was a child of thirteen when his father, Baldwin III died, so a regent had to be appointed, which meant the weakness of a minority, while Baldwin IV himself unfortunately was a leper. The extent of his illness was not realised in 1174, or he might have been passed over as ruler. Raymond III of Tripoli, Baldwin IV's closest male relation, was chosen as regent. Raymond had spent ten years as a prisoner of the Muslims and thus was something of an outsider in Jerusalem. Raymond III was the patron of William of Tyre, the chronicler, who gives a very favourable portrayal of Raymond. Baldwin IV came of age in 1176 and Raymond III returned to Tripoli. The young king renewed the alliance with Byzantium and planned yet another attack on Egypt.

As Baldwin IV's illness took hold he became blind and the bacteria destroyed his nose. Eventually, he lost the use of his arms and legs and had to be carried in a litter. It was thus vital to find a husband for Sibylla (*c*.1160–90), his sister. The choice fell on William, son of the Count of Montferrat (died 1177), who came from a crusading family and was related to the French kings. He married

## Baldwin IV 1161–85

Baldwin was educated by William of Tyre, who noticed when Baldwin was only nine that the boy had no feeling in one of his arms. Doctors were consulted but were reluctant to diagnose leprosy as knights and nobles afflicted with the disease were expected to join the Knights of St Lazarus. He succeeded his father in 1174 when he was thirteen and Raymond of Tripoli acted as regent. Despite his illness and increasing disfigurement, he was a good horseman and an intrepid fighter. He held Saladin back in five attacks and won an unexpected victory when he made a sortie from Ascalon, where he was under siege, and defeated Saladin at Mont Gisard. He continued the alliance with Byzantium against the Turks. In 1179 he was unhorsed resisting another invasion, which probably was the result of his increasing poor health, and by 1182 he could not ride and led his troops from a litter. But even in 1183, when the High Court of Jerusalem refused to follow Guy de Lusignan as their commander, he went to relieve the siege of Kerak and Saladin withdrew at his approach. In that year he crowned his nephew as Baldwin V with Raymond of Tripoli and Joscelin III of Courtenay as regents. His character appears in the 2005 Ridley Scott film *Kingdom of Heaven*.

Sibylla in 1176, but died a year later. Sibylla was pregnant and so unable to be regent when Baldwin IV became ill again. The unlikely new regent was Reynald of Châtillon, now released by the Muslims, as Manuel I had paid much of his ransom. He planned to invade Egypt in collaboration with the Byzantines and Philip I of Flanders (1143–91), who was a cousin of Baldwin IV. Philip I had come east in 1177, hoping to find a bride among the princesses who would have a claim to the throne if Baldwin IV died childless. But the expedition fell apart even before it had begun, in disputes over who would rule Egypt when it was taken. The Greeks went home in disgust and Philip I went off to fight in Syria.

The unstable conditions on both Christian and Muslim sides were reflected in a two-year truce agreed in 1180. William of Tyre lamented that, for the first time, the terms of the truce were concluded on equal terms, and this showed the declining impact of the crusaders. A further destabilising factor came with the death of Manuel I in 1180. He left an eleven-year-old son, for whom his mother, Maria, was to be regent. Maria was the daughter of Constance of Antioch and so, for the time being, the Byzantine Empire remained friendly towards the crusaders.

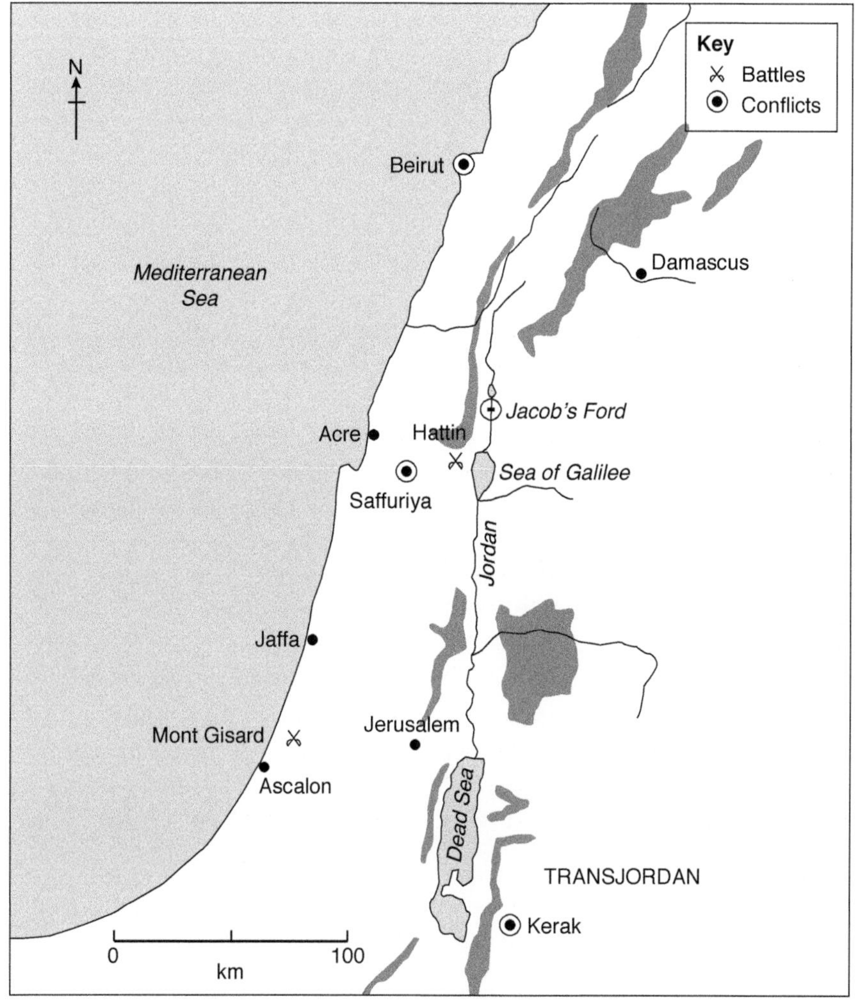


**Figure 6.1** Sites of battles and conflicts in the Middle East between the crusaders and Muslims in the years between 1174 and 1187.

## Saladin and Baldwin IV at Mont Gisard

In 1178 Saladin suffered a rare defeat at the hands of Baldwin IV and Reynald at Mont Gisard, near Ibelin, when he was caught unawares. His army had heavy casualties and many were taken prisoner. The Christians also had heavy losses, but Baldwin IV had shown that he was not entirely useless. The victory raised morale but may also have convinced observers in the west that the situation in the east was not as dismal as the crusaders tried to suggest. Saladin was convinced, as a result, that the forces of Syria and Egypt were not enough to defeat the Christians. To do that, he needed the support of Mosul and Aleppo.

**KEY FIGURE**

**Guy de Lusignan (c.1150–94)**

Guy was from a noble Poitevin family, who had been involved in earlier crusades. He went to the Near East following a summons from his brothers, who saw him as a possible consort for the widowed sister and heiress of Baldwin IV, Sibylla. They married, and in 1186 took over the kingship from the dead Baldwin V. The following year Guy led the crusader forces at Hattin, where they were defeated. He was released by Saladin in 1188 and soon began the siege of Acre. In 1190, with Sibylla's death, any claims he had to the throne came to an end. However, he was later recompensed with Cyprus, where he died.

**ONLINE EXTRAS**
Pearson Edexcel WWW

Get to grips with the concepts of similarity and difference by completing Worksheet 24 at **www.hoddereducation.co.uk/accesstohistory/extras**

### Jordan 1179

The crusaders, buoyed up by their success, began to build a castle, at Jacob's Ford, on the River Jordan. This was extremely expensive and used up vast resources, but the hope was that it would protect the approaches to Jerusalem. However, as it was only 80 kilometres from Damascus it was seen as a provocative act. It was to be garrisoned by 80 Templars and could hold up to 1000 fighting men. Saladin saw how threatening this was and made a huge effort to take it, capturing it in five days. Recent excavations at the site, and the discovery of the remains of some of the troops, reveal some vicious wounds and testify to the brutality of the warfare. The Templars were all executed when the castle was captured.

### Back in Jerusalem

Sibylla's child by William had been a boy, another Baldwin. The nobles now felt that she should marry again to provide a spare heir. This led to further divisions in Jerusalem over the best choice. Raymond III of Tripoli, who was Lord of Galilee as a result of his marriage and so a key baron in the kingdom, and Bohemund of Antioch came to Jerusalem and pressed for Sibylla to marry one of Raymond's men. Baldwin IV, although unwell again, saw this as a threat to his crown and arranged very rapidly for Sibylla to wed **Guy de Lusignan** (*c*.1150–94), a newly arrived French knight. Such was the urgency in his view that they were married during Holy Week 1180. The resulting tensions between Raymond III and Guy only added to the factions now dominating the court. Guy was from Poitou and his brother, Aimery, was a close associate of the family of Agnes Courtenay. He may even have been her lover (her personal life was vivid and notorious, at least according to William of Tyre). Their party now placed their nominees in all the key posts, Heraclius (*c*.1128–90/1) the Archbishop of Jerusalem, and another of Agnes' alleged lovers, becoming the patriarch, and Guy receiving extensive lands. But all this intrigue and instability did not make for a kingdom which could defend itself well against a skilled general like Saladin.

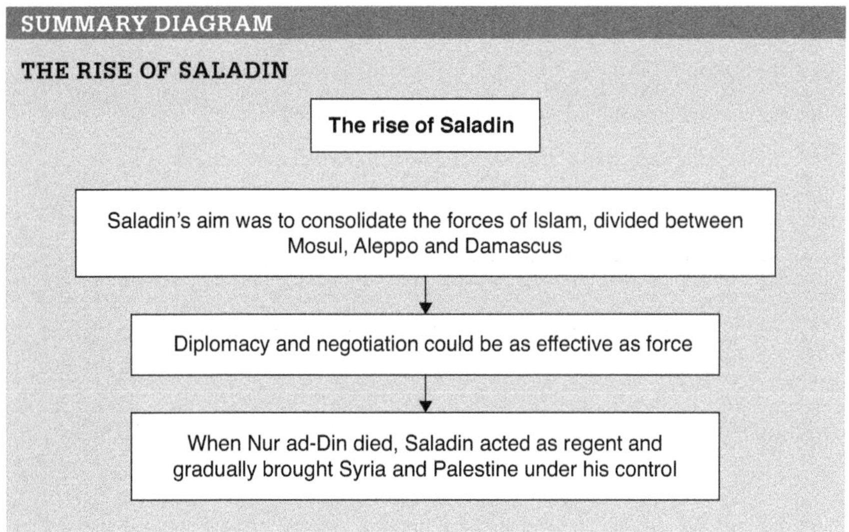

SUMMARY DIAGRAM
THE RISE OF SALADIN
The rise of Saladin
Saladin's aim was to consolidate the forces of Islam, divided between Mosul, Aleppo and Damascus
Diplomacy and negotiation could be as effective as force
When Nur ad-Din died, Saladin acted as regent and gradually brought Syria and Palestine under his control


# 5 The victory of Saladin at Hattin and his conquest of Jerusalem

- *How far were internal or external factors the key to the crusaders' defeat at Hattin in 1187?*

Saladin's victory at Hattin in 1187 was hardly unexpected, after the events of the 1180s:

- In 1183 Saladin finally occupied Aleppo. In the autumn he campaigned in Galilee and then besieged the castle of Kerak.
- Also in 1183, a raid by Reynald of Châtillon had even reached as far as the Red Sea and disrupted the annual pilgrimage to Mecca. Saladin's fury at this bold move was shown when he took two of the captured Franks to Mecca and ritually cut their throats in front of an approving crowd.
- In 1186 he took Mosul and thus completed his encirclement of the crusader territories. A truce he had made with the Christians had given him the chance to pursue his goal of uniting the Muslims undisturbed.

However, the continued factional strife in Jerusalem was also a factor in preventing any kind of realistic resistance being mounted against Saladin.

## Background to the Battle of Hattin

There was a complicated series of events that led up to the battle in 1187. These are outlined in Table 6.1 (see page 138).

**Table 6.1** Timeline leading to the Battle of Hattin

| Year | Event |
|---|---|
| 1183 | Baldwin IV appeared to be dying and appointed Guy de Lusignan as his regent<br>Guy was blamed for the limited challenge to Saladin<br>Guy was stripped of the regency and Baldwin's nephew, also Baldwin, aged five, named instead. Raymond III of Tripoli commanded the army<br>Guy refused to go quietly and, with Sibylla, held out in Ascalon |
| 1184 | Baldwin IV had a relapse and Raymond III of Tripoli became regent. He was to rule for ten years until young Baldwin came of age. If Baldwin died in the meantime, an international panel would assess the rights of Sibylla (daughter of Amalric I by his wife Agnes of Courtenay) and Isabella (1172–1205) (daughter of Amalric I by his second wife Maria Comnena) |
| 1185 | Baldwin IV died. Raymond III remained as regent for Baldwin V |
| 1186 | Baldwin V died. Raymond III hoped to be elected king but Sibylla outmanoeuvred him and was made queen, with the support of the patriarch and the Templar leader. Sibylla agreed to divorce Guy as long as she was given a free choice about whom she should marry next. She then surprised everyone by choosing Guy. Raymond III proposed that the husband of Isabella, Humphrey of Toron (*c.*1166–98), should be king and the Ibelins backed him, but Humphrey would not agree, leaving Raymond III isolated. As a result Raymond III left to take service under Bohemund III of Antioch (*c.*1148–1201) leaving Guy and Sibylla as king and queen |

## The campaign of 1187

Guy had made a truce with Saladin but this was broken in 1186, when Reynald of Châtillon attacked a caravan travelling from Egypt to Damascus. Saladin demanded compensation and Guy agreed but Reynald refused to obey. This made war inevitable. Raymond III of Tripoli remained adamant in his opposition to Guy and renewed his truce with Saladin, which included his wife's lands in Galilee. Guy sent a deputation to Raymond III, which included Gerard of Ridfort (died 1189), Grand Master of the Templars, who was a personal enemy of Raymond III and whose agreement to any settlement was vital. At the same time, a Muslim force under Saladin's son was crossing Galilee with Raymond III's permission and the two forces met, unintentionally, at Cresson, where most of the Templars were killed. Raymond III blamed himself for this tragedy and thus made his peace with Guy.

Saladin was able to call on troops from Aleppo and Mosul, and his army was the largest he had ever commanded. Guy summoned all his vassals to meet at Acre. The Templars and Hospitallers sent virtually their entire knightly forces. The Templars even released the funds sent by Henry II of England as part of his penance after the murder of Becket, which were meant to be awaiting the English king's arrival to crusade. This allowed more mercenaries to be hired. Even Bohemund III of Antioch sent troops in the end. The relic of the True Cross was brought from the Holy Sepulchre, but not by Heraclius, who claimed to be too ill but was generally believed to be enjoying the favours of his latest mistress. The Bishop of Tyre was entrusted with the most sacred relic.

Saladin crossed the Jordan on 1 July and his troops attacked and took Tiberias on the Sea of Galilee. Raymond III's wife and children were in the castle at Tiberias and held out there, sending increasingly frantic messages to Raymond III. King Guy then came to a disastrous decision:

- In council at Acre, Raymond III argued that the summer heat made an attack very unwise and that Saladin would soon have to withdraw. Reynald and Gerard took the opposite view and accused Raymond III of being in Saladin's pay. Guy agreed with Reynald and Gerard.
- Guy decided to attack. His troops camped at a well-watered site. Guy recalled that four years earlier he had refused to advance against the Muslims from such a site and been condemned as a coward. This time would be different, he hoped.
- Guy changed his mind. Despite the plight of Raymond III's wife, Raymond III persisted in his advice not to advance, and this time Guy agreed.
- Guy changed his mind again. Gerard, the Grand Master of the Templars, came to Guy at night and persuaded Guy to reverse his decision.
- Guy attacked. On 3 July the crusaders left their well-watered camp and marched on Tiberias across the Galilean hills. Saladin waited at Hattin, a village where the road came down to the Sea of Galilee.

Catastrophe ensued. The heat meant that the crusader army was desperate for water and forced to halt on the slopes of a rocky hill called the Horns of Hattin. The well there was dry. Saladin's army set fire to the scrub on the hill and so the Christians had to face the smoke along with their thirst. Overnight Saladin surrounded Guy's forces. Guy's troops fought as best they could, charging the enemy. Raymond III of Tripoli's men rode at the Muslims, who opened their ranks to let them through and then closed up. Thus, Raymond III was cut off from the battle and could take no further part. He retreated to Tripoli.

Guy and his officers moved to the top of the hill and, when the Muslims finally reached them, the Christians were so exhausted that they were lying defenceless on the ground. They were taken to Saladin, who personally gave Guy water. But Saladin saw Reynald as an enemy and attacked Reynald before his bodyguard finished the job, cutting off Reynald's head. The other barons were treated with respect but the Templars and Hospitallers were all slaughtered, apart from Gerard the Grand Master. The lesser folk were sold in the slave market, where this sudden glut of prisoners brought prices down to a very low level. The Bishop of Tyre had died and the True Cross was lost forever.

**ONLINE EXTRAS** WWW
AQA

Learn how to assess the importance of an individual by completing Worksheet 24 at **www.hoddereducation.co.uk/accesstohistory/extras**

**ONLINE EXTRAS** WWW
OCR

Learn how to plan an effective essay by completing Worksheet 31 at **www.hoddereducation.co.uk/accesstohistory/extras**

## Why were the crusaders defeated at Hattin?

A further cause of the defeat at Hattin was the failure of deputations to the west. In 1181 the Templars had sent envoys to Alexander III and he appealed to Philip II of France (1165–1223) (Louis VII died in 1180) and to Henry II of England. The pope blamed poor leadership for the problems in the east and considered Baldwin IV's leprosy to be the result of the sinfulness of the settlers. But Philip II, as a new king, and Henry, as an old one, did not respond positively.

In 1184 the crusaders tried again, sending Heraclius himself along with the masters of the Templars and Hospitallers. But, for a second time, neither Philip nor Henry would commit to a crusade, although they sent money. A few crusaders did arrive in response but were disillusioned to discover that a truce had been made with Saladin. Apart from the situation in western Europe throughout the 1170s and 1180s which prevented kings from going crusading, there was some feeling that the settlers in the east were too accommodating towards Islam. The easy everyday relationships and the trade and other contacts between Christians and Muslims surprised and sometimes appalled western visitors, who failed to appreciate the realities of the situation.

**ONLINE EXTRAS**
Pearson Edexcel WWW

Learn how to analyse the effectiveness of key individuals by completing Worksheet 25 at **www.hoddereducation.co.uk/accesstohistory/extras**

### The situation in western Europe

Henry II, the Angevin King of England, and the King of France, Louis VII and then Philip Augustus, were bitter enemies and did not trust each other and, therefore, were unwilling to leave their lands. Henry had married Louis' first wife, Eleanor of Aquitaine, which caused resentment between the two. The two kings were reconciled in 1170, but then Thomas Becket, Archbishop of Canterbury, was murdered by some of Henry's knights. Henry was condemned for encouraging the murder and that ended the feeling of unity, which prevented them both from departing.

The penance imposed by the pope on Henry was to provide knights for the Holy Land. But yet again, as he was about to depart for the Holy Land in 1174, he faced a rebellion at home led by his eldest son, Henry the Younger. The rebellion was supported by Henry the Younger's brothers, Henry II's wife and Louis.

Finally, when there was a further appeal for help in 1181, Henry II was worried that as he was the closest male heir to Baldwin, he would be forced to stay for years. He was also concerned that the new King of France, Philip Augustus, was scheming with Henry's sons to recover lands in France and, therefore, was unwilling to depart.

## Other factors in the defeat at Hattin: no help from Byzantium

Furthermore, the change in the outlook of Byzantium meant that no help could be expected from the eastern empire. Events in Constantinople were as fast moving as in Jerusalem and similarly complex. Manuel I, who died in 1180, had held his empire together by his own determination, but had failed to make provision for the future. He had believed a prophecy which claimed that he had fourteen more years to live and rule. The new emperor was Alexius II (1169–83), aged eleven. His mother was Maria (1152–82), the daughter of Constance of Antioch and so associated with the Latins. This did not make her more popular in Constantinople, where the destructive passage of crusaders had twice disrupted the city, while the Italian merchants who lived there were becoming rich on the trade they controlled. Maria was advised by Alexius Comnenus, a nephew of her husband, who was also rumoured to be her lover.

The opposition found a leader in Andronicus Comnenus (*c*.1118–85), a cousin of Manuel I, who rallied support and in 1182 reached Constantinople, where the people had already risen and murdered all the Italians they could find. He rapidly took control. Alexius II was imprisoned and blinded. Maria was strangled and then Alexius II was murdered. Andronicus became emperor aged 62 and married Alexius II's widow, Alice of France (1171–1204 at least), who was twelve. Andronicus saw his chief enemies as being in Europe, namely in Sicily and Germany, so he wanted to secure his eastern frontiers. Thus, he made a treaty with Saladin, promising Saladin a free hand against the Franks in return for protection from the Seljuk Turks. However, in 1185 Andronicus was overthrown in turn by his cousin, Isaac Angelos (1156–1204), who proved to be an ineffectual ruler.

## Other factors in the defeat at Hattin: no help from Antioch

This sudden decline in the power of Byzantium left the crusaders without an ally who could harass Saladin from the west. It also led Bohemund III of Antioch to abandon his Greek wife and marry a lady of doubtful reputation in Antioch. This action brought the rage of the patriarch, Aimery, down on him and Heraclius had to come to Antioch to broker a peace. Those of Bohemund III's nobles who disliked his marriage the most fled to the Prince of Cilicia in Asia Minor, who took the opportunity of unrest in Antioch to extend his own territories. Bohemund III felt it wise under the circumstances to make a truce with Saladin.

**ONLINE EXTRAS** WWW
AQA

Get to grips with making links across the period by completing Worksheet 25 at **www.hoddereducation.co.uk/accesstohistory/extras**

**ONLINE EXTRAS** WWW
AQA

Test your understanding of continuity and change across the period by completing Worksheet 26 at **www.hoddereducation.co.uk/accesstohistory/extras**

**ONLINE EXTRAS** WWW
OCR

Learn how to assess the role of factors by completing Worksheet 32 at **www.hoddereducation.co.uk/accesstohistory/extras**

**ONLINE EXTRAS** WWW
Pearson Edexcel

Learn how to address the concept of significance by completing Worksheet 26 at **www.hoddereducation.co.uk/accesstohistory/extras**

**ONLINE EXTRAS** WWW
AQA

Get to grips with exam-style questions by completing Worksheet 27 at **www.hoddereducation.co.uk/accesstohistory/extras**

## The fall of Jerusalem

The aftermath of Hattin brought more disaster to the crusaders. There were few men left to resist Saladin, so he was able to capture forts and castles, numbering 52 according to one account. Saladin kept his word when terms of surrender were agreed, which encouraged defenders to give in. He took Acre and Ascalon and, after a fortnight's siege, Jerusalem. The inhabitants were mostly allowed to pay a ransom and leave. The al-Aqsa Mosque was reinstated, but some Christian services continued to be held in the Church of the Holy Sepulchre and pilgrims were still allowed to visit. All that remained under the rule of the crusaders were the cities of Tripoli, Antioch and Tyre, and the castles belonging to the Templars and Hospitallers in Tripoli. Saladin's reaction is reflected in Source B.

**SOURCE QUESTION**

In what ways is the celebration in Source B by Saladin similar to crusaders' reactions to successes?

**SOURCE B**

**From a letter from Saladin about the fall of Jerusalem, quoted in S.J. Allen and Emilie Ant, editors, *The Crusades: A Reader*, University of Toronto Press, 2010, p. 162.**

*The land of Jerusalem has become pure … God is become one God and he was three. The houses of the infidel are cast down. The Muslims have taken possession of the fortified castles. Our enemies will not return to them for they are branded with the seal of weakness and degradation. God has placed beauty where deformity was … The servant [Saladin] will change the weeds of error for the good seed of the true faith. He will cast down the crosses of the churches and will cause the summons to prayer to be heard. He will change altars into pulpits and of churches he will make mosques … God has driven them out of this territory and has cast them down. He has favoured the partisans of the truth and has shown his anger against the infidels … The word of God has been exalted. The tombs of the prophets which the infidels had stained have been purified.*

Raymond III of Tripoli died in late 1187 and left his country to Raymond, the son of Bohemund III of Antioch. Bohemund III, however, transferred it to his second son, another Bohemund, fearing that Tripoli and Antioch would be too much for one man to defend. Guy was joined by Sibylla in prison and Saladin released them both some time in 1188. Saladin's exploits were lauded in the works of his secretary, Imad ad-Din al-Isfahani, and his friend, Baha' ad-Din Ibn Shaddad. He stressed his role as the heir to Nur ad-Din's *jihad* by placing Nur ad-Din's **minbar** in the al-Aqsa mosque in Jerusalem as Nur ad-Din had wanted.

**KEY TERM**

**Minbar** A pulpit from which sermons are preached in the mosque.

In Europe, the news of the fall of Jerusalem was received with horror and disbelief. Pope Urban III (*c.*1105–87) was said to have died from the shock. Inevitably, a new crusade was proposed.

**SUMMARY DIAGRAM**

**THE VICTORY OF SALADIN AT HATTIN AND HIS CONQUEST OF JERUSALEM**

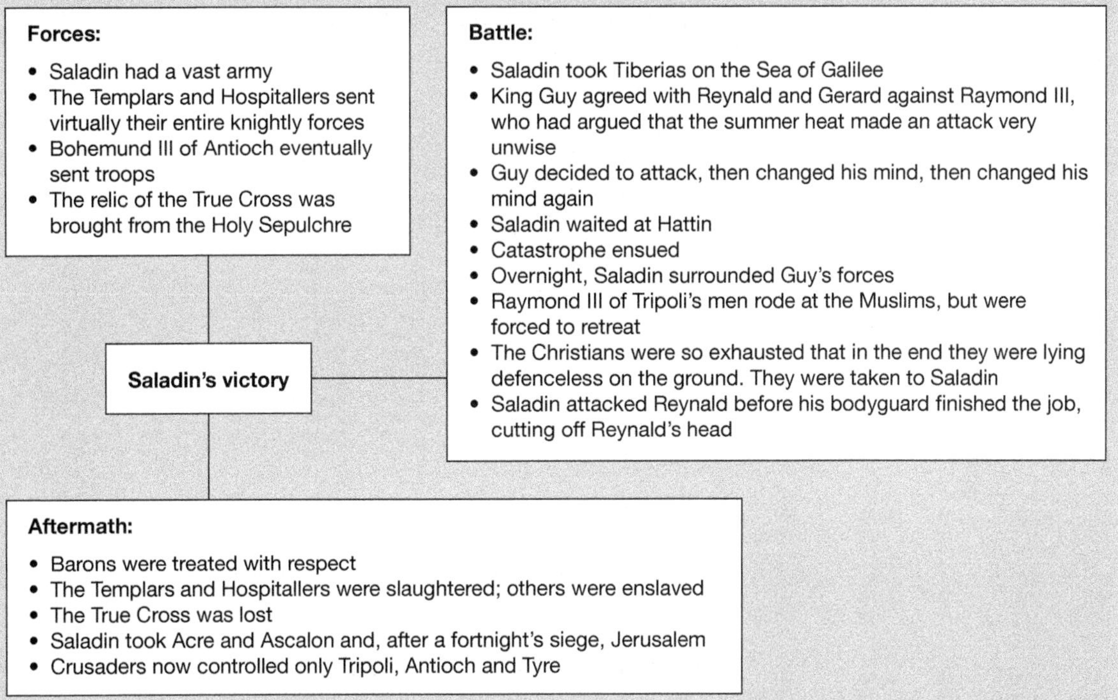

**Forces:**

- Saladin had a vast army
- The Templars and Hospitallers sent virtually their entire knightly forces
- Bohemund III of Antioch eventually sent troops
- The relic of the True Cross was brought from the Holy Sepulchre

**Battle:**

- Saladin took Tiberias on the Sea of Galilee
- King Guy agreed with Reynald and Gerard against Raymond III, who had argued that the summer heat made an attack very unwise
- Guy decided to attack, then changed his mind, then changed his mind again
- Saladin waited at Hattin
- Catastrophe ensued
- Overnight, Saladin surrounded Guy's forces
- Raymond III of Tripoli's men rode at the Muslims, but were forced to retreat
- The Christians were so exhausted that in the end they were lying defenceless on the ground. They were taken to Saladin
- Saladin attacked Reynald before his bodyguard finished the job, cutting off Reynald's head

**Saladin's victory**

**Aftermath:**

- Barons were treated with respect
- The Templars and Hospitallers were slaughtered; others were enslaved
- The True Cross was lost
- Saladin took Acre and Ascalon and, after a fortnight's siege, Jerusalem
- Crusaders now controlled only Tripoli, Antioch and Tyre

# 6 Key debate

*How should Saladin be viewed?*

The debate about Saladin is well outlined in Jonathan Phillips' book (2019), where he explains that views of Saladin largely varied according to who was writing about him. Contemporary Muslim writers who knew Saladin personally praised his virtues; Ibn al-Athir, who was sympathetic to Zengi's dynasty, was critical of him. Shi'ite authors, too, have criticised Saladin for ending the Fatimid caliphate of north Africa. More recent Arab perspectives have seen Saladin as a hero who united the Muslim world in an effort to liberate Jerusalem and Palestine from the invading crusaders. In modern historiography, he became an icon of Arab nationalism, with leaders from Nasser to Saddam Hussein lauding his achievements and using his name to keep alive the memory of the crusading era. In the west, Saladin received much praise for his chivalrous qualities from near-medieval contemporaries: Dante gives Saladin a place among the virtuous non-Christians in the First Circle of Hell. In addition, nineteenth-century authors writing heavily romanticised accounts of the crusades, such as Walter Scott in *The Talisman* (1825) and Stanley Lane-Poole in *Saladin and the Fall of*

*Jerusalem* (1898), portrayed Saladin in a similar way. One reason for western versions being more favourable is that Richard I, one of the foremost warriors of his day, was unable to defeat Saladin and so the sultan was endowed with special powers to account for this failure.

Modern interpretations by historians recognise that Saladin was not a perfect military commander. He showed his shortcomings at Mont Gisard, Tyre, Acre, Arsuf and Jaffa. He could be savage, as in his treatment of rebels in Egypt or towards Reynald of Châtillon and the Military Orders after Hattin. Against this are his impressive victory at Hattin and his capture of Jerusalem, which makes him such a hero for the Arabs, alongside his many acts of generosity.

A more hostile view comes from Andrew Ehrenkreutz, an American scholar writing in 1977, who deplored Saladin's rule in Egypt as merely exploiting the situation for his own selfish ambitions. He further denigrated the sultan as an opportunist who was ready to abandon religious principles for political expediency.

Recent research has focused on exploration of a wide range of sources, many of them translated from Arabic for the first time, so that interpretations of Saladin continue to evolve.

Extract 1 outlines views of Saladin in Europe after the defeat of the Crusader States at the Battle of Hattin.

**INTERPRETATION QUESTION**

Which of these two extracts, Extract 1 or 2, provides the more convincing interpretation of the role of Saladin in the years 1182–93?

### EXTRACT 1

**From Jonathan Phillips, *The Life and Legend of the Sultan Saladin*, Bodley Head, 2019, p. 317.**

*An angry and vicious Latin poem presented the sultan as a man of lowly origins, also responsible for the murders of the Fatimid caliph plus Nur al-Din and his son as well as the rape of Nur al-Din's wife … The opening chapters of one of the earliest accounts of the Third Crusade, the* Itinerarium peregrinorum, *accused the sultan of living off the earnings of prostitutes in Damascus and killing the caliph: he was characterised as a fortuitous, opportunistic chancer. Saladin was often described as a stick, a scourge sent by God to beat the Christians for their sins or, as one writer put it, if Nur al-Din was a stick, then Saladin was a hammer. To compound these spiritual matters, the sultan's victories in the Holy Land prompted the kings of England and France to launch the 'Saladin Tithe', a punishing 10% levy on revenues and movables; to have one's name attached to a major tax rarely constitutes an attractive legacy.*

**ONLINE EXTRAS** AQA **WWW**

Develop your analysis of historical interpretations by completing Worksheet 28 at **www.hoddereducation.co.uk/accesstohistory/extras**

Extract 2 has a more favourable view of Saladin.

### EXTRACT 2

**From Steven Runciman, *A History of the Crusades, Volume III*, Penguin Books, 2016, first published 1954, p. 65.**

*Of all the great figures of the Crusading era Saladin is the most attractive. He had his faults. In his rise to power he showed a cunning and ruthlessness that fitted ill with his later reputation. In the interests of policy he never shrank from bloodshed.*

**ONLINE EXTRAS** AQA **WWW**

Develop your analysis of interpretations by completing Worksheet 29 at **www.hoddereducation.co.uk/accesstohistory/extras**

*He slew Reynald of Châtillon, whom he hated, with his own hand. But when he was severe it was for the sake of his people and his faith. He was a devout Muslim. However kindly he felt towards his Christian friends, he knew that their souls were doomed to perdition. Yet he respected their ways and thought of them as fellow-men. Unlike the Crusader potentates, he never broke his word when it was pledged to anyone, whatever his religion. For all his fervour, he was always courteous and generous, merciful as a conqueror and a judge, as a master considerate and tolerant. Though some of his emirs might resent him as a Kurdish parvenu and though preachers in the West might call him Antichrist, there were very few of his subjects that did not feel for him respect and devotion, and few of his enemies could withhold admiration from him.*

**ONLINE EXTRAS** WWW
Pearson Edexcel

Develop your analysis of interpretations by completing Worksheet 27 at **www.hoddereducation.co.uk/accesstohistory/extras**

# CHAPTER SUMMARY

Although the Muslims defeated the crusaders at Hattin and took back Jerusalem, this should not be seen as inevitable. The crusaders did not lack ability or courage but they suffered from a series of problems which, when taken together, were too much for them. These included a run of succession problems among the ruling families which led to disunity and rivalries among the feudal nobility, who often put their own interests before those of the States. Other factors contributed, such as coming up against two skilful Muslim leaders in Nur ad-Din and Saladin, who were both inspired by the idea of *jihad*. Moreover, the refusal of monarchs in Europe to become involved in sending aid to the east and the chaotic circumstances in Byzantium, where the authority of the emperors was severely challenged, made the situation for the crusaders worse. The antics of men such as Reynald of Châtillon and Raymond III of Tripoli were extremely unhelpful and represented the way in which some of the settlers put their own interests before the common good. Guy de Lusignan tried his best to hold on to Jerusalem but could not overcome all the circumstances which piled up against him.

## Refresher questions

Use these questions to remind yourself of the key material covered in this chapter.

**1** What was the impact of *jihad* on the crusading movement?

**2** What were the main achievements of Nur ad-Din?

**3** How damaging was the rift between Melisende and Baldwin III?

**4** What were the results of the capture of Ascalon?

**5** Why did Amalric attack Egypt?

**6** What were Saladin's strengths as a leader?

**7** Why was aid from Europe not given?

**8** What advantages did Saladin have at Hattin?

## Question practice: AQA

### Essay questions

**1** To what extent was the weakness of the Fatimids the main reason for the rise of Islamic power in the years 1144–87? [A level]

**EXAM HINT** You will need to analyse the various factors that explain the rise of Islamic power, and assess how important the given factor was in relation to them all. Outline your overall argument in the introductory paragraph.

**2** 'The loss of Jerusalem was due to divisions among the Franks.' Assess the validity of this view with reference to the years 1164–87. [A level]

**EXAM HINT** Analyse the given statement and then consider other possible factors. Make sure you have a clear overall plan and effective judgement.

## Question practice: OCR

### Essay questions

**1** Which of the following was of greater importance in Muslim/Arab advances before the Third Crusade? i) Nur ad-Din. ii) Saladin. Explain your answer with reference to both i) and ii). [A level]

**EXAM HINT** The importance of the two individuals in Muslim/Arab advances before the Third Crusade should be explained and a supported judgement reached as to which was more important.

**2** How important were internal divisions within the Crusader States in bringing about their decline? [A level]

**EXAM HINT** Responses should consider a range of reasons for the decline of the States. A good paragraph should be written on internal divisions, analysing the role they played before considering other issues, such as Muslim strengths. A judgement as to the relative importance of the factors should be reached.

## Question practice: Pearson Edexcel

### Essay question

**1** To what extent was Saladin's military leadership the main reason for the Muslim recapture of Jerusalem in 1187? [A level]

**EXAM HINT** Examine Nur ad-Din's successes from 1149, and Saladin's growing power in Egypt, noting the importance of his victory at Hattin. Compare Muslim success with the growing weakness and divisions among the Crusader States, and the succession crisis from 1185.

# CHAPTER 7

# The Third Crusade

The events of 1187 led to a revived crusading movement in Europe. This involved better financing, often through taxation, and greater emphasis on the redeeming power of the True Cross. The Third Crusade was notable for the quality of its leadership and for its military achievements, although these fell short of reconquering Jerusalem. This chapter examines the events leading up to the Third Crusade and its outcome by focusing on the following themes:

- The preaching of the Third Crusade
- The roles of Frederick Barbarossa, Philip II and Richard I in the Third Crusade
- The results of the Third Crusade

The key debate on page 164 of this chapter asks the question: What did the Third Crusade achieve?

**KEY DATES**

| | |
|---|---|
| **1187** | Papal bull *Audita tremendi* (*On hearing with what terrible [and severe judgement]*) issued by Gregory VIII |
| **1189** | Siege of Jerusalem by King Guy |
| | Departure of Frederick Barbarossa |
| **1190** | Death of Frederick Barbarossa |
| | Departure of Philip II and Richard I |
| **1191** | Capture of Acre and return home of Philip II |
| **1192** | Failure to take Jerusalem |
| | Battle of Jaffa |
| | Truce between Richard I and Saladin, and return home of Richard I |

## 1 The preaching of the Third Crusade

*Why was the preaching of the Crusade greeted with such a favourable response?*

There was some very rapid reactions to the fall of Jerusalem. The first of these, even before Pope Gregory VIII's papal bull was published, came from Conrad of Montferrat (died 1192), a powerful nobleman from northern Italy, who was related to William, who had been briefly married to Sibylla (see page 138). Conrad landed at Tyre and was instrumental in preventing the city from falling to Saladin. This meant the Christians maintained a port, which would be useful for bringing in both troops and supplies and which could be a way in to the Levant. While King Guy was still in captivity, Conrad took control of what remained of the kingdom of Jerusalem. His exploits were celebrated in the ballads of the wandering troubadours and used as an example to encourage others to follow. Some did, and William II of Sicily (1153–89), a fleet from Pisa and a fleet from England all arrived over the next months.

### Key figures of the Third Crusade

Pope Gregory VIII
Frederick Barbarossa
Philip II
Richard I
Saladin

## The *Audita tremendi* 1187

Pope Gregory VIII issued the *Audita tremendi* (*On hearing with what terrible [and severe judgement]*) in October 1187. This was within ten days of his election as pope, suggesting that it had actually been drawn up before the death of Urban earlier in the month. The papacy responded very rapidly to the loss of the Holy City (see page 142) as news had reached Rome of its fall through merchants from Genoa and they had been followed swiftly by Joscius, the Archbishop of Tyre. Joscius arrived in ships with black sails and drawings showing Saladin's horses stabled in the Church of the Holy Sepulchre. Pope Gregory summarised what had happened. He described the 'barbarous ferocity, thirsting for the blood of Christians', which characterised the Muslims, and their readiness to 'profane the holy and erase the name of God from that land'. He urged his readers to accept the challenge from God, in the same way that Bernard of Clairvaux had with the Second Crusade (see page 100). However, the main focus was on a call to repentance, with the Crusade as a penitential exercise and as part of their duty to protect fellow Christians, and making it very clear that it was a just cause. The papal bull included biblical quotations to ram the message home and argued that the recent disasters were a punishment for the sins, not only of the settlers in the Crusader States but of all Christians. The pope also encouraged people to sign up for the Crusade by promising a full indulgence and with the expectation that they would gain a place in heaven. On earth, their goods would be under his protection, but they were expected to fast on Fridays and eat no meat on Wednesdays and Saturdays.

### Responses to the *Audita tremendi*

It was not surprising that the reception of this message was so striking. The fall of Jerusalem and the loss of the True Cross were depicted everywhere as catastrophic events. Jerusalem had been hugely popular as a pilgrimage destination and was familiar to many in Europe through travellers' tales, songs and representations in stained glass. The dreadfulness of the event needed to be matched by an equally strong response. Charter evidence shows that crusaders were prepared to sell all their goods, often to local monasteries, so they could join the Crusade.

### Organisation of the appeal

The message of the papal bull was consistently applied by all preachers to make it more effective. Care was also taken to ensure that the papal legates used local churchmen to assist in their preaching tours. This ensured that there were no language barriers, even though the legate sent to Germany, Henry, Bishop of Albano (*c*.1136–89), was reputed to know no German. Members of the Cistercian order such as Henry or Archbishop Baldwin of Canterbury (*c*.1120–90), who was in charge of the English side of the operation, were often prominent. Peter of Blois (*c*.1130–*c*.1211), who was Baldwin's secretary, wrote a series of tracts in England urging Englishmen to join the Crusade, while some abbots targeted particular members of the nobility to shame them individually into taking part. Conrad of Montferrat sent a banner showing in vivid detail the atrocities committed by Saladin and his army, which was used at meetings where the Crusade was being preached. Some preachers were accompanied by returned crusaders who could add personal testimony, often including descriptions of the carnage after Hattin. Much of the preaching was carefully timed to coincide with the penitential season of Lent and the festivities of Christmas and Easter, which were centred on the person of Christ. The feasts of the Holy Cross were also popular days to preach the Crusade, as not only did large numbers attend church, but the concept of taking the cross was also closely linked to the concept of crusading and would therefore have particular resonance with the congregation.

## The recruitment of monarchs

One of the key factors in the response to the appeals for another crusade was the example of some of the leading monarchs of Europe. Some made impetuous promises. Richard (1157–99), the eldest surviving son of Henry II of England, took the cross at Tours without even asking permission from his father. In Germany, Frederick I Barbarossa (*c*.1123–90) made his pledge at an assembly at Mainz in 1188, which encouraged many other German princes to follow suit. Henry II of England had made various vague promises previously to go on a crusade and had sent money to the Holy Land (see page 140). Possibly aware that his excuses were not all that convincing, he sent more cash from the profits of the shrine of Becket. More importantly, early in 1188, Henry and his arch-rival Philip II met at Gisors on the edge of territory disputed between them, where Archbishop Joscius persuaded them to agree to go on crusade and to raise special taxation to help defray costs. This consisted of a ten per cent tax on movable goods, which became known as the Saladin Tithe. Those who went on the Crusade were exempt from the tax, which may have been an inducement for them to join. Most of the nobility of northern France were influenced into joining the Crusade. It was further agreed that the French should wear red crosses, the English white crosses, and the **Flemish** green crosses.

## Settlements of outstanding issues

A further factor encouraging the monarchs to crusade was that ongoing disputes between some of the parties were shelved. Thus, Henry II and Philip II adjourned their quarrels to another time, while Frederick I Barbarossa extended the offer of peace to all his opponents, even **Henry the Lion**. He offered Henry the choice of coming on the Crusade, all expenses paid, or exile. Henry chose the latter.

### KEY TERM

**Flemish** Relating to Flanders, the region covering present-day northern Belgium, part of France and the Netherlands.

### KEY FIGURE

**Henry the Lion (1129/30–95)**

A Welf and Duke of Saxony. He also claimed Bavaria. When Frederick I was elected as German king in 1152, he made peace with the Welfs and Henry supported the king in his Italian campaigns. He married Matilda, daughter of Henry II of England, and in 1172 went on pilgrimage to Jerusalem. In 1176 he quarrelled with Frederick I over his rights as duke and was deprived of his lands. He spent time in England with Henry II as an exile, returning to Germany later. When he refused to join the Crusade he was exiled again. After Frederick I died, Henry made his peace with the new emperor in 1190.

**ONLINE EXTRAS** OCR **WWW**

Get to grips with assessing the importance of an issue by completing Worksheet 33 at **www.hoddereducation.co.uk/accesstohistory/extras**

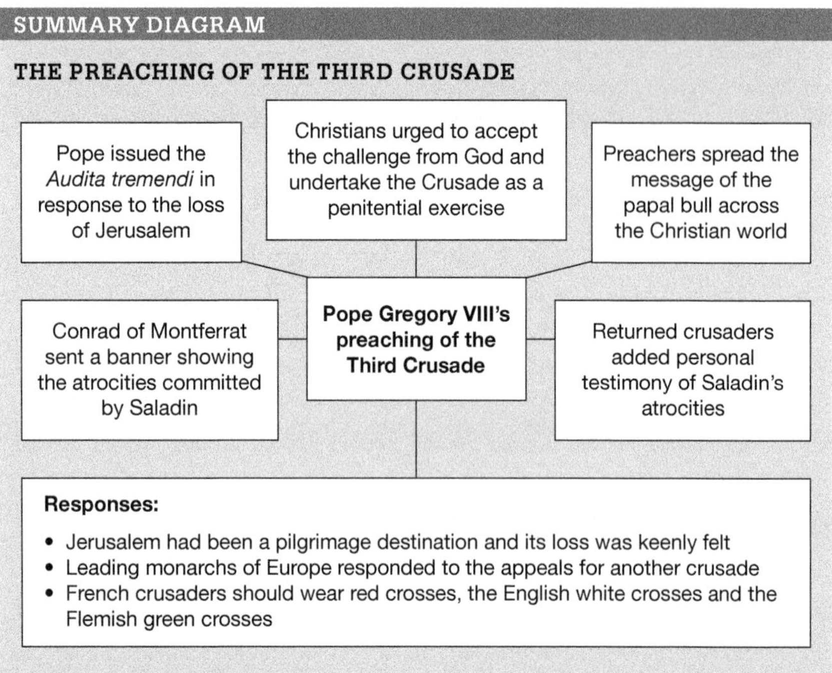

SUMMARY DIAGRAM
THE PREACHING OF THE THIRD CRUSADE
Pope issued the Audita tremendi in response to the loss of Jerusalem
Christians urged to accept the challenge from God and undertake the Crusade as a penitential exercise
Preachers spread the message of the papal bull across the Christian world
Conrad of Montferrat sent a banner showing the atrocities committed by Saladin
Pope Gregory VIII's preaching of the Third Crusade
Returned crusaders added personal testimony of Saladin's atrocities
Responses:
• Jerusalem had been a pilgrimage destination and its loss was keenly felt
• Leading monarchs of Europe responded to the appeals for another crusade
• French crusaders should wear red crosses, the English white crosses and the Flemish green crosses


# 2 The roles of Frederick Barbarossa, Philip II and Richard I in the Third Crusade

- *What part did Frederick I Barbarossa, Philip II and Richard I take in the Crusade?*

All three men played significant parts in the Third Crusade.

## Frederick I Barbarossa

Frederick I Barbarossa was the most powerful ruler ever to go on a crusade and his influence was immense. He had been elected in 1152, so was a very experienced ruler, and much of his reign had involved warfare in Germany, Italy and Poland. He had been on the Second Crusade (see page 96), but he was nearing 70 years of age. In March 1188 he took the cross in Mainz at the hands of Henry, Bishop of Albano (*c*.1136–89), and other German princes followed his example. His army was large, with possibly as many as 15,000 men, of whom 3000 may have been mounted knights, over twice the number that had fought for the Christians at Hattin (see pages 138–9). In strong contrast with the two previous crusades, he made his way from Regensburg to the Byzantine Empire.

However, before departing, he ensured that his territories at home were secure. His great rival, Henry the Lion, duke of Saxony (1129/30–95) was given the choice of ceding his rights over part of his lands, going on the Crusade, or going into exile for three years. He chose the latter and went to his father-in-law in England.

Frederick was accompanied by his son, and many bishops and German counts. The German Church, which had been hostile, was won over by Frederick's reconciliation with the pope. Thanks to the discipline he maintained, the army covered about twenty kilometres a day. He had prepared his way by negotiating with the rulers through whose lands he would pass, writing to the rulers of Hungary, Byzantium and Asia Minor, asking for safe passage. He had also ensured that the numbers of hangers-on was limited by making those who took part pay their own way. This degree of organisation and preparation was in strong contrast with some of the earlier Crusades. He left Germany in May 1189.

Frederick's progress was not entirely unhindered as the Byzantine emperor was hostile and the Turkish sultan in Anatolia went back on his word, but a combination of threats and diplomacy saw Frederick continue on his way. He won a considerable victory fighting off the Turks in Iconium, which led the

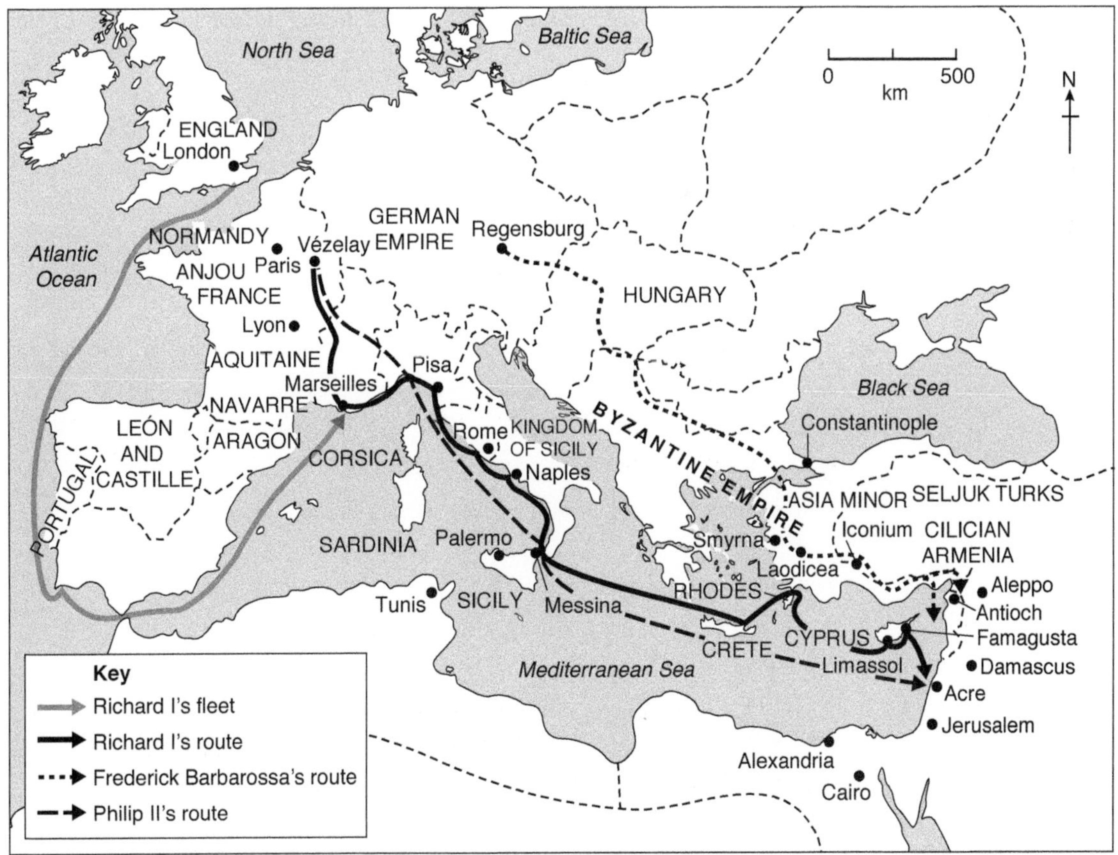


**Figure 7.1** Routes taken to the Third Crusade.

## Frederick I Barbarossa c.1123–90

Frederick was Duke of Swabia by birth. His mother was a Guelf and his father a Ghibelline so he was seen as uniting the rival factions in Germany. He went on the Second Crusade with his uncle, Conrad III. He was elected German king in 1152 and crowned emperor in 1155 at Rome. His long red beard gave him the nickname Barbarossa. He was determined to limit papal power and increase his own sovereignty, but had mixed success. He led five expeditions to Italy to force the Italians to acknowledge his power, but even as he defeated them, they remained defiant. One of his vassals, Henry the Lion, Duke of Saxony, refused to join him in Italy and was removed from his dukedom as a result. Frederick was more effective in reducing the power of the great barons in Germany and in ending the long-running civil war. He was enthusiastic about the Third Crusade and raised 15,000 men to fight, Unfortunately, he was drowned crossing the River Saleph. It is not clear how he fell into the river. He may have been trying to cool down, he may have had a heart attack and fallen in or the shock of the cold water may have killed him. As he was in his late sixties he was an old man in medieval terms. Legend has it that he rests sleeping in a cave with his knights and will rise again to restore German greatness. This is perhaps the reason Hitler called his attack on Russia in 1941 Operation Barbarossa.

sultan to come to terms. Disaster overtook the Germans when Frederick I was drowned crossing a river in southern Cilicia in June 1190. His son, Frederick VI of Swabia (1167–91), took over, but lacked his father's commanding presence. The remnants of the army either sailed for home or marched on to Antioch. Here they were virtually wiped out by disease that spread through their ranks. The few who survived joined the rest of the crusaders at Tyre.

While it is just speculation to argue that the loss of Frederick was crucial in the outcome of the Crusade, it is true that his army had shown itself to be highly capable. It is also true that Frederick had immense prestige and that the inter-crusader rivalries which disfigured the Crusade might not have broken out so viciously had he still been alive. It can, therefore, be argued that his death was a disaster for the Crusade:

- The morale of the German army was destroyed.
- The army began to disintegrate, with some returning home from Cilician or Syrian ports.
- A few soldiers joined the crusaders at Tyre.
- Frederick of Swabia took his father's body to Antioch with the remnants of the army.
- An outbreak of plague further reduced the numbers.
- Duke Frederick did eventually join the defenders of Acre (see page 156), but made little difference to their efforts.

Frederick was the most powerful ruler in western Europe and his participation had added to the prestige of the Crusade, but his large force had worried Saladin, who had begun to build up his defences.

## Richard I 1157–99

Richard was the third son of Henry II and Eleanor of Aquitaine, and succeeded to the Duchy of Aquitaine as a boy. He was famed for his military prowess and his ability to control the unruly barons of his duchy. He joined with his brothers in rebellion against their father in 1173–4. In 1183 the death of his older brother Henry made him heir to the English throne. His father wanted him to surrender Aquitaine to his younger brother, John, but Richard refused and did homage to Philip II, joining the French king in fighting Henry II, who was defeated and died. As king, Richard's main aim was to go on crusade after Saladin had recaptured Jerusalem. He raised the necessary money in any way he could and left in 1190. He travelled via Sicily, where he restored his sister Joan to her rights after the death of her husband, the ruler of Sicily. He conquered Cyprus and married Berengaria of Navarre there. He reached the Holy Land to assist in the siege of Acre, which fell in 1191, and he defeated Saladin at Arsuf. Twice he came within a few miles of Jerusalem but realised he could not hold it, even if he took the city, and arranged a truce with Saladin so that pilgrims could visit the Holy Places freely. On his way home, travelling through Germany in order to avoid France as he had quarrelled with Philip II, he was captured by Duke Leopold and handed over to Henry VI. His whereabouts were unknown in England and the story goes that he was found by his minstrel, Blondel, whom he heard singing a favourite song beneath his prison window. He was ransomed at a huge cost and returned home to take up arms again against Philip II and to regain the lands he had lost while he was absent. England was governed by Hubert Walter. Richard died at the siege of Chalus and was buried at Fontevraud Abbey. He was renowned for his skill as a soldier and as a poet and the hero of the troubadours. There is debate as to whether he was homosexual, as he seemed to have little interest in women. He is commemorated by a Victorian statue outside the Houses of Parliament.

## Richard I

Richard of Poitou had become Richard I on the death of his father, Henry II, in 1189. This, and the revival of war, accounted for some of the delays which affected his preparations. The truce that had been agreed at Gisors did not last and Philip II encouraged Richard to rebel against his father. Fighting went on through 1188–9, until a truce was agreed in July 1189, under which the two monarchs agreed to leave for the Crusade in February 1190. However, very shortly after this, Henry II died and the departure date was deferred until April.

Richard was another highly experienced warrior who had overcome the proud lords of Poitou. He also knew how important it was to have adequate supplies. The Angevins were able to use their effective administration to raise large sums, particularly through the Saladin Tithe. It was even reported that Richard said he would sell London if a buyer could be found. Even without this, he was able to raise sufficient funds so that he could hire an army of perhaps 6000 men. He also decided to take the sea route. Over 100 ships were hired or bought. The troops included a contingent of Welsh archers. Going by sea also eliminated the presence of camp followers, who slowed the progress of a crusading army and ate up scarce resources. He sent his ships in advance to meet him at Marseilles, while he joined forces with Philip at Vézelay in July 1190.

## Philip II

Philip II of France, known as Augustus (1165–1223), had been King of France since 1180 and was intent on continuing the work of his father, Louis VII, to build up the power of the French monarchy. His chief enemies were the Angevin

## Philip II 1165–1223

Philip was one of the most successful medieval French kings, carrying on the work of strengthening the monarchy begun by his father, Louis VII. He exploited the tensions in the Angevin family and encouraged the sons to rebel against Henry II. He went on the Third Crusade with some reluctance and seized an excuse to return home early. He was able to overrun some of Richard's French lands and to conspire with Richard's brother and heir, Prince John. When Richard returned the lands were reconquered and Philip was less successful, but after the death of Richard in 1199, King John proved easier to bring down. In 1204 Philip took Normandy and by 1208 John held only parts of Poitou. Philip completed the defeat of John with victory at Bouvines in 1214 over a coalition of his enemies. He was equally effective in reforms in France, where he made Paris a worthy capital, increased his revenue and centralised the administration. He was given the title 'Augustus' by one of the chroniclers, probably to suggest that his achievements mirrored those of Augustus, the first Roman emperor. When he died he was the richest and most powerful European ruler.

rulers of England and much of France. It was significant that Joscius met Philip and Henry II, the English king, at Gisors in the Vexin, a disputed area on the borders of France and Normandy, the latter of which was ruled over by the Angevins. Philip agreed to a truce with Henry and to the raising of taxation to fund the Crusade. However, Philip was less enthusiastic about the Crusade than Fredrick Barbarossa, even though it would promote his prestige, and was determined that he would go only if all his rivals went, including the English king and the major French nobles. In March 1188 Philip held a meeting in Paris to authorise the collection of the tax, with those who agreed to go on the Crusade granted exemption from paying it. Although large numbers of clergy and nobles attended the meeting and were caught up in the so-called 'Great Movement' to journey to Jerusalem, the Saladin Tithe was so unpopular in France that Philip was forced to cancel it.

Philip II did not depart for the Crusade immediately as he was short of funds and there was also the problem of the Angevins (see page 140). Philip meanwhile had mustered about 650 knights and 1300 squires, and arranged for ships from Genoa to transport his army. The two kings met at Vézelay in July 1190, where they agreed to share any gains equally and moved off, Philip II to Genoa and Richard I to Marseilles, where the English ships met him. They then met up again at Messina in Sicily and spent the winter there. The combined force now came together for the first time and numbered about 17,000. The delay in reaching the Levant seems surprising, given the urgency of the situation, but Richard I saw a way to add to his resources. He maintained he was owed money by Tancred, the ruler of Sicily (1138–94), arising from the marriage of Richard's sister, Joanna (1165–99), to William II (1153–89), the previous ruler of Sicily. He used a mixture of force and diplomacy to get his dues, which added to his resources.

### Conflict between Richard I and Philip II

Both Philip and Richard have been criticised for their slow response to the call for the Crusade. Even at the time, the well-known troubadour Bertran de Born castigated them for their slow progress. In their defence it can be argued that raising the money and troops took time. Both also had personal reasons for delay. Philip's wife died in childbirth in 1190, along with the twins she was expecting, while Richard had the aftermath of his father's death to deal with. It should also be remembered that both monarchs were taking risks. Philip's heir was a three-year-old child, Prince Louis, and the king was now a widower. Richard's heir was John, both unreliable and ambitious. Moreover, there were a number of issues between the two kings (see page 140). Chief of these was Richard I's reluctance to marry Alice (1160–*c*.1220), Philip's sister, to whom he had long been betrothed. One explanation for this was that Henry II had taken her for his mistress while she was at the English court and so lessened Richard I's desire to marry her. In any case, Richard I saw no political benefit in marrying her and instead took as his bride Berengaria of Navarre (*c*.1163–1230). Navarre would help to secure his lands in southern France, and his mother, Eleanor of Aquitaine, had brought Berengaria to Sicily. This quarrel was to have a decisive impact on the outcome of the Crusade and Philip II left Sicily alone in March 1191, with Richard I following the next month.

Richard made use of his time in Sicily, extorting money from Tancred, the ruler of Sicily. Richard claimed that his sister, Joanna, the widow of the previous ruler of Sicily, was entitled to her dowry. By a mixture of force and diplomacy he persuaded Tancred to give him 40,000 gold ounces, but he did give Philip a third of it. However, this apparent spirit of cooperation did not last, largely because of the issue of Richard's marriage.

As Richard I's fleet passed Cyprus, it became caught in a storm and some of his ships were driven ashore on Cyprus. The ruler of Cyprus was Isaac (*c*.1155–95/6), a minor member of the Comnenus family. He took some of the crusaders prisoner and ill-treated them, which led Richard to take control of the whole island. Isaac was an ally of Saladin so Richard felt justified in taking lands belonging to a Christian ruler. The conquest of Cyprus was useful to the crusaders in the long term as a base from which they could advance and to which they could retreat. Richard imposed a tax on all the inhabitants and soon sold the island to the Templars, rather than have to govern it. He also married Berengaria while in Cyprus.

Events in Cyprus also contributed to another cause of disagreement between Philip II and Richard I. While Richard I was in Cyprus he was visited by King Guy, who wanted his support. Guy was a Poitevin and so one of Richard's vassals. His rival, Conrad of Montferrat, had secured the backing of Philip II, to whom Conrad was related.

**ONLINE EXTRAS** WWW
OCR

Learn how to assess the importance of an individual by completing Worksheet 34 at **www.hoddereducation.co.uk/accesstohistory/extras**

## The events of the Third Crusade

Saladin's siege of Tyre had been unsuccessful, thanks to the vigour of Conrad of Montferrat, and the forces sent by William of Sicily also contributed to encouraging Saladin to seek some kind of settlement. In the summer of 1188 he agreed to release the prisoners taken at Hattin, most of whom then went to either Tyre or Tripoli. These included Guy de Lusignan (King Guy). This may have looked like very generous behaviour from Saladin, but it showed his insight. Saladin hoped this action might lead to divisions among the crusaders and he certainly did not lose from the following events as the crusaders resumed their infighting. Guy went to Tyre and expected Conrad to hand over the city, but Conrad refused. Guy, in order to prove his credentials, then began to besiege Acre in the autumn of 1189 with a small army and, in turn, came under attack from Saladin. This was an unexpected move as Acre was well defended and Saladin's forces were well rested and close by. Guy's unexpected vigour and spirited defence, as well as help from contingents recently arrived from Pisa and Sicily, won him more support, so that Conrad recognised him as King of Jerusalem. Guy received some help from small parties of recently arrived crusaders from England, Germany and the Netherlands, but the remnants of Barbarossa's force who arrived were so demoralised that most of them went back home.

In the winter of 1189–90 the fighting continued, although at times the ground was so muddy that a truce was called. Disease took hold and Queen Sibylla and her daughters died. This left a problem as Guy's claim to be King of Jerusalem was through his wife. The heir was Isabella, daughter of Amalric I and Maria Comnena. Conrad was determined to marry her and secure the throne, and he did so. He persuaded a French bishop to authorise her divorce from Humphrey of Toron and conveniently ignored suggestions that he had at least two other wives elsewhere. Conrad had support from Leopold of Austria (1157–94), who had taken over as leader of the Germans. Thus, yet another dispute over the succession to the crown destabilised a Crusader State and ensured that there was no chance that Guy and Conrad would be reconciled, particularly with the birth of a daughter to Isabella in 1191.

These events illustrate the fragmented nature of the crusader campaigns, the personal ambition of many of those involved, but also their success against the odds. But even so, by the spring of 1191 the attack on Acre was in dire difficulties with food scarce and Saladin's forces in wait. So the arrival of both Philip's and Richard's fleets, in April and June, respectively, was crucial. It was nearly four years since the defeat at Hattin before the request for help was finally answered.

## The siege of Acre

Richard I arrived in Acre in June 1191 and was greeted with celebration and much telling of the stories of ancient heroes, suggesting that Richard was another such. Philip II had been there since April and had taken the lead in pressing on with the siege; helped by the siege engines he brought with him, he was making some progress against the city walls. However, the general belief that the city would not be taken until Richard I arrived did not make Philip II's relations with Richard I any better.

Acre fell in July 1191 for a number of reasons:

- Saladin had never been able to stop supplies arriving by sea for the attackers, so was almost bound to fail to hold the city.
- Richard's arrival boosted morale.

- Richard brought with him more and stronger siege engines, such as catapults and big wooden towers, and these were too powerful for the defenders.
- The siege engines brought or constructed by the crusaders proved too much for the defenders, although they responded with a barrage of missiles.
- The crusaders may have numbered 25,000 and Saladin's defending army was much smaller.
- Richard I hired mercenaries with his accumulated funds and offered payments for every stone which was removed from the walls of Acre.

The events of the siege had not led to a better relationship between the two kings. Both had been ill, Richard I seriously, and their tempers were short. Richard I refused to counter any suggestion that he should share Cyprus with Philip II under the terms of their agreement. He outbid Philip II in paying mercenaries and so recruited more. The Count of Flanders died and Richard I stepped in to acquire his siege machines. This stress on Richard's better resources was a constant irritant to Philip II, who continued to push for Conrad to be recognised as King of Jerusalem, which Richard I resisted.

When it came to the division of the spoils of Acre, the kings were more of one mind. They would take it all between the two of them. This led to protests from the Germans who were not attached to either army, and Duke Leopold, their leader since the death of Frederick, went home in indignation. It was said that Leopold was already aggrieved because he had planted his banner on the captured walls of Acre only to have it torn down by Richard I. Agreement was reached between Richard and Philip on one other issue. In a compromise, Guy was to remain King of Jerusalem with Conrad recognised as his heir. The revenues would be divided between them and Conrad was given lands near Tyre. This did not entirely satisfy Conrad and made him difficult to work with.

## Philip II's departure

Philip II left for home at the beginning of August, handing his share of the spoils of Acre to Conrad and taking an oath to do no harm to Richard I's lands in France. The Duke of Burgundy took over the leadership of the French. Philip II left for several reasons:

- He was still unwell and, in fact, never fully recovered. As a confirmed hypochondriac this weighed heavily with him.
- The death of the Duke of Flanders meant that there was an unstable situation in northern France and he felt he needed to be there to deal with it.
- He was worried about the health of his infant son and heir. Richard I had told him at one point that the little boy had died. This false information had upset Philip II considerably.
- Playing second fiddle to Richard I gave him no pleasure.
- Despite his oath, there was the chance that he might be able to gain an advantage in the long-running rivalry with the Angevins.

**ONLINE EXTRAS** AQA **WWW**

Get to grips with making links between factors by completing Worksheet 30 at **www.hoddereducation.co.uk/accesstohistory/extras**

**ONLINE EXTRAS** Pearson Edexcel **WWW**

Learn how to write a balanced argument by completing Worksheet 28 at **www.hoddereducation.co.uk/accesstohistory/extras**

Philip left his troops behind, so his departure could be seen as making little difference to the Crusade. But, back in western Europe his activities, combined with the plotting of Prince John (1166–1216), Richard I's younger brother, were a huge factor in making Richard I reluctant to stay any longer than he need in the Holy Land. An unidentified chronicler gives their account in Source A (see below).

**SOURCE QUESTION**

On what grounds does the writer in Source A condemn Philip for his decision? To what extent is this view a balanced assessment?

**SOURCE A**

From the *Book of King Richard's Expedition to the Holy Land of Jerusalem*, Folio Society, 1958, pp. 72–3. This book is an English translation of the *Itinerarium Peregrinorum et Gesta Regis Ricardi*, considered the best chronicle of the Third Crusade, written anonymously in the thirteenth century.

*A rumour began to spread among the army that the king of France (on whom the hope of the people rested) intended to return home and was making active preparations for his journey. O how wicked and insulting a proceeding, to wish while as yet so much work remained on hand, to go away, when his duty was to rule so large a multitude of people, and when his presence was necessary to encourage the Christians to so pious a work! O why did he come so long a way, with so much toil, if he intended to return almost immediately! O wonderful performance of his vow, merely to enter the Holy Land and contend against the Turks with such small triumph. The king of France alleged sickness as the cause of his return and said he had performed his vow as far as he was able. Indeed it must not be denied that he expended much labour and money in the Holy Land in assaulting the city, that he gave aid to many and by the influence of his presence hastened the capture of Acre. But when his inflexible determination to return became known, the French, had they been able to, would have renounced their subjection to him.*

## Prisoners

Richard decided to march south to Jaffa. It had been agreed that the defenders of Acre be ransomed, but when Saladin was slow to pay up, Richard I had 3000 of them killed. This was in stark contrast with the magnanimity of Saladin at the capture of Jerusalem, but Richard I's supporters have argued that he had little choice as the prisoners needed food and lodging, nor would it be sensible to release them to fight on for the Muslims. The massacre had the effect that Saladin became less ready to spare Christian prisoners.

## Richard I as sole commander

### The Battle of Arsuf and its significance

Saladin was bound to try and stop Richard's march and the two armies met at Arsuf in September 1191. Saladin had been building up his forces and wanted a pitched battle which he hoped would be decisive. The crusaders were suffering from the heat, but were well supplied as the fleet had sailed down the coast to accompany them, as ordered by Richard. The battle was won by a cavalry charge which broke Muslim resolve and helped to atone for Hattin. The charge was led by two Hospitaller knights, in defiance of Richard's instructions, but Richard reacted quickly and changed his tactics, ordering a general advance. The victory showed that Saladin could be beaten, and the crusaders thought the tide was now in their favour and a march on Jerusalem would succeed.

## The failure to take Jerusalem

Richard I's aim was to restore the Crusader States, but he was not so devoted a soldier that he was bent on fighting all the way, if more could be achieved by negotiation. Admittedly, western Europe was expecting a great military victory, but, as the man on the spot, Richard I would act as he saw fit. He had been in touch with Saladin soon after his arrival. The Muslim general was feeling the strain of the action and his failure to save Acre had harmed his reputation, so he was ready to negotiate. But he had some issues on which he would never give way in discussion: Jerusalem must remain in his hands and so must Transjordan, as the essential link between Egypt and Syria.

Richard himself enjoyed several successes in his remaining months in the Holy Land:

- He came within nineteen kilometres of reaching Jerusalem in January 1192; however, he did not advance any further.
- He made a realistic settlement over Jerusalem, given Guy's continuing unpopularity. Conrad was crowned as king and Guy was given Cyprus as compensation. (This foundered when Conrad was murdered on the streets of Tyre by two Assassins dressed as monks. The story went that he had left his house to dine with a friend because his own meal was not ready as his wife, Isabella, was still in her bath!)
- He approved the marriage of Isabella to Henry of Champagne (1166–97), which took place within a week of Conrad's death. Henry was related to Richard I and an experienced crusader.
- In May 1192 he again approached Jerusalem.
- In September he signed a three-year truce with Saladin. The Christians kept the coastline from Jaffa to Tyre, but gave up Ascalon. Pilgrims could visit Jerusalem but Richard I would not go himself while it remained a Muslim city.

## Why did Richard not take Jerusalem?

- Richard's preferred strategy was to attack Egypt and deprive Saladin of its wealth, but he could not persuade his fellow crusaders to back this plan.
- His campaign to take Jerusalem was held back in part by wet weather and therefore progress was slow.
- Richard insisted on fortifying the castles along the route and securing his supply lines, which made progress even slower.
- He realised that if he captured Jerusalem, it would be very difficult to hold as most of the crusaders expected to return home and not stay and garrison the city.

**Figure 7.2** The marches on Jerusalem, 1191–2.

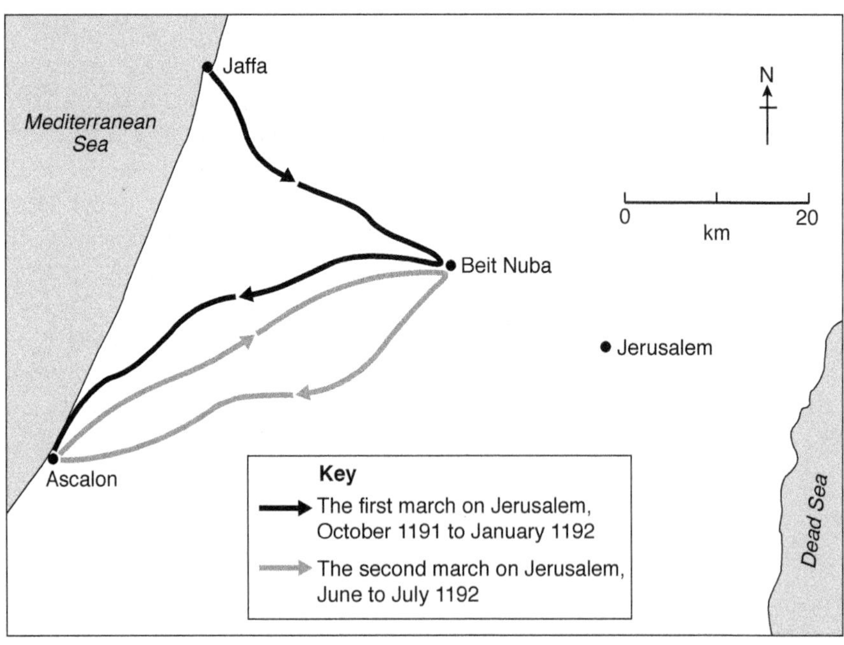


- The Military Orders were more interested in holding on to the coastal areas.
- The loss of German troops reduced the numbers available to Richard and made conquest impossible.
- Richard was concerned about developments in England and France, where Philip was threatening Normandy and John was causing trouble in England, despite papal protection for absentee crusaders and Richard having granted John vast estates before he left, including six counties, numerous lordships and castles. John's marriage to Isabella of Gloucester only added to his power and although he was expected to maintain peace there were disputes between him and Richard's chancellor.

> **ONLINE EXTRAS** AQA WWW
> Develop your skills at assessing the importance of an individual by completing Worksheet 31 at **www.hoddereducation.co.uk/accesstohistory/extras**

> **ONLINE EXTRAS** OCR WWW
> Learn how to support an argument by completing Worksheet 35 at **www.hoddereducation.co.uk/accesstohistory/extras**

> **ONLINE EXTRAS** OCR WWW
> Learn how to plan an effective essay by completing Worksheet 36 at **www.hoddereducation.co.uk/accesstohistory/extras**

> **ONLINE EXTRAS** OCR WWW
> Get to grips with assessing the impact of an event by completing Worksheet 37 at **www.hoddereducation.co.uk/accesstohistory/extras**

## The end of the Third Crusade

- A second approach to Jerusalem in May 1192 again reached Beit Nuba and Richard actually saw the city, but the same reasons prevented an assault and its capture.
- Saladin attacked Jaffa and captured it, but Richard retook the city in August 1192 and therefore ensured that the crusaders retained control of the coast.
- Saladin attacked Ascalon but was driven back by Richard's army.

The chronicler describes Richard I's exploits at Jaffa in Source B.

**SOURCE B**

From the *Book of King Richard's Expedition to the Holy Land of Jerusalem*, Folio Society, 1958, pp. 146–7.

*The word was forthwith given [to attack Jaffa] and the galleys were pushed to land. The king, dashing forward into the waves with his thighs unprotected by armour and up to his middle in water, soon gained firm footing on the dry shore ... The Turks stood to defend the shore, which was covered with their numerous troops. The king, with an arbalest [a crossbow of an advanced design] which he held in his hand, drove them back left and right; his companions pressed upon the retreating enemy, whose courage failed when they saw it was the king and they no longer dared to meet him. The king brandished his fierce sword, allowing them no time to resist him. Yielding before his fiery blows, they were driven off in confusion by the king's men, until the shore was entirely cleared of them ... The brave king had no sooner entered the town than he caused his banners to be hoisted on a hill so that they might be seen by the Christians being besieged in the tower. Taking courage at the sight they rushed forth in arms from the tower to meet the king, throwing the Turks further into confusion ... If we examine the deeds of the ancients and all the records left us by former historians, we shall find there was never a man who so distinguished himself in battle as king Richard did that day.*

**SOURCE QUESTION** 

What was the special contribution of Richard to the success at Jaffa, according to the writer of Source B? Do you have any doubts about the reliability of this source?

The Christian and Muslim armies had reached a stalemate. Neither Saladin nor Richard was in good health. Both were also facing challenges from their domestic enemies. Therefore, a three-year truce was signed at Jaffa in September 1192. They agreed that:

- The Christians would keep the coastline from Jaffa to Tyre.
- Ascalon would be handed over to the Muslims.
- Christian pilgrims would be allowed to visit Jerusalem freely.

The treaty itself was the result of a drawn-out process of negotiation. Both Richard and Philip had been in talks with Saladin from the moment of their arrival at Acre in June 1191, contact that was sustained by members of the local nobility who kept up communication with the Muslim leader.

## SUMMARY DIAGRAM

### THE ROLES OF FREDERICK BARBAROSSA, PHILIP II AND RICHARD I IN THE THIRD CRUSADE

**Frederick I Barbarossa:**
- Most powerful leader to go on a crusade
- German king and Holy Roman Emperor
- Enthusiastic crusader
- Well prepared
- 15,000 men
- Elderly, and his death weakened the German forces

**Richard I:**
- Experienced warrior
- Travelled by sea and avoided bringing followers
- Welsh archers
- Had issues with Philip

**Monarchs of the Third Crusade**

**Philip II:**
- French king
- Successful monarch
- Reluctant crusader
- Had issues with Richard
- Went home early

# 3 The results of the Third Crusade

■ *How far was the Third Crusade a success?*

The Crusader States survived for another 100 years, but Jerusalem was not taken. The short-term results were as follows:

- The question of the remainder of the kingdom of Jerusalem was settled at a council. Conrad was recognised as King of Jerusalem and Guy was given Cyprus as consolation. The Templars had found it hard to govern and were happy to hand it over; however, Conrad was murdered by two Assassins disguised as monks, on the streets of Tyre.
- Isabella was quickly married to Henry of Champagne in April 1192, a popular choice as the nephew of both Philip II and Richard and an experienced crusader. This provided some stability.

From Richard I's point of view, a further failure, for which he was only partly responsible, came on his return journey. He was strongly suspected of being involved in the commissioning of the murder of Conrad, so he travelled in disguise. In Vienna he was recognised and taken captive. He was handed over to the Duke of Austria in December 1192. Leopold passed him on to Emperor Henry VI (1165–97). It took until February 1194 for Richard I to be released, on the payment of a vast ransom. However, Richard's actions during the Third Crusade had gained him great prestige in the Muslim world and, as it was believed he would return with another crusader army, the acquisition and control of the coast provided a platform from which to attack the Muslims.

As for Saladin, he died in March 1193, aged 55, and his empire broke up on his death. Richard's defeats of Saladin at the battles of Acre, Arsuf and Jaffa had damaged Saladin's reputation.

Henry VI went on to gather forces for another expedition, possibly hoping to be successful where his father had failed, in 1196. He gained support from the papacy and the emperor in Byzantium, and a large army gathered at Bari in Italy in 1197. The crusaders managed to capture Beirut, adding to the coastal possessions of the Christians and maintaining control of the sea. But, in late 1197, they received the news that Henry VI had died and so they returned to Germany. These events did, however, lay the foundations for a greater German presence in the Holy Land, which had, hitherto, been very much the preserve of the French. Henry VI also founded a Military Order, called St Mary of the Germans at first, but which later became the **Order of the Teutonic Knights**.

**ONLINE EXTRAS AQA** WWW

Develop your skills at making comparisons by completing Worksheet 32 at **www.hoddereducation.co.uk/accesstohistory/extras**

**ONLINE EXTRAS AQA** WWW

Learn how to write a balanced essay by completing Worksheet 33 at **www.hoddereducation.co.uk/accesstohistory/extras**

**ONLINE EXTRAS OCR** WWW

Learn how to write an argument rather than an assertion by completing Worksheet 38 at **www.hoddereducation.co.uk/accesstohistory/extras**

**ONLINE EXTRAS OCR** WWW

Learn how to plan a balanced essay by completing Worksheet 39 at **www.hoddereducation.co.uk/accesstohistory/extras**

**KEY TERM**

**Order of the Teutonic Knights** A religious order which played a major role in eastern Europe in the Middle Ages.

## SUMMARY DIAGRAM

### THE RESULTS OF THE THIRD CRUSADE

The Crusader States survived for another 100 years, but Jerusalem was not taken. Richard I could not see how the city could be held for the crusaders

↓

Richard I was distracted by news coming from home

↓

Richard could not persuade the crusaders to attack Egypt. He believed its wealth would make conquering Jerusalem easier, but the men were not going to be diverted from their main focus

↓

Saladin died in March 1193, aged 55, and his empire broke up on his death

↓

Henry VI went on to gather forces for another expedition in 1196. He gained support from the papacy and the emperor in Byzantium, and a large army gathered at Bari in Italy in 1197

↓

In late 1197 they received the news that Henry VI had died and so they returned to Germany (although there was now a greater German presence in the Holy Land, including the new Order of the Teutonic Knights)

**ONLINE EXTRAS** WWW
Pearson Edexcel

Learn how to plan an effective essay by completing Worksheet 29 at **www.hoddereducation.co.uk/accesstohistory/extras**

**ONLINE EXTRAS** WWW
Pearson Edexcel

Develop your analysis of the Third Crusade by completing Worksheet 30 at **www.hoddereducation.co.uk/accesstohistory/extras**

**ONLINE EXTRAS** WWW
Pearson Edexcel

Get to grips with your analysis of consequence by completing Worksheet 31 at **www.hoddereducation.co.uk/accesstohistory/extras**

# 4 Key debate

■ *What did the Third Crusade achieve?*

Contemporaries, as well as historians, had different views about how worthwhile the Crusade had been. In Extract 1, Steven Runciman argues that not much had been achieved, while in Extract 2, Christopher Tyerman considers that the Third Crusade helped to ensure a Christian presence in the Holy Land for some years and influenced the way later crusades were organised.

**INTERPRETATION QUESTION**

Which of Extracts 1 and 2 do you find more convincing as an explanation of the outcome of the Third Crusade?

**EXTRACT 1**

From Steven Runciman, *A History of the Crusades, Volume III*, Penguin Books, 2016, first published 1954, p. 66.

*The kingdom of Jerusalem was a very small kingdom; and though its kings were in name kings of Jerusalem, Jerusalem lay out of its grasp. All that they owned was a strip of land, never as much as ten miles wide, stretching for ninety miles by the sea from Jaffa to Tyre. Further north Bohemond's judicious neutrality had preserved for him his capital [Antioch] and a little land around, down to the port of Saint Symeon. His son retained Tripoli itself and the Hospitallers held Krak des Chevaliers and the Templars Tortosa under him. It was not much to have salvaged from the Crusade.*

**ONLINE EXTRAS**
**Pearson Edexcel** www

Practise your interpretation analysis by completing Worksheets 32, 33 and 34 at **www.hoddereducation.co.uk/accesstohistory/extras**

**ONLINE EXTRAS**
**AQA** www

Develop your interpretation analysis by completing Worksheets 34 and 35 at **www.hoddereducation.co.uk/accesstohistory/extras**

**EXTRACT 2**

From Christopher Tyerman, *God's War: A History of the Crusades*, Penguin Books, 2007, p. 473

*The capture of Acre proved a major triumph, providing the restored kingdom of Jerusalem with a commercial centre of international importance. The effective conquest of significant parts of the coastal plain allowed for the establishment of a territorial state that lasted intact to the 1260s. The incorporation of Cyprus into Christian Outremer provided a new base and source of wealth and aristocratic opportunity. The Treaty of Jaffa of 1192 acted as a model for future diplomacy. For most of the next seventy years truces determined the relations between the Christian rulers of mainland Outremer and their Muslim neighbours. Only unreflective or partisan westerners regarded the practice as irreligious.*

# CHAPTER SUMMARY

The Third Crusade was a reaction to the fall of Jerusalem, which had horrified Europe. The Crusade was preached by high-ranking churchmen and they drew in three monarchs, Frederick Barbarossa, Philip II and Richard I. Frederick was a very powerful ruler and much was hoped from him. His drowning before even reaching the Holy Land was a big blow. Philip II and Richard I were rivals and never likely to cooperate but various events worsened their ill-feeling towards each other. Although they captured Acre, Philip II went home early. Richard I showed much skill and courage but could not capture Jerusalem and had to come to terms with Saladin. The Crusade showed how difficult it would be for the crusaders to win back Jerusalem but it did preserve the Crusader States for another century.

## Refresher questions

Use these questions to remind yourself of the key material covered in this chapter.

1. How did the preachers win over their listeners?
2. What happened to Frederick Barbarossa?
3. What were the results of the German failure?
4. Why were Philip II and Richard I on bad terms?
5. Why were the crusaders able to take Acre?
6. Why did Philip II go home?
7. What successes did Richard I have?
8. Why could the crusaders not take Jerusalem?

## Question practice: AQA

### Essay question

1. 'The fundamental weaknesses of Outremer explain the failure to recapture Jerusalem in 1189.' Assess the validity of this view with reference to the years 1164–89. [A level]

**EXAM HINT** You must examine the various factors that explain the failure to recapture Jerusalem and then argue which you believe the most important were. It may be that the factors actually link together.

## Question practice: OCR

### Essay questions

**1** Which of the following was of greater importance in the outcome of the Third Crusade? i) Philip II of France. ii) Richard I. Explain your answer with reference to both i) and ii). [A level]

**EXAM HINT** The importance of the two individuals in the outcome of the Third Crusade should be explained and a supported judgement reached as to which was more important.

**2** How successful was the Third Crusade? [A level]

**EXAM HINT** Responses should establish criteria against which to judge success, such as achieving their aims. The Third Crusade should then be judged against each of the criteria, allowing a judgement to be reached as regards the success of achieving each of the criteria; this will allow an overall judgement to be reached as to the overall success of the Crusade.

## Question practice: Pearson Edexcel

### Essay question

**1** How far do you agree that the rivalry between Richard I and Philip II was the most important factor which determined the limited success of the Third Crusade? [A level]

**EXAM HINT** Explain the growing rivalry between Richard and Philip, and the reasons for Philip's return to France in 1191. Note also the death of Frederick Barbarossa, and its impact on the Crusade as a whole, and the reasons for Richard's failure to take Jerusalem in 1191–2.

CHAPTER 8

# The Fourth Crusade

The Fourth Crusade owed much to the initiative of a new pope, Innocent III. He became pope in 1198 and, in his late thirties, was unusually young for the role. The end of the Third Crusade (see Chapter 7) convinced him that another crusade was needed and that Egypt should be its initial target. In the end, the Crusade diverted to Constantinople and took and sacked the city in 1204, an everlasting blot on the reputation of crusading. This chapter examines the events of the Fourth Crusade and its outcome by focusing on the following themes:

- The role of Pope Innocent III
- The Treaty of Venice
- The attacks on Constantinople
- The results of the Fourth Crusade

The key debate on page 185 of this chapter asks the question: Why did the crusaders attack Constantinople?

**KEY DATES**

| | |
|---|---|
| **1198** | Innocent III became pope and issued the papal bull *Post miserabile* (*Sadly after*) |
| | Truce with Saladin |
| **1199** | Many knights took the cross |
| **1201** | Agreement with Venice for transport |
| | Boniface of Montferrat recognised as leader |
| **1202** | Attack on Zara |
| **1203** | First attack on Constantinople; Alexius IV made co-emperor with Isaac II |
| **1204** | Overthrow of Alexius IV. Capture of Constantinople by the crusaders |

## 1 The role of Pope Innocent III

■ *What was the role of Innocent III in instigating the Crusade?*

Innocent believed that the pope had supreme power, over both spiritual and secular matters and, therefore, rulers should do as he commanded. This helps to explain his attitude towards the Fourth Crusade. He would personally take control of every aspect of the undertaking, including its financing and its leadership. Innocent had no intention of consulting with kings or nobles: he expected them to follow his commands. This was a fundamental mistake that would have repercussions for the Crusade and contributed to its failure.

Pope Innocent III was convinced that the crusading movement had divine approval and saw it as the duty of all Christians to support the drive to recapture Jerusalem. In August 1198 he issued a new appeal, *Post miserabile* (*Sadly after*), which referred to the loss of Jerusalem, the massacre of Christians, the invasion

### Key figures of the Fourth Crusade

Pope Innocent III
Alexius IV
Boniface of Montferrat
Count Baldwin of Flanders
Count Louis I of Blois
Count Thibaut III of Champagne
Dandolo
Geoffrey de Villehardouin
Simon de Montfort

## Innocent III c.1160–1216

Elected pope in January 1198 at the age of 37, Innocent III had been educated at some of Europe's finest centres of learning. These had instilled in him an exalted view of the papacy and its role in the world. For Innocent, the pope was Christ's representative on earth, with supreme power, not only in the spiritual world of the Church, but also in the temporal world. His claim was a breathtaking one: he believed that papal power exceeded that of the rulers of states, and that they should bend to his will in all things. He played a crucial role in the reform of the Church through his **decretals** and the Fourth Lateran Council, which led to a refinement in canon law. He also used interdict to try and force rulers to obey his will, although this was not always successful. He extended the scope of Crusades to include attacks on Muslim Spain, and the Albigensian Crusade against the Cathars in southern France. The disastrous Fourth Crusade served only to increase the divisions between the Greek and Latin Churches.

**KEY TERMS**

**Decretals** Papal decrees concerning a point of canon (Church) law.

**Apostolic See** The papacy.

by Muslims of the land where Christ had walked and the loss of the True Cross as disasters which needed to be overcome. He depicted the **Apostolic See** as grieving to the extent that 'It cried out and wailed to such a degree that due to incessant crying out, its throat was made hoarse, and from incessant weeping its eyes almost failed.' Pope Innocent III went on to urge everyone to put their trust in God, to remember how Christ had sacrificed himself for them and to think of the treasure they would store up for themselves in heaven by supporting the Crusade. Innocent further made it clear that everyone could get involved. Churchmen and those also unable to go in person could pay for or towards someone else going and receive the same spiritual benefits as those who went.

Determined to play a key role in the Crusade, in the same way as Urban II had done in the First Crusade, Innocent III wrote to all his archbishops and suggested they should summon councils to discuss the need for the Crusade to recapture Jerusalem. This was to be achieved by first capturing the Egyptian Ayyubid sultanate, which was the most powerful at the time. Some did so and councils granted up to three per cent of diocesan incomes for the Crusade. But, within a year, Innocent III realised that this would be insufficient and sent further instructions, ordering that the Church pay a fortieth as an income tax (2.5 per cent).

## The response to Pope Innocent III's appeal

Innocent had hoped that his appeal would lead the two most powerful western European kings, Richard I of England and Philip II of France, to make their peace and again go crusading. This was very unlikely to happen as they had been fighting one another since Richard I returned from the Third Crusade to find that Philip II had occupied much of Normandy. In any case, Richard died in April 1199 from a wound inflicted by a bolt from a crossbow, while Philip II remained at odds with the pope. Philip II had put aside his wife, Ingeborg (1174–1237), and the pope refused to acknowledge Philip's second marriage as legal. Moreover, the Spanish monarchs were also at war with each other and the King of Leon had even made an alliance with the Muslims.

In Germany, the death of Henry VI had left an underage heir and disputes had broken out over the succession.

However, the knights of northern France, where there was a very strong crusading tradition, were more responsive. The Crusade was preached at Écry-sur-Aisne in Champagne at a tournament in late 1199. This was rather surprising as tournaments were condemned by the Church for leading to the sins of pride, envy and murder. But they were the places where fighting men could be found, and the evenings, after the action of the day was over, were noted for feasting and celebration. Such events often involved recitations of the epics of the First Crusade such as the *Chanson d'Antioche*. On hearing the appeal, two men came forward, **Count Thibaut III of Champagne** and **Count Louis I of Blois**. Both came from families which had featured in former Crusades. Thibaut III's father had been Henry of Champagne, who had ruled in Jerusalem until his death in 1197, while Louis I may have been on the Third Crusade. Other nobles joined them, such as Simon de Montfort (*c*.1175–1218), who had already fought in the Holy Land, and **Count Baldwin of Flanders**. Another was **Geoffrey de Villehardouin**, who would write an account of his experiences, which is valuable as the view of a layman, rather than the usual monkish chroniclers.

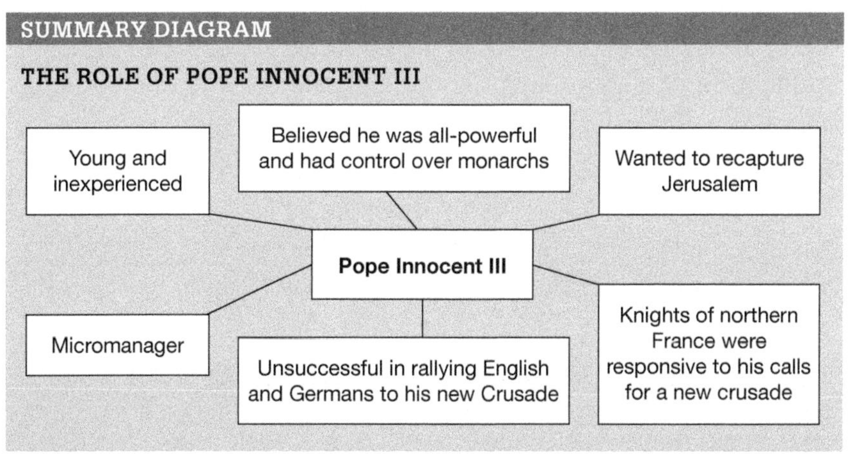
SUMMARY DIAGRAM
THE ROLE OF POPE INNOCENT III
Young and inexperienced
Believed he was all-powerful and had control over monarchs
Wanted to recapture Jerusalem
Pope Innocent III
Micromanager
Unsuccessful in rallying English and Germans to his new Crusade
Knights of northern France were responsive to his calls for a new crusade

## 2 The Treaty of Venice

■ *How significant was the Treaty of Venice?*

The crusaders met at Soissons early in 1200 and here they made what proved to be a vital decision. They agreed to travel overland to Italy and then to hire transport from the Republic of Venice to travel by sea. The crusaders sent representatives, who included Villehardouin, to negotiate with the ruler of the city-state, the **doge**. This decision was made for a number of reasons:

- Genoa and Pisa were engaged in a civil war.

### KEY FIGURES

**Count Thibaut III of Champagne (1179–1201)**

His father had fought in the Second Crusade and ruled Jerusalem until his death in 1197 when he fell from a balcony. Thibaut was related to the royal houses of both France and England.

**Count Louis I of Blois (1172–1205)**

Like Thibaut, he was also related to the French and English royal families and his father had died at the siege of Acre.

**Count Baldwin of Flanders (1172–1205)**

He and his wife, Marie, took the cross in Bruges in early 1200. Baldwin's family had been heavily involved in crusading, while Marie was sister to Thibaut. Their decision to take the cross encouraged other Flemings to join.

**Geoffrey de Villehardouin (c.1150–1213/18)**

He wrote an account of the Crusade. He was in his early fifties and was a senior adviser to the Count of Champagne. He had taken part in the Third Crusade and spent four years in a Muslim prison. He was closely involved in the planning and main decision-making of the Crusade.

### KEY TERM

**Doge** Chief magistrate of the Republic of Venice

- Venice was one of the largest and richest urban centres in Europe, with a population of 60,000.
- It had a trade agreement with Byzantium which gave its merchants favourable terms, while its geographical position meant that the city controlled the major Mediterranean trade routes.
- The land route involved going through Byzantine territory and the emperors were hostile.
- The number of crusaders was not sufficient to be able to fight their way across Asia Minor.
- It was much faster to travel by sea.
- Richard I and Philip II had used this route successfully in the Third Crusade.

The doge at the time was Enrico Dandolo (*c.*1107–1205), a remarkable figure, who had been blinded by an accident in the 1170s and had ruled Venice since 1192, despite being in his late eighties when he took over.

The envoys arrived in the city in early 1201 and began negotiations with the doge and his closest advisers.

## The Treaty of Venice

The negotiation resulted in the Treaty of Venice, which was drawn up in 1201 and included these terms:

- The Venetians would provide transport for 4500 horses, 9000 squires, 4500 knights and 20,000 foot soldiers.
- The Venetians would provide food for these people for nine months.
- The crusaders would pay four marks per horse and two marks per man.
- The terms would be valid for twelve months.
- Venice would provide 50 armed galleys for the love of God.
- Anything captured on sea or land would be divided equally between Venice and the crusaders.
- The total cost would be 85,000 silver marks, to be paid in instalments by April 1202.

## Enrico Dandolo c.1107–1205

Dandolo was born into one of the leading families in Venice and sent on diplomatic missions. Some of these were to Constantinople, where he defended the interests of Venice so strongly that the emperor had him blinded, in one story. In fact, a head injury caused his poor sight. He was ambassador to Sicily in 1174 and Ferrara in 1191 and then, aged about 85, was elected as doge in 1192. He was a keen reformer, despite his age, and issued a new legal code and revised the coinage. He promoted Venetian trade very successfully and his role in the Fourth Crusade reflected his interests and his diplomatic skills. He persuaded the crusaders to attack Zara in return for funds and then to capture Constantinople, much to the benefit of Venice. He stayed in the Byzantine capital to protect Venetian interests and died there, being buried in the Church of St Sophia.

This was a huge undertaking for the Republic and represented how much it was ready to commit to the cause. Its normal commercial activities would need to be suspended to meet these obligations. Up to this point, the Venetians had taken little part in the Crusades, except for their contribution to the siege of Tyre in 1124, in which several members of Dandolo's family had been involved. The average sailing ship carried about 600 passengers and needed a crew of 100 sailors, so about half the adult population of Venice would be needed on the ships. As for the horse transports, they needed to be specially adapted with slings to carry the horses and low-level doors so the knights could charge straight out into battle.

In agreeing to the treaty, the crusaders' representatives made a number of fatal miscalculations:

- The target of 33,500 crusaders was a very optimistic figure, especially since recruitment had been slow so far.
- It was assumed that the whole crusading force would travel together from Venice: in reality, many planned to travel overland or make their way to the Holy Land from their local ports.
- The money due to Venice was a huge sum.
- No rulers were planning to join the Crusade, and so national treasuries could not provide any funding.

## Why did the Venetians take part?

The motives of Venice could be seen by the cynical observer to have been commercial. The amount of money the Venetians would receive was twice the annual income of the French or English monarchs. They were not overcharging, however, as the figures were similar to the amount paid by Philip II to the Genoese in the Third Crusade. It was the vast numbers who were expected on the Crusade that made the difference. Another factor lay in the secret agreement that the Crusade would start by attacking Egypt, rather than the Holy Land. There were good reasons for this decision (see below), but it could be viewed as a betrayal of the aims of the Crusade. However, for the Venetians, the lure of the great port of Alexandria was the real attraction. If they could establish themselves there, they would be pre-eminent over Genoa and Pisa, their main rivals, and Dandolo's reputation as doge would be secured.

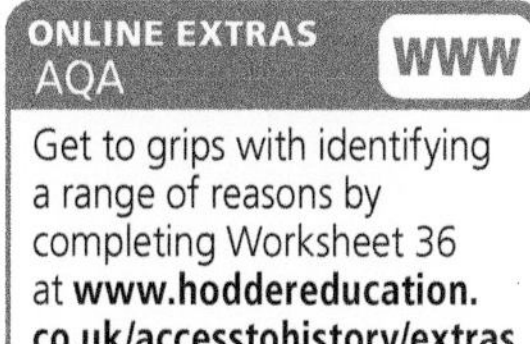

ONLINE EXTRAS
AQA
WWW
Get to grips with identifying a range of reasons by completing Worksheet 36 at **www.hoddereducation.co.uk/accesstohistory/extras**


## Another attack on Egypt

There was nothing new about a wish to invade Egypt. King Amalric I had tried to do so and Richard I had wanted to attempt it. It was a sound strategic move with the vast resources of Egypt at stake, while possession of its ports would ensure control of the eastern Mediterranean for the Christians. Should the crusaders take Egypt, it would make it much harder for the Muslims to drive them out of the Holy Land. Lastly, the Kingdom of Jerusalem had made a truce with Muslim Syria, so the Christians could not fight there, but Egypt was excluded from the truce.

## The impact of the death of Thibaut of Champagne

In May 1201 Thibaut was taken ill and died, aged only twenty. His death was a major blow to the Crusade's prospects. Thibaut was a popular and charismatic leader, who was likely to inspire many French nobles and thousands of foot soldiers to accompany him on the Crusade. With his death, many were deterred from signing up as there were concerns about the stability of Champagne, which would now be under a female regency.

**KEY FIGURE**

**Boniface, Marquis of Montferrat (c.1150–1207)**

Boniface had plenty of family crusading credentials. His brother William had married Sibylla of Jerusalem, and another brother, Conrad, had married her half-sister, Isabella (see page 138). The family was linked to both the French and German royal houses and it is possible that it was Philip II who had suggested Boniface as a leader.

The crusaders met again at Soissons and decided to approach **Boniface, Marquis of Montferrat**, with the offer to command the whole army. He accepted the command and, after a visit to Citeaux, he went to the court of Philip of Swabia (1177–1208) at Hagenau for Christmas.

## The weakness of the Byzantine Empire

Philip of Swabia, the King of Germany, was related by marriage to the Byzantine house of Angelos as his wife, Irene (*c*.1181–1208), was the daughter of the former emperor, Isaac II Angelos (see page 141). Isaac II Angelos had been overthrown in 1195, blinded and held in captivity along with his son, Prince Alexius (*c*.1182–1204), while Irene's uncle, another Alexius (*c*.1153–1211), had taken the crown as Alexius III Angelos. Prince Alexius had escaped from prison and turned up at Hagenau. There has been speculation that Boniface and Prince Alexius made secret plans while at Hagenau to divert the Crusade from Alexandria to Constantinople and there achieve a regime change which would clearly benefit Alexius the prince. This view seems unlikely as the Angelos dynasty was not popular as it had savagely overthrown the Comnenus emperors and Isaac the emperor had made an alliance with Saladin. This also seems to be an argument based more on hindsight than on any real evidence. When Prince Alexius took his case to the pope, Innocent made it clear that he was not interested and that he would have made the same point as forcibly to Boniface or Philip, had they suggested a different aim for the Crusade.

# The gathering in Venice

From May 1202 crusaders began to assemble in Venice, but problems emerged:

- The number of men mustering fell far short of the projected 33,500: by midsummer only 12,000 troops had arrived.
- The proceeds of the fortieth, the tax imposed by the pope, had not arrived (and were not likely to do so as there was much resistance to paying it).
- Despite their best efforts, the Crusade's leaders could scrape together only 50,000 marks, leaving a massive shortfall of 34,000 marks.
- Some crusaders had set off on their own from Flanders, Marseilles and even Genoa, while others refused to travel and returned home.
- The Venetians had built the ships and prepared the fleet and were determined that they would be paid.

- The muster proceeded so slowly that it was too late in the year to sail for Egypt by the time all the participants had arrived.
- With the arrival of summer, disease began to take its toll.

The situation was not good, therefore, and all-round humiliation for the crusaders and for Venice loomed. It was Dandolo who suggested a solution. He did not want to be remembered as the doge who had bankrupted the Republic, nor did he want a resentful and bored crusader army in Venice. His plan was to attack the city of Zara (now Zadar in Croatia). He was prepared to wait for his money and be paid out of the spoils from Zara. This city was close by, only 265 kilometres to the south-west, and its people had recently broken free from Venetian rule, so Dandolo had every incentive to mount an assault on the city. It was not an ideal solution. For one thing, the people of Zara were Christians and their overlord was King Bela III of Hungary (*c.*1148–96). Bela had taken the cross, so his lands should have been under the protection of the Church. The fact that the crusaders agreed to the scheme shows how desperate they were.

However, not all crusaders accepted the plan. Once the pope found out, he ordered his legate, Peter of Capuano, to forbid the crusaders to attack Zara and to **excommunicate** any who defied papal orders. But the legate saw at first hand the dilemma facing the crusaders and chose not to take any action. Simon de Montfort bluntly refused to fight other Christians and Boniface of Montferrat paid a diplomatic visit to Rome so as not to be involved. Many churchmen with the crusaders also wanted to leave and had to be persuaded to stay by the papal legate, who feared the crusaders might end up with no spiritual guidance.

**KEY TERM**

**Excommunicate**
To exclude a member of the Church from taking the sacraments.

## Zara

The siege of Zara was carried out efficiently by the crusaders. They sailed from Venice in October 1202 with a fleet of about 200 ships, led by the doge's vermillion-coloured vessel. After the army landed, they received a letter from the pope forbidding them to attack Zara in terms which expressed his utter distaste and disgust very strongly. But Innocent III was in Rome and unable to influence events in Zara. Even his threats of excommunication were ignored. In late November the city fell to the besieging army and the spoils was shared between the crusaders and the Venetians. Although this resolved the immediate financial problems, it had created other issues:

- The pope had to be placated and a four-man embassy was sent to Rome.
- The attack on Zara further delayed the crusaders and therefore they had to spend the winter in the city.
- There were disturbances between the crusaders and the Venetians which led to some deaths.
- The financial gains from the attack on Zara were not enough to finance an attack on Egypt.

It was this final issue that would ultimately lead to the crusaders being willing to entertain the proposal of Prince Alexius.

**ONLINE EXTRAS**
Pearson Edexcel 

Learn how to write effective opening sentences by completing Worksheet 35 at **www.hoddereducation.co.uk/accesstohistory/extras**

SUMMARY DIAGRAM

**THE TREATY OF VENICE**

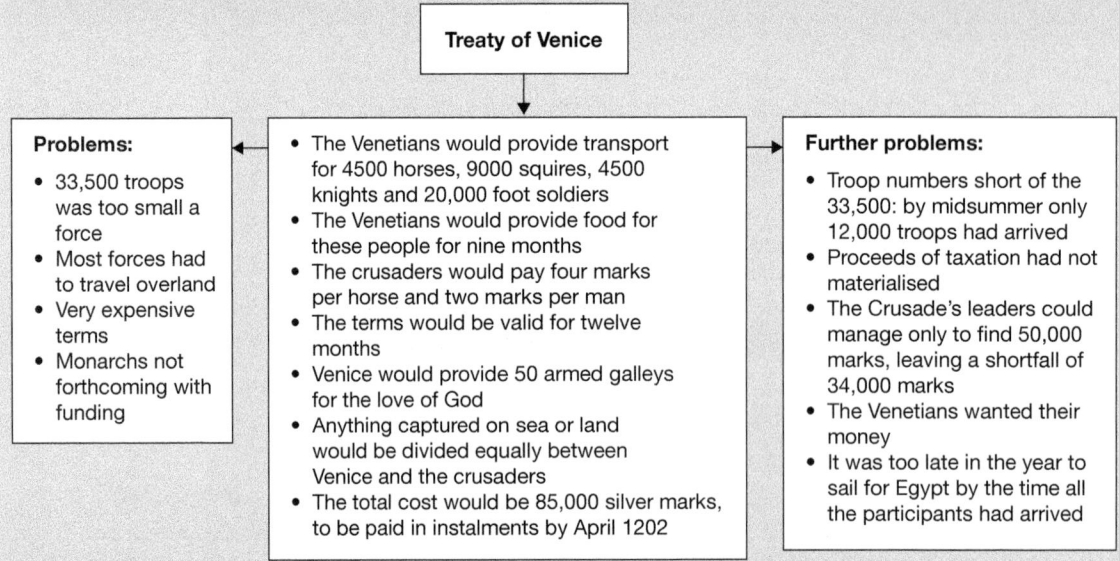

**Treaty of Venice**

- The Venetians would provide transport for 4500 horses, 9000 squires, 4500 knights and 20,000 foot soldiers
- The Venetians would provide food for these people for nine months
- The crusaders would pay four marks per horse and two marks per man
- The terms would be valid for twelve months
- Venice would provide 50 armed galleys for the love of God
- Anything captured on sea or land would be divided equally between Venice and the crusaders
- The total cost would be 85,000 silver marks, to be paid in instalments by April 1202

**Problems:**

- 33,500 troops was too small a force
- Most forces had to travel overland
- Very expensive terms
- Monarchs not forthcoming with funding

**Further problems:**

- Troop numbers short of the 33,500: by midsummer only 12,000 troops had arrived
- Proceeds of taxation had not materialised
- The Crusade's leaders could manage only to find 50,000 marks, leaving a shortfall of 34,000 marks
- The Venetians wanted their money
- It was too late in the year to sail for Egypt by the time all the participants had arrived

# 3 The attacks on Constantinople

*Why did the crusaders decide to attack Constantinople?*

The moral flexibility of the crusaders had not gone unnoticed. Envoys on behalf of Prince Alexius came to them while they spent the winter in Zara and suggested that they might further their cause by restoring his family to the throne of Byzantium. Strong inducements were offered. Prince Alexius and his father would force the Patriarch of Constantinople to submit to papal authority, something much longed for by the Roman Church. Payment of 200,000 silver marks would be given to the crusaders and the Venetians, which would cancel out all debts and finance the next stage of the operation. The army would be supplied by the Greeks for another year. Alexius would join the Crusade if desired, and anyway would provide 10,000 Greek soldiers and a permanent force of 500 knights for Palestine. One version of these events is given in Source A (see page 175).

**SOURCE A**

**From Geoffrey de Villehardouin, *The Conquest of Constantinople*, translated by Caroline Smith, Penguin Books, 2008, pp. 20–1.**

*Now you will hear about one of the most amazing and momentous occurrences of which you have ever been told. At that time there was an emperor at Constantinople whose name was Isaac. He had a brother whose name was Alexius, whom he had ransomed from a Turkish prison. This Alexius seized his brother the emperor, put the eyes out of his head and made himself emperor through the treacherous act of which you were just told. Alexius kept Isaac in captivity for a long time, with one of his sons who was also called Alexius. This son later escaped from prison and fled in a boat to a coastal city called Ancona. From there Alexius went to King Philip of Germany who had married his sister. He came to Verona in Lombardy and stayed for a while in that town, where he encountered numerous pilgrims who were on their way to join the army. The people who had helped Alexius escape and who remained with him, said to him, 'Sir, take note that there is an army close by at Venice of the finest men and the best knights in the world who are going overseas. You should appeal to them to take pity on you and your father who were so unjustly dispossessed. If they are willing, you should do whatever they ask of you. There's a chance they might be moved by your plight.' Alexius said that he would do this very gladly and that their advice was sound.*

**SOURCE QUESTION** 

How does Villehardouin in Source A portray events to reflect credit on the crusaders?

There was some merit in Prince Alexius' proposal. Alexius needed help to overthrow his uncle, while the crusaders needed money and men. The Byzantines pointed out that Prince Alexius' father had been unjustly deprived of his lands, and that one of the reasons put forward by Pope Urban II for the First Crusade had been the unjust way that the Christians had lost their lands. The crusader debts would be wiped out and they would gain supplies for the immediate future. The extra men would also help to compensate for those who had left. In the longer term, the presence of a garrison force in the Holy Land would solve the continual problem of the shortage of manpower in defending the Christian kingdom. The Crusade would be able to continue, thus avoiding the dreadful humiliation of its breaking up at such an early stage. Moreover, the Venetians welcomed the chance to obtain good trading terms in Constantinople as the power behind the restoration of the emperor and to be able to call on Byzantine resources in the assault on Alexandria. For the papacy, it was the chance to achieve its long-held aim of reuniting the Greek and Latin Churches.

The ultimate aim of Egypt was not forgotten. Indeed, the King of Jerusalem sent a small expedition south in 1204 as a preliminary to the arrival of the crusaders whom he expected.

## The use of force

A difficulty facing the crusaders was that the only way to establish Isaac and Alexius in Constantinople was by force, and the pope had expressly forbidden force against other Christians. Some crusaders, such as Simon de Montfort, were so disgusted by the suggestion of attacking Constantinople that they left and made their own way to the Holy Land. Reinforcements from Flanders similarly decided to go straight to Syria. There was also the problem of the excommunication which had come into operation when the crusaders disobeyed the pope and attacked Zara. The bishops who were with the army sent a group to Rome to explain the realities of the situation to the pope. This placed Innocent III in a difficult position. He had long prayed for a crusade and he did not want to be the person to call a halt. Therefore, he agreed to absolve the crusaders, provided they restored what they had taken and did not invade any more Christian lands unless 'a just or necessary cause should, perhaps, arise'. He would not do the same for the Venetians, whom he blamed for the events.

But enforcing obedience proved too much of a challenge. Zara was not given back to Hungary. Boniface refused to publish the bull excommunicating the Venetians, asserting that it would lead to the break-up of the Crusade, although he did agree that if Innocent III really insisted, then he would publish it. But messages to and from Rome took some weeks. By the time Innocent III's reply arrived, saying that the bull should be published and that the crusaders were not to attack any more Christian lands, and especially not the Byzantine Empire, it was too late. The fleet had set sail for the capital city of the Greek Empire, leaving Zara in April 1203.

## The first attack

Prince Alexius joined the crusaders at Corfu and from there they sailed for Constantinople in May 1203. When they saw the walls of the Byzantine capital, they soon realised how hard it would be to capture the city if it did not accept Alexius voluntarily. The army made its base near what is now Scutari and in July a fleet sailed along by the sea walls of Constantinople demonstrating its strength. Some onlookers shouted abusive comments but mostly Prince Alexius' presence was ignored. This was not really surprising as he was little known in the empire and therefore had little support, while the emperor had made it clear that Alexius was proposing to subordinate the Greeks to the pope. Given the lack of support for Alexius and Greek hostility to subordination to the Roman Church it had become obvious that the only way to take Byzantium was by force. Backing for the ruling emperor had not crumbled as the crusaders had hoped, despite there having been numerous uprisings against rulers in recent years.

The fleet crossed the Bosphorus and prepared to attack Galatea on the northern bank of the Golden Horn. The army was divided into seven units, each geographically organised so that men fought alongside those they already knew. Prayer was offered before the assault began. The amphibious landing was a considerable achievement; the doors of the ships opened as planned and the knights charged out. They were soon able to take the Tower of Galatea and to break the vast chain which protected the entrance to the Golden Horn. The Venetian ships now came up and moored off the walls, using scaling ladders from their ships for their advance, while the French fought on land in the northern sector of the city.

## Byzantine resistance

Up to this point, Alexius III Angelos had done very little to defend his city. He had not even tried to attack the crusaders as they landed, the moment at which they were the most vulnerable. Now his soldiers began to send out raiding parties, which were successful in stopping supplies reaching the attackers. By July the crusaders were short of food and began to bombard the walls more fiercely. The doge, Dandolo, set an example by forging ahead in his galley and being carried on to the shore. His men followed. Alexius III countered with his crack troops, the Varangian Guard. The crusaders responded by setting fire to the area they had taken. Encouraged by a strong wind, the fire spread rapidly. Full battle was then begun by Alexius III, whose army was far bigger than that of the depleted crusaders, who may have had as few as 3000 men to fight.

**ONLINE EXTRAS** AQA **WWW**

Develop your analysis of an individual by completing Worksheet 37 at **www.hoddereducation.co.uk/accesstohistory/extras**

Source B (below) describes the exploits of Dandolo.

**SOURCE B**

**From Geoffrey de Villehardouin, *The Conquest of Constantinople*, translated by Caroline Smith, Penguin Books, 2008, p. 46.**

*Now you will hear of a wondrous and brave feat; the doge of Venice, who was an old man and could not see a thing, was in the prow of his galley, fully armed and with the banner of St Mark before him. He called out to his men that they should put him ashore; if they refused he would punish them harshly. So they brought the galley to land and themselves leapt forth, taking the banner of St Mark ahead of the doge. When the Venetians saw that the banner of St Mark had landed and that their lord's galley had reached land before them, each of them felt himself ashamed and they all went ashore. Those in the transports leapt out as and when each saw his chance and made their way to land. Then you would have seen an astounding assault. Geoffrey de Villehardouin, the marshal of Champagne who composed this work is your witness that more than forty people told him honestly that they saw the banner of St Mark on one of the towers, although no one knew who had carried it there.*

**SOURCE QUESTION** 

How useful is Source B for a historian studying the attack on Constantinople?

The outcome of this encounter was unexpected. Despite possessing a superior force, Alexius III withdrew behind the walls of his city. The crusaders attributed their victory to the fear the sight of them had inspired in the Byzantine forces. Alexius III's decision was inexplicable as not only did he outnumber the crusaders but he knew they were short of food. It was also crucial as his support dwindled away and on 17 July he fled from the city.

## The return of Isaac II and Alexius IV

Byzantine officials went to offer the throne to Isaac II, although by custom a blind man could not become emperor. The crusaders also sent a deputation under Villehardouin to negotiate with Isaac. When the terms of the agreement that Prince Alexius had made with the crusaders were explained to Isaac II, he was appalled as he knew how much resistance there would be in Constantinople. Despite this, Prince Alexius was crowned as his co-emperor, Alexius IV Angelos. In the meantime, the Greeks continued to supply the crusading army, camped out near Galatea, with food, while some of the crusaders went sightseeing in the city, and, no doubt, saw all its wealth and splendour for themselves. They agreed to stay on over the winter to help prop up the new regime. In Europe there was much rejoicing at the easy victory and the prospect of the reunification of Christendom. The only problem was that Constantinople had made no formal submission to Rome as yet. But Innocent III remained hopeful and was assured by the crusaders that they would set out for Egypt in the spring. He wrote to them in February 1204 reproving them for their actions and ordering them to carry on with the Crusade. The bishops with them were told to ensure everyone performed acts of penance.

### Rioting and disorder

The relationship between Alexius IV and the crusaders began to fall apart for a number of reasons:

- There was great resentment within the city from the native population, egged on by their clergy, to the presence of the westerners.
- Rioting and disorder broke out and a mosque was attacked by the crusaders.
- A major fire, started by the Christians, destroyed many of the wooden buildings in a large part of the city. This action led to the westerners becoming so unpopular that the traders living in Constantinople all had to flee to the camp near Galatea for safety.
- Alexius IV delayed payment of the promised money to the army. In November the crusaders told him to pay up or face the consequences. Insults were exchanged on both sides.
- Dandolo's efforts to broker a settlement failed in the hostile atmosphere. The result was worse rioting and disorder, culminating in a Byzantine attempt to destroy the Venetian fleet with fireships. Only the skilful seamanship of the Venetian sailors saved their navy.

Alexius IV was increasingly unpopular with his subjects, mostly because of the heavy taxation needed to meet the demands of the crusaders. He had even melted down treasure from some of the city churches. He was eventually overthrown in January 1204, by a member of the Comnenus family, who was a great-great-grandson of Alexius I and took the title Alexius V (*c*.1140–1204). He showed his hostility to the crusaders by hanging three unfortunate Venetians who had been captured from hooks in front of the city walls and then setting them alight. Fearing a movement to restore Alexius IV, he had him strangled. Isaac II, his father, had already died. It was as a result of these circumstances that the second attack on Constantinople developed.

## The second attack on Constantinople

The crusaders held a meeting in March 1204 and decided that an attack on Constantinople was their only option, for the following reasons:

- They had very few viable alternatives. They were far from home with little food and so could neither proceed to Egypt nor go back to western Europe.
- The murder of Alexius IV, their ally, needed to be avenged.
- The clergy asserted that the Greek Church was in schism and so the attack was right and just.

They then drew up an agreement about how the spoils would be divided:

- All the loot would be pooled and the Venetians would be paid what they were owed as a priority.
- Then what was left would be shared equally between the Venetians and the other crusaders.
- A committee of six Frenchmen and six Venetians would decide who was to be the next emperor and patriarch.
- Another group would decide how the Byzantine lands should be allocated, while the Venetians were promised they would have trading dominance.
- The campaign to the Holy Land would be deferred to 1205.
- All took an oath that violence to women and churchmen was to be avoided.

There were three phases to the attack:

- 9 April: the fleet crossed the Golden Horn and scaling ladders and siege engines were used against the walls. The defenders reacted strongly with missiles and boiling oil, while an unfavourable wind made the attack harder. This forced the crusaders to withdraw.
- 12 April: a second assault was launched which was more effective as the wind had changed. Some Venetian ships got right up against one of the towers and men were able to get a foothold on the walls. French foot soldiers then broke down a small bricked-up door and entered the city through a hole about the size of a fireplace. The defenders fled and the Frenchmen were able to find a gate which they opened so that the knights could ride in. The emperor now fled from the city and the officials left in charge surrendered, hoping to prevent any more destruction.

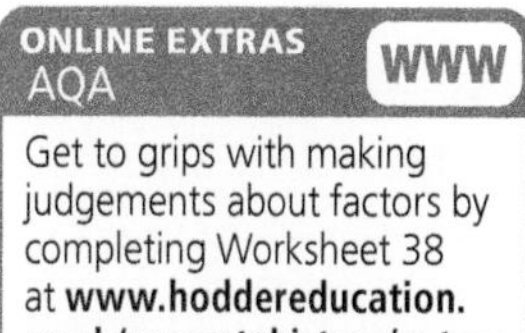

ONLINE EXTRAS
AQA
WWW
Get to grips with making judgements about factors by completing Worksheet 38 at www.hoddereducation.co.uk/accesstohistory/extras

ONLINE EXTRAS
Pearson Edexcel
WWW
Get to grips with the concept of causation by completing Worksheet 36 at www.hoddereducation.co.uk/accesstohistory/extras

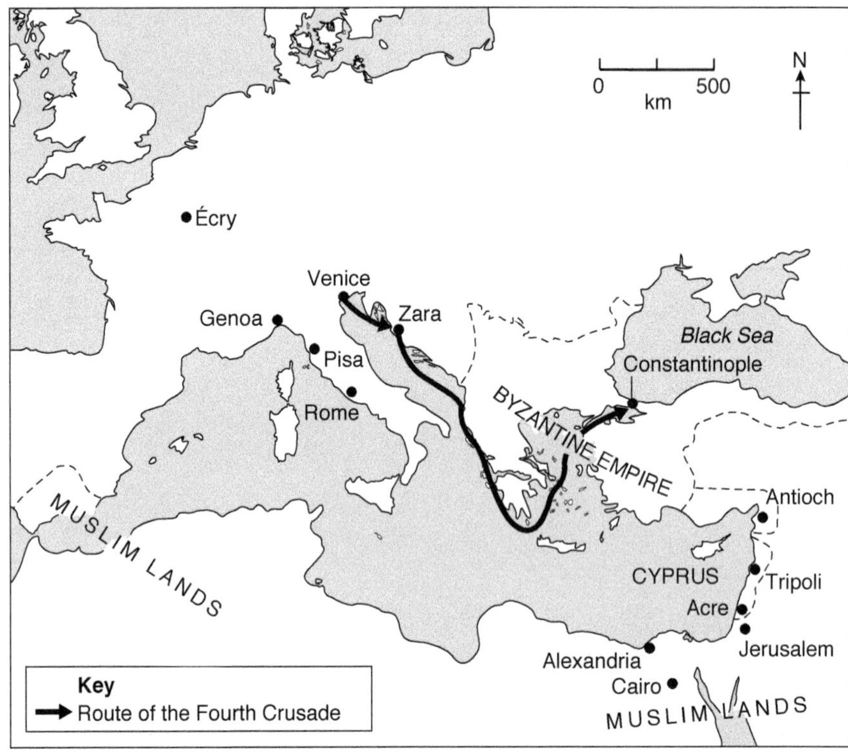


**Figure 8.1** The route of the Fourth Crusade.

- 13 April: the leaders took over the palaces, amazed at the vast riches they contained, while the rank-and-file of the army ransacked the rest of the city for three days, even defiling the great Church of Hagia Sophia. They found gold, silver, tableware, precious stones, silk cloth, garments of fur and ermine and 'all the fine things that were ever found on earth', according to Villehardouin.

**SOURCE QUESTION**

What evidence is there in Source C to suggest that God had given the crusaders victory?

**SOURCE C**

**From Geoffrey de Villehardouin, *The Conquest of Constantinople*, translated by Caroline Smith, Penguin Books, 2008, p. 67.**

*Each man chose lodgings that pleased him, and there were plenty to go round. And so the army of pilgrims and Venetians established their quarters. There was great rejoicing at the honour and victory that God had granted them, for those who had been in poverty were now in wealth and luxury. Thus they celebrated Palm Sunday and the following Easter Sunday in God-given honour and joy. And they certainly should have praised Our Lord, since they had no more than 20,000 armed men, and they had conquered 400,000 men or more in the strongest city in the world, a great city and the best fortified.*

## The destruction in Constantinople

Greek writers such as Nicetas Choniates (*c.*1155–1217) and Nicholas Mesarites (*c.*1163/4–after 1214), who both witnessed events in Constantinople, were horrified by what happened and described drunken soldierly and sexual assaults. However, they did also note that some Greeks were treated with respect. But Choniates also pointed to the contrast with the way Saladin had behaved when he took Jerusalem (see page 142), thus implying that a Muslim had treated Christians better than fellow-Christians had. The total death toll was about 2000 people, less than one per cent of the population, and the violence against the inhabitants was largely curbed after the first day. Some of the looted treasure was collected in three of the churches to be distributed according to the March agreement. But this was probably only about half of what was taken. The value of the plunder has been estimated as 500,000 marks, which would have been the equivalent of the income of a medium-sized European state over ten years. But it was distributed among thousands of individuals who had fought in the siege.

## The removal of relics

One of the aspects of the plundering which upset the Greeks most, and caused very long-lasting resentment, was the removal of the holy relics with which Constantinople was so richly supplied. Churchmen such as Bishop Nivelo of Soissons, Bishop Conrad of Halberstadt and Abbot Martin of Pairis in Alsace led the way in seizing relics which would enrich their churches. Nivelo's haul included the head of St Stephen, the first martyr, a thorn from the Crown of Thorns and the finger of St Thomas, which he had placed in the side of Christ. Conrad had parts of the True Cross, the head of St James, the brother of Christ, and many other parts of the bodies of the disciples and early saints. Abbot Martin terrorised a monk in the monastery of Christ Pantocrator into giving him their valuables stored in an iron chest. In 2004, 800 years after the siege, Pope John Paul II (1920–2005) returned the remains of St Gregory the Theologian and St John Chrysostom, two important Orthodox saints, to the Patriarch of Constantinople.

From the loot, the Venetians were paid what they were owed and then the knights all received twenty marks, clergy and mounted sergeants ten marks, and foot soldiers five marks. This was in addition to what individuals had managed to hoard for themselves. The Republic of Venice had been much influenced in the past by Byzantine art and the Basilica of St Mark was modelled on the Church of the Holy Apostles in Constantinople but was now enriched with other looted objects. The most notable plunder was the sculpture of the four horses, the Triumphal Quadriga, which had been in the Hippodrome of Constantinople and can now be seen inside St Mark's Basilica.

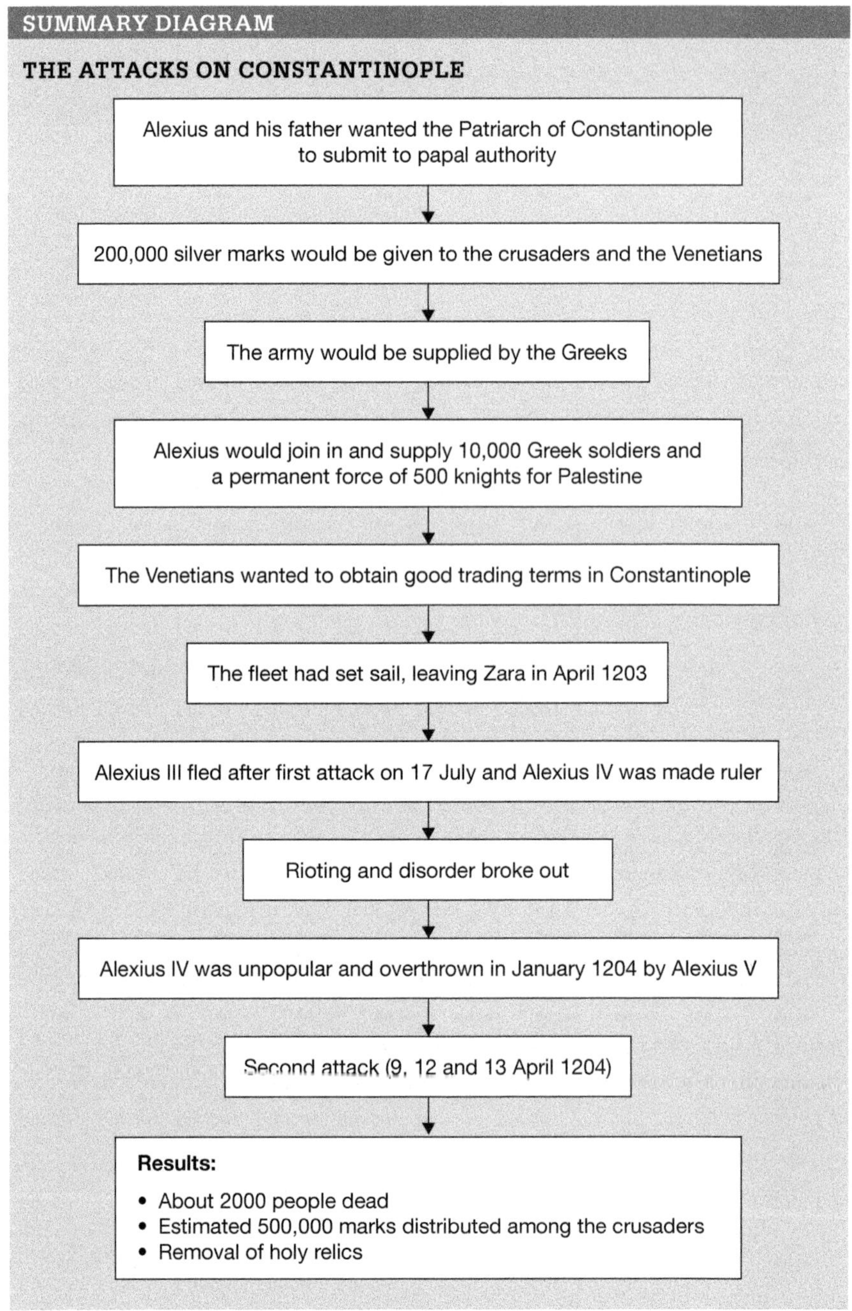
SUMMARY DIAGRAM
THE ATTACKS ON CONSTANTINOPLE
Alexius and his father wanted the Patriarch of Constantinople to submit to papal authority
200,000 silver marks would be given to the crusaders and the Venetians
The army would be supplied by the Greeks
Alexius would join in and supply 10,000 Greek soldiers and a permanent force of 500 knights for Palestine
The Venetians wanted to obtain good trading terms in Constantinople
The fleet had set sail, leaving Zara in April 1203
Alexius III fled after first attack on 17 July and Alexius IV was made ruler
Rioting and disorder broke out
Alexius IV was unpopular and overthrown in January 1204 by Alexius V
Second attack (9, 12 and 13 April 1204)
Results:
• About 2000 people dead
• Estimated 500,000 marks distributed among the crusaders
• Removal of holy relics

# 4 The results of the Fourth Crusade

■ *What were the consequences of the capture of Constantinople?*

There were several consequences of the capture of Constantinople.

## Baldwin as emperor

Count Baldwin of Flanders was elected as the first Latin emperor, Baldwin I, and duly crowned and enthroned by the assembled Catholic bishops. Boniface of Montferrat was disappointed not to be elected, especially as he was betrothed to Isaac II's widow, but the Frenchmen who were chosen to be on the electoral committee did not all favour him and the Venetians were hostile. He had some compensation in being allowed to seize the city of Thessalonica.

## The expansion of the Venetian Empire

Dandolo had asked Innocent III to be released from his vow to go to the Holy Land in view of his age and blindness. Innocent III blamed Dandolo for the attack on Zara and refused to agree, arguing that Dandolo was vital to the success of the Crusade. However, Dandolo died in Constantinople in 1205.

Venice gained control of Crete and Corfu, which was very profitable to their trading empire, and later extended their holdings to Euboea and trading posts such as Methone and Coron.

## The Patriarch of Constantinople

A Venetian was made the Patriarch of Constantinople. As a result, Innocent III looked forward to the union of the two Churches and saw the victory of the small crusading army of 20,000 men over one of the greatest cities in the world as a clear sign of divine favour. He was ready to give full crusading privileges to those who would stay to defend the Latin Empire. But gradually his enthusiasm lessened. The legate on the Crusade had absolved those remaining from their vows to go on to the Holy Land, which meant there was no prospect of a crusade to Egypt. Moreover, accounts of what had happened at the capture of the city began to filter back to Rome. Innocent III was upset by the apparent grasping behaviour of the crusaders and condemned them for breaking their vows and fighting Christians. As a realist, he saw that there was no hope of a reunion of the Church while the Greeks felt so hostile to the Latins and blamed them for the fate of Constantinople.

## Other consequences

The new Latin empire proved as hard to defend as the Crusader States. Like them, it suffered from a lack of manpower and was difficult to hold together.

The new emperor, Baldwin I, was more or less in control in mainland Greece but even here faced resistance in Epirus. In Asia Minor, the area around Smyrna and Nicaea broke away and, on the Black Sea, Trebizond opted for warlord rule. The ruler of Bulgaria was in open revolt. The shrinking of his territories limited Baldwin I's income. Appeals for help attracted little response and the Venetians were of little assistance as their strength was at sea and not on land.

In 1205 Baldwin I was defeated and captured at Adrianople, fighting the Greeks and Bulgarians. Louis I of Blois died and Baldwin I was later probably killed in prison. He left only an infant daughter and so was succeeded by his brother, Henry (*c.*1176–1216). Boniface of Montferrat was killed in 1207 and Thessalonica annexed by Epirus.

In the longer perspective, the Fourth Crusade had permanently damaged both the Holy Land and Byzantium, even though it was taken back by the Greeks in 1261, because the political fragmentation proved to be permanent and confirmed the east–west schism. The security of the Holy Land was weakened as its settlers flocked to Byzantium, as they saw greater opportunities to gain wealth there. As a result, the position of the Muslims in the Near East was strengthened. The Byzantine Empire was considerably weakened and this paved the way for later Muslim conquests in Anatolia and the Balkans in the future.

Develop your analytical skills by completing Worksheet 39 at **www.hoddereducation.co.uk/accesstohistory/extras**

**ONLINE EXTRAS**
Pearson Edexcel WWW

Develop your understanding of the developments of the Fourth Crusade by completing Worksheet 37 at **www.hoddereducation.co.uk/accesstohistory/extras**

Those in the west who benefited the most were the monasteries and churches which received the relics from the plunder of Constantinople. They could display these relics, become centres of pilgrimage and make money from offerings. Miracles allowed them to make their fortunes and to build better and bigger churches to accommodate their holy objects, thus providing work for craftsmen and builders and stimulating the local economy. This was not quite the result for which Innocent III had yearned.

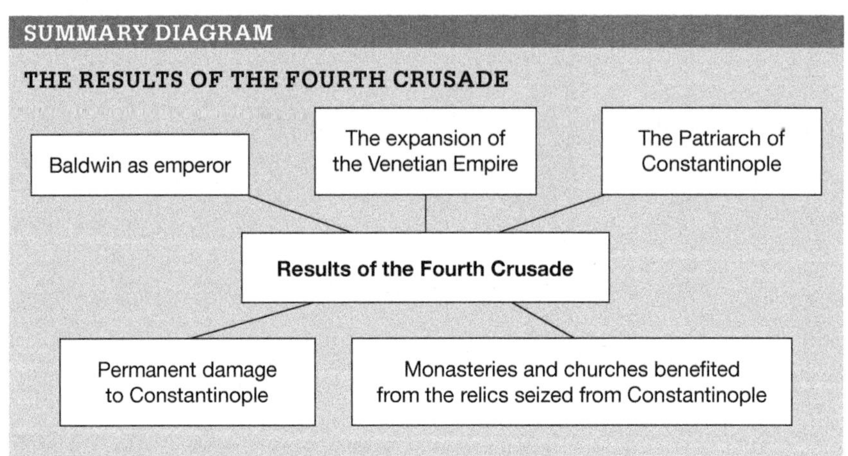

# 5 Key debate

- *Why did the crusaders attack Constantinople?*

Understanding why the crusaders decided to attack Constantinople has exercised a number of historians. The outcome of the assault, namely the savage sacking of the city, is a huge blot on the reputation of the crusading movement and so exoneration is pursued as much as explanation. For some time the 'clash of civilisations' theory was generally accepted, as propounded by Steven Runciman. He argued that the arrival of the first crusaders in 1096 had alarmed the Byzantines so that conflict was the inevitable outcome. This view was criticised as untenable since the Byzantine emperors were generally on good terms with the west and many Latins served in their armies and were prominent in defending Constantinople in 1203. In addition, there was no great enthusiasm in the west for an attack. Many rank-and-file crusaders went on to the Holy Land rather than take a Christian city and few volunteered to serve in the armies of Baldwin and his successors. Indeed, by 1261, Byzantium had retaken most of its empire. Studies by Michael Angold (2003) and Paul Stephenson (2010) have shown that the Byzantine Empire was coming under pressure in the Balkans and in Cyprus and so they suggest that it might have broken up in any case.

It is now generally accepted that the crusaders did not intend to capture Constantinople at the outset and the reasons why they changed their minds are the subject of discussion. Christopher Tyerman (2019) argues that the diversion to Constantinople was seen as a means towards eventually campaigning in the Holy Land as the Crusade was meant to do, while the Venetians looked to develop trading opportunities and thus defray some of the vast costs the Crusade had entailed. Problems arose when it became clear that Alexius IV had little support in Constantinople and so was unable to assist the crusaders in achieving their aims.

Michael Angold (2003) argues that the refusal of Alexius to honour his undertakings was the main reason for the breach with the crusaders and also suggests that it was the malign influence of Mourtzouphlos (who would become Alexius V) which lay behind Alexius' intransigence.

For Jonathan Phillips (2004), it was the murder of Alexius which precipitated the attack on Constantinople and he argues that this was the point at which a crusader conquest of Constantinople became the aim of the expedition, as other options were not open to them. Tyerman adds that a further consideration was the way that doubts about attacking fellow Christians were stilled by the clergy. The argument was made that the Byzantines were schismatics who had broken away from the Roman Catholic Church, they were regicides who had killed Alexius, their emperor, and they were oath-breakers who had refused to make good their obligations to the crusaders. Thus, they were holding up the meritorious cause of the conquest of the Holy Land, and those who died in the fighting would earn indulgences.

The first interpretation suggests that the attack on Constantinople was inevitable.

**INTERPRETATION QUESTION**

Which of the two interpretations, Extract 1 or 2, do you find the more convincing?

**EXTRACT 1**

From Jonathan Phillips, *The Fourth Crusade*, Jonathan Cape, 2004, p. 235.

*The murder of Alexius marked an irrevocable break between the Byzantines and the crusaders. Despite the problems between the young emperor and the westerners, while Alexius remained alive there was always a possibility that his need for support and his moral and contractual obligations towards the crusaders might prevent open war. The two sides had teetered on the brink of conflict since November 1203. Now there was no further room for manoeuvre. Mourtzouphlous was known to have killed the emperor and he refused to fulfil his victim's promises to the crusaders. Both sides realized that war was a certainty and they began to prepare for battle. The crusaders' position was desperate. They had tied themselves ineluctably [unavoidably] to Alexius and his death left them completely exposed, thousands of miles from home and camped outside a hostile city. His failure to deliver the anticipated financial backing meant that the Venetians remained substantially underpaid for continuing to provide the fleet, and the crusaders themselves lacked the money to mount an effective campaign in the Holy Land.*

A second interpretation argues that the crusaders could have left, but were tempted by the riches of Constantinople.

**EXTRACT 2**

From Michael Angold, *The Fourth Crusade*, Longman, 2003, p. 99.

*The murder of Alexius IV Angelus shocked the crusaders and confirmed their view that regicide was a peculiarly Byzantine vice. It brought to the surface stereotypes that had been festering in Latin minds since the usurpation of the tyrant Andronicus Comnenus. The hardening of attitudes towards the Byzantines is important, but the crusade leaders could have extricated themselves without too much difficulty from Constantinople. They seemed reluctant to take the opportunities to depart that were offered. Moral and religious grounds will certainly have played their part, but it would have dawned on the crusaders that Constantinople was a prize there for the taking. They represented the only effective military and naval power. The imperial court had little real influence on the streets of Constantinople, which were in the hands of the mob. The crusader army was now rather stronger than it had been when it first arrived. It had been joined by the Latins of Constantinople, estimated at about 15,000. In addition, some of the crusaders who had sailed directly to Syria, but had found nothing to do, arrived in dribs and drabs over the autumn and early winter of 1203.*

**ONLINE EXTRAS** AQA **WWW**

Practise your interpretation analysis by completing Worksheet 40 at **www.hoddereducation.co.uk/accesstohistory/extras**

**ONLINE EXTRAS** Pearson Edexcel **WWW**

Practise your interpretation analysis by completing Worksheets 38, 39 and 40 at **www.hoddereducation.co.uk/accesstohistory/extras**

# CHAPTER SUMMARY

The Fourth Crusade resulted from pressure from Innocent III as expressed in his papal bull, *Post miserabile*. It was led by initially by Thibaut III of Champagne and Louis I of Blois, who made an agreement with the Venetians, led by the doge, Dandolo, for transport to Egypt. When Thibaut died he was replaced by Boniface of Montferrat. The crusaders could not produce the money they had promised Venice and so were persuaded to attack Zara to acquire some loot. They were then enlisted by Prince Alexius to help to restore him to the Byzantine throne. Innocent III did not back this diversion and excommunicated disobedient crusaders. They attacked Constantinople and the emperor fled. The new emperor, Alexius IV, became unpopular and was overthrown, so the crusaders besieged Constantinople and took and sacked it. Innocent III was horrified at the way events turned out. The Crusade achieved very little and the sack of Constantinople was widely condemned in Europe.

## Refresher questions

Use these questions to remind yourself of the key material covered in this chapter.

1. What were the aims of the Fourth Crusade?
2. What were the terms of the agreement between the crusaders and Venice?
3. Why did the Venetians want to attack Byzantium?
4. Why did the crusaders attack Zara?
5. What was the reaction of Innocent III to the attack on Zara?
6. Why was Constantinople attacked the first time?
7. Why was Constantinople attacked the second time?
8. What were the main results of the Crusade?

## Question practice: AQA

### Essay questions

1 To what extent was poor leadership the most significant reason for the failures of the crusaders in the years 1187–1204? [A level]

**EXAM HINT** You need to examine the importance of poor leadership alongside other factors. Make sure you have a thematic approach and avoid descriptions of events.

2 'A complete failure for all Christians.' Assess the validity of this view of the Crusades in the years 1187–1204. [A level]

**EXAM HINT** Consider the Crusades in this period as a complete failure – but then also consider mitigating factors which might provide a partial argument against the quotation given in the question.

## Question practice: Pearson Edexcel

### Interpretations questions

1 Historians have different views about the reasons for the failure of the Fourth Crusade. Analyse and evaluate Extracts A and B (page 189), and use your knowledge of the issues, to explain your answer to the following question: How convincing do you find the view that Innocent III was responsible for the failure of the Fourth Crusade? [AS level]

**EXAM HINT** Analyse points made in Extract A (on Innocent's failures) and Extract B (on the Venetians' ambitions). Use your own knowledge to support the view in the question, and then to modify or counter it.

2 In the light of differing interpretations, how convincing do you find the view that the Fourth Crusade failed because 'Innocent's conception of crusading was fundamentally flawed' (Extract C)? To explain your answer, analyse and evaluate the material in both Extracts B and C (page 189), using your own knowledge of the issues. [A level]

**EXAM HINT** Analyse points made in Extract B (on the lack of men and the Venetian contract) and Extract C (on Innocent's ambition to direct the Crusade). Use your own knowledge to support the view in the question, and then to modify or counter it.

**EXTRACT A**

From Jamie Byrom and Michael Riley, *The Crusades*, Hodder Education, 2013, p. 121.

*Innocent called his crusade plans 'the business of the cross'. He adopted a business-like approach to identifying problems that might weaken the Crusade. Many of these problems had grown up over the previous century and other Popes had tried to tackle them, but Innocent believed that his systematic response would help raise the most powerful crusading force yet seen. His mistake was in believing that strengthening papal control of the Crusade would deepen religious commitment and guarantee success.*

*In the autumn of 1198 Pope Innocent sent his officially approved preachers to call people to crusade. ... But the response was slow. There was no rush to join the Crusade, and clergy were reluctant to pay the new [church] tax.*

**EXTRACT B**

From Jonathan Phillips, *The Fourth Crusade and the Sack of Constantinople*, Pimlico, 2005, pp. 311–12.

*The reason why the Fourth Crusade went to Constantinople in the late spring of 1203 was, ironically, in response to an invitation of a Greek – the appeal by Prince Alexius to help him and his father to secure what they regarded as their rightful position as rulers of the Byzantine Empire. Had this request not been made, there is no convincing evidence to suggest that the expedition would have turned towards Constantinople. To explain why the westerners' fleet sailed down to the Bosphorus, rather than heading towards Egypt and the Holy Land, one has to ask why the prince's offer was accepted.*

*Herein lay the Achilles heel of the whole enterprise: the lack of men and money. These were hardly new considerations and were, indeed, two prime causes of the collapse of the Second Crusade in 1148. ... The Fourth Crusade, however, possessed an additional constituent – the contract between the French and the Venetians – and it was the need to make good the terms of this agreement that became a powerful force in driving and shaping the expedition.*

**EXTRACT C**

From Thomas Asbridge, *The Crusades*, Simon & Schuster, 2012, pp. 524, 525 and 526.

*... Innocent sought to launch a new crusade to the Holy Land, ... issuing a calls to arms [in] August 1198. He visualised a glorious endeavour – the preaching, organisation and prosecution of which would be under his direct control – imagining that so orderly and sacred an expedition could not fail to win divine approval.*

*Yet, despite ... the assurance of Innocent's vision, all his ... efforts elicited only a muted response: the anticipated hordes of enthusiastic warriors did not enlist ... [and] the donation chests strewn across the West failed to fill.*

*In fact, Innocent's conception of crusading was fundamentally flawed. Absolutist in tone, it made no provision for interactive collaboration between the Church and the secular leaders of ... society. The pope imagined that he would simply bend the kings and lord of ... Christendom to his will. ... But this proved to be entirely unrealistic. ... When ... it became obvious that there would be no [royal] involvement [in the Crusade], Innocent did not attempt to consult or recruit ... leaders from the upper aristocracy. He probably believed that the members of this class would flock to his cause of their own volition, eager to serve at his beck and call – but he was wrong, and this lapse of judgement would have tragic consequences for Christendom.*

CHAPTER 9

# Conclusion (AQA): The Age of the Crusades, c1071–1204

In this unit, AQA wants you to prove an understanding of the process of change over time, and that you use a knowledge of shorter periods in order to prove this broader awareness. You should consider wider themes or periods in this course as the basis of your learning and revision.

This study in breadth should encourage an understanding of the following:

- The nature of cause and consequences, of change and continuity, and of similarity and differences over a long period.
- The links between perspectives, such as political, economic, social or religious, as well as appreciating developments relating to the perspectives separately over time.
- The role played by individuals, groups, ideas or ideology.

To help you, AQA has introduced six key questions that identify these broader issues and perspectives. As a basis for your work, you might consider the following points related to each of these key questions:

1 What were the motives of the crusaders and the counter-crusaders?

2 What problems faced the States in Outremer and how successfully were these problems addressed?

3 How important were faith and ideas for Christians and Muslims?

4 What was the impact of the Crusades on the Muslim Near East?

5 How did the Byzantine Empire, Outremer and the Latin West change and what influenced relations between them?

6 How important was the role of key individuals and groups and how were they affected by developments?

Each of these six key questions is considered in more detail below.

## 1 What were the motives of the crusaders and the counter-crusaders?

Many candidates look at this key question by considering the motives for the First Crusade. While this is entirely reasonable, it is useful to remember that this study in breadth requires an understanding of themes over time. Therefore, a good appreciation of how motives changed is crucial. Some awareness of how difficult it is to prove motivation by anything other than an individual's actions is also needed.

An obvious starting point is the Battle of Manzikert in 1071. Reaction to the threat posed by the Seljuk Turks might be used as the basis for considering the broader theme of the reaction to a military threat across the period. By the Fourth Crusade you might argue that the crusaders were themselves concocting the military threat in order to provide justification for an attack on a range of perceived enemies. It is not difficult to find specific evidence to support this concept of military threat. This might include the death of Sulayman and the re-emergence of the Turkish threat in the 1090s, Zengi's capture of Edessa in 1144, the Battle of Hattin in 1187 and the threat posed by King Bela of Hungary to Venetian interests in 1202. The origin of the military threat may have changed, but the theme is a consistent one across the period and sets the crusaders more in the cast of defenders than of military aggressors, which is a useful point for further discussion. Indeed, this theme might also be used to explain the motives of the counter-crusaders. Muslim reaction to the military threat posed by the Latin West can be contrasted with the internal military threat created by Muslim factions, which might itself be illustrated by the rise of Nureddin in Egypt and, of course, by Saladin. Indeed, the removal of factionalism under Saladin merely shifted the origin of perceived military threat to the Crusader States. This again allows for consideration of change and continuity over time.

Undoubtedly, discussion of military threat will also include the emergence of *jihad* under Zengi and the extent to which religion motivated the Latin crusaders. Again, it is easy to become fixated on Urban II and the Council of Clermont in 1095 and to forget the broader themes of this course, as it is to forget that individual crusaders were motivated by individual histories. Raymond of Toulouse did not have the same objectives as Bohemund of Taranto. It may not even be valid to suggest that a participant in the Peasants' Crusade was motivated by the same religious awareness and objectives as King Richard on the Third Crusade. Did religion really offer a sense of community and common understanding in such a diverse and geographically disparate adventure as the Crusades, and one which stretched across the full date range of this course? It is perhaps even flawed to argue that the counter-crusaders were motivated by a common appreciation of Islamic theology.

Religion as a theme might very easily be identified with the interests of those on the First Crusade. The Holy Lance and the True Cross are both powerful symbols of the importance of religious imagery to the crusaders during and beyond 1099 as this imagery remained important at Hattin in 1187, when the True Cross was captured by Saladin. However, it is much more difficult to argue a consistent religious theme by the time of the Fourth Crusade, when the attacks on Zara and on the Byzantine Empire itself appear to counter the importance of religion. However, caution should be exercised. The religious objectives of the papacy were somewhat different from those exercised by the crusaders themselves. The papal desire to heal the schism in the Church and the willingness to 'accept' the subservience of the eastern to the western Church was a fear articulated by Alexius in the 1090s, a fear which might simply be considered to have been realised by the early thirteenth century.

Material motivation is another theme that should be developed across the period. Baldwin of Boulogne and Tancred of Hauteville's Armenian interlude during the First Crusade, and Bohemund's fixation with Antioch can be compared with the motivations of those on the Fourth Crusade, where a nebulous desire for military glory faced the realities of needing money to finance what was an exceptionally expensive adventure. The struggle to finance a crusade is well illustrated by the debt run up with the Venetian Empire, but these are themes which must surely be considered across the whole period, and remind us to consider how an expensive and highly dangerous exploit such as a crusade must have been motivated by deeply held beliefs, if not faith.

## 2 What problems faced the States in Outremer and how successfully were these problems addressed?

An initial exercise should be to consider which problems were consistent ones across the period and which were not. The specific turning points should be identified with a discussion about the extent to which each changed the nature of the problem or threat posed.

A prominent issue was that of recruitment for permanent settlement. Once the opportunity for military glory had passed, and the promise of papal indulgence faded, what motivated individuals to settle? The absence of the prospect of material award might explain the problems behind later recruitment and can indeed be used to reinforce the impression that crusaders were motivated mainly by greed and ambition. However, the existence of the Military Orders and the continued influx of pilgrims provide a useful counter-balance to the notion that Outremer was simply abandoned by the west after each crusade.

The military vulnerability of Outremer is a major theme and joins the broader problems of recruitment. The position of Edessa, distanced and vulnerable as it was, was a consistent early concern, but only became focused with the emergence of powerful and increasingly united opposition. The initial successes of the crusaders, such as the capture of Antioch, might reasonably be attributed to factional disputes, for example between Ridwan and Duqaq. The slow emergence of a united Muslim opposition is thus a useful theme, but one in which major developments are still concentrated in relatively short periods of time. The death of Zengi in 1146, or that of Nureddin in 1174, may be argued to have been important in the long-term development of a united Muslim interest in the area, but such discussions should then be firmly linked to how this affected the security of Outremer. This theme can be linked to the key questions addressing the impact of individuals, and especially the role that Reynald and Saladin had in cementing an oppositional alignment. Indeed, questions should be asked about the degree to which the emergence of a united Muslim presence should by necessity have meant an anti-Outremer alignment.

The issue of success over time might then be linked to these broader themes. The capture of Jerusalem may suggest that the issues had not been addressed successfully; however, this supposes that the events of 1187 were a result of longer-term trends. It might well be argued that it was the short-term events and the issues of a disputed inheritance and a sickly king, or even more specifically the military tactics at the Horns of Hattin, that was a much more significant factor. Indeed, the course of the Third Crusade and especially of Richard's advance through Outremer, proves that the problems facing Outremer were far from insurmountable. Those who argue that the fall of Outremer was inevitable might like to consider at what chronological point such an inevitability existed.

## 3 How important were faith and ideas for Christians and Muslims?

This theme should already have been addressed when considering motivation in question 1. However, this key question presents an excellent opportunity to assess how this theme changed over time. The religious motives provided by the papal indulgence in the 1090s are at variance with the motives of crusaders fearing a resurgent Islam in the 1180s. Bernard of Clairvaux's restrained preaching of the Second Crusade, made more emotive by Radulf, might itself have simply provided reason for a popular interpretation of Christianity based on a fear of the unknown, and culminating in the targeting of European Jewry. This difference between popular Christianity and that of the leaders might be further explored by a study of the German crusades. It is useful in this context to consider how a historian might measure faith. The fall of Edessa in 1144 prompted much soul searching within the Christian west and was commonly interpreted as a trial of faith. This might be contrasted with those who took the crusaders' oath in the 1090s, who seemed more convinced of the inevitable, divinely inspired, success of their venture. Were such views of the inevitability of success as prominent in the motivation of those on the Fourth Crusade, and if not, how might this lack of conviction be proven? Consideration of breadth might, therefore, question the extent to which religious conviction of the crusaders decreased over time. It was perhaps difficult to explain away the defeat at Hattin and the fall of Jerusalem for those believing in divine direction.

From a Muslim perspective there appears to be a very simple narrative of the slow development throughout this period of a more coherent expression of faith. However, the fundamental divisions between Sunni and Shi'ite remained and simply re-emerged when strong leadership was absent. How far the concept of *jihad* provides a convincing explanation for Muslim resurgence should be debated. Is the simple chronology of an increasingly fractured Christianity, contrasted with an increasingly united Muslim faith through the years 1071–1204, convincing and, if so, can it be proven?

## 4 What was the impact of the Crusades on the Muslim Near East?

Consideration of what changed and of what stayed the same across the whole period is an excellent means to address breadth for this key question. For much of the early period the relationship between crusader and Muslim was reasonably harmonious. Many of the Crusader States relied on trade. In any case, much of the hinterland beyond the crusader cities was still heavily influenced or even controlled by local atabegs. It is unlikely that Islamic interests considered the presence of the crusader army as anything other than a Byzantine relief force simply regaining lost territory, and anyway this Christian army rapidly disappeared soon after 1100. The emperor was keen to distance himself from the more aggressive religious sentiment expressed by the crusaders as he needed the Byzantine Empire to continue peaceful trade in the region. Indeed, it was with some trepidation that Alexius saw the Crusades advance beyond the fairly narrow confines of regaining Byzantine territory from the Seljuk Turks. That the Fatimids were willing to allow Christian pilgrimage to the holy sites was enough for Alexius to consider an end to his support of any further Latin advance southwards and he reacted angrily to the western desire to push home an attack against a close trading partner in the Fatimids. A fairly symbiotic relationship between settlers and locals subsequently developed over time, and rival Muslim potentates could easily find themselves on either side of Christian factionalism, fighting each other. That this changed, and how, should form part of the consideration of this key question. While it is difficult to attribute blame, there is a sense in many histories of the period that poor leadership, especially from the early leaders of Outremer, meant that any opportunity for peaceful settlement was missed. A broader understanding of the politics of the region, and especially the intense factionalism between different interest groups, might, however, counter the simplistic notion of the crusaders arriving in a peaceful and well-governed region which they subsequently destabilised. A more nuanced understanding might link to key question 6 and consider the extent to which Zengi, Nureddin and Saladin had a far more dramatic impact on the Muslim Near East than the presence of a handful of Crusader States. That Outremer suffered ever more destructive political factionalism should serve to challenge the impression of the Crusader States as having anything other than a relatively minor impact on the Muslim Near East.

## 5 How did the Byzantine Empire, Outremer and the Latin West change and what influenced relations between them?

This is a very useful key question to consider alongside key question 4. While change to the Muslim Near East might have been less dramatic, it is clear that, for Outremer at least, this whole period saw establishment, development and a subsequent move towards virtual destruction. Why this might have occurred and whether it was slow and gradual or the result of dramatic short-term events is something that should be considered.

The thesis of a slow and gradual decline is appealing, although this can come close to seeing an unhistorical inevitability behind events. Valid links might be made with conclusions reached for question 2. The lack of a unified military structure and of an effective government led to further secular weakness. The rise of the Military Orders, for example when stepping in to defend Outremer under monarchs such as Baldwin IV, seems to support the slow decline thesis. However, this should not be taken too far. The Battle of Ascalon in 1153 proves just how close Outremer could come to reversing decline. In fact, much might be made of the view that Outremer was subject to short sharp shocks that ultimately proved fatal. The deaths of both Baldwin IV and Baldwin V provide just this sort of event that caused permanent damage to the interests of Outremer in the longer term. Even the accession of Baldwin III at the age of thirteen might be considered to have led to short-term damage, which proved very difficult to recover from. Indeed, the rule of Melisende might illustrate the degree to which change occurred, not because of longer-term weaknesses, but simply because of unforeseeable events.

The attack on Constantinople during the Fourth Crusade can be used to suggest that the narrative of the Byzantine Empire was similar, at least in the final outcome, to that of Outremer. Starting from a strong position in which the Seljuks were in retreat, the Byzantines appeared to become even stronger, especially after the Treaty of Devol. However, internal division led to collapse and occupation. Similar arguments to those used about inevitability might be deployed here; certainly Alexius Comnenus considered the huge crusading army of the First Crusade to be close to becoming an army of occupation, not of liberation. This developing mutual suspicion should be a theme that is explored across the whole period. However, here again specific evidence should be deployed so that arguments about perceived Byzantine duplicity, for example in recovering Antioch, or in signing treaties with the Fatimids, can be proven. An easy route to this is to consider how individuals drove the interests of Outremer and of wider politics in the Near East.

## 6 How important was the role of key individuals and groups and how were they affected by developments?

This key question requires that you go much further than simply learning the individual biographies of notable individuals. It is the effect that individuals had, often in conjunction with other factors, that should also be explored. In addition, the relationship between key individuals might be considered to be the key driving force in the politics of the Near East in this period. Tancred and Baldwin, Bohemund and Alexius, Saladin and Richard are obvious initial contrasts and at least provide some specific evidence that can contribute to this theme. However, broader questions about how far individual ambition affected the development of events across longer periods of time should also be considered. How, for example, does the ambition of Reynald link with the longer-term weaknesses of the Kingdom of Jerusalem to explain its eventual collapse? Was there an overarching papal ambition to control the Orthodox Church, or was the call to arms more a reflection of the individual aspirations of each pope? Is it convincing to interpret the First Crusade as one in which Urban II remained firmly in control, while by the Fourth Crusade Innocent III had become the puppet of secular ambition and of the crusaders' financial necessity? If there really was a decline in papal authority across the period, then to what extent was this a consequence of the mistakes made by individual popes? In considering the Byzantine Empire, Alexius Comnenus appears to be largely responsible for the resurrection of Byzantine fortunes, but attention should be given to other factors and especially to the increasing weakness and factionalism of the Seljuk Turks. How significant was Alexius when he is contrasted with the whole range of other factors? Moreover, if the emperor is responsible for the early successes of the Byzantium, then is it also valid to assert that other emperors are to blame for its eventual decline and occupation? A final consideration might be to question the extent to which individuals in this period were ever in a position to truly influence events – as the key question intimates, to what extent were individuals the product rather than the agents of change?

**CHAPTER 10**

# Conclusion (OCR): The Crusades and the Crusader States 1095–1192

In this unit, OCR wants you to have an understanding of continuity and change over time so that you can see issues in a wider perspective. You will be able to ask significant questions about important issues and developments.

The length of the study should encourage an understanding of the following:

- The nature of cause and consequence, of change and continuity.
- Change and development over time.
- The study of a range of different perspectives, including cultural, economic, ethnic, political, religious and social issues.
- The role played by individuals, societies, ideas and events.

To help you, OCR has introduced four key topics that identify the broader issues and perspectives. These are:

1. The First Crusade.
2. The Crusader States in the twelfth century.
3. The Second Crusade.
4. The Third Crusade.

When studying each of the topics it might be helpful to consider the following points related to each of the key topics.

## 1 The First Crusade

It would be useful to have an understanding of the situation in western Europe, Byzantium and the Islamic Near East in the eleventh century, as this will be helpful in comprehending why there was a call for a crusade and why the call attracted such large-scale support. This will also encourage you to consider whether the First Crusade was a response to long-term or short-term developments within the region.

Crusades were a holy war and, therefore, it will be helpful to have an understanding of the concept and how it developed, particularly as this is often seen as a motivating factor for many of the crusaders. This long-term development can then be weighed up against the appeal of Alexius for aid, not in the immediate aftermath of the Battle of Manzikert in 1071, but following political developments in 1095. Alexius' appeal was readily seized on by Urban and it is important to be aware of why he responded to the call. Was it for religious motives or were there political considerations at play, particularly in light of the schism and the split with the east? Did Urban see a crusade as a chance to reassert papal authority in western Europe and also to unite the Christian Church, which would help strengthen his own position?

An understanding of his motives in calling for a crusade can be examined through his appeal at Clermont and the subsequent preaching tours that were undertaken in western Europe. It might be helpful to consider why Urban made his appeal at Clermont and the response to his speech, as that sheds light on the nature of society at the time.

The nature of Urban's appeal at Clermont might lead to a fixation on religious motivation, but it is important to remember that the motives of those who went on the First Crusade varied considerably; Raymond of Toulouse did not have the same motives as Bohemund. It is also worth considering whether those who went on the People's Crusade under Peter the Hermit had the same motivation as those on the First Crusade.

Religion as a motive for those going on the First Crusade might be seen in the events surrounding the Holy Lance and the True Cross and the genuine conviction of many to free their fellow Christians from the rule of the infidel. However, it is important to remember that these religious motives were somewhat different from those of the papacy.

It is also important to consider material and economic motivation. This can be seen in the actions of some of the leaders of the First Crusade, with Tancred and Baldwin's Armenian interlude and Bohemund's capture of Antioch. The desire to establish kingdoms in the Near East can be contrasted with the main body of crusaders who may simply have wanted some land given the issue of primogeniture and a land shortage in western Europe.

You should be aware of why the People's Crusade failed and it might be helpful to compare this with the success of the First Crusade. There were a number of possible reasons for the success, and an understanding of the political situation within the Muslim world will help you to understand how divided they were and the impact that this had at various stages of the Crusade. There should also be some awareness of the psychological shock that the Crusade must have had on the Muslim world and how this might have affected the outcome. These issues should be compared with the strength of the crusader forces and the tactics used by both sides to explain how it was that the crusader force was able not only to cross Anatolia, but also to capture Edessa, Antioch and, ultimately Jerusalem.

## 2 The Crusader States in the twelfth century

This section of the specification centres around the establishment, development and survival of the Crusader States in the twelfth century. It is important to understand the chronology of the establishment, development and losses of the States, as that will allow you to analyse the various factors that resulted in the varied pattern that emerged. As the first key topic suggested, many of the nobles who participated in the First Crusade were looking for the opportunity to establish kingdoms in the Middle East. However, the establishment of these kingdoms was a challenge as the number of crusaders who returned home after the First Crusade was significant, leaving only a small number to hold these important lands. The survival of the States was due to a number of reasons and it is important to be able assess the importance of issues, such as the strength and weaknesses of the various rulers, help from the west, Muslim disunity, and the role of both castles and the Military Orders in their survival. These issues will also make you aware of some of the challenges that the kingdoms faced and be able to analyse how far they were able to overcome such issues. In considering this, it is important to think about the challenge of the climate and also how the States were organised in order to compensate for the lack of numbers. This will make you aware of the military vulnerability of the States and will combine with the problem of recruitment. It was difficult for the States to recruit people for permanent settlement. This was made worse by the lack of military opportunity and the fading appeal of papal indulgence. The absence of material reward may explain the problem of recruitment, but might also help you to understand the motives of those who undertook the First Crusade. The position of Edessa is important as its distance made it vulnerable and was of consistent concern in the early period, particularly when faced with increasingly united opposition. The growing Muslim unity was also important in threatening the States. Although there were struggles between the Christians and Muslims, some attention should also be given to the symbiotic relationship between settlers and the locals which developed during the twelfth century. There were also Muslim rulers who made alliances with Christian rulers and therefore found themselves on either side of Christian factionalism. However, there should also be consideration of the weaknesses of the States, and issues such as the problems of succession and the internal rivalries of Baldwin III and Melisende played a role in the decline. It is also important to be aware of the lack of help from both Byzantium and the west, which further weakened the States. It would also be worth considering whether the decline of the States was the result of a longer-term trend, although the success at Ascalon in 1153 suggests otherwise, or whether it was the result of short-term actions of men such as Reynald and Saladin.

## 3 The Second Crusade

Your understanding of the developments and difficulties facing the early Crusader States will help you to understand the events of the 1130s and 1140s which led to the Second Crusade. The growing unity of Muslim forces and the concept of *jihad* were important in raising concerns for the States, but it was the capture of Edessa in 1144 that ultimately led to the calling of the Crusade, causing much soul-searching in the west and being seen as a trial of faith. An understanding of the message of Bernard of Clairvaux's preaching is valuable in appreciating the reasons for a further crusade. However, it is also worth being aware of other crusades to Lisbon, against the Wends, and the attacks on Jews in Europe, as this will help you to understand how perhaps the motives of those who went had changed from the First Crusade. These other diversions will also help you to begin to understand whether the religious zeal that characterised the First Crusade was in decline and perhaps played a role in the failure of the Second Crusade. Discussions over the actual goal of the Crusade suggest that there was a lack of a clear aim once it was realised that retaking Edessa was pointless. The choice of Damascus might be seen as controversial and the actions of the crusaders outside the city walls could be seen as the main reason for the failure. However, this will need to be balanced against a consideration of the events of 1147–8 in Anatolia, Antioch and Acre. After the success of the First Crusade it might be argued that the crusaders expected the same success, but the surprise and shock of a crusading army had gone and the Muslims were in a stronger position following Zengi. The failure of the Second Crusade had a considerable impact on the west, the Crusader States and the east, destroying the concept of the invincibility of crusader forces and encouraging a resurgence among Muslims. However, the emergence of a united Muslim interest and its impact on the security of the States should not be exaggerated. There were still Muslim factions, seen with the rise of Nur ad-Din in Egypt and by Saladin, and these divisions did allow some recovery of the States, seen at Ascalon, so to see the Second Crusade as the beginning of the end can be considered an exaggeration.

## 4 The Third Crusade

Some of the themes of the previous two key topics will be continued in this section with the development of the concept of *jihad* and the impact of Zengi, Nur ad-Din and Saladin. How far *jihad* explains Muslim resurgence might also be considered. It was the events of 1187, in particular, that sparked the call for the Third Crusade and it is important to consider how far these events were the result of the actions of the rulers of the Crusader States or of a growing sense of confidence among Muslim forces. The Battle of Hattin and loss of Jerusalem were the actual catalysts, but the extent to which the Muslims were taking advantage of the weaknesses and divisions within the Kingdom of Jerusalem is also worth considering. The importance of religious imagery also played a role in the launching of the Third Crusade, with the loss of the Holy Cross. The success of Muslim forces in this period also suggests that the problems faced by the Crusader States had not been overcome, but again this supposes that the failures in 1187 were the result of longer-term developments rather than the short-term problem of a disputed inheritance and a sickly king or the military tactics at Hattin. The ease with which Richard I was able to advance through the area suggests that the problems facing the States were not insurmountable and therefore their decline was not a foregone conclusion.

The events of the Third Crusade suggest that the death of Frederick Barbarossa was the key reason why the Crusade did not retake Jerusalem. This should lead to a consideration of the roles of the three leaders and how far the rivalry, particularly between Richard I and Philip Augustus, was responsible for the failure to capture Jerusalem. This can then be broadened out into a consideration as to whether the Crusade should be seen as a failure, given that its goal, the capture of Jerusalem, was not achieved. This failure would need to be balanced against a range of other achievements, such as the events at Acre and Jaffa. It might also be argued that the Crusade was a success both in the long and short term, as not only were there negotiations with Saladin, but the Crusade did ensure the survival of the States. The impact of the Crusade on the west and east should also be considered so that a balanced assessment of its impact can be made.

CHAPTER 11

# Conclusion (Pearson Edexcel): The Crusades c1095–1204

In the years 1095–1204 crusading armies set out from Europe to the Holy Land with the aim of recovering the holy places of Christendom from the Muslims. Although the First Crusade did achieve its objective of taking the city of Jerusalem, the later crusades were not as successful, with the Second Crusade ending in failure and the Third Crusade being only moderately successful. The Fourth Crusade started with high hopes, but ended with the sack of Constantinople, an act of sheer brutality which is still remembered today with bitterness by Muslims and Orthodox Christians alike. This concluding chapter will investigate the key themes which link all four crusades, and will examine the following:

1 Why men went on crusades.
2 The role of the papacy in the Crusades.
3 The leadership provided by European rulers and princes.
4 The successes and failures of the Crusader States of Outremer.
5 The changing nature of the Muslim response to the crusading armies.

## 1 Why men went on crusades

### Religious motives

The mindset of medieval men and women was dominated by strongly held religious beliefs. Life spans were short. If people managed to survive childbirth and childhood they could expect to live for 30 or 40 years: concerns about the afterlife were, inevitably, never far from their minds. The Christian Church played a central role in everyday life, and priests instilled in their parishioners the idea of an afterlife which promised heaven for some and eternal damnation in hell for others.

During their lifetimes, people tried to ensure that they would gain a passage to heaven when they died. The Christian Church had developed the practice of confession: people would admit their sins to a priest, and they would be given a **penance** which would absolve them from their guilt. Usually, penance took the form of prayers, but sometimes it would involve undertaking a pilgrimage to a particular holy place. There were many such places in medieval England, one of the most famous being the Holy Well at Walsingham in Norfolk. Rome was a popular destination for pilgrims and penitents, and in the eleventh century the journey to Santiago de Compostela in present-day Spain grew in importance as a pilgrimage route. The concept of pilgrimage was thus well established by the time of the First Crusade, and Jerusalem was an irresistible destination.

**KEY TERM**

**Penance** A punishment imposed by a priest on someone who has confessed to their sins.

Forgiveness of sins was an important aim for medieval Christians, which explains why the promise of a plenary indulgence for crusaders was so attractive. Urban II promised all those who took part in the crusade, and who had confessed their sins, full remission of the penance they would be expected to perform. The plenary indulgence was a powerful and attractive offer and was promised by successive popes in all four crusades.

The Ten Commandments include the unambiguous command 'thou shalt not murder', which appeared irreconcilable with the invitation to crusade in the Near East and slaughter men in opposing armies. Christians sought to develop ideas which would reconcile these opposing concepts. Prominent thinkers, notably St Augustine in the fifth century, provided a theoretical justification for the concept of the Just War. Augustine stated that a Just War was one which had a clear moral justification and could be waged if all other attempts at resolving conflicts had been exhausted. If war was the last resort, it had to be carried out with the least possible violence. 'Mission creep' was forbidden. War was to be carried out based on clearly defined aims which could not be changed during the course of the campaign.

The four crusades were all clearly inspired by religious aims. They were not intended as wars against Islam, nor of conquest for its own sake. Most crusaders were motivated by a desire to free the holy places of Jerusalem from Muslim control, and in so doing gain the spiritual benefits of a pilgrimage. The Church of the Holy Sepulchre was believed to be the site of Jesus' crucifixion, burial and resurrection. This was a prize worth fighting for.

## Political motives

Europe in the tenth and eleventh centuries was a society dominated by violence. The centralising power of the Holy Roman Empire had been lost after the death of Emperor Charlemagne in the early ninth century, and by 850 the empire had been divided into several territories. The central power and authority of most rulers was very weak, allowing individual nobles and knights to attack each other and plunder at will in their localities in order to extend their power and their lands. Both the papacy and European rulers hoped that crusading would channel this violent culture away from Europe and into the Near East.

Territorial concerns were an important reason for the first two crusades. By the late eleventh century, the Byzantine Empire was in pronounced decline and was under threat from several hostile forces. The most important of these were the Seljuk Turks from Asia, who had overrun Byzantine lands in Asia Minor. Their actions prompted Emperor Alexius I to seek help from the west in resisting the Seljuk threat. He sent ambassadors to several European rulers, but his most important appeal reached Urban II. His request was pivotal in persuading the pope to preach the First Crusade.

The Second Crusade was also called for territorial reasons. Zengi's capture of Edessa in 1144 seemed to Europeans to mark the beginning of an all-out assault on the Crusader States. It prompted Pope Eugenius III to summon the Second Crusade but, ironically, not a single crusader army reached the County of Edessa.

## The changing concept of knighthood

In the eleventh century a knight was simply a man who had enough money to equip himself for (usually local) warfare, with his own weaponry and horse. Bands of knights were feared throughout Europe for pillaging local communities and killing their inhabitants.

In the tenth and eleventh centuries **codes of chivalry** developed throughout Europe. In England, tales of the legendary King Arthur and his Knights of the Round Table were well known, and European understanding of the code of chivalry owed much to the French song of Roland. Under the chivalric code, a knight was charged with defending the Church, protecting the weak, respecting women and fighting against injustice. Several orders of knights developed during and after the First Crusade. The most notable of these were the Knights Templar and the Knights Hospitaller, formed to protect Christians on their pilgrimages to the Holy Land, and to protect the poor and sick.

There were other reasons why men went on the Crusades. Personal and financial gain proved attractive to some, others sought to escape from domestic troubles, and it is likely that many were compelled into crusading by family or local pressures. Crusading was a very expensive undertaking, and it is possible that men were largely impelled to **take the cross** for genuine religious reasons.

**KEY TERMS**

**Codes of chivalry** Moral codes of conduct. These were not written documents and they varied slightly from one region to another.

**Take the cross** Crosses were simply fashioned out of two pieces of cloth and were worn as a badge of honour by crusaders.

**Pontificate** The period of office held by a pope.

# 2 The role of the papacy in the Crusades

The papacy played a key role in all four crusades and, in the process, strengthened the power of both the papacy itself and the Catholic Church.

## The papal reform movement

Until the eleventh century the Catholic Church was a decentralised organisation. Papal power and authority were essentially limited to Rome and the surrounding area. Bishops and abbots of monasteries were appointed, not by the pope, but by secular rulers, the emperor and the various monarchs of individual states. This state of affairs was challenged by one of the great reforming popes of the Middle Ages, Gregory VII (1073–85). Gregory was a firm believer in the idea that the Christian Church was a divinely created organisation which should therefore be more powerful and influential than any secular institution. During his **pontificate**, he carried out a programme of sweeping reforms, attacking corrupt practices which had crept in over many years, including the marriage of priests and the purchase of offices within the Church. In this way, Gregory intended to increase the power of the papacy by centralising all Church power and authority in Rome. This papal reform movement inevitably involved clashes with secular rulers, most notably with the German Emperor Henry IV, but Gregory's lead was followed by later popes, especially Urban II.

## Urban II and the First Crusade

A cardinal under Gregory VII, Urban II (1088–99) was an active participant in Gregory's reform movement, and a strong supporter of the idea of papal supremacy. In the early years of his pontificate, he toured northern Italy and France, holding several Church councils where he addressed clerical abuses. Urban seized on Alexius I's request for assistance against the Seljuk Turks as a means of promoting papal power throughout Europe, and as an invaluable project which would cement the role of the papacy as the leader of Christian Europe. This explains his speech at the Council of Clermont in 1095 when he summoned all Christians, nobles and people alike, to fight the Turks and take control of the Holy Land. Mindful of the violence which had blighted Europe for many years, Urban had harsh words for the knights, calling them 'oppressors of children and plunderers of widows'. He urged them to be concerned for their souls and advance as 'knights of Christ' to the Holy Land. Urban's call for a crusade increased the power of the papacy and gave a strong boost to the papal reform movement.

## Eugenius III and the Second Crusade

In 1144 Zengi overran the County of Edessa, the first of the Crusader States. The news caused consternation in Europe, and it was feared that the remaining states, and Jerusalem itself, might be seized by Muslim forces. Pope Eugenius III (1145–53), aware of the fragile condition of Outremer, took the unusual step of issuing a papal letter, *Quantum praedecessores,* addressed to Louis VII of France, calling for a further crusade. The initial response was lukewarm, since Jerusalem remained in Christian hands, but it was given a powerful boost by Bernard of Clairvaux, whose inspirational preaching persuaded thousands of men to respond to the pope's appeal and take up the cross. Bernard undertook a preaching campaign in France and Germany and was instrumental in persuading the German King Conrad III and his nephew Frederick Barbarossa to journey to the Holy Land. However, the failure of the Crusade served only to weaken the position of Outremer and gave a significant boost to the morale of Muslim forces.

## The papacy and the Third Crusade

Gregory VIII's pontificate lasted for just 57 days in 1187, but he was responsible for the papal letter *Audita tremendi,* which called for a crusade to avenge the disastrous Battle of Hattin in 1197. His successor, Clement III (1187–91), took a close interest in the Crusade, but had little influence over its course and outcome thanks to the involvement of two prominent rulers, Philip II and Richard I.

## Innocent III and the Fourth Crusade

Innocent III (1198–1216) was heavily involved in the papal reform movement instituted by Gregory VII. This caused him many problems in his relationships with kings and princes, because he firmly believed that papal power outweighed the power of secular rulers. He issued the papal letter *Post miserabile* soon after becoming pope. This was not a response to events in the Holy Land but was rather a bureaucratic template full of instructions on how a crusade should be organised. For Innocent, previous crusades had not succeeded completely because their organisation and direction were faulty. His own instructions were clear. Crusaders had to serve for at least two years, and plenary indulgences would be offered to those who paid for a substitute to take their place on a crusade. One unwelcome innovation was that the whole Church would have to pay taxes to pay for the military–religious enterprise. Innocent was prepared to lead the enterprise in person, but his appeal was ignored by European kings, who felt that his attitude towards them was too high-handed, and it was left to a few nobles to answer the call to crusade. The Fourth Crusade failed to overcome its lacklustre beginnings: it never reached the Holy Land and was wrecked with the sack of Constantinople in 1204.

Papal appeals for European Christians to go on crusades were often very successful, attracting thousands of followers to wage a 'war of the cross'. Although popes were in theory the leaders of the Crusades, they lost control of each conflict, and the direction of each became the responsibility of secular rulers and princes. In the end, successive popes were mere spectators in conflicts over which they had no real control.

## 3 The leadership provided by European rulers and princes

One reason for the varying outcomes of the four crusades was the leadership provided by different kings and princes. While successive popes claimed theoretical command of each crusade, it was the military leaders who made decisions on the ground.

### The First Crusade

For European rulers, Urban's appeal at Clermont fell on deaf ears. The rulers of England, France and Germany were unable, for various reasons, to risk leaving their kingdoms for what was likely to be a number of years. William II of England and Philip of France had several domestic concerns to deal with, and Henry IV of Germany was involved in a long-running quarrel with the papacy dating back to the time of Gregory VII. It was left to prominent members of the European nobility to take the lead. Godfrey of Bouillon, Baldwin of Boulogne, Stephen of Blois, Bohemund of Taranto and Raymond of Toulouse were all powerful nobles who brought with them four armies, from France, Flanders, Germany and Italy. Baldwin left the Crusade to carve out a territory of his own, the County of Edessa, and Stephen of Blois soon returned to Europe, believing that the Crusade could not succeed. The remaining nobles maintained a fragile unity, but achieved their desired objective, the taking of Jerusalem.

## The Second Crusade

Louis VII of France and Conrad III of Germany were the first kings to lead a crusade. They were aware of the danger of leaving their kingdoms for any period of time and placed loyal subjects in control while they were away. It was the lack of a unified command which contributed to the failure of the Crusade. Their large armies took separate routes to Constantinople, and both suffered considerable losses at the hands of the Seljuk Turks in southern Europe. Conrad reached Constantinople first, but decided not to wait for Louis' forces, and crossed into the Near East. Since Edessa remained under the firm control of Muslim forces, attempts to reclaim it were not an option. Conrad's armies suffered massive defeats at Iconium and Dorylaeum, and when both forces finally united in 1148 they were unable to overcome Muslim forces at the siege of Damascus. Conrad fell ill and was forced to leave the Crusade for Constantinople, and the Second Crusade ended in humiliating failure. The divided leadership of the two kings, coupled with their different ambitions, were major factors in its failure.

## The Third Crusade

The Third Crusade got off to a promising start under the leadership of the three leading European monarchs. However, this unity was an illusion. The German Emperor Frederick Barbarossa never reached the Holy Land: he drowned in June 1190 while fording a river. Philip II of France and Richard I of England were involved in bitter rivalry over control of the Angevin territories in France and were never able to overcome the tensions that existed between them. Both kings were successful at Acre in 1191, but Philip decided to return to France, citing ill-health as a reason. Richard continued the Crusade alone. He attempted on two occasions to fulfil the aim of the Crusade, the recapture of Jerusalem, but the loss of both Barbarossa and Philip meant that his forces were too weak to defeat Saladin's armies. When he received news that his treacherous brother Prince John had allied with Philip, he signed a truce with Saladin and the remnants of the crusading armies withdrew.

## The Fourth Crusade

The Third Crusade had demonstrated that the presence of kings would not guarantee success. When Innocent III announced the Fourth Crusade, not a single monarch responded. It was left to several nobles to undertake the enterprise, although it suffered a severe blow with the death of the popular Thibaut of Champagne, which lost the Crusade thousands of his supporters, as well as much-needed funds. The leadership made several very costly blunders which contributed to its speedy collapse:

- They massively overestimated the number of crusaders and incurred crippling expenses by ordering far too many ships, supplies and weapons from Venice.

- They allowed Doge Enrico Dandolo to use the crusading armies to attack Zara, a Christian city and a target for the Venetians.
- They were taken in by the Byzantine Prince Alexius' extravagant promises of financial rewards if they restored his family to the throne of Byzantium. When the prince failed to keep his promises, the crusaders attacked and looted Constantinople in 1204. The following year the armies returned home: they had not even managed to leave European soil.

## 4 The successes and failures of the Crusader States of Outremer

The Crusader States were established fairly speedily in the aftermath of the First Crusade. Baldwin of Boulogne took the initiative with the founding of the County of Edessa in 1098. Three further States were established: Tripoli, Antioch and, the most powerful State of all, the Kingdom of Jerusalem.

Edessa was a landlocked State in the far north, but the other States were established on a narrow strip of land, with the Mediterranean to the west and the barren deserts of Syria to the east. There were no defensible frontiers to protect the States against Muslim forces, and the boundaries between each Christian State were not clearly defined.

Outremer was the first example of Europeans establishing States outside Europe itself, and their very survival seemed unlikely. Initially, there were little more than a handful of scattered outposts controlled by a few European knights, but they gradually established themselves as prosperous and stable societies.

The lands which comprised the Crusader States were agricultural in nature and relatively prosperous. Trade and trade routes were an essential feature of their economy. Long-established trade routes from Aleppo and Damascus carried silk, cotton and spices via overland caravans to the ports of the western Mediterranean. From here goods were carried by ships, most of them Italian, to Europe and Byzantium.

There were two important reasons for the survival of the States of Outremer in the early twelfth century:

- Although the States were surrounded by hostile Muslim forces, the Muslims were divided among themselves. The religious split between Sunni and Shi'ite Muslims was irreconcilable, and they were distracted by internal political and dynastic rivalries.
- Two military–religious orders were founded for the protection of the States, the Templars and the Hospitallers. These were originally set up to protect major thoroughfares for pilgrims, especially those leading to Jerusalem, where the Hospitallers maintained a hospital for sick and needy pilgrims. From these simple beginnings, both orders exploded in size, influence and wealth. Supported by wealthy patrons in Europe, and by the papacy, they were joined by many Europeans who possessed the military skills necessary to defend the States. Over time they took control of many castles and fortifications, which were usually free from local control.

### The decline of the Crusader States

Edessa was the first State to succumb to Muslim forces. It was a poor and sparsely populated territory, with no outlet to the sea, and it was surrounded by hostile Muslim forces. Its borders were frequently attacked, and it received very little support from the other States, or from the Byzantine Empire. In 1144 it was rapidly overrun by the Muslim warrior Zengi. His victory sparked the Second Crusade, although its forces made no attempt to free it from Muslim control.

Tripoli, Antioch and Edessa itself were all closely dependent on the powerful Kingdom of Jerusalem. Although economically strong, Jerusalem was increasingly riven by dynastic rivalries which weakened it politically. Baldwin I and Baldwin II established a strong monarchy with well-defended frontiers, but the strength of the monarchy was not to last. Baldwin II's daughter, Melisende, ruled jointly with her husband, Fulk of Anjou. Fulk was very unpopular with many nobles, and his rule led to palace intrigues and divisions among the nobility. The decline of the monarchy was accelerated by Baldwin III's ambition to rule alone without his mother, and by the 'leper king' Baldwin IV's failure to produce an heir. As court life became increasingly chaotic, the kingdom was delivered a fatal blow by Saladin, who destroyed Jerusalem's army at the Battle of Hattin in 1197, took Jerusalem itself, and occupied the whole kingdom.

The Third Crusade was unable to return Jerusalem to Christian control, and the Crusader States were reduced to a handful of separate territories.

## 5 The changing nature of the Muslim response to the crusading armies

The Muslim response to the Crusades changed considerably between the First and Third Crusades. One of the reasons for this was partly due to the changing strength of both sides but it was also driven by the leadership of the Muslim forces.

### Malik Shah

Malik Shah died in 1092, several years before the First Crusade, but his legacy was important in accounting for the success of that Crusade. Between 1072 and 1092 he ruled over the massive Seljuk Empire, which stretched from present-day Turkey deep into central Asia. Following his death in 1092 a period of dynastic and political instability ensued as his family squabbled over the succession and the division of the empire's territories. This chaotic disunity meant that the Seljuk Turks were incapable of mounting a unified response to the First Crusade. The Sultan Kilij Arslan underestimated the strength of the Christian armies and suffered a heavy defeat at Nicaea in 1097. Subsequent defeats led to the capture of Jerusalem and victory for the First Crusade.

### Zengi

Zengi was active during the 1130s as he enhanced his power in both Syria and Iraq. Muslim chroniclers described him as 'violent, powerful and awe-inspiring', and he struck fear into friends and foes alike. In 1144 the city of Edessa was left relatively undefended by its ruler. Zengi seized the opportunity and attacked the city, capturing it and overrunning the entire Crusader State.

### Nur ad-Din

Zengi was assassinated in 1146 and was succeeded in Syria by his son Nur ad-Din. Nur consolidated his power in Syria, and by 1154 had conquered the key cities of Aleppo and Damascus. He was a deeply religious man whose ambition was to expel the Christians from Outremer and establish Muslim control over the whole region. He believed that the best way of achieving this was through uniting Sunni Muslims in Syria and Shi'ite Muslims in Egypt under a single ruler. His dream was realised in 1169 when his generals took control of Egypt and handed over the territory to Nur.

### Saladin

Saladin was an ambitious general in Nur's army who was partly responsible for the successes of the Egyptian campaigns. He controlled Egypt, theoretically on behalf of Nur. When Nur died in 1174 Saladin began to extend his own power in Syria, and by 1183 he had gained control over the whole region.

In 1187 Saladin had his most dramatic successes. He destroyed a Christian army in battle at Hattin, took Jerusalem later that year, and sparked the Third Crusade. He had few military successes during that Crusade, but his forces were strong enough to ensure that the crusading armies were unable to take Jerusalem. In 1192 Saladin and Richard I of England concluded a truce. Jerusalem would remain in Muslim hands, but the city would remain open to pilgrims and traders alike. Saladin died in 1193 and, like Malik Shah before him, left a large empire which fragmented thanks to infighting over the succession.

## Conclusion

Crusading did not come to an end with the Fourth Crusade: during the thirteenth century a further five crusades were undertaken. Perhaps the most successful of these was the Fifth Crusade, when the Emperor Frederick negotiated the return of Jerusalem to Christian hands. This success was short lived since Muslim forces regained control of the city in 1244. As for the Crusader States themselves, they continued to fragment until they were finally extinguished in 1291.

The influence of the Crusades remains alive today. For the Greek Orthodox Church, the sack of Constantinople remains a live and a bitter issue. In the 1950s the Egyptian President Nasser described himself as the new Saladin. In 2001, with remarkable ineptitude, US President George W. Bush described the war against Iraq as 'this crusade, this war on terrorism'. The influence of Nur ad-Din lives on today. Since 2011 a rebel group has been working to overthrow the regime of the Syrian President Assad. The group is named after Nur ad-Din.

# Exam focus: AQA

## Introduction to a breadth study

Component 1A, The Age of the Crusades, is a breadth study, demanding a different approach to the deployment of knowledge and skills from that seen in the depth paper.

In the breadth paper, exam questions address a much broader chronological range and typically cover 20–25 years, although it is perfectly possible for a question to cover a greater date range even than this. Questions on the breadth paper test understanding of a theme or an issue across an extended period. Effective preparation for the AQA exam on this topic should, therefore, include practising the skills related to a study in breadth, combined with subject knowledge of the key themes and broader concepts specific to a study of the Age of the Crusades.

### Skills

The study of breadth requires a good understanding of the nature of change and continuity over a long period of time. This should mean that you are able to identify what has changed and what has stayed the same within extended chronological periods. You should prepare to use this terminology of similarity and difference or of long and short term to emphasise that you are considering the wider picture of a period and that you are not simply focusing on one very specific incident within a 20–25-year span. This requirement for a broad understanding of a period does not mean that there should be an equal treatment across the whole date range of the question – to do this would be plainly historically inappropriate. Most questions will, in fact, expect you to focus on key events, as these provide the specific support necessary to substantiate your judgements, but you should also place these key events within the general pattern of change across the period. Imagine yourself in a helicopter surveying the overall landscape of a period, and landing every so often at specific points in order to investigate these in more depth. This is as good an analogy of what makes an outstanding breadth response as any other.

In addition to showing a command of the whole period set in a question, the breadth paper might also expect you to show knowledge of different themes, such as political, economic, social, religious and the role of chance. Indeed, writing an answer in this thematic manner might make it even easier to consider patterns of change over time. For example, look at this question:

**In the context of the years 1071–95, how far was the letter from Alexius the most significant factor in the calling of the First Crusade?**

It is perfectly possible, in response to this question, to have an opening paragraph which details the letter, another paragraph that considers the role of Manzikert, and another that considers the Council of Clermont. This might appear to be an appropriate breadth response as the key events mentioned lie at the beginning, in the middle and at the end of the date range set in the question. However, this episodic approach does not powerfully address concepts such as change and continuity. If a more thematic approach is adopted – considering themes such as religion, individuals and political ambition – then broader patterns can be seen within each. A paragraph on religion might include the letter from Alexius as the main evidence, suggesting that this is or is not the key evidence in proving the overwhelming significance of religion as a long-term factor in the calling of the First Crusade. If possible, an awareness of how these themes interact and which is the most significant across the period will also strengthen a breadth response.

### Knowledge

The study of breadth requires a broad awareness of patterns which should be proven by means of specific subject knowledge. This unit does not expect you to have less knowledge than on the depth paper – simply that you are able to use your knowledge to prove more general patterns over time. Indeed, this unit is titled the 'Age of the Crusades' to emphasise that learning should not simply be about each individual crusade in turn, but that the whole period should be considered. AQA has provided six key questions to assist in the development of this type of broader knowledge:

- What were the motives of the crusaders and the counter-crusaders?
- What problems faced the States in Outremer and how successfully were these problems addressed?
- How important were faith and ideas for Christians and Muslims?
- What was the impact of the Crusades on the Muslim Near East?
- How did the Byzantine Empire, Outremer and the Latin West change and what influenced relations between them?
- How important was the role of key individuals and groups and how were they affected by developments?

These key questions should prove the basis of your preparation for the exam and also for your notes throughout the two years of study. It may be useful, for example, to collate your notes according to these questions, or at least to provide answers to these questions every half term.

In addition to collating your knowledge with these six key questions in mind, you should be mindful of what type of question you are most likely to be asked in the exam. You may, for example, try to learn intricate detail about the events of the Second Crusade, or learn the individual biography of a significant individual. However, it is very unlikely that a question asking about such specific events will be asked as these detailed points do not fit into the requirements of the breadth paper. Hence, a key task when reading up on the Second Crusade, for example, might be to consider how this specific event might be placed within a broader question.

On the Second Crusade a more typical question might be:

**'It was the military failure of Outremer in the years 1119–44 that was the main reason for the calling of the Second Crusade.' How valid is this view?**

This question clearly requires a broad understanding of patterns over the whole period 1119–44 and not just of events immediately prior to the calling of the Crusade. Your reading should therefore focus on providing the detail necessary to support this type of broader approach.

With practice, it is possible to see these broader patterns more clearly and to devise your own date ranges in which certain themes can be identified and questioned. It soon becomes apparent that learning the specifics of, for example, the Fourth Crusade, is a less effective use of time than placing the event in a broader contextual range. For example, asking about the legacy of the Crusades by 1204 but expecting knowledge of the Fourth Crusade to be used as part of the broader conceptual answer.

# Interpretations guidance

Section A of the examination for AQA Component 1: Breadth Study: The Age of the Crusades 1071–c1204 contains extracts from the work of historians. This section tests your ability to analyse different historical interpretations. Therefore, you must focus on the interpretations outlined in the extracts. The advice given here is for both the AS and the A level exams:

- For the AS exam, there are two extracts and you are asked which is the more convincing interpretation (25 marks).
- For the A level exam, there are three extracts and you are asked how convincing the arguments are in relation to a specified topic (30 marks).

An interpretation is a particular view on a topic of history held by a particular author or authors. Interpretations of an event can vary, for example, depending on how much weight a historian gives to a particular factor and largely ignores another one.

Interpretations can also be heavily conditioned by events and situations that influence the writer. For example, judging the merits or otherwise of Richard I will tend to produce different responses. Someone writing long ago may view Richard as a national hero. Someone writing in more modern times might adopt a more critical view.

The interpretations that you will be given will be largely from recent or fairly recent historians, and they may, of course, have been influenced by events in the period in which they were writing.

## Interpretations and evidence

The extracts will contain a mixture of interpretations and evidence. The mark scheme rewards answers that focus on the *interpretations* offered by the extracts much more highly than answers that focus on the *information or evidence* mentioned in the extracts. Therefore, it is important to identify the interpretations:

- *Interpretations* are a specific kind of argument. They tend to make claims such as 'Saladin's leadership was the most important reason for the Muslim capture of Jerusalem in 1187'.
- *Information or evidence* tends to consist of specific details. For example: 'Saladin's deployment of troops at the Battle of Hattin in 1187 tempted the crusader forces into a battle in which Saladin had the tactical advantage of well-fed and watered troops'.
- *Arguments and counter-arguments*: sometimes in an extract you will find an interpretation which is then balanced in the same paragraph with a counter-argument. You will need to decide with which your knowledge is most in sympathy.

### The importance of planning

Remember that in the examination you are allowed an hour for this question. It is the planning stage that is vital in order to write a good answer. You should allow at least one-quarter of that time to read the extracts and plan an answer. If you start writing too soon, it is likely that you will waste time trying to summarise the *content* of each extract. Do this in your planning stage – and then think how you will *use* the content to answer the question.

## Analysing interpretations: AS (two extracts)

The same skills are needed for AS and A level for this question. The advice starts with AS simply because it involves only two extracts rather than three.

**With reference to these extracts and your understanding of the historical context, which of these two extracts provides the more convincing interpretation of the motivation of those travelling to the east in the years 1095–1119? (25 marks)**

Extracts A and B are used for the AS question. Extracts A, B and C are used for the A level question.

**EXTRACT A**

Adapted from T. Asbridge, *The First Crusade*, Free Press, 2005, p. 68.

*Some crusaders did at least entertain the possibility that they might end up settling in the Holy Land. However, the reality was that most crusaders were inspired by a complex combination of motives; many must have harboured hopes that in the course of this devotional pilgrimage they might reap some personal gain. But perhaps the most significant insight into the medieval mentality is the demonstration that authentic Christian devotion and a heartfelt desire for material wealth were not mutually exclusive impulses in the eleventh century. Greed cannot have been the dominant motive among the First Crusaders not least because, for most participants the expedition promised to be utterly terrifying and cripplingly expensive for the crusader. The prospect of such a massive journey into the unknown left many almost paralysed with fear.*

**EXTRACT B**

Adapted from J. Riley-Smith, *The First Crusade and the Idea of Crusading*, Continuum, 2009, p. 47.

*It is hard to believe that crusaders were motivated by crude materialism. Given their knowledge and expectations and the economic climate in which they lived, the use of assets to invest in the fairly remote possibility of settlement in the East would have been a stupid gamble. It makes much more sense to suppose that they were moved by an idealism, which must have inspired not only them but also their families. Behind many crusaders stood a large number of men and women who were prepared to make financial sacrifices to help them go. Crusaders were fired by the prospect of making a penitential pilgrimage to Jerusalem but also of fighting in a holy cause.*

**EXTRACT C**

Adapted from J. Phillips, *Holy Warriors*, Vintage Press, 2009, p. 4.

*Some crusaders would need to remain in the Levant to hold the territory; there was very little point in taking Jerusalem if everyone then returned home. The First Crusade was in part, therefore, a war of Christian colonisation, as well as Christian liberation. For those prepared to take a chance it offered a new life. However, as it turned out, while huge numbers were willing to become crusaders, relatively few would remain in the East afterwards. If the hope of plunder and riches helped to draw people towards this great adventure, in the event, the acquisition of wealth proved far harder than it had appeared before they set off.*

## Analysing Extract A

From the extract:

- Some crusaders were hoping to settle in the east.
- Crusaders went eastwards for a variety of reasons, including materialism, often in combination with other factors.
- The Crusade was very expensive and so it is unlikely that material motives were dominant.

Assessing the extent to which the arguments are convincing:

- deploying knowledge to establish the numbers that did in fact settle
- deploying knowledge to support the assertion of a 'devotional pilgrimage'
- deploying knowledge to indicate that individuals such as Tancred did 'reap personal gain'
- deploying evidence of the seizure of Edessa and the siege of Antioch as evidence to challenge the premise of 'cripplingly expensive'
- deploying evidence of the extent to which individuals did indeed travel long distances in the medieval world, for example pilgrimage.

## Analysing Extract B

From the extract:

- The crusaders were not motivated by materialism.
- Crusaders were motivated by idealism, as were their families.
- Crusaders were very well supported by those who stayed at home.
- The Crusade was a pilgrimage and a chance to fight for God.

Assessing the extent to which the arguments are convincing:

- deploying knowledge to agree with the notion of the Crusade as a pilgrimage (and agreeing with Extract A)
- deploying knowledge to evaluate the argument that crusaders were not motivated by materialism (disagreeing, at least in part, with Extract A)
- deploying knowledge about the Crusade as a chance to fight in a holy cause
- deploying knowledge to evaluate the role of those who stayed in Europe.

Comparing the analysis of each extract should give the direction of an overall conclusion and judgement about which of the extracts is more convincing. In this case it may be that Extract A is more convincing because it does try to present a balanced view, and accepts that people were motivated by a variety of factors.

## The mark scheme for AS

The mark scheme builds up from Level 1 to Level 5, in the same way as it does for essays:

- Do not waste time simply describing or paraphrasing the content of each source.
- Make sure that when you include your knowledge it is being used to advance the analysis of the extracts – not as knowledge in its own right.
- The top two levels of the mark scheme refer to 'supported conclusion' (Level 4) and 'well-substantiated conclusion' (Level 5).
- For Level 4, a 'supported conclusion' means finishing your answer with a judgement that is backed up with some accurate evidence drawn from the source(s) and your knowledge.
- For Level 5, a 'well-substantiated conclusion' means finishing your answer with a judgement which is very well supported with evidence, and, where relevant, reaches a complex conclusion that reflects a wide variety of evidence.

## Writing the answer for AS

There is no one correct way! However, the principles are clear. In particular, contextual knowledge should be used *only* to back up an argument. None of your knowledge should be standalone – all your knowledge should be used in context.

For each extract in turn:

- Explain the evidence in the extract, backed up with your own contextual knowledge.
- Explain the points in the extract where you have evidence that contradicts the writer.

Then write a conclusion that reaches a judgement on which is more convincing as an interpretation. You might build in some element of comparison during the answer, or it might be developed in the last paragraph only.

# Analysing interpretations: A level (three extracts)

For the AQA A level exam, Section A gives you three extracts (see page 214), followed by a single question.

**Using your understanding of the historical context, assess how convincing the arguments in each of these three extracts are in the reasons why people travelled to the east in the years 1095–1119. (30 marks)**

An analysis of Extracts A and B has already been provided for the AS question (see page 214).

## Analysing Extract C

From the extract:

- Christian settlement of the east was an important objective of the Crusade.
- The Crusade was a war of Christian liberation.

- The Crusade offered the opportunity for crusaders to make a new start.
- The promise of material gain was not realised.

Assessing the extent to which the arguments are convincing:

- deploying knowledge to corroborate the extent of Christian settlement of the east
- deploying knowledge to explain the notion of Christian liberation
- deploying knowledge of those who did settle and leave the west behind in the pursuit of a new start
- deploying knowledge of the extent to which the failure of material gain affected the movement of others eastwards.

### Writing the answer for A level

First, make sure that you have the focus of the question clear. Then you can investigate the three extracts to see how convincing they are.

You need to analyse each of the three extracts in turn. A suggestion is to have a large page divided into nine blocks.

| Extract's main arguments | Knowledge to corroborate | Knowledge to contradict or modify |
|---|---|---|
| A | | |
| B | | |
| C | | |

- In the first column, list the main arguments each uses.
- In the second column, list what you know that can corroborate the arguments.
- In the third column, list what might contradict or modify (you might find that you partly agree, but with reservations) the arguments.
- You may find, of course, that some of your knowledge is relevant more than once.

## Planning your answer

Decide how you could best set out a detailed plan for your answer:

- Briefly refer to the focus of the question.
- For each extract in turn, set out the arguments, corroborating and contradictory evidence.
- Do this by treating each argument (or group of arguments) in turn.
- Make comparisons between the extracts if this is helpful. The mark scheme does not explicitly give credit for doing this, but a successful cross-reference may well show the extent of your understanding of each extract and add to the weight of your argument.
- An overall judgement is not required, but it may be helpful to make a brief summary, or just reinforce what has been said already by emphasising which extract was the most convincing.

### The mark scheme for A level

For each of the three extracts, the mark scheme makes it clear that a good answer will:

- Identify the arguments presented in each extract.
- Assess the extent to which the arguments are convincing, using own knowledge.
- Take every opportunity to make a balanced answer wherever this is appropriate, by corroborating and contradicting the arguments in each extract.

The mark scheme progresses upwards like this:

- Level 1: general comments about the three extracts or accurate understanding of one extract.
- Level 2: some accurate comments on the interpretations in at least two of the three extracts, but with limited comments or with description.

- Level 3: some supported comments on the interpretations, putting them in their historical context. Some analysis of the content of the extracts, but little attempt to evaluate them.
- Level 4: good understanding of the interpretations provided in the extracts, with knowledge to give a good analysis and some evaluation.
- Level 5: very good understanding and strong historical awareness to analyse and evaluate.

Notice that there is no reference in the mark scheme to *comparing* the extracts or reaching a judgement about the most convincing.

# Exam focus: OCR

## Essay guidance

The assessment of OCR Unit Y203: The Crusades and the Crusader States 1095–1192 for the A level is as follows:

- you will answer one essay question from a choice of two, and one shorter essay question also from a choice of two.

The guidance below is for answering the A level essay questions. Guidance for the shorter essay question is at the end of this section.

For A level History essays the skills are made very clear by the mark scheme, which emphasises that the answer must:

- focus on the demands of the question
- be supported by accurate and relevant factual knowledge
- be analytical and logical
- reach a developed and supported judgement about the issue in the question.

There are a number of skills that you will need to develop to reach the higher levels in the marking bands:

- understand the wording of the question
- plan an answer to the question set
- write a focused opening paragraph
- avoid irrelevance and description
- write analytically
- make a supported judgement about the relative importance of the issue you are discussing
- write a conclusion which reaches a supported judgement based on the argument in the main body of the essay.

These skills will be developed in the section below, but are further developed in the 'Period Study' chapters of the *OCR A level History* series for both Units 1 and 2.

### Understanding the wording of the question

To stay focused on the question set, it is important to read the question carefully and focus on the key words and phrases. Unless you directly address the demands of the question you will not score highly. Remember that in questions where there is a named factor you must write a good analytical paragraph about the given factor, even if you argue that it was not the most important.

| Types of A level questions you might find in the exams | The factors and issues you would need to consider in answering them |
|---|---|
| 1 Assess the reasons why the First Crusade was a success | Weigh up the relative importance of a range of factors as to why the First Crusade was a success. This is developed below and a range of issues that might be discussed is outlined |
| 2 To what extent was Muslim weakness responsible for the victory of the crusaders in the First Crusade? | Weigh up the relative importance of a range of factors, including comparing the importance of Muslim weakness with other factors such as religious zeal, aid from Byzantium, military tactics and leadership |
| 3 'The role of castles was the most important reason for survival of the Crusader States in the twelfth century.' How far do you agree? | Weigh up the relative importance of a range of factors, including comparing the importance of castles with other issues to reach a balanced judgement. Castles might be compared with Muslim weakness and divisions, the role of the Military Orders, the leadership of the Crusader States and early expansion, and aid from Byzantium and the west |

| Types of A level questions you might find in the exams | The factors and issues you would need to consider in answering them |
|---|---|
| 4 How successful was the Third Crusade? | This question requires you make a judgement about the success of the Third Crusade. Instead of thinking about factors, you would need to think about issues such as:<br>• The acquisition of Jerusalem<br>• The treaty with Saladin<br>• The gaining of ports<br>• The raising of forces<br>• The securing and protection of the remaining States. |

## Planning an answer

Many plans simply list dates and events: this should be avoided as it encourages a descriptive or narrative answer, rather than an analytical answer. The plan should be an outline of your argument; this means you need to think carefully about the issues you intend to discuss and their relative importance before you start writing your answer. It should therefore be a list of the factors or issues you are going to discuss and a comment on their relative importance.

For question 1 in the table, your plan might look something like this:

- Military leadership: the reputation and importance of Bohemund.
- Military tactics: the Muslims were not familiar with them, siege warfare, heavy cavalry.
- Religious zeal: drove the crusaders on when the military situation was poor, importance of the Holy Lance, determination to reach Jerusalem, withstand sieges.
- Muslim disunity: most important as when the Muslims were united later, the Crusades failed.
- Aid from Byzantium: help of emperor got them through Anatolia so fewer troops lost by the time they reached the Holy Land.

## The opening paragraph

Many students spend time 'setting the scene'; the opening paragraph becomes little more than an introduction to the topic – this should be avoided. Instead, make it clear what your argument is going to be. Offer your view about the issue in the question – what was the most important reason for the success of the First Crusade – and then introduce the other issues you intend to discuss. In the plan it is suggested that Muslim disunity was the most important factor. This should be made clear in the opening paragraph, with a brief comment as to why – perhaps that this meant the crusaders never faced the full Muslim force, as would happen later when other Crusades failed. However, although Muslim disunity was the most important factor, it is worth just briefly mentioning the other factors that you intend to discuss and giving a brief comment as to your view about their relative importance. This will give the examiner a clear overview of your essay, rather than it being a mystery tour where the argument becomes clear only at the end. You should also refer to any important issues that the question raises. For example:

> *There are a number of reasons why the First Crusade was a success, including leadership, military strength and help from Byzantium***[1]***. However, the most important reason was Muslim disunity***[2]***. This was particularly important as it meant that the crusader forces never had to face the full might of Muslim forces***[3]***. Although not as important, religious zeal still played a crucial role as it provided the motivation to survive the siege of Antioch and keep going to Jerusalem. The crusaders were strengthened even further by the help they received, particularly from Byzantium, as this allowed the crusaders to gain some of the resources they needed and to be guided through Anatolia***[4]***.*

**1** The student is aware that there were a number of important reasons.

**2** The student offers a clear view as to what they consider to be the most important reason – a thesis is offered.

**3** There is a brief justification to support the thesis.

**4** Some of the factors and their relative importance are briefly stated.

## Avoid irrelevance and description

Hopefully, the plan will stop you from simply writing all you know about why the Crusade was successful and force you to weigh up the role of a range of factors. Similarly, it should also help prevent you from simply writing about or describing the events of the First Crusade rather than explaining why the crusaders were successful. You will not lose marks if you do that, but neither will you gain any credit, and you will waste valuable time.

Look at the paragraph below written in answer to the question: 'How important was religious zeal in the outcome of the First Crusade?'

*Religious zeal was one of a number of factors that was important in the success of the First Crusade***[1]***. Many had gone on the Crusade because of their desire to achieve remission for the sins they had committed and the desire to help their fellow Christians in the east***[2]***. Religious zeal was seen throughout the Crusade, but particularly at Antioch, where a pilgrim named Peter Bartholomew claimed to have a vision where St Andrew revealed to him the whereabouts of the Holy Lance. It was claimed that whoever found the lance would be successful in battle. Peter excavated under a church and found it; whether it was real or not it provided the crusaders with motivation. The discovery led the crusaders to force the invading army to flee and the Muslim defenders within the citadel of Antioch also surrendered***[3]***. Religious zeal was therefore important in the success of the crusader armies***[4]**.

1. The answer acknowledges that religious zeal was important.
2. The answer describes why many had gone on the Crusade but does not explain why religious zeal led to success.
3. The descriptive approach continues with, at best, a hint that it led to the defeat of the Muslim forces at Antioch, but it is still not well linked to the success of the Crusade.
4. The response asserts that it was a major factor, but this has not been clearly shown.

There is no real explanation as to how the religious zeal led to the success of the crusaders which would be needed to reach Level 3, and certainly no evidence of either evaluation or judgement that would be needed for the higher levels.

## Write analytically

This is perhaps the hardest, but most important skill you need to develop. An analytical approach can be helped by ensuring that the opening sentence of each paragraph introduces an idea, which directly answers the question and is not just a piece of factual information. In a very strong answer it should be possible to simply read the opening sentences of all the paragraphs and know what argument is being put forward.

If we look at the second question on the importance of Muslim weakness (see page 218), the following are possible sentences with which to start paragraphs:

- Muslim weakness was crucial as it created a power vacuum which the crusaders were able to exploit. …
- Muslim divisions meant that their leaders were unaware of the aims of the crusading armies. …
- Crusader military tactics in both battles and sieges were important in securing victories. …
- Support from Byzantium in the early stages of the Crusade was vital for success. …

You would then go on to discuss both sides of the argument raised by the opening sentence, using relevant knowledge about the issue to support each side of the argument. The final sentence of the paragraph would reach a judgement on the role played by the factor you are discussing in the crusader victory. This approach would ensure that the final sentence of each paragraph links back to the actual question you are answering. If you can do this for each paragraph you will have a series of mini essays, which discuss a factor and reach a conclusion or judgement about the importance of that factor or issue. For example:

*Muslim divisions were crucial, particularly in the early stages, for the success of the First Crusade. The division between Sunni and Shi'ite was so great that they hated each other more than they hated the newly arrived crusaders. When the crusaders first arrived they found that there were a series of petty rulers fighting each other and this made it much easier for the crusaders to defeat them as they were not as* *strong numerically***[1]**. *As a result of the divisions that followed the death of Malik Shah in 1092 and other caliphs and viziers there was a power vacuum in Anatolia. These leaders seemed unaware of the aim of the Crusade and therefore did not put up serious resistance***[2]**.

1 **The sentence puts forward a clear view that Muslim divisions were crucial, but does qualify it and suggest that this was particularly true in the early stages.**

2 **The claim that it was important in the early stages is developed and some evidence is provided to support the argument.**

The paragraph above explains the importance of Muslim divisions in securing victory for the crusaders, but explaining their role will take you only to Level 3 or 4 depending upon how well developed and how well supported your explanation is. At this level, answers will produce a list of reasons as to why the crusaders won. Answers that are not that developed or are poorly explained will be placed in Level 3, while those that are well developed will reach Level 4. The quality of the answer above, if repeated in other paragraphs, would certainly reach Level 4.

In order to reach Levels 5 and 6 there needs to be clear evidence of the evaluation of factors – how important were the factors in securing crusader victory? The paragraph above does start to move towards that as it argues that Muslim divisions were important in the early stages of the war, allowing the crusaders to take Anatolia with little resistance. The paragraph also provides some support for that claim and it is this that turns an assertion that they were important into a judgement and takes the response to the higher levels.

At Level 5, the judgement is likely to be present only in the conclusion, as shown in the example below. However, responses that reach Level 6 will make a judgement about the importance of each factor as they explain their role, so that there will be a series of interim judgements which are then pulled together in an overall conclusion.

## Questions for practice

Write six opening sentences for the following:

- 'The lack of a clear aim was the main reason for the failure of the Second Crusade.' How far do you agree?
- Assess the reasons why so many people went on the First Crusade.
- How effective a leader of the Third Crusade was Richard I?
- 'Muslim divisions were the most important reason for the survival of the Crusader States in the twelfth century.' How far do you agree?

## The conclusion

The conclusion provides the opportunity to bring together all the interim judgements to reach an overall judgement about the question. Using the interim judgements will ensure that your conclusion is based on the argument in the main body of the essay and does not offer a different view. For the essay answering question 1 (see page 218), you can decide which was the most important factor in the success of the First Crusade, but for questions 2 and 3 you will need to comment on the importance of the named factor – Muslim weakness or castles – as well as explain why you think a different factor is more important, if that has been your line of argument. Or, if you think the named factor is the most important, you would need to explain why that was more important than the other factors or issues you have discussed.

Consider the following conclusion to question 2: 'To what extent was Muslim weakness responsible for the victory of the crusaders in the First Crusade?'

*Although the leadership of Bohemund and the military skill of the crusaders allowed them to defeat the Muslim forces, it would not have been possible to defeat a united, and much larger, Muslim force***[1]**. *The crusaders were fortunate that, given their vastly reduced numbers, they were faced only by mostly weak, individual Muslim leaders and that the political situation in the region was such that they did not face a leader such as Malik Shah or Saladin***[2]**.

**1** This is a strong conclusion because it considers the importance of the named factor – Muslim weakness – and offers a clear view as to which factor was the most important.

**2** It supports its claim that Muslim weakness was the most important factor and is therefore not simply an assertion.

## How to write a good essay for the A level short answer questions

This question will require you to weigh up the importance of two factors or issues in relation to an event or a development. For example:

**Which of the following was of greater importance in the survival of the Crusader States in the twelfth century? i) Aid from the west. ii) Muslim disunity. Explain your answer with reference to both i) and ii).**

As with the long essays, the skills required are made very clear by the mark scheme, which emphasises that the answer must:

- analyse the two issues
- evaluate the two issues
- support your analysis and evaluation with detailed and accurate knowledge
- reach a supported judgement as to which factor was more important in relation to the issue in the question.

The last point is particularly important as many students write all they know about the two named events, individuals or factors but do not relate it back to the actual question, in this instance the survival of the Crusader States.

The skills required are very similar to those for the longer essays. However, there is no need for an introduction, nor are you required to compare the two factors or issues in the main body of the essay, although either approach can still score full marks.

For example, an introduction could be:

*In general, particularly after the failure of the Second Crusade, both men and money from the west were in short supply. Aid was sporadic and the number of settlers who were needed, if the area was to be colonised, was never large enough to be able to settle the region. This was even more of a problem in the second half of the period***[1]***. However, this can be contrasted with the support, military help and money that was given to the Military Orders of the Knights Templars and Hospitallers, who played a vital role in the survival of the Crusader States. The aid given to them was important as the orders were feared by the Muslims, who saw them as their fiercest enemies, and their resources and manpower helped in the survival of the States***[2]***. However, the States were always short of manpower and this was reflected in the general determination to avoid battle whenever possible. Moreover, links with the west were weak and despite appeals for more manpower this did not materialise and weakened the States in the second half of the period***[3]***.*

**1** The answer explains the problems of obtaining aid from the west.

**2** However, a further aspect of aid is discussed.

**3** The wider implications are hinted at and this is linked back to the question of survival.

The answer could go on and argue how Muslim disunity affected the survival of the Crusader States in both the short and long term.

Most importantly, the conclusion must reach a supported judgement as to the relative importance of the factors in relation to the issue in the question. For example:

*Muslim disunity was more important than aid from the west as aid was so limited, and the breakdown in relations with Byzantium limited it further***[1]***. Muslim disunity was more important because once the Muslims were united they were able to defeat the Crusader States, as was seen by Saladin's invasion of the Kingdom of Jerusalem in 1187. This can be contrasted with earlier in the century when Muslim disunity made it much easier for the Crusader States to seize land in the period from 1100 to 1144. Although the shortage of manpower was eased by the aid given to the*

*Military Orders, this was not enough to resist the Muslim forces when they were united at the end of the period, showing that Muslim disunity was the more important factor***[2]**.

1 The response explains the relative importance of the two factors and offers a clear view.

2 The response supports the view offered in the opening sentence and therefore reaches a supported judgement.

## Questions for practice

- Which of the following had the greater impact on the outcome of the Third Crusade? i) Richard I. ii) Philip II of France. Explain your answer with reference to both i) and ii).
- Which of the following was of greater importance in encouraging people to go on the First Crusade? i) The desire for remission of sins. ii) Economic gain. Explain your answer with reference to both i) and ii).

# Exam focus: Pearson Edexcel

## Overview

Pearson Edexcel's Paper 1, Option 1A: The Crusades, c1095–1204, is assessed by an exam comprising three sections:

- Sections A and B test your knowledge of the period 1095–1192. The questions test your breadth of knowledge of four key themes:
  - reasons for the Crusades, 1095–1192
  - leadership of the Crusades, 1095–1192
  - the Crusader States of Outremer, 1100–92
  - the changing Muslim response to the crusaders, 1095–1192.
- Section C tests your depth of knowledge regarding a key historical debate: What explains the failure of the Fourth Crusade?

## Sections A and B

Section A of the exam paper contains two questions, and you have to complete one. Questions in Section A will test the breadth of your knowledge by focusing on at least ten years.

Section B of the exam paper also contains two questions, and you have to complete one. Questions in Section B will test the breadth of your knowledge by focusing on at least one-third of the period you have studied: 32 years.

Neither Section A nor B requires you to read or analyse either sources or extracts from the work of historians.

### Skills

Section A and B questions require you to deploy a variety of skills. The most important are focus on the question, selection and deployment of relevant detail, analysis and, at the highest level, prioritisation.

Questions in Sections A and B will focus one of the following concepts:

- cause
- consequence
- change/continuity
- similarity/difference
- significance.

Therefore, the questions will typically begin with one of the following stems:

- How far …
- How accurate is it to say …
- To what extent …
- How significant …
- How successful … .

## Section C

Section C of the exam paper is different from Sections A and B. While Sections A and B test your own knowledge, Section C tests both your own knowledge and your ability to analyse and evaluate interpretations of the past in the work of historians. Section C contains two extracts from the work of historians, and there is one compulsory question.

Section C focuses on an interpretation related to the following controversy:

**What explains the failure of the Fourth Crusade?**

It looks at the following aspects of the interpretation:

- Innocent III's plans for the Crusade and the significance of their failure.
- The significance of the size and leadership of the crusading forces.
- The impact of the role of Venice and of the priorities of the Doge Enrico Dandolo.
- The significance of the failure of Prince Alexius and of the sack of Constantinople.

### Skills

Section C tests your ability to analyse and evaluate different historical interpretations in the light of your own knowledge. Therefore, it tests a variety of skills, including:

- identifying the interpretation
- writing a well-structured essay
- integrating extracts with own knowledge
- reaching an overall judgement.

# The AS level exam

## Paper 1

The AS exam tests the same content as the A level exam and is structured in exactly the same way. However, there are differences between the two exams.

## Sections A and B

There are three key differences between A level and the AS in Sections A and B.

### Wording

The wording of AS level questions will be less complex than the wording of A level questions. For example:

| A level question | AS level question |
|---|---|
| How far do you agree that the revival of Muslim military power was the main reason for the failure of the Second Crusade? | Was the poor leadership of Louis VII and Conrad III the main reason for the failure of the Second Crusade? Explain your answer. |
| 'Religious enthusiasm was the most important reason why people joined the First and Second Crusades.' How far do you agree with this statement? | How far do you agree that lack of support from the Byzantine Empire was the main reason for the Muslim recapture of Jerusalem in 1187? |

### Focus

Section A questions can focus on a more limited range of concepts at AS than at A level. Specifically, at AS level Section A questions can focus only on *cause* and *consequences* (including success and failure), whereas A level questions can focus on a wider variety of concepts.

### Mark scheme

The A level mark scheme has five levels, whereas the AS level mark scheme has only four. This means that full marks are available at AS for an analytical essay, whereas sustained analysis is necessary for full marks at A level.

## Section C

Section C of the AS exam focuses on the same aspects of the same debate:

**Study Extracts 1 and 2 (page 228) before you answer this question. In the light of differing interpretations, how convincing do you find the view that the Fourth Crusade failed because 'Innocent's conception of crusading was fundamentally flawed' (Extract 1). To explain your answer, analyse and evaluate the material in both extracts, using your own knowledge of the issues.**

As in the A level exam, you have to answer one compulsory question based on two extracts. The AS level exam is different from the A level exam in the following ways.

### The question

The AS level question is worded in a less complex way than the A level question. For example:

| A level | AS level |
|---|---|
| In the light of differing interpretations, how convincing do you find the view that Alexius III's actions were the main reason for the sack of Constantinople in 1204?<br>To explain your answer, analyse and evaluate the material in both extracts, using your own knowledge of the issues | Historians have different views about the reasons for the failure of the Fourth Crusade. Analyse and evaluate the extracts and use your knowledge of the issues to explain your answer to the following question:<br>How far do you agree with the view that the crusaders' agreements with Venice in 1201 wrecked the Fourth Crusade's chances of success? |

### The extracts

At AS, the extracts will be slightly shorter and you may get extracts taken from textbooks as well as the work of historians. In this sense, the extracts at AS level should be slightly easier to read and understand.

# Essay guidance for Sections A and B

## Understanding the question

In order to answer the question successfully you must understand how the question works. Each essay question has three components:

- An invitation to reach a judgement …
- … on a subject from your course of study …
- … and a clearly defined time period.

For example:

**How far do you agree that … the leadership of Nur ad-Din and Saladin was the most important reason for the decline of the Crusader States … in the years 1154–87?**

Overall, *all* Section A and B questions ask you to make a judgement about the extent of something, in a specific period. In order to focus on the question, you must address all three elements. The most common mistakes come from misunderstanding or ignoring one of these three key elements.

All of your examined essays will be judged on how far they focus on the question, and the quality of their structure. The better your focus and the clearer your structure, the better your chance of exam success.

Your essay should be made up of three or four paragraphs, each addressing the changing style of leadership. Your essay plan might look something like this:

- Paragraph 1: the role of Nur ad-Din, 1154–74.
- Paragraph 2: the role of Saladin, 1174–87.
- Paragraph 3: internal divisions within the Crusader States.
- Paragraph 4: lack of aid and supplies from the west.

In addition to your three or four main points, you should begin your essay with a clear introduction and end with a conclusion that contains a focused summary of your essay.

Here is an example introduction in answer to the question above:

> In the years 1149-74 Muslim military leadership was provided by Nur ad-Din and, after his death in 1174, by Saladin**[1]**. Both leaders mounted several campaigns against the Crusader States which had two objectives: the weakening of the power of the Christian forces and the extension of their own power in both Syria and Egypt, which culminated in 1187 with Saladin's recapture of Jerusalem**[2]**. During these years the Crusader States were weakened by internal rivalries, which allowed the Muslims to seize the initiative on several occasions. Most importantly, the Christian states had very little support from the west, either in financial aid or in providing supplies of men and military equipment**[3]**.

1 The answer is clearly focused on the question from the outset.

2 Explains the twin ambitions of Muslim leaders in the years to 1187.

3 The essay considers the stated factor, and also makes a judgement on the relative importance of factors.

## Reaching an overall judgement

In addition to focus and structure, and the level of relevant detail and analysis, your exam essays will be assessed on how far you reach a supported overall judgement. The clearer and better supported your judgement, the better your mark is likely to be.

The mark scheme distinguishes between five levels of judgement:

| | |
|---|---|
| Level 1 (low) | No overall judgement |
| Level 2 | Stated overall judgement, but no support |
| Level 3 | Overall judgement is reached, with weak support |
| Level 4 | Overall judgement is reached and supported |
| Level 5 (high) | Overall judgement is reached and supported by consideration of the relative significance of key factors |

As you know, your essays are judged on the extent to which they analyse. The mark scheme distinguishes between five different levels of analysis:

| | |
|---|---|
| Level 1 (low) | Simplistic or no analysis |
| Level 2 | Limited analysis of key issues |
| Level 3 | Some analysis of key issues |
| Level 4 | Analysis of key issues |
| Level 5 (high) | Sustained analysis of key issues |

The key feature of the highest level is sustained analysis: analysis that unites the whole of the essay.

Below is a sample paragraph for the essay title on page 226. This paragraph highlights the use of relevant detail, analysis and a well-supported judgement.

While it is true that Muslim military leadership played an important role in the decline of the Crusader States in these years, problems of geography, defence, government and aid from the west also weakened the States**[1]**. The States possessed no natural boundaries to the east, which made them difficult to defend. For example, in 1149 Nur ad-Din was able to seize Apamea and Harib, and thus threaten the security of Antioch. Muslim forces seized a number of Mediterranean ports, cutting off trade routes from Europe. The defence of the States was largely entrusted to the military religious orders of Templars and Hospitallers, who established defensive control via a network of castles and border fortifications. The orders were lavishly funded by European nobles but were not controlled by local rulers. As a result, they were able to purchase large tracts of land which were largely independent from the rulers of the States. Moreover, many castles were not built as a means of defence but were administrative centres or used to defend local agriculture only**[2]**. The States received very little support from Byzantium or from European kings or nobles. After the disastrous Second Crusade, Baldwin III asked for help from Europe, but none was forthcoming. A further appeal in 1184 was equally fruitless. The rulers of the Byzantine Empire showed no interest in protecting the Crusader States at all. Perhaps the most important reason for the decline of the States in these years was the internal rivalries and growing divisions within the ruling elites, as well as several succession crises**[3]**. When Baldwin II of Jerusalem died in 1131, he was succeeded by his daughter Melisende, her husband Fulk, and their infant son Baldwin III. Fulk refused to rule jointly with Melisende, which provoked a rebellion by Hugh of Jaffa. A major crisis developed from 1174 when the 'leper king' Baldwin IV became monarch. Factions emerged within the elites, supporting either Raymond of Tripoli or Guy of Lusignan as future claimants to the throne. Internal divisions were at their worst with the deaths of Baldwin IV and Baldwin V in quick succession in 1185–6. This caused a major crisis of government at a time when Muslim power under Saladin was rapidly increasing. These divisions meant that the States could not adopt a united front against Muslim attacks**[4]**.

**1** Identifies other relevant reasons for the decline of the States.

**2** Detailed examination of problems of defence.

**3** Criteria established on the relative importance of factors.

**4** Developed substantiation here, with relevant names and dates.

## Interpretation guidance for Section C

### Identify the interpretations

Section C is different from Sections A and B. It presents two extracts from the works of historians. You are expected to use the extracts and your own knowledge to examine the views presented in the extracts and reach conclusions in answer to the question.

The questions for Section C are not concerned with source analysis. You are not required to consider matters such as reliability or usefulness but should analyse and evaluate the two interpretations.

The following guide may be helpful in framing your answer:

- Analyse and evaluate the points made by the author of the first extract.
- Analyse and evaluate the points made by the author of the second extract.
- Use your own knowledge and the material in the extracts to support the proposition made in the question.
- Use your own knowledge and the material in the extracts to modify or challenge the proposition made in the question.

For the highest levels of attainment, use the two extracts as a set and draw reasoned conclusions on the question.

Here is a sample Section C question with a worked answer to guide you.

**Study Extracts 1 and 2 before you answer this question. In the light of differing interpretations, how convincing do you find the view that the Fourth Crusade failed because 'Innocent's conception of crusading was fundamentally flawed' (Extract 1). To explain your answer, analyse and evaluate the material in both extracts, using your own knowledge of the issues.**

**EXTRACT 1**

From Thomas Asbridge, *The Crusades*, Simon & Schuster, 2012.

*Innocent sought to launch a new crusade to the Holy Land, issuing calls to arms in August 1198. He visualised a glorious endeavour – the preaching, organisation and prosecution of which would be under his direct control – imagining that so orderly and sacred an expedition could not fail to win divine approval. Yet, despite the assurance of Innocent's vision, all his efforts elicited only a muted response: the anticipated hordes of enthusiastic warriors did not enlist, and the donation chests strewn across the West failed to fill.*

*In fact, Innocent's conception of crusading was fundamentally flawed. Absolutist in tone, it made no provision for interactive collaboration between the Church and the secular leaders of society. The pope imagined that he would simply bend the kings and lords of Christendom to his will. But this proved to be entirely unrealistic. When it became obvious that there would be no royal involvement in the Crusade, Innocent did not attempt to consult or recruit leaders from the upper aristocracy. He probably believed that the members of this class would flock to his cause of their own volition, eager to serve at his beck and call – but he was wrong, and this lapse of judgement would have tragic consequences for Christendom.*

**EXTRACT 2**

From Jonathan Phillips, *The Fourth Crusade and the Sack of Constantinople*, Pimlico, 2005.

*The reason why the Fourth Crusade went to Constantinople in the late spring of 1203 was, ironically, in response to an invitation of a Greek – the appeal by Prince Alexius to help him and his father to secure what they regarded as their rightful position as rulers of the Byzantine Empire. Had this request not been made, there is no convincing evidence to suggest that the expedition would have turned towards Constantinople. To explain why the westerners' fleet sailed down to the Bosphorus, rather than heading towards Egypt and the Holy Land, one has to ask why the prince's offer [to wipe out the debts owed to the Venetians] was accepted.*

*Herein lay the Achilles heel of the whole enterprise: the lack of men and money. These were hardly new considerations and were, indeed, two prime causes of the collapse of the Second Crusade in 1148. The Fourth Crusade, however, possessed an additional constituent – the contract between the French and the Venetians – and it was the need to make good the terms of this agreement that became a powerful force in driving and shaping the expedition.*

An example answer:

The extracts provide contrasting views on the reasons for the failure of the Fourth Crusade. Extract 1 suggests that Innocent's vision involved the pope himself taking direct control of the Crusade, which would make for centralised control of the enterprise, and of its planning and organisation. As a result, he failed to consult with kings and nobles, which almost doomed the expedition before it even got under way. In contrast, Extract 2 suggests that it was problems during the course of the Crusade that caused it to fail, notably sending the crusaders to Constantinople to help restore Alexius and his father to the throne. The extract also refers to two other crucial factors: the lack of men and of money. Since it considers more than one factor to explain failure, I believe that Extract 2 is more convincing than Extract 1**[1]**.

Innocent III called the Fourth Crusade a few months after he was elected pope in 1198. His attitude towards the Crusade was a straightforward one. He identified the problems that had weakened the crusades of the previous century and decided that the solution was to place every aspect of the enterprise under his direct control. One of his main interests was to stamp out heresy in Europe, and he believed that the Crusade would ignite religious enthusiasm, and thus guarantee its success. However, one fundamental error was Innocent's determination to establish absolute personal control over the Crusade. This reflected his wider view of the papacy itself. He claimed universal supremacy over all people and nations, and declared that the pope was above all men, and answerable only to God. As a result, he would not work with kings or nobles, nor would he discuss his plans with them: he expected that they would follow his plans without question. In this he was mistaken for, as Extract 1 reveals, there was no rush of crusaders eager to enlist, nor were substantial funds and voluntary contributions made available. When he wrote to Richard I of England and Philip II of France asking for their support, they refused point-blank, as did the Byzantine emperor. Thus, all the evidence suggests that the pope's conception of crusading was 'fundamentally flawed'**[2]**.

Extracts 1 and 2 both agree that the Fourth Crusade lacked both men and money, with Extract 2 claiming that these shortages were 'the Achilles heel of the whole enterprise'**[3]**. One reason for the shortage of men was the sudden death in 1201 of Thibaut of Champagne. He was a popular and inspiring ruler who could have become the leader of the whole crusade, but his death meant that many nobles and thousands of men failed to join the Crusade.

The Crusade was perhaps fatally weakened by the agreement made between the French and the Venetians in 1201, mentioned in Extract 2**[4]**. The crusaders had to estimate the final number of crusaders so that the Venetians could supply sufficient ships and supplies. They decided on a figure of 33,500 men, and Doge Enrico Dandolo set the cost to Venice of 85,000 marks. The number of men was a wild overstatement: in the end, only 13,000 turned up, with several thousands of men heading directly towards Acre. Moreover, the absence of powerful European rulers who could help finance the Crusade placed it under tremendous financial strain. This explains the point made in Extract 2, that the crusaders should sail, not towards Egypt and the Holy Land, but towards Constantinople. Doge Dandolo's chief concerns were the interests of his city rather than of the Crusade. He offered to postpone debt repayments if the crusaders attacked Zara on his behalf and restore it to Venetian control. Although the city was a Christian one, the crusaders accomplished this in November 1202. Furthermore, the Byzantine Prince Alexius made a number of extravagant promises, including an undertaking to pay off the entire Venetian debt, if the crusaders restored his family to power in Constantinople. After the Crusade reached the city Alexius failed to keep his promises. In response, the crusaders sacked and looted the city, an action which wrecked and ended the Fourth Crusade**[5]**.

In conclusion, the evidence suggests that the most important reason for the failure of the Fourth Crusade was the lack of adequate funds. Extract 1 reveals that 'the donation chests strewn across the West failed to fill', showing that papal funds for the Crusade were not very large. Extract 2 confirms that the lack of money was a serious problem, and that the contract with Venice was 'a powerful force in driving and shaping the expedition'**[6]**.

1 Identifies the points made in both extracts, and reaches an initial judgement.

2 Detailed understanding, which places Innocent's attitude towards the Fourth Crusade within the context of his overall claims of papal supremacy.

3 Uses the extracts as a set, an important skill.

4 Considers the relative significance of factors.

5 Strongly focused on financial difficulties, well supported by own knowledge.

6 Reaches a convincing and substantiated overall judgement.

# Timeline

| Year | Crusade events | Events elsewhere |
|---|---|---|
| 1054 | | Schism between eastern and western Churches |
| 1071 | | Battle of Manzikert |
| 1073 | | Gregory VII became pope |
| | | Start of Investiture Crisis |
| | | Seljuk Turks captured Jerusalem |
| 1076 | | Henry IV, Emperor of Germany declared Gregory VII deposed |
| 1080 | | Clement III made anti-pope by Henry IV |
| 1081 | | Alexius I Comnenus became Emperor of Byzantium |
| 1088 | | Election of Urban II as pope |
| 1092 | | Death of Malik Shah |
| 1094 | Church Council at Piacenza | |
| 1095 | Alexius I requested help from the pope in fighting the Turks | |
| 1095 | Church Council at Clermont | |
| 1095–9 | First Crusade | |
| 1095 | People's Crusade departed for the Holy Land | |
| 1096 | First Crusade, second wave | |
| | Nicaea attacked | |
| | Massacre of Jews in Germany | |
| 1097 | Nicaea fell to the crusaders | |
| | Battle of Dorylaeum | |
| 1098 | Siege of Antioch | |
| | Kerbogha defeated by the crusaders | |
| | Capture of Edessa by the crusaders and establishment of first Crusader State by Baldwin of Boulogne | |
| | Antioch established by Bohemund | |
| 1099 | Raymond of Toulouse departed for the Holy Land | Death of Urban II, succeeded by Paschal II |
| | Jerusalem captured by the crusaders | |
| 1100 | Baldwin I became King of Jerusalem | |
| 1101 | Defeat of Raymond of Toulouse in Asia Minor by the Turks | |
| | Capture of Caesarea by the crusaders | |
| 1104 | Capture of Acre | |
| 1109 | Capture of Tripoli | |
| 1110 | Capture of Beirut and Sidon | |
| 1113 | Hospitaller Order became independent | |
| 1119 | Battle of the Field of Blood | |
| | Founding of the Templars | |

| Year | Crusade events | Events elsewhere |
|---|---|---|
| 1124 | Capture of Tyre | |
| 1127–52 | | Conrad III King of Germany |
| 1128 | Zengi occupied Aleppo | |
| 1129 | Templar Order given official Church support | |
| 1133–89 | | Henry II King of England |
| 1137–80 | | Louis VII King of France |
| 1144 | Fall of Edessa to Zengi | |
| 1145 | Eugenius III issued *Quantum praedecessores* | |
| 1146 | Preaching tour of Bernard of Clairvaux | Death of Zengi |
| 1147–9 | Second Crusade | |
| 1147 | German Crusade against the Wends | Byzantine Empire made truce with the Turks |
| | Siege of Lisbon | |
| | Departure of Conrad III and Louis VII | |
| | German army defeated in Asia Minor | |
| 1148 | Council of Palmarea decided to attack Damascus | |
| | Failure of Second Crusade to capture Damascus; Conrad returned to Germany | |
| 1149 | Return of Louis VII to France | |
| | Nur ad-Din defeated crusaders at Inab | |
| 1152 | | Election of Frederick Barbarossa as German king |
| 1153 | Crusaders captured Ascalon | |
| 1155 | | Frederick Barbarossa crowned emperor in Rome |
| 1163 | King Almaric started attacks on Egypt | |
| 1174 | | Death of Nur ad-Din |
| | | Saladin in control in Damascus |
| 1176 | | Defeat of Manuel I at Myriocephalum |
| 1179 | Capture of Jacob's Ford by Saladin | |
| 1180–1223 | | Philip II Augustus King of France |
| 1187 | Battle of Hattin | |
| | Saladin captured Jerusalem | |
| | *Audita tremendi* issued by Gregory VIII | |
| 1189–92 | Third Crusade | |
| 1189 | Siege of Jerusalem by King Guy | |
| | Departure of Frederick Barbarossa | |
| 1189–99 | | Richard I King of England |
| 1190 | Death of Frederick Barbarossa | |
| | Departure of Philip II Augustus and Richard I | |
| 1191 | Battle of Arsuf | |
| | Crusaders captured Acre | |

| Year | Crusade events | Events elsewhere |
|---|---|---|
| | Philip II returned home | |
| | First march on Jerusalem turned back | |
| 1192 | Second march on Jerusalem turned back | |
| | Battle of Jaffa | |
| | Truce between Richard I and Saladin | |
| | Richard I returned home | |
| 1198 | Innocent III issued the papal bull *Post miserabile* | Innocent III became pope |
| | Truce with Saladin | |
| 1199–1216 | | John King of England |
| 1199 | Many knights took the cross | |
| 1201 | Agreement with Venice for transport | |
| | Boniface of Montferrat recognised as leader | |
| 1202 | Attack on Zara | |
| 1202–4 | Fourth Crusade | |
| 1203 | First attack on Constantinople | |
| | Alexius IV made co-emperor with Isaac II | |
| 1204 | Overthrow of Alexius IV | |
| | Capture of Constantinople by crusaders | |

# Glossary of terms

**Absolution** The act of forgiveness, which only a priest could undertake.

**Angevin** The Angevins were a royal house that ruled England and much of France in the twelfth and early thirteenth centuries; its monarchs were Henry II, Richard I and John.

**Anti-pope** A rival pope elected by opponents of a current pope. Each pope built up support where he could.

**Apostolic See** The papacy.

**Ascetic life** A simple life characterised by denial of the pleasures of the secular world.

**Atabeg** Hereditary Turkish noble title, given to the ruler of a province.

**Caliph** The head of an Islamic state, seen as a successor to Muhammad.

**Charter evidence** Evidence from charters, which are medieval records of, for example, grants, sales or exchanges of land or rights, an agreement between two parties, or even a list of possessions.

**Christendom** The Christian parts of the world, largely in Europe at this time.

**Clerical celibacy** The belief that the clergy should not be married or have sexual relationships, so their focus was always on God.

**Clerical marriage** Marriage for priests and bishops was (in theory) forbidden in the Roman Catholic Church, but not in the Greek Orthodox Church.

**Codes of chivalry** Moral codes of conduct. These were not written documents and they varied slightly from one region to another.

**Confession** The prayer in which worshippers asked for forgiveness for the sins they had committed.

**Danishmends** A Turkish tribe ruling in Anatolia.

**Day of Judgement** The day when Christ would return to earth and everyone would be judged and be sent to either heaven or hell.

**Debased coinage** Where the metal content of coins is less than their face value. The process leads to higher prices.

**Decretals** Papal decrees concerning a point of canon (Church) law.

**Depose** To remove of a ruler or pope from their position.

**Doge** Chief magistrate of the Republic of Venice

**Ergotism** A disease prevalent in areas where rye bread was eaten. It was caused by eating rye that was affected by a fungus. Symptoms included convulsions, hallucinations and gangrene. Sufferers often died.

**Excommunicate** To exclude a member of the Church from taking the sacraments.

**Flemish** Relating to Flanders, the region covering present-day northern Belgium, part of France and the Netherlands.

**Frankish knights** Men from the landowning classes and influenced by the code of chivalry and the legends of the past. Chivalry in this sense was the honourable conduct expected from a knight, such as courtesy to ladies and undertaking of worthy tasks. (It was more notable for the theory than for the observance.) The Frankish knights fought on horseback, and their equipment and entourage were expensive to maintain.

**Franks** Collective word for people who lived in France at the time.

**Great Mosque** A centre of religious life for the Muslims which dated back to 634.

**Heresy** A belief that goes against the beliefs of the established Church.

**Holy Sepulchre** The burial place of Christ, and included a church built by Constantine, a sacred site.

***Jihad*** Meaning 'struggle' in Arabic; one of the duties of Muslims was to fight for the defence of their religion against non-Muslims or the infidel. The term was used to whip up enthusiasm for the war against the crusaders.

**Mecca** The birthplace of Muhammad and the holiest city in Islam.

***Milies sancti Petri* or vassals of Saint Peter** Knights throughout the Christian West who were bound by oath to offer armed service to the Church and to the pope as its head.

**Minbar** A pulpit from which sermons are preached in the mosque.

**Moors** Used by medieval and early modern Europeans to variously describe Arabs, north African Berbers and Muslim Europeans.

**Muslim Near East** The area near the eastern end of the Mediterranean Sea, approximately equivalent to what we know today as Greece, Turkey, Syria, Lebanon, Palestine, Israel and Egypt.

**Order of the Teutonic Knights** A religious order which played a major role in eastern Europe in the Middle Ages.

**Outremer** French for overseas. The term came into use after the First Crusade and described the County of Edessa, the Principality of Antioch, the County of Tripoli and the Kingdom of Jerusalem. It was later used more broadly to cover the Levant or the Holy Land.

**Papal bull** Public decree issued by a pope.

**Patriarch** A bishop, in some eastern Churches.

**Peace and Truce of God** From about 1000, local nobles had begun to make agreements not to attack churches, unarmed persons and clergymen and by 1040 this had developed so that fighting was forbidden on certain days of the week. 'Assemblies of peace' met to swear oaths to keep the peace, and 'leagues of peace' made up of clergy and nobles enforced this. The centre of this movement was the monastery of Cluny, where Urban had been a monk and was probably influenced by such developments.

**Pechenegs** A Turkish tribe who had migrated from central Asia. They were much given to war with their neighbours but were finally defeated in 1091 by a combined force of their enemies.

**Penance** A punishment imposed by a priest on someone who has confessed to their sins.

**People of the Book** An Islamic term referring to Jews, Christians and Sabians, or converts to Islam.

**Pillaging** During war, stealing or robbing a place or something.

**Plenary indulgence** Absolved someone from all punishments incurred by their sins.

**Pogrom** The deliberate persecution of an ethnic or religious group.

**Polity** A form of civil government.

**Pontificate** The period of office held by a pope.

**Power of the Keys** The power given to St Peter in the Gospels to forgive sins, which was passed on to all the popes as heirs of St Peter.

**Primogeniture** The right of succession belonging to the firstborn son. This was common in western Europe, where the eldest son inherited all the lands of his parents.

**Qur'an** The central text of Islam, believed to have been directly revealed to Prophet Muhammad by God in Arabic over a period of 23 years (609–32).

**Relic** A body part or a belonging from a holy person, kept as an object of reverence.

**Retinues** Followers such as guards, soldiers and servants. The wealth and power of a lord were reflected in the size of his retinue.

**Saint Denis** The burial place of Denis, the first Bishop of Paris, martyred in about 250 on the hill of Montmartre. An abbey was established there and most French kings were buried there, so it was a very sacred site.

**Seljuk Turks** A tribe from central Asia who moved west in the tenth century and converted to Sunni Islam. They captured Baghdad in 1055 and set up the Seljuk Empire. Under Alp Arslan and Malik Shah they extended their rule to include Iran, Mesopotamia, Syria, Palestine and the Sultanate of Rum. But they were later pushed back by the crusaders and attacked in the east by the Mongols.

**Simony** Paying to get an office or job in the Church.

**Sultan** A powerful ruler under the authority of the caliph.

**Supply train** Horses carrying supplies to help the crusaders.

**Surcoat** A garment worn over medieval armour, often embroidered with heraldic arms.

**Take the cross** Crosses were simply fashioned out of two pieces of cloth and were worn as a badge of honour by crusaders.

**Trinity** The belief that God is one but has three persons: the Father, the Son and the Holy Spirit.

**True Cross** Believed to be the cross on which Christ had been crucified. It had been found by Helena, the mother of Emperor Constantine, in about 327.

**Viziers** Chief ministers of a Muslim ruler.

**Warlords** Powerful nobles who recruited mercenary forces and controlled the land around their strongholds. They fought one another much of the time.

**Wattle** Woven strips of wood forming panels used for fencing or for walling.

**Western Wall** Also called Kotel or the Al-Buraq Wall: the site where Muhammad tied his steed on his Night Journey to Jerusalem before ascending to paradise, and the holiest place where Jews are allowed to pray.

# Further reading

## General

There are numerous books that deal with most or all of the crusading period, some of which are referred to specifically below when they are of particular value in dealing with an aspect of a crusade. However, some more general works include:

**Amin Malouf, *The Crusades Through Arab Eyes* (Saqi Essentials, 2006)**

An ideal counter to the western views that are seen in most books. This work uses contemporary Arab chroniclers to examine the Crusades and explain the conflicts within the Arab world and its reaction to an encounter with an alien culture

**Jonathan Phillips, *Holy Warriors: A Modern History of the Crusades* (Vintage Press, 2010)**

A useful study of the crusading impulse which challenges traditional views

**Jonathan Phillips, *The Crusades 1095–1197* (Longman, 2002)**

A short, single-volume history of the first three Crusades, it provides an ideal introduction for students and a useful collection of documents

**Jonathan Riley Smith, *The Crusades: A History* (Continuum, 2009)**

A single-volume history of the crusading movement, it not only provides an account of the Crusades but also details their organisation and what it was like to take part

**Jonathan Riley Smith, *What were the Crusades?* (Ignatius, 2002)**

A valuable introduction to the Crusades, the work attempts to define 'the crusade'. In particular it is useful in defining the concept of a penitential war

**Christopher Tyerman, *How to Plan a Crusade* (Allen Lane, 2015)**

An interesting work that gives valuable insights into the planning funding and raising of the crusader armies

## Chapter 1

**Toby Purser, *The First Crusade and the Crusader States 1073–1130* (Heinemann, 2010)**

Provides some useful background to the situation in Europe and the Middle East, allowing students to place events in context

## Chapter 2

**Hans Eberhard Mayer, *The Crusades* (Oxford University Press, 1988)**

A traditional interpretation which considers the importance of the inheritance practice in motivating crusaders

**Jonathan Riley Smith, *The First Crusade and the Idea of Crusading* (Continuum, 2009)**

This work takes a similar line to Mayer in discussing the importance of the inheritance practice

## Chapter 3

**Thomas Asbridge, *The First Crusade* (Free Press, 2004)**

This authoritative study stresses the importance of religious fervour and argues that it was the culmination of the reform movement which played a key role

**John France, *The Crusaders and the Expansion of Catholic Christendom 1000–1714* (Routledge, 2005)**

A valuable contribution in explaining the success of the First Crusade, this work puts emphasis on the military effectiveness of the crusader army, which it argues developed as the Crusade progressed

**Peter Frankopan, *The First Crusade* (Vintage, 2013)**

A detailed study of the situation in Byzantium at the time of the First Crusade, this work argues that the aid the crusaders received from Byzantium was crucial in the success of the Crusade

**Moshe Gill, *A History of Palestine* (Cambridge University Press, 1997)**

In explaining the victory of the crusaders, this book focuses on the divisions within the Muslim world

**Thomas Madden, *The Concise History of the Crusades* (Rowman & Littlefield, 2013)**

An account which highlights the genuine concern of western Christians to liberate oppressed believers in the east

**Jonathan Riley Smith, *The First Crusade and the Idea of Crusading* (Continuum, 2009)**

Although stressing the religious motives, this work put greater emphasis on the ideological pull of Jerusalem

## Chapter 4

**Malcolm Barber, *The Crusader States* (Yale University Press, 2014)**

Most works on the establishment of the States consider similar issues such as disunity in the Muslim world, the import of feudal structures from the west and further conquests allied to strong leadership, but Barber also emphasises the importance of establishing ports to bring in supplies

**Alan Forey, 'The Military Orders 1120–1312' in Jonathan Riley-Smith, editor, *The Oxford History of the Crusades* (Oxford University Press, 1999)**

Helpful in explaining how the Military Orders contributed to the crusading movement

**Christopher MacEvitt, *The Crusaders and the Christian World of the East* (University of Pennsylvania Press, 2009)**
In explaining the early success of the States this book also suggests that coexistence between Christians and Muslims alongside the links with Italian city-states were important

## Chapter 5

**Aharon Ben-Ami, *Change in a Hostile Environment: The Crusaders' Kingdom of Jerusalem* (Princeton University Press, 1969)**
Takes a very different perspective and considers the importance of the Muslim counter-crusade in defeating the crusaders

**Jonathan Phillips, *The Second Crusade* (Yale University Press, 2007)**
A detailed study of the Second Crusade in which Phillips argues that the failure was the result of the reluctance of magnates to commit to the campaign and the political disorder within the empire

**Jason Roche, *The Second Crusade: Holy War on the Periphery of Latin Christendom* (Brepols, 2015)**
Much like Runciman, this work argues that treachery and duplicity were vital in explaining the failure of the Crusade

**Steven Runciman, *A History of the Crusades, Volume II* (Penguin, 1954)**
Argues that it was Byzantine trickery and duplicity that played a vital role in the failure of the Crusade

**Christopher Tyerman, *A New History of the Crusades* (Penguin, 2007)**
Looks beyond events in the Middle East and considers the impact of a lack of clear aims for the Crusade and how targets outside the Levant weakened the movement

## Chapter 6

**Marshall Baldwin, *A History of the Crusades: The First One Hundred Years* (University of Wisconsin Press, 2006)**
Similar in approach to Richard, but probably less available

**Bernard Hamilton, *The Leper King and His Heirs* (Cambridge University Press, 2008)**
A detailed study of one of the most important kings of Jerusalem and his impact on the States

**Alan Murray, *From Clermont to Jerusalem: The Crusades and Crusader Society 1095–1500* (Brepols, 2016)**
A detailed study which looks at the make-up of the nobility of the kingdom of Jerusalem

**Helen Nicholson, *The Knights Hospitaller* (Boydell Press, 2013)**
As the title suggests, this looks in detail at the role of one of the Military Orders

**Jean Richard, *The Crusades c1071–1291* (Cambridge University Press, 1999)**
This work builds on debate about the coexistence of Christians and Muslims, adopting an 'assimilationist model' that was popular with nineteenth-century French historians who were influenced by colonial thought

**R.C. Smail, *Crusading Warfare 1097–1193* (Cambridge University Press, 1972)**
This work contrasts with Richard and Baldwin and suggests that the French presence was repressive and exploitative, with the French behaving as a distinct ruling class

## Chapter 7

**Thomas Madden, *The Concise History of the Crusades* (Rowman & Littlefield, 2013)**
While accepting the failure of the Crusade to capture Jerusalem, the work is useful in examining the success of the Crusade in strengthening the Crusader States

**Jonathan Phillips, *The Life and Legend of the Sultan Saladin* (Bodley Head, 2019)**
Although this goes beyond the Third Crusade and looks at the impact of Saladin through time, as well as considering his role in the Crusade, it offers a balanced perspective

## Chapter 8

**Jonathan Harris, *Byzantium and the Crusades* (Bloomsbury, 2014)**
Harris challenges the view of Runciman and Norden, viewing the Crusade as an accident

**Jonathan Phillips, *The Fourth Crusade and the Sack of Constantinople* (Pimlico, 2015)**
A detailed study of the Crusade

**Steven Runciman, *A History of the Crusades, Volume III* (Penguin, 1954)**
Building on the work of Walter Norden (not listed as written in German), Runciman sees the Crusade as an almost inevitable clash between two civilisations. The book places the Crusade in the wider context of the crusade movement and sees the clash as a culmination of the difficult relationship between the east and west

# Index